D0301566

Also by **Ashgate:**

DARREN OLDRIDGE
Religion and Society in Early Stuart England

Also in the Variorum Collected Studies Series

CHARLES DUGGAN
Decretals and the Creation of 'New Law' in the Twelfth Century

PATRICK McGURK
Gospel Books and Early Latin Manuscripts

JAMES McKINNON
The Temple, the Church Fathers and Early Western Chant

ANNA SAPIR ABULAFIA
Christians and Jews in Dispute: Disputational Literature and the Rise of Anti-Judaism in the West (c. 1000–1150)

JAMES MULDOON
Canon Law, the Expansion of Europe, and World Order

KATHLEEN HUGHES
Church and Society in Ireland, A.D. 400–1200

GILES CONSTABLE
Culture and Spirituality in Medieval Europe

JOHN GILCHRIST
Canon Law in the Age of Reform, 11th–12th Centuries

JAMES McEVOY
Robert Grosseteste, Exegete and Philosopher

PAUL FREEDMAN
Church, Law and Society in Catalonia, 900–1500

GABRIELE WINKLER
Studies in Early Christian Liturgy and its Context: Byzantium, Syria, Armenia

BRIAN CROKE
Christian Chronicles and Byzantine History, 5th–6th Centuries

GERALD BONNER
Church and Faith in the Patristic Tradition: Augustine, Pelagianism, and Early Christian Northumbria

VARIORUM COLLECTED STUDIES SERIES

Liturgical Calendars, Saints, and Services in Medieval England

Professor Richard W. Pfaff

Richard W. Pfaff

Liturgical Calendars, Saints, and Services in Medieval England

Ashgate
VARIORUM

Aldershot · Brookfield USA · Singapore · Sydney

Published in the Variorum Collected Studies Series by

Ashgate Publishing Limited
Gower House, Croft Road,
Aldershot, Hampshire GU11 3HR
Great Britain

Ashgate Publishing Company
Old Post Road,
Brookfield, Vermont 05036–9704
USA

ISBN 0–86078–677–3

British Library CIP Data
Pfaff, Richard W.
Liturgical Calendars, Saints, and Services in Medieval England —
(Variorum Collected Studies Series: CS610).
1. Catholic Church—Liturgy—History—Congresses. 2. England—Church History—
1066–1485. I. Title.
264'.02'00902

US Library of Congress CIP Data
The Library of Congress Catalog Card Number is pre-assigned as 98–071752.

The paper used in this publication meets the minimum requirements of the American National Standard for Information Sciences – Permanence of Paper for Printed Library Materials, ANSI Z39.48–1984. ∞ ™

Printed by Galliard (Printers) Ltd, Great Yarmouth, Norfolk, Great Britain

VARIORUM COLLECTED STUDIES SERIES CS610

CONTENTS

This volume contains xii + 268 pages

PREFACE

This collection of pieces differs from many in the Variorum Reprints series in two ways. First, it has a larger than usual proportion of previously unpublished papers. Secondly, it contains a rather substantial Introduction, written in order both to set the pieces in an overall context and to provide a basic historiographical and bibliographical overview. I hope that the latter may give this Introduction some usefulness quite apart from the papers it is meant to introduce. I am thankful to John Smedley, editor of the Variorum series, for his willingness to have four papers read at learned meetings included here. Owing to other preoccupations of mine, not least of an administrative sort, these did not see the light of publication in journals as would normally have been the case, and it is gratifying to be able to offer them now to a possibly wider audience than those who first heard them.

The pieces reprinted here have appeared over a span of nearly twenty-five years. It has not seemed either useful or, in a sense, fair to subject them to revision or to attempt any updating. I try to explain to students that it is essential to give the original date of publication when citing an article from a volume of reprinted pieces, a principle that requires original and reprinted formats to be as close to identical as possible. With the unpublished papers, however, I have felt free to refer occasionally to important work more recent than the dates the papers were read.

The formulas by which manuscripts are specified vary somewhat from piece to piece, depending on the styles mandated by the original formats, but where possible I have tried to use simplified forms; no readers of these papers are likely to be puzzled by abbreviations as obvious as BL (for London, British Library), Bodl. (for Oxford, Bodleian Library), or CUL (Cambridge, University Library). Likewise, among slightly diverse reference abbreviations, HBS always stands for Henry Bradshaw Society publications.

I am grateful to Ruth Peters of Variorum and to Nicholas Rogers of Sidney Sussex College, Cambridge, for close scrutinies given to the unpublished papers, and to the original editors of the volumes and journals in which the published articles appeared. Support for the research on which the pieces included here are based has come from the University of North Carolina at Chapel Hill (University Research Council), the National Humanities Center (through funds provided by the Andrew W. Mellon Foundation), and Magdalen College, Oxford, where I matriculated forty years ago and which elected me to a Visiting Fellowship in 1989-90.

* * * * * * * * *

This volume is dedicated to my daughter-in-law, Emily.

RICHARD W. PFAFF

Chapel Hill
November 1997

ACKNOWLEDGEMENTS

Grateful acknowledgement is made to the following persons, editors, publishers, institutions and journals for their kind permission to reprint the articles included in this volume: Paul Watkins, Stamford (II); The Hambledon Press, London (III, XII); Peeters, Leuven (V, X); *Mediaevalia* and the Center for Medieval & Early Renaissance Studies, Binghamton (VII); Boydell & Brewer, Suffolk (IX); the Medieval Academy of America, Cambridge, MA (XIII).

PUBLISHER'S NOTE

The articles in this volume, as in all others in the Collected Studies Series, have not been given a new, continuous pagination. In order to avoid confusion, and to facilitate their use where these same studies have been referred to elsewhere, the original pagination has been maintained wherever possible.

Each article has been given a Roman numeral in order of appearance, as listed in the Contents. This number is repeated on each page and quoted in the index entries.

I

Introduction: The Study of Medieval Liturgy

As with other volumes in this series, the rationale for the present one is primarily that of authorship - all the contents were written by one person - and secondarily that of theme or topic. Although I cannot pretend that the pieces collected here were all written consciously to a single theme, let alone purpose, they do all cluster around the Latin liturgy of the middle ages, most often in England. That statement would seem to need as little glossing as if it were made about a comparably large field like medieval agrarian history or, to take a much smaller area of study, medieval metrology. I have for a long time been aware, however, that this is far from being the case, and that what even informed listeners understand when they hear the words 'medieval liturgy' is not at all a single entity. What justification there may be for offering the present collection as a whole must to a degree lie in an attempt, to be made partly in this Introduction and partly through the pieces themselves, to draw out some dimensions of what is meaningfully to be understood by those words, 'medieval liturgy': a phrase with different connotations from those of 'liturgy', which used by itself tends to mean, understandably, rites of worship as practised in modern communities of the faithful.

This difference of connotation, and the resulting divergence in understanding, can be expressed succinctly as that between the study of liturgy as a basic sub-field within medieval studies (as well as being one of the 'auxiliary sciences' [*Hilfswissenschaften*] for medievalists) and the same study as a segment of a seminarian's preparation for ordination. Although, as will be indicated presently, in practice the distinction does not always have to be strictly maintained, it may be useful to make plain at the outset that the pieces collected here are largely irrelevant to this second understanding of 'liturgy.' Nor do they fairly fall under the heading of what is sometimes referred to as 'liturgiology,' a word with rather fusty overtones. The *Oxford English Dictionary* gives as its first use the title of J.M. Neale's *Essays in Liturgiology*, published in 1863, and the term seems to have been appropriated almost wholly by Anglican Ritualists. Certainly it was the case that many liturgical scholars of the past century and a half have been personally sympathetic to either Anglo- or Roman Catholic efforts towards the revival of worship; some will be noticed in a subsequent paragraph. But it should be easy enough to distinguish the kinds of questions that exercised 'liturgiologists' a hundred years or so ago - for example, is blue the 'authentic' colour for Advent, should a proper 'English' altar have riddell posts and curtains - from the sorts of investigations pursued in the present volume.

Rather than expatiating further on what I think is *not* meaningfully connoted by the phrase 'the study of medieval liturgy,' I ought now to try to indicate what I think *is* involved. This seems to me to be a matter of two basic aspects: liturgical books and the 'system' of medieval liturgy as represented in the realities of specific services at specific places and specific times. For the student, these two aspects are the proverbial chicken-and-egg. That is, the student encounters the liturgical books as primary data in modern libraries, and with the aid of them (and, it is vital to remember, of many other kinds of sources) tries to re-create mentally the services for which they were compiled; but pragmatically the services themselves should be understood as the primary data, for it is possible in some cases to have Christian liturgical services without books and it was likely in many instances that services were conducted from such books but not strictly in accordance with what was specified in them (see especially no. XII). Whichever is thought of as in any individual case 'coming first,' each requires a word of explanation.

'Liturgical books' are virtually synonymous with 'service books.' Either term refers mainly to books out of which individual services can be conducted, but also to those that simply tell the performer(s) what do without providing the texts or formulas to be read; these latters books are variously called ordinals, ordinaries, and sometimes customaries (*consuetudines*, though this term is most often used for full collections of the practices of monastic life at a particular religious house). They may of course be extant only in highly fragmentary form; there are cases where from the survival of scraps of parchment with only a few lines of writing an entire service book must be inferred. They are mostly in manuscript form, so much so that the medievalist is tempted to write - as I fear I have sometimes done - 'liturgical manuscripts' when referring to the broader category of medieval liturgical books: the point at issue being the service books printed in the late fifteenth and early sixteenth centuries. (As the primary focus of the present volume is on the middle ages in England, it is natural to take as the practical as well as intellectual terminus of investigation the imposition of the first Book of Common Prayer by act of Parliament in 1549; put baldly, for liturgical purposes the middle ages can be taken to end in England in that year.)

The 'system' of services which can to a large extent be reconstructed from the surviving liturgical books is in all its details a matter of considerable complexity, but for purposes of basic understanding a simple threefold classification remains the easiest approach. Services were either the eucharist - in the Latin middle ages generally called the mass, *missa* - or the eight-part divine (alias daily) office or what is sometimes called pastoral or occasional offices; the latter may usefully be subdivided into those specific to a bishop and those which a simple priest could perform. This Introduction would not be the appropriate place to lay out either the nomenclature or the sequence of the parts of these various services, and it must be presupposed that the reader either knows or can look up definitions of such fundamental terms as missal, breviary, psalter, and pontifical, as well as proper of time (*temporale*), proper of saints (*sanctorale*), and common of saints. The point here is simply that in considering any specific liturgical detail or incident - the kinds of things that form the matter of the papers in this volume - the student should always be aware of its setting in the entire context of services which formed a totality.

A trio of specific examples may help to explain the importance of this notion of a 'totality' (possibly a better term than 'system') of the medieval services. Behind three of these papers there lies the idea of what I like to call the 'liturgical person' (indeed, I have changed the title of no. IX to make this dimension plain): the sensibility of one whose life patterns are rooted in liturgical observance and who at the same time either studies the liturgy or makes active choices about it, or both. So in no. V, William of Malmesbury, a Benedictine monk of the first half of the twelfth century, lives within a context of daily mass and (probably quite elaborate) monastic office, with the bishop coming on certain special occasions and the abbot, or a deputy, performing certain pastoral services - especially, within a monastery where baptism, marriage, and (one hopes) the ordeal would have played little part, visitation of the sick and burial of the dead: the context out of which he makes his abridgement of a commentary on the *Liber offficialis* of the Carolingian liturgist Amalarius of Metz. Similarly, St Hugh (no. IX) spent many years in a monastic liturgical context, that of the Carthusians, and then, after reluctantly becoming bishop of Lincoln in 1186, in the markedly different contexts of a secular cathedral establishment of great wealth and self-consciousness and of a diocesan bishop who was also, *ipso facto*, a major royal vassal; his quite marked liturgical individuality, to put it politely, can be assessed only against this multiformity of contexts. And in no. XI, the 'doodlings,' as I think of them, on an old psalter-manuscript made by (as I strongly suspect) Ralph Baldock, successively dean of St Paul's and bishop of London around 1300, must be seen in the light of that secular cathedral establishment which, though proud, never got its liturgical practices quite worked into a discrete 'use' in the sense that was both true and widely known to be true of its rival at (New) Sarum or Salisbury.

The approach that I have been describing, that which combines the study of individual liturgical books with (I hope) an awareness of their context in the totality of the services for which the books are at least in theory intended, may appear to run the risk of donwplaying or even neglecting the dimension of 'religious sentiment' which would seem to be inherent in all liturgical worship. Again the old riddle about chicken and egg may be apposite. The problem here, expressed in the often-cited proposition *Lex orandi fiat legem credendi*, is the degree to which liturgical changes and developments create changes in religious sentiment as opposed to reflecting them, and vice versa. An obvious example (one not mentioned otherwise in these pages) is the emergence of the cult and feast of Corpus Christi in the late thirteenth century and early fourteenth century. Another is liturgical expression of concern for the condition of individual souls after death so often remarked on as a feature of late medieval religiosity: but the specific interest drawn out from the study of St Gregory's Trental (no. XIII) is the way a microcosm of the liturgical year is somehow supposed to intensify the value of the thirty masses offered for a specific soul. This is a good case in point because, while the study does little to illuminate that major feature of medieval spirituality (roughly, purgatory), it highlights another such feature, less-studied but clearly discernible, that of late medieval attitudes to the liturgical year.

Allied to religious sentiment in general and finding principal expression(s) liturgically is the cult of saints. Hagiography is both an ancient and a highly developed study, with strong thrusts in directions pursued in academic contexts of departments of religious studies and of literature, as well as of history. As with the broader considerations of spirituality, for present purposes the aspect mainly involved here, the incorporation of saints' days into liturgical worship, can help students to understand matters not themselves hagiographical. Specifically, analysis of the saints included for liturgical commemoration, of the relative importance ('gradings') they are given, and of the texts used for their feasts, may often provide prime data for localizing or dating (or both) of the books under study. Once again it is worth stressing the interrelatedness of subject and text: that, as study of the hagiographical component of service books can help us to get a surer grasp on those books, so firm information about the books themselves can be a considerable aid in developing an adequately contexted view of the growth of a saint's cult. In item IV, a study of the puzzling discrepancy as to whether a (largely early) medieval feast on 19 January was that of Mary and Martha or of Mary and Marius along with their sons Audifax and Abbacuc, the lining up of witnesses - entries in calendars, martyrologies, and massbooks - turns out to be as helpful in understanding the witnesses as in resolving in the (admittedly unsolved) hagiographical enigma. Number VIII, on the other hand, sheds some light on the way Becket's martyrdom was kept alive in the narrowly focused shape of a martyrological notice, or rather of several different notices, the multiplicity of which provide useful data about, once more, both the books in which these notices are found and the growth of the murdered archbishop's cult. Number X, which is a bit of a *jeu d'esprit*, approaches the cult of a saint - very minor as a saint, absolutely major as an historical figure, Bede - through the stylings that male, non-martyr saints receive in calendars and headings; the implication here is that the stylings themselves deserve attention towards the dual effort of understanding both books and cults.

Liturgical calendars can either be studied as the aggregate of the occasions entered in them or used as quarries out of which to extract information about a particular entry or group of entries. While the piece just mentioned, about the stylings used for Bede, is a small example of the second kind of use for an individual figure, no. III centers on a group of saints often said to have been 'purged' by Lanfranc as part of his programme as William the Conqueror's archbishop of Canterbury. Analysis of their fate in a number of post-Conquest calendars and related documents suggests that that chestnut should be laid to rest. This may be regarded as a use of liturgical data towards demonstrating a wider point. The same approach is apparent in no. II, 'set' in the same locale, Christ Church, Canterbury, as no. III but a couple of generations earlier. Although the treatment of the celebrated scribe Eadui Basan was meant as an overall survey of a figure who turns out to be a highly substantial one in the early history of that monastic establishment, and the palaeographical observations are offered both tentatively and timorously (as from one easily cowed by the palaeographically expert), the liturgical inferences to be drawn from the books we know that he worked on can provide a useful starting point for awareness of the liturgy at the metropolitical church of the southern English province.

Some information about liturgical sensibility at Canterbury and also about ways the English past may have been preserved there is the point of a third piece in this collection, no. VII, which also brings in another dimension vital for medieval liturgical studies, that of iconography. The *mis-en-scène* here is a particularly fascinating and complex one: the necessity, and opportunity, of drawing up the scheme for the virtually ground-level windows around the choir and eastern transepts of the rebuilt (after the terrible fire of 1174) east end of Canterbury cathedral. That the designer(s) should in at least three cases have incorporated details which can only come from Old English sources - in one instance clearly misunderstood - throws an interesting backward-looking glance into a situation that would seem to be marked by the new: new architectural style (that brought by William of Sens into his rebuilding of the choir), new shrine, new saint (Becket, canonized in 1173). This is to be sure a limited investigation, but when the time comes for a truly synoptic view of the development of the liturgical calendar at Christ Church from the time of Dunstan in the late tenth century until the end of the middle ages, the evidence suggested by this backward-lookingness will have to be taken into account - as well, of course, as that of the surviving calendars.[1]

The phenomenon of the liturgical calendar itself, so heavily depended on by (among others) art historians, seems to have been thought about surprisingly little, and no. VI is an attempt to address the fundamental question of why a

---

[1] See also my chapter on 'The Calendar' in *The Eadwine Psalter. Text, Image, and Monastic Culture in Twelfth-Century Canterbury*, ed. M.T. Gibson, T.A. Heslop, and R.W. Pfaff (London and Iniversity Park, PA 1992), 62-87; and T.A. Heslop, 'The Canterbury Calendars and the Norman Conquest,' in *Canterbury and the Norman Conquest. Churches, Saints and Scholars 1066-1109*, ed. R. Eales and R. Sharpe (London 1995), 53-85.

liturgical book which in the high and later middle ages is commonly equipped with that feature, the psalter, has one at all. This piece can be taken to underline in particular the value of trying to maintain the dual approach alluded to above, of taking with equal seriousness the specific liturgical details of any document at hand and its overall historical and cultural context.[2]

A Brief Historiographical and Bibliographical Overview

Even if it is intellectually possible to make a distinction between, on one hand, study of the liturgy in (especially) medieval England as an aspect of the broader history of either England or the middle ages and, on the other, study of such aspects of the liturgy as pertain to contemporary worship, in terms of the modern literature on liturgy the distinction is much harder to maintain; for while the fustiness that surrounds the term 'liturgiology' seems to render its approach entirely dated, the modern study of liturgy is a vast and flourishing field - so much so that the phrase 'liturgical studies' now has as its primary connotation that which bears on present-day worship in a variety of Christian communions. Something like the following brief historiographical-cum-bibliographical overview, therefore, seems necessary to address what can be a source of (often unrealized) confusion: what is not, as well as what is, likely to be useful for the student of medieval liturgy in the way of modern resources. In addition, because I am not given to vast bibliographical footnotes, some such overview may be desirable in itself as prolegomenon to the present collection of studies. Because they deal overwhelmingly with English matters, the items here

2 The work of Francis Wormald in producing his extremely valuable and extensively referred-to collections of calendars (*English Kalendars before A.D. 1100*, HBS 72, 1934; *English Benedictine Kalendars after A.D. 1100*, i. *Abbotsbury-Durham* and ii, *Ely-St Neots*, HBS 77, 1939 and 81, 1946) has been deleterious in one respect: as published they are virtually without context, in that in the first volume Wormald assigned a location and date for each of the twenty that he included, without any explanation for his assignments, and in the second and third volumes provided only scanty discussion of the witnesses he collated for each of the monastic houses covered; he also omitted all obits from his editions. In fairness it should be noted that he intended a volume of commentary, which was never completed; but in the event, the effect has been that students in a variety of disciplines have cited these calendars without having had much help in the vital matter of context.

discussed will be almost wholly confined to those of pertinence to the liturgy in medieval England.

In the years around 1980 I compiled a 'select' bibliography of about one thousand titles (the notional limit permitted by the series) exclusively on the subject of medieval Latin liturgy for the Toronto Medieval Bibliographies series.[3] It was in the course of the work of selection and organization for that book that I became aware of the extent to which the study of the history of medieval liturgy has been affected by concern with the liturgical renewal of our own day. To begin with, we should note that most of the principal introductory tools and big manuals which the searcher after some bit of medieval liturgical knowledge consults reflect strongly the influence of the movement for contemporary liturgical renewal. This is true of such works as H.A.P. Schmidt's *Introductio in liturgiam occidentalem*,[4] the collaboration edited by A.G. Martimort as *L'Eglise en Prière* (later translated into English and German, then revised and further translated),[5] the comparable work edited by three British scholars as *The Study of Liturgy*,[6] Theodor Klauser's *Kleine abendländische Liturgiegeschichte* (the English translation of which sold so well as to qualify for reprinting in paperback),[7] and above all the immensely influential *Missarum Sollemnia* of J.A. Jungmann.[8]

Beyond the level of these general tools and manuals, moreover, many of those who have furthered the study of the medieval liturgy most notably have been deeply involved in the processes of modern liturgical revision: not only

3 Richard W. Pfaff, *Medieval Latin Liturgy: a Select Bibliography*. Toronto Medieval Bibliographies 9 (Toronto 1982).

4 Rome 1960.

5 The entire bibliographical history need not be given here. The first (French) edition was published in Paris in 1961, the third (post-Vatican II) in 1965; the current English translation, as *The Church at Prayer* (Collegeville, Minn. 1986-7) is from the fourth edition, 1983.

6 Edited by Cheslyn Jones, Geoffrey Wainwright, and Edward Yarnold (London and New York 1978; 2nd edn 1992).

7 Again, the printing history is complicated. The German text of 1965 was used for John Halliburton's English version, *A Short History of the Western Liturgy* (Oxford 1969, with supplementary material added to the 1979 paperback reissue; but an earlier German version appeared as long ago as 1944.

8 The story here is even more complicated than with the previous two items, for the 'current' English translation by Francis Brunner in 2 vols (*The Mass of the Roman Rite*, New York 1951-55) is of the second German edition, 1949, whereas the latest German version is the sixth (Vienna 1966; Jungmann died in 1975).

Jungmann, Klauser, and Martimort, but also scholars like Pierre Salmon, Bernard Capelle, and Anton Hänggi. (And of course some - Odo Casel, Joseph Pascher, Louis Bouyer - have been far more deeply concerned with the Liturgical Movement than with historical studies *per se*.) And this is true not only on the Continent but also in the English-speaking world, where W.H. Frere's name and influence have bulked large.[9]

This aspect should, however, be balanced by notice of another, largely earlier, tradition, one of a concern with the medieval liturgy without regard for any particular relevance to twentieth-century worship. This tradition has been perhaps strongest in England, where, as well as the 'liturgiological studies' referred to above, serious, text-based medieval liturgical scholarship came of age around the turn of the present century through the work of (above all) Edmund Bishop and of many of the editors of early Henry Bradshaw Society volumes. In England this approach might without obloquy have been termed antiquarian; that is, its practicioners have tended to be Fellows of the Society of Antiquaries as much as, or as well as, clerks in holy orders: outstanding figures include J.W. Legg, H.A. Wilson, J.B.L. Tolhurst, and Francis Wormald, along with more recent representatives like Christopher Hohler and Derek Turner. On the Continent such scholars have tended to be members of the Order of St. Benedict, and to have had a strong interest in codicological matters: André Wilmart, Cunibert Mohlberg, Alban Dold, Robert Amiet, Jean Deshusses. (Not all, of course, have been monks: Cyrille Vogel and the immensely prolific Klaus Gamber were secular priests.)

The century or so spanned by the publications of the scholars mentioned above - Edmund Bishop's earliest substantial work came out in 1886,[10] the English translation and revision of Vogel's *Introduction aux sources de l'histoire du culte chrétien au moyen âge* in 1986[11] - has also been the century of learned journals. Summary notice of a few of the principal journals in which contributions to medieval liturgical history can be found will, as well as being necessary in itself, illustrate how little the study of medieval liturgy has seemed

9 See especially *Walter Howard Frere. A Collection of his Papers on Liturgical and Historical Subjects*, ed. J.H. Arnold and E.G.P. Wyatt. Alcuin Club Collections 35 (London 1940).

10 See the bibliography in Nigel Abercrombie, *The Life and Work of Edmund Bishop* (London 1959), 492-508.

11 Translation and revision of the French original (Spoleto 1981) by W.G. Storey and N.K Rasmussen as *Medieval Liturgy: an Introduction to the Sources* (Washington 1986).

to have a discreteness comparable to that of, say, Old English literature or medieval canon law. For a long time the only journal solely, or even chiefly, devoted to liturgical studies was *Ephemerides Liturgicae*, begun in 1887. Its approach was originally rubrical and modern, as its close connection with the Congregation of Sacred Rites would have made likely. But in the late 1920s the journal took a markedly more scientific and historical turn, and published a lot of scholarship in medieval liturgy throughout the next three and a half decades (and throughout the vicissitudes of World War II). With the Second Vatican Council, however, the journal's character shifted noticeably; and though there are still historical articles from time to time, for the last fifteen years or so the concerns of modern liturgical revision have clearly predominated.

Liturgical scholarship of a high order has also been published from time to time in three other journals started in the late nineteenth century: the *Analecta Bollandiana* begun in 1882, the *Revue Bénédictine* in 1885 - from the standpoints respectively of the Bollandists and Black Monks, nearly *sub specie aeternitatis* in each case - and in England the splendidly austere *Journal of Theological Studies* in 1900 (although recently there has been little in the way of liturgical scholarship in its pages). The principal organ for liturgical scholarship in Germany was founded just after the 1914-18 War in direct association with the aims of the Liturgical Movement and in even more direct connection with the *Mysterientheologie* advocated by its founder and editor, Odo Casel. Although this journal, the *Jahrbuch für Liturgiewissenschaft*, died amidst the strains of Nazi Germany (the last volume, ostensibly for 1935, finally appeared in 1941), its animating forces remained, and under the auspices of the Abt-Herwegen Institut für liturgisches und monastisches Forschung headquartered at Maria-Laach the journal reappeared in 1950 as *Archiv für Liturgiewissenschaft*. Since its founding it has published many distinguished contributions of an historical sort, some of them quite lengthy; but medieval questions have never been the primary object, and as with the *Ephemerides Liturgicae*, recent volumes have tended to include less rather than more medieval matter. Purely historical concerns sometimes of a liturgical sort are reflected in *Sacris Erudiri: Jaarboek voor Godsdienstwetenschappen*, published by the monks of Steenbrugge in conjunction with their monumental work on the various series of the Corpus Christianorum, which gives the journal a naturally patristic emphasis; despite its subtitle; in some volumes there are no directly liturgical contributions. The most recent organ (1984), and in some ways the most promising, is *Ecclesia Orans*, published under the auspices of the Faculty of Sacred Liturgy of the Pontifical University of Sant' Anselmo in Rome; this contains many studies, often in English and sometimes commendably short, of historical as well as contemporary concern, and in particular has printed many contributions by Antoine Chavasse.

As this quick review has shown, there is no one periodical which devotes itself solely, or even predominantly, to the subject of medieval Latin liturgy - nothing, that is, as single-minded as the *Bulletin of Medieval Canon Law* or *Archivum Latinitatis Medii Aevi* or *Gesta* (the journal of the International Center for Medieval Art), to name only three. General medieval journals do publish a few items of liturgical interest from time to time - especially *Speculum* and *Studi Medievali*, and, outstandingly for its limited subject area, *Anglo-Saxon England*) - as do some of the general ecclesiastical history journals and also some organs of national or local church history, most conspicuously *Hispania Sacra*. In addition, outstanding articles have occasionally been published in the journals sponsored by the Continental theological faculties to which their authors happen to belong; only by having access to the *Revue de Science Religieuse*, *Zeitschrift für katholische Theologie*, *Gregorianum*, or *Bulletin de Littérature Ecclésiastique* can one avoid missing much of the work of Michel Andrieu, Jungmann, Schmidt, and Martimort respectively. Aside from this principle, itself almost haphazard, there is no rhyme or reason as to where articles dealing with the medieval liturgy are likely to appear. When the field is widened to include the bibliographical and codicological journals (above all *Scriptorium*), the art-historical and musicological journals (among which *Etudes grégoriennes* is particularly important), and the numerous literary and historical periodicals and those published by individual religious orders, it becomes even clearer that our subject is a widely-diffused rather than efficiently-concentrated one. Finally, several journals devoted primarily to pastoral or modern liturgy - *Questions liturgiques*, *La Maison-Dieu*, *Jahrbuch für Liturgik und Hymnologie*, *Liturgisches Jahrbuch*, *Studia Liturgica*, *Worship*, and the like - do occasionally have contributions or reviews relating to medieval liturgy.

Journals, of course, provide only a limited amount of the kinds of material that scholars most need, source material. Fortunately, three or four scholarly series are devoted entirely or in part to editions of texts of a liturgical sort. Easily the most important among them for our purposes are the publications of the Henry Bradshaw Society. These began in 1890 and, after a rather fallow period a quarter century or so ago, have in the recent past included fine editions, usually with collation tables, of a wide range of liturgical texts, many of Anglo-Saxon interest.[12] On the Continent there are two main series currently producing texts, Liturgiewissenschaftliche Quellen und Forschungen from Münster and Spicilegium Friburgense from Fribourg in Switzerland (a series from Rome begun in 1950, Rerum ecclesasticarum documenta, which in its 'series maior' produced several standard editions of cardinal Continental service books, has issued nothing since 1985); none of these publications has been of a source primarily English. The standard parallel-edition (Latin-English) series begun as Nelson's and continued as Oxford Medieval Texts has been the venue for several publications of specifically English works which, though not themselves liturgical texts, are sources of the first importance: notably, the *Regularis concordia*,[13] Lanfranc's *Monastic Constitutions*, [14] and Wulfstan of Winchester's *Life of St Æthelwold*.[15]

At the beginning of my first book, published in 1970, I supplied a two-page note entitled 'Principal Modern Editions of Medieval English Secular Liturgical Texts.'[16] Although all of the information there need not be repeated, it may be useful to have the bare bibliographical data, updated and supplemented with corresponding data about a few editions of monastic books and books for episcopal and pastoral offices. (Discussion of what is conventionally meant, and what can sensibly be understood, by the familiar terms Sarum Use, or York, or Hereford, cannot be entered into here; I hope to treat this subject at length in the history of the liturgy in medieval England on which I am currently working.) Modern editions of the whole range of 'Sarum' liturgical books are available. There are two editions of the Sarum Missal, F.H. Dickinson's of 1861-83, based on a collation of early printed editions (primarily that of 1526),[17] and J.W. Legg's of 1916, from three thirteenth- and early fourteenth-century

---

12 HBS publications through volume 106, 1991 are inventoried in detail and discussed in Anthony Ward, *The Publications of the Henry Bradshaw Society*, Bibliotheca 'Ephemerides Liturgicae' Subsidia 67 (Rome 1992).

13 Edited by Thomas Symons (Edinburgh 1953).

14 Edited by David Knowles (Edinburgh 1951); revised edn in Corpus Consuetudinum Monasticarum 3 (Siegburg 1967).

15 Edited by Michael Lapidge and Michael Winterbottom (Oxford 1991).

16 Richard W. Pfaff, *New Liturgical Feasts in Later Medieval England* (Oxford 1970), xvii-xviii. This was disfigured by two stupid errors in the very first item: 'F.W.' Dickinson for F.H. and 'W.G.' Legg for J.W.

17 F.H. Dickinson, ed. *Missale ad usum insignis et praeclarae ecclesiae Sarum* (Burntisland 1861-83).

manuscripts.[18] The late medieval breviary is a highly complicated book, and the presentation of the 1531 Paris edition of the 'Great' (fullest format) Sarum breviary by Francis Procter[19] and Christopher Wordsworth compounds the complexity in a modern edition which is extraordinarily difficult to use.[20] A slightly younger contemporary of Legg's and of comparable stature to him and to Edmund Bishop as a liturgical scholar, W.H. Frere, produced under the auspices of the Plainsong and Medieval Music Society facsimiles of both a Sarum gradual[21] and a Sarum antiphoner,[22] and a more straightforward edition of three related kinds of texts under the composite title *The Use of Sarum*.[23] The Sarum manual has been edited, largely from the 1543 printed edition, by A.J. Collins,[24] and there are two editions of the Sarum processional, both mainly from sixteenth century printed texts (that book is quite rare in manuscript form), a conventional one by W.G. Henderson and a facsimile by Richard Rastall.[25]

The standard editions of York service books were all produced under the auspices of the Surtees Society, the principal local history society for Northumbria, between 1874 and 1883; not surprisingly, all leave something to be desired by late twentieth-century standards. Editions of the York missal and (together in one volume) of the manual and processional were published by W.G. Henderson,[26] and of the York breviary by S.W. Lawley.[27] In all these

18 J.W. Legg, ed. *The Sarum Missal, edited from three early manuscripts* (Oxford 1916).

19 Procter's name is very often misspelled, which can be fatal in the age of computerized catalogues. In one of the pieces reprinted below my correct spelling of it was carefully altered by the editors of the volume, both genuinely learned persons, to 'Proctor' throughout!

20 F. Procter and C. Wordsworth, ed. *Breviarium ad usum insignis ecclesiae Sarum*. 3 vols. (Cambridge 1879-86).

21 W.H. Frere, ed. *Graduale Sarisburiense*. 2 vols. (London 1891-4).

22 W. H. Frere, ed. *Antiphonale Sarisburiense*. 3 vols. (London 1901-25).

23 W. H. Frere, ed. *The Use of Sarum*, I. *The Sarum Customs as set forth in the Consuetudinary and Customary*, and II. *The Ordinal and Tonal*. 2 vols (Cambridge 1898-1901); the Tonal, not really a separate book, was supplied in a Appendix.

24 A.J. Collins, ed. *Manuale ad usum percelebris ecclesie Sarisburiensis*, HBS 91 (1958).

25 W.G. Henderson, ed. *Processionale ad usum insignis ac praeclarae ecclesiae Sarum* (Leeds 1874; Henderson's name is not on the title-page, only at the end of the preface); G. Richard Rastall, ed. *Processionale ad usum Sarum 1502* (Clarabricken, Ireland 1980).

26 W.G. Henderson, ed. *Missale ad usum insignis ecclesiae Eboracensis*, Surtees Soc. 59-60 (1874), and *Manuale et processionale ad usum insignis ecclesiae Eboracensis*, Surtees Soc. 63 (1875).

cases the sources primarily drawn on were the early printed editions. The same is true of the Hereford books, which are even scarcer in manuscript than those of York: the missal edited by Henderson, [28] the breviary by Frere and L.E.G. Brown.[29]

Surprisingly, perhaps, given the self-consciousness that marks much 'regular' or 'religious' life, monastic liturgical texts have been edited less extensively than these secular ones. The distinctions and variations among the uses of the various groups (conventionally called 'orders,' especially after the legislation of the Fourth Lateran Council in 1215) need not concern us a great deal here.[30] The 'monastic' (for these purposes, mainstream Benedictine) breviary has been well presented in an extensive edition of a composite manuscript from Hyde Abbey in Winchester of about 1300,[31] and there is a large, although not quite complete, facsimile edition of a mid-thirteenth century Worcester antiphoner, mainly the work of the fine scholar Dame Laurentia McLachlan (anonymously; there is no name on the title-page).[32] There is also a somewhat truncated edition of a late fourteenth-century breviary with English rubrics used by Bridgettine nuns.[33] The difference in mass liturgy between monastic and secular rites is much less than in the daily office; it is nonetheless noteworthy that the fullest edition of any English missal is that of a monastic book: the late fourteenth-century missal of Westminster Abbey by J.W. Legg, a

27 S.W. Lawley, ed. *Breviarium ad usum insignis ecclesiae Eboracensis*, Surtees Soc. 71, 75 (1880-3).

28 W.G. Henderson, ed. *Missale ad usum percelebris ecclesiae Herfordensis* (Leeds 1874); a single important manuscript, Oxford, University Coll. 78A, was also heavily drawn on.

29 W. H. Frere and L.E.G. Brown, ed. *The Hereford Breviary*, HBS 26, 40, 46 (1904, 1911, 1915).

30 The main exception would be the usages of the Carthusians; these are dealt with in the one piece below to which they are relevant, no. IX.

31 J.B.L. Tolhurst, ed. *The Monastic Breviary of Hyde Abbey, Winchester*. 6 vols, HBS 69, 70, 71, 76, 78, 80 (1932-42). Volume VI bears the title, *Introduction to the English Monastic Breviaries*, and, although an extensive treatment of many aspects of its subject, leaves much to be desired in the clarity and thoroughness of its exposition.

32 *Antiphonaire monastique. XIIIe siècle. Codex F.160 de la Bibliothèque de la Cathédrale de Worcester*, Paléographie musicale, 1st series 12 (Solesmes 1922-4).

33 A.J. Collins, ed. *The Bridgettine Breviary of Syon Abbey*, HBS 96 (1969).

great monument of liturgical scholarship.[34] An early thirteenth-century book from the Augustinian abbey of Lessness in Kent is also available.[35]

The reason that 'pre-Conquest' was specified above is because of the tendency, in some ways regrettable, for those who study Anglo-Saxon England (increasingly understood, and defined, as extending to about 1100) to be a world unto themselves.[36] In recent years a considerable number of Henry Bradshaw Society publications have been of Anglo-Saxon texts. Two of these are of massbooks, one from the New Minster, Winchester,[37] and one probably from Winchcombe abbey.[38] The fine 1896 edition of the so-called Missal of Robert of Jumièges has recently been reprinted by the same society.[39] Antedating the Bradshaw Society's existence is the equally excellent edition of the most important (and complex) surviving Anglo-Saxon massbook, F.E. Warren's of the Leofric Missal.[40] Texts of the expanded mass-chants called tropes can be found in an edition by Frere, who was a pioneer in the study of medieval liturgical music as well as of other aspects of the liturgy.[41]

Several HBS volumes have dealt in one way or another with the daily office in the Anglo-Saxon church, although the length and complexity of the manuscripts to be edited, especially when they include the entire psalter, mean that partial rather than full editions tend to be the rule. Despite the resulting difficulty in using them, we do have such presentations of mid- to late-eleventh

34 J.W. Legg, ed. *Missale ad usum Ecclesie Westmonasteriensis*. 3 vols. HBS 1, 5, 12 (1891-7).

35 Philip Jebb, ed. *Missale de Lesnes*, HBS 95 (1964).

36 T he entire field, with survey of MSS and cumulative bibliography, is treated in Richard W. Pfaff, ed. *The Liturgical Books of Anglo-Saxon England*, Old English Newsletter Subsidia 23 (Kalamazoo 1995); this a free-standing version of what, revised, is meant eventually to be part of the multi-volume enterprise Sources of Anglo-Saxon Literary Culture.

37 D.H. Turner, ed. *The Missal of the New Minster*, Winchester, HBS 93 (1962).

38 Anselme Davril, ed. *The Winchcombe Sacramentary*, HBS 109 (1995).

39 H.A. Wilson, ed. *The Missal of Robert of Jumièges*, HBS 11 (1896; repr. Woodbridge 1996).

40 F.E. Warren, ed. *The Leofric Missal* (Oxford 1883; repr. Farnborough 1968).

41 W.H. Frere, ed. *The Winchester Troper, from MSS of the Xth and XIth Centuries*, HBS 8 (1894). The ongoing Swedish-based enterprise Coropus Troporum (Stockhom 1975-) is giving a new and vastly expanded dimension to the study of tropes. See also A.E. Planchart, *The Repertory of Tropes at Winchester*. 2 vols (Princeton 1977).

century compilations associated with Leofric of Exeter[42] and with St Wulstan of Worcester,[43] the tenth-century 'Durham' collectar,[44] and an early eleventh-century liturgico-devotional miscellany from Winchester Old Minster,[45] along with another, slightly less liturgical, miscellany from the same context.[46] Not used regularly in the office but common to several liturgical services at special times or for special circumstances is the litany of the saints, the Anglo-Saxon corpus of which has appeared as another HBS publication.[47]

Although none of the papers in the present volume deals with bishops' liturgies as contained in pontificals and benedictionals (published work of mine on those subjects is subsequent to the latest date these papers represent, early 1995), it may nonetheless be useful to furnish the same modicum of information about such books as has just been offered for mass- and office-books. (A benedictional is a separate presentation of the special blessings pronounced by the bishop at communion; if not so presented, the blessings tend to be a component of the pontifical proper.) Again, the Anglo-Saxon period seems the best represented, with editions as far back as 1903 and 1910, these being respectively of two books associated with the reforms of Æthelwold of Winchester.[48] Subsequent editions of pre-Conquest books include a Canterbury benedictional of the second quarter of the eleventh century,[49] a pontifical named after Lanalet in Cornwall but possibly used at Wells,[50] a late tenth-century pontifical long mis-ascribed to the eighth-century archbishop of York Egbert[51] and (in the same volume) a fragmentary book possibly made at Winchester but

42 E.S. Dewick and W. H. Frere, ed, *The Leofric Collectar....* 2 vols, HBS 45, 56 (1914, 1921). The two volumes have different subtitles, that of vol. II being the more accurate: *compared with the Collectar of St Wulfstan, together with kindred documents of Exeter and Worcester.*

43 Anselm Hughes, ed. *The Portiforium of Saint Wulfstan.* 2 vols, HBS 89-90 (1958-60).

44 Alicia Corrêa, ed. *The Durham Collectar*, HBS 107 (1992).

45 Beate Günzel, ed. *Ælfwine's Prayerbook*, HBS 108 (1993).

46 B.J. Muir, ed. *A Pre-Conquest English Prayer-Book*, HBS 103 (1988).

47 Michael Lapidge, ed. *Anglo-Saxon Litanies of the Saints*, HBS 106, 1991.

48 H.A. Wilson, ed. *The Benedictional of Archbishop Robert*, HBS 24, 1903; G.F. Warner and H.A. Wilson, ed. *The Benedictional of St Æthelwold*, Roxburghe Club (London 1910), a regrettably rare volume. The former is misnamed, being in fact more a pontifical than a benedictional.

49 R.M. Woolley, ed. *The Canterbury Benedictional*, HBS 51 (1917).

50 G.H. Doble, ed. *Pontificale Lanaletense*, HBS 74 (1937).

51 As in the now obsolete edition of William Greenwell, *The Pontifical of Egbert, Archbishop of York, A.D. 732-66*, Surtees Soc. 27 (1853).

later used at Durham,[52] and three fragmentary pontificals, two of them Anglo-Saxon, now in the same British Library Cottonian manuscript.[53]

Modern study of post-Conquest episcopal books depends from two fine older works, that of W.G. Henderson on a thirteenth-century book owned by a sixteenth-century cardinal archbishop of York,[54] and of H.A. Wilson on the late twelfth-century Magdalen College pontifical.[55] Subsequently only one such book, a sixteenth-century benedictional, has been put into print.[56] Modern editions of post-Conquest pontificals are much to be desired; indeed, extensive study of many subjects relating to them will not be possible until more such editions exist.

The matter of ordinals, directories, and other collections of instruction about the conduct and content of liturgical services has hitherto been mentioned only in connection with Frere's *Use of Sarum*. Under this heading should be grouped two quite distinguishable types of works. One is cumulated prescriptions for individual liturgical units, be they dioceses, religious houses, or entire orders. Outstanding in this respect is the Exeter Ordinal of c. 1337, largely the work of Bishop John de Grandisson, to which is attached a set of Legenda for the daily office and a martyrology.[57] An ordinal for the distinctively English order of St Gilbert has been edited, along with the office for its founder, a calendar, and something of a missal.[58] Degrees of specificity within documents for individual houses called ordinals or customaries vary widely; some are extremely instructive as to minute liturgical details, others are more concerned with the daily regimen of the house. Here it will have to suffice to notice the range of such documents as presented in several Bradshaw Society volumes: those for St Augustine's, Canterbury and St Peter's,

52 H.J. Banting, ed. *Two Anglo-Saxon Pontificals (the Egbert and Sidney Sussex Pontificals)*, HBS 104 (1989).

53 D.H. Turner, ed. *The Claudius Pontificals* (HBS 97, 1971).

54 W.G. Henderson, ed. *Liber Pontificalis Chr. Bainbridge Archiepiscopi Eboracensis*, Surtees Soc. 61 (1875).

55 H.A. Wilson, ed. *The Pontifical of Magdalen College, with an appendix of extracts from other English MSS of the twelfth century*, HBS 39 (1910).

56 R.M. Woolley, ed. *The Benedictional of John Longlonde, Bishop of Lincoln*, HBS 64 (1927).

57 J.N. Dalton, ed. *Ordinale Exon.* ..., 4 vols. HBS 37, 38, 63, 79 (1909-40). G.H. Doble was co-editor of the fourth volume.

58 R.M. Woolley, ed. *The Gilbertine Rite*. 2 vols, HBS 59 (1921).

Westminster,[59] the nunnery at Barking,[60] St Mary's, York,[61] Norwich cathedral priory,[62] and Bury St Edmunds.[63]

The other type consists of works which, although privately compiled, are meant to serve as instructions or manuals for priests throughout, at least, the Sarum province. Outstanding among these is the treatise called *Ordinale Sarum sive Directorium Sacerdotum*, an influential private compilation by one Clement Maydeston, which borders on liturgical commentary rather than rubrical prescription.[64]

Finally, it is necessary to notice a small range of secondary literature, that is, monographs and articles In this general bibliographical overview they must bulk relatively small, for in comparison with the amount of source material at the student's disposal there is less published secondary scholarship on the history of the liturgy in medieval England than might have been expected. Much of what there is has tended to be literary in thrust, focusing on liturgical influences in a particular work or author.[65] Art historians tend to be specially interested in calendars and litanies of saints, those being the liturgical components likeliest to help them in dating specific manuscripts (and, by comparison, other artefacts like metalwork or windows).[66] Historians of music

59 E.M. Thompson, ed. *Customary of the Benedictine Monasteries of Saints Augustine, Canterbury and Saint Peter, Westminster*. 2 vols, HBS 23 and 28 (1902-4).

60 J.B.L. Tolhurst, ed. (with notes by Laurentia McLachlan) *The Ordinale and Customary of the Benedictine Nuns of Barking Abbey*. 2 vols, HBS 65-6 (1927-8).

61 The Abbess of Stanbrook (Laurentia McLachlan) and J.B.L. Tolhurst, ed. *The Ordinal and Customary of the Abbey of Saint Mary, York*. 3 vols, HBS 73, 75, 84 (1936-51).

62 J.B.L. Tolhurst, ed. *The Customary of the Cathedral Priory Church of Norwich*, HBS 82, 1948.

63 Antonia Gransden, ed. *The Customary of the Benedictine Abbey of Bury St Edmunds*, HBS 99 (1973).

64 C. Wordsworth, ed. (transcribed by W. Cooke), *Ordinale Sarum*... 2 vols, HBS 20, 22 (both 1901).

65 For example, T.D. Hill, 'A Liturgical Source for *Christ* I.164-213,' *Medium Aevum* 46 (1977), 12-15, and Susan Rankin, 'The Liturgical Background of the. Old English Advent lyrics; a repappraisal,' in *Learning and Literature in Anglo-Saxon England: essays ... to P. Clemoes*, ed. M. Lapidge and H. Gneuss (Cambridge 1985), 317-40.

66 Particularly to be mentioned here is such work of Nigel Morgan's as his 'Notes on the Post-Conquest Calendar, Litany, and Martyrology of the Cathedral Priory of Winchester with a Consideration of Winchester Diocese Calendars of the pre-Sarum Period,' in *The Vanishing Past. Studies of Medieval Art, Liturgy and Metrology presented to Christopher*

are likely to be concerned with a wider range of liturgical texts,[67] and their interest in 'chant traditions' sometimes yields valuable synoptic conclusions.[68] For the pre-Conquest period, palaeographical studies have informed liturgical investigations and vice versa,[69] but the further one advances from 1066, the less interest there seems to be in the palaeography of liturgical manuscripts. Indeed, the one area in which there is at present (1997) the greatest vigor in pursuit of the liturgy in medieval England is in Anglo-Saxon studies, focused on both the annual periodical *Anglo-Saxon England* (as noted above) and the series Cambridge Studies in Anglo-Saxon England.[70]

While this overview has meant to demonstrate some of the range of liturgical scholarship available to the (predominantly Anglophone) student of the medieval liturgy, it can also serve to indicate the main outlines of what has appeared during the period - roughly the past thirty years - covered by the work reflected in the pieces included below. As these papers deal with matters both pre- and post-Conquest and approach their subjects from a variety of points of view, it may seem especially useful to have supplied some sense of the broad context of scholarship out of which they have arisen. In addition, to have included here the names of some of the pioneers and giants among modern liturgical scholars gives me a bit of the feeling that public recitation of the

---

Hohler, ed. A. Borg and A. Martindale, British Archaeological Reports, International Series 111 (Oxford 1981), 133-71.

67 A noteworthy recent volume is *Music in the Medieval English Liturgy: Plainsong and Mediaeval Music Society Centennial Essays*, ed. Susan Rankin and David Hiley (Oxford 1993); most of the contributions are intensely musicological.

68 See for instance David Hiley, 'Thurstan of Caen and Plainchant at Glastonbury: Musicological Reflections on the Norman Conquest,' *Procs. Brit. Acad.* 72 (1986), 57-90.

69 Most signally in the work of David Dumville, as currently summed up in two books, *Liturgy and the Ecclesiastical History of Later Anglo-Saxon England* (Woodbridge 1992) and *English Caroline Script and Monastic History: Studies in Benedictinism A.D. 950-1030* (Woodbridge 1993).

70 For example, vol. 17, Inge B. Milfull, *The Hymns of the Anglo-Saxon Church. A Study and Edition of the 'Durham Hymnal'* (Cambridge 1996). This was originally a Munich dissertation directed by Helmut Gneuss, whose *Hymnen und Hymnarien im englischen Mittelalter*, Buchreihe der Anglia 12 (Tübingen 1968) and subsequent publications, many in English, form the most important body of contributions by a German scholar to our field.

diptychs in the liturgy of the early church must have provided: a consciousness of summing up and an awareness of great gratitude.[71]

---

71 To stand alongside the quartet of those whose work is discussed above whom I hold in the greatest reverence - Bishop, Frere, Legg, and Wormald - I must mention also two great masters in the field of English manuscript studies whose names often occur in the following articles: M.R. James, whose life I have spent a fair amount of mine studying (see my *Montague Rhodes James* [London 1980] and Neil Ker, from whose personal influence and kindnesses I, like many others of my generation, have benefitted greatly (see my 'N.R. Ker and the Study of English Medieval Manuscripts,' in *Basic Readings in Anglo-Saxon Manuscripts*, ed. Mary P. Richards [New York 1994], 55-77).

II

Eadui Basan: Scriptorum Princeps?

In the last twenty years or so there has emerged a monk of Christ Church, Canterbury, who now seems a discernible, perhaps a major, figure in the cultural history of eleventh-century England.[1] That there was a monastic scribe called Eadui Basan whose autograph appears at the end of an eleventh-century English Gospel book in Hanover has been known since at least the beginning of the present century.[2] A local habitation for this scribe was provided in 1935, when it was recognized that a fragmentary flyleaf in a Lambeth Palace manuscript (430) belonged to the widely-known Christ Church obituary in BL Cotton MS Nero C.ix, so that there was now placed in a plausible context 'Eadwius sacerdos et monachus'.[3]

But the emergence of Eadui as a figure of some magnitude is owed almost entirely to the discerning eye of T. A. M. Bishop, who in his *English Caroline Minuscule* (1971) provided a list of eleven specimens of that scribe's hand.[4] He described it as 'round, upright, deliberate, and artificial but not mannered, with characteristic g, &, ct, ra, question mark, and various forms of cedilla'. This 'deliberate hand' he spoke of in his preface as marking 'the beginning at Christ Church, Canterbury, of the "formalism" seen in other English manuscripts of the period' (p. xxiii). It was, as he had put it a few years earlier, 'a clear, carefully formed, slightly denatured script... well calculated

1 I am indebted for assistance and advice to Janet Backhouse, Michelle Brown, Richard Gameson, Elizabeth Teviotdale, and especially to T. A. Heslop, who generously sent me proofs of his *Anglo-Saxon England* article. Abbreviations used in the notes are as follows: Bishop, *ECM* = T. A. M. Bishop, *English Caroline Minuscule* (Oxford, 1971); Bishop, 'Notes' = 'Notes on Cambridge Manuscripts', *Trans. Cambridge Bibliographical Soc.* 1953-63 (7 parts); Brooks = Nicholas Brooks, *The Early History of the Church at Canterbury* (Leicester, 1984); Heslop = T. A. Heslop, 'The Production of *de luxe* Manuscripts and the Patronage of King Cnut and Queen Emma', *ASE*, 19 (1990), 151-95; Ker, *Catalogue* = N. R. Ker, *Catalogue of Manuscripts containing Anglo-Saxon* (Oxford, 1957); Temple = Elzbieta Temple, *Anglo-Saxon Manuscripts, 900-1066* (London, 1976).

2 S. Beissel, *Geschichte der Evangelienbücher* (Freiburg, 1906), p. 137, citing C. Graeven, 'Die drei ältesten Handschriften des Michaelisklosters', *Zeitschrift des historische Vereins für Niedersachsen* for 1901, 284-85. Beissel surmised that this scribe might have come from Winchester.

3 A. Boutemy, 'Two Obituaries of Christ Church, Canterbury', *EHR*, 50 (1935), 292-99, at p. 295. The date of this Eadwius's death is said to be 22 September, but there is of course no indication of year.

4 Bishop, *ECM*, p. 22.

to set off the elaborate ornament of manuscripts':[5] an acute assessment, as we shall see, though in what sense it is 'slightly denatured' is not clear to me.

The current foundation of our knowledge of Eadui then is Bishop's list; but it would of course be naive to suppose that the eleven items on it represent anything like Eadui's *oeuvre* as a scribe. This is simply what has both survived and been identified by one distinguished scholar. Grateful as we are for the list, it may perhaps be added to in the future. I do not think it possible to establish a chronology of the surviving specimens of his writing purely on palaeographical grounds. Bishop speaks of one piece as seeming 'to be the late and degenerate work' of Eadui,[6] and Janet Backhouse, finding the script in another 'uneven and sometimes almost quavering', thinks it 'perhaps not too imaginative to see it as the work of an elderly or infirm man';[7] but it would be a perilous set of judgements which tried to go beyond that.

Instead, I propose to notice the surviving specimens of his work according to the kind of text they represent. We have from his hand the following: three Gospel books or lectionaries of which he seems to be the sole scribe, and a fourth in which he wrote a single page; one complete psalter (i.e. written completely by him, though it has since been altered considerably), part of another, and a third, much earlier one, for which he supplied a missing quire; finally a few charters.[8] These items may not seem like a great deal on which to base even an assessment, let alone a claim; but they represent a considerable amount to have been identified as the work of one named scribe of the eleventh century. Brief consideration of each of them may set us some way towards being able to surmise something about Eadui's stature.

As has been mentioned, we are able to assign a name to this distinctive hand because of the autograph that survives at the end of the Hanover Gospels (Pl. 40): 'Pro scriptore precem ne tempnas fundere pater. Librum istum monachus scripsit EADUUIUS cognomento BASAN. Sit illi longa salus. Vale seruus dei .N. & memor esto mei.'[9] It is so exciting to have his signature in this helpful way that it is easy to ignore the wording of this closing formula; but it does tell us quite plainly that the book has been

5 *Idem*, 'Notes on MSS in Cambridge, part vii', *Trans. Cambridge Bibliographical Soc.*, III (1963), 413-22, at p. 420.

6 See below, note 32.

7 See below, note 18.

8 There is a further item in Bishop's list, identified as Cambridge, Gonville and Caius College MS 732/734, 'leaf from a service book'. But nothing in the library of that college seems to correspond to this (I am grateful to the entire staff for an exhaustive but fruitless search), and further enquiry has not yielded any result.

9 Hanover, Kestner-Museum Hs. W.M. XII[a], 36 (f. 183v). Temple, no. 67.

written for a specific 'pater .N.' – and also provides the basic fact that this scribe is himself a monk. The 'servus dei .N.' can be interpreted in two ways. T. A. Heslop maintains that this 'suggests that Eadui was working for an intermediate patron. The book's ultimate recipient was unknown to him by name, indeed perhaps he had not yet been chosen.' But this seems to be not very flattering to that ultimate recipient, especially if, as the same scholar also supposes, such a book as this may have been used as a present by Cnut in the course of his trip to Rome in 1027.[10] An alternative possibility which seems to me preferable is that Eadui is writing this book for a recipient yet to be elected – a bishop or abbot to be chosen to fill a vacancy. Such a person could plausibly be thought to be grateful for the book personalized in this way rather than 'depersonalized' in the setting Heslop suggests, and indeed likelier to pray for the scribe who so carefully names himself. The book was in Germany already in the later eleventh century;[11] how it got there is not known.

How the Gospel lectionary now in Florence[12] got to its first home outside England is also a mystery, though again, since Bishop has noted added matter in an eleventh-century Continental hand, it presumably did so quite early. It has only one illustration, a drawing of Christ enthroned and flanked by Peter and Paul. Though the text of the book proper is unquestionably in Eadui's hand, Heslop finds this drawing very similar in style to the Matthew portrait in the Pembroke Gospels (Cambridge, Pembroke College, MS 301), and suggests that 'while the monumental capitals beneath the drawing in Florence are by Eadwig, the uncials and rustic capitals on the same folio are also entirely within the tradition of scribes B and C' (p. 173), these being the now customary designations for those who wrote, among other books, the sacramentary of Robert of Jumièges (Rouen, Bibl. mun. MS Y.6) and the Kederminster Gospels (BL Loan MS 11). I do not find this notion very realistic, supposing as it does that Eadui wrote the third line while a second scribe wrote lines 1, 5, and 8 and another wrote 2, 4, 6, and 7. The weak link here seems to be the supposition that the three words 'In illo tempore' are written by Eadui; they are not much to go on in the assigning of scripts, and it would seem preferable to suppose that Eadui was supplied with the title page complete and began his work on f. 1v.

10 Heslop, pp. 176, 180.

11 *The Golden Age of Anglo-Saxon Art, 966-1066*, ed. J. Backhouse, D. H. Turner, L. Webster (London, 1984), no. 56. Cf. Temple, no. 67: 'German additions (ff. i, 183v, 194) of 11th and 12th centuries indicate that the volume left England at an early date.'

12 Florence, Bibliotheca Medicea-Laurenziana MS Plut. XVII.20. Temple, no. 69.

The third of Eadui's books of this kind, that called the Grimbald Gospels (BL Add. MS 34890), is a very grand book indeed.[13] It has come by its nickname because of a letter supposedly from Archbishop Fulk of Reims recommending Grimbald of St Bertin's to Alfred the Great. The hand which added the letter is apparently slightly later than Eadui's, and, as Temple has pointed out, may indicate no more than that this book was made for the New Minster, Winchester (to which Ker assigns it, with a query).[14] As, however, this localization is made on the basis of the letter about Grimbald, who was a great New Minster figure, the argument is a rather circular one.

Still, it is relevant to consider whether the Grimbald Gospels (there is no reason to discard the conventional name) represents Eadui writing on commission, so to speak, for another great monastic house, or whether the book should be seen as one of a series of Gospel texts, to which an interesting addition happens to have been made but which was not written to order. Though there can be no certainty, signs of incompleteness in this otherwise sumptuous book rather suggest that it was being made against some pressure of time. In the evangelist portraits, their 'books' are blank – perhaps incomplete, perhaps awaiting the evangelistic pens; but the scrolls carried by the human symbol of Matthew and bovine symbol of Luke are likewise devoid of writing, and there is a puzzling blank green surface to the right of the evangelist John. Furthermore, though the book is written almost flawlessly to the end of the Fourth Gospel, in the Gospel list which follows (f. 145v-57) every other initial is omitted (they have subsequently been pencilled in, with a good attempt at imitation of the original letter forms). It is reasonable to wonder whether the book was not sent off – as it were, to meet a deadline – before these last, not very time-consuming, details could be finished.

It is, therefore, possible to suggest that Eadui was asked to write a Gospel book for a rich and proud house, one which cannot be thought to have lacked scribes of its own. If this should be the correct understanding of the Grimbald Gospels, it would help us also to understand one of the major puzzles surrounding Eadui's career: his writing of a single, oddly isolated, leaf in the York Gospels.[15] What happened can be stated simply, but explanation is both complicated and controverted. The verso (23v) of the first, display page of Mattthew's Gospel (which faces the Evangelist portrait on 22v) was originally left blank; and the missing words, from 'Esrom' through 'qui uocatur Christus' in the Matthean genealogy, were subsequently supplied by

13 Temple, no. 68.

14 N. R. Ker, ed. *Medieval Libraries of Great Britain*, 2nd edn, (London, 1964), p. 103; see under Hyde.

15 York Minster, MS Add. 1. A facsimile edition, edited by Nicolas Barker with four substantial introductory essays, was published for the Roxburghe Club in 1986.

Eadui. The questions raised by this curious manner of proceeding begin with why the page was left blank in the first place and how long the interval was between when f. 23 (and, apparently, the rest of the codex) was written and when Eadui filled in the blank space. Michelle Brown has dealt with these problems admirably in a recent review of the facsimile.[16] The salient point for our purposes is her questioning of the long-held assumption that the York Gospels (which seem quite clearly to have reached York by *c.*1020-23) was written – save for f. 23v – in the late tenth century and that a gap of some twenty years or more supervened before Eadui wrote his page. Brown sees 'fewer obstacles to viewing Eadui's work as part of the original campaign, with his contribution forming the final stage in the work' (p. 554) - though this does not explain why the filling in of the blank page should have constituted the final stage. On balance she favours moving the dating of the volume to the early eleventh century, thus casting Eadui's role as part of 'a continuous working sequence'. Even so, we are left with the question with which we started: roughly, is it Eadui's eminence or his 'juniority' which was responsible for his being chosen to fill in the blank?

Heslop agrees that the idea that this book should have been in production for twenty to thirty years is inherently implausible, but does not speak in terms of filling a blank space. He reminds us that Bishop once suggested that Eadui had actually, as the writer of the first page of Gospel text proper, 'established the mise-en-page merely, the rest of the Gospels being written in a clear but non-calligraphic hand,' though later Bishop seemed to change his mind. As a new way out of the dilemma, Heslop suggests ingeniously that 'scribes of different ages were working side by side'[17] – a suggestion which incidentally reinforces the one made just above about the little signs of haste in the Grimbald Gospels.

A similar question about Eadui's involvement in a collaborative work confronts us with an even more famous codex, the Harley Psalter.[18] This extraordinarily complicated book is not only incomplete but unfinished, despite (or perhaps because of) the efforts of at least three scribes and some eight artists.[19] As the book has come down to us it has seventy-three folios;

16 M. P. Brown in *The Book Collector*, 38 (1989), 551-55.

17 Heslop, p. 169. The reference to Bishop is from part ii of the 'Notes', 1955, p.186.

18 BL Harley MS 603. Temple, no. 64. See most recently J. Backhouse, 'The Making of the Harley Psalter', *British Library Jnl*, 10 (1984), 97-113; also of interest are R. Hasler, 'Zu zwei Darstellungen aus der ältesten Kopie des Utrecht-Psalters,' *Zeitschrift für Kunstgeschichte,* 44 (1981), 317-39, and an unpublished doctoral thesis by Judith Duffey, *The Inventive Group of Illustrations in the Harley Psalter* (Univ. of California, Berkeley, 1977). Further light is expected to be shed in the forthcoming thesis of William Noel.

19 The numbering of the artists is that of Francis Wormald, *English Drawings of the*

there is no prefatory matter, and it stops in the middle of Psalm 143, at the end of a gathering. One scribe wrote ff. 1-27 and from the middle of 54v to 73; another wrote a brief section, ff. 50-54v; and Eadui wrote four gatherings in the middle, ff. 28-49. Though some leaves are now missing, his section seems to begin at Psalm 49 and to end at Psalm 97.[20] The following section (Psalms 100 to 105.25), that begun by the third scribe, provides one of the major enigmas of the Psalter, for it is in the Gallicanum version whereas the other parts of the text – both the initial scribe's section and Eadui's – are basically in the Romanum.[21] Indeed, it looks as though the third scribe was replaced summarily by the original one when it was realized that he was writing the 'wrong' version.

But some uncertainty about versions is also apparent in Eadui's section. In several places he has written a Gallicanum reading – for example, in Psalm 95.2 the Gallicanum 'benedicite nomini' rather than the Romanum 'benedicite nomen', in 51.11 a 'quia' instead of 'quem', in 52.6 a 'quoniam' in place of a probable Romanum 'quia'. These tiny instances suggest that Eadui may have in some way been 'thinking Gallicanum', as the third scribe definitely was. This is intrinsically not very surprising, since the Utrecht Psalter, on which the illustrations are clearly based, is itself Gallicanum.

The major curiosity about Eadui's section is in any case not his slight textual wavering but the fact that it was in his time virtually not illustrated. A few faint initials are all that seem to have been accomplished in his part in the early eleventh century, though some decades later an artist did illustrate the first of the folios he wrote (28) and in the twelfth century, probably around the middle, ff. 29-35 were elaborately illustrated (but again not completely, there being only faint sketchwork on ff. 34-35). The last fourteen of Eadui's folios have no illustration whatever.

From such indications as these we can hazard the following guess about Eadui's role in the making of this book. Clearly he is neither the starting nor the principal figure. Another scribe begins the psalms; it is this scribe rather than Eadui who takes over when the third has to be replaced. And whatever part Eadui may have had in the decoration of some of the books he wrote, he does not have such a part here. It seems reasonable to suppose that he is a somewhat junior figure in the scriptorium when he works on the Harley Psalter, and the date most often assigned to it, the first ten or so years of the eleventh century, seems consonant with this – though again the danger of circular reasoning must be kept in mind: is this book to be dated then partly

---

Tenth and Eleventh Centuries (London, 1952), no. 34.

20 These are quires V to VIII, of six, eight, six, and two leaves (as they now stand) respectively.

21 Brooks, p. 381 n. 28, says that the Gallicanum text of pss. 100-105.25 was supplied at the end of the 11th century, but this is simply wrong.

because Eadui seems to work on it in a subsidiary capacity or do we regard his part as secondary because we have otherwise assigned an early date?[22]

Janet Backhouse advances a different line of argument.[23] She points out that Eadui's section is written on inferior vellum, that the pages are not laid out like those in the earlier part of the book, and that there is no illustration by the artist who busily filled gaps in parts one, three, and four but not in (Eadui's) part two. In short, she feels, his section has 'every appearance of being a later substitute for a lost or damaged portion of the original work'. She tends to prefer a rather late date for the inception of the book, toying intriguingly with a time as late as *c.*1020, which would put Eadui's section quite far along in his career as a scribe, and cast him in the light not of a relatively junior member of the scriptorium but as a senior, even elderly, figure. Indeeed, this is where Backhouse maintains that his hand is 'uneven and sometimes almost quavering', and concludes that 'it is perhaps not too imaginative to see it as the work of an elderly or infirm man', whose part of the book could have been written as late as the 1040s. I find this rather difficult to accept, simply because there is not a shred of evidence which otherwise places any of Eadui's work later than 1023: which of course is not to say that he stopped writing then. And if the arguments rehearsed earlier about the York Gospels hold water, his *floruit* is even more firmly established in the second decade of the century. In this as in other respects the key document in interpreting his importance is probably the Arundel Psalter.

Here no questions about collaborative involvement arise. The Arundel Psalter (BL Arundel 155) is almost certainly datable to the period 1012-23, and was written solely (in its original state) by Eadui.[24] The dating framework comes from the presence as an original entry in the calendar of 'Passio sancti Ælfheahi archiepiscopi' (martyred 19 April 1012) and from the absence of his translation on 8 June 1023.[25] Such a clear framework helps to make the Harley Psalter seem earlier, though there is in theory no absolute reason why it has to be. Whatever may be the relationships of time or causation between the two books, it is clear that Arundel is not only a one-man but a very individual production. Indeed, it should more fittingly be

22 This discussion assumes that the Harley Psalter was made at Christ Church and not at St Augustine's. Again the danger of circular argument exists, but Eadui's role does seem one of the deciding factors for Christ Church. Backhouse also favours this location (note 18).

23 Backhouse, 'Harley Psalter', p. 106. The article makes several stimulating suggestions about the book as a whole.

24 Temple, no. 66.

25 The calendar is printed in F. Wormald, ed. *English Kalendars before A.D. 1100* (Henry Bradshaw Society 72, 1933), pp. 169-81.

called the Eadui Psalter, for it bears his stamp in three distinctive ways beyond his merely having written it: textual, liturgical, and iconographic.

The first aspect relates again to the textual question that arose with the Harley Psalter. Though, as we saw, Eadui seems to have had some Gallicanum readings in his head while he was writing his section of Harley, the Arundel Psalter is once more of the Romanum – that is, old-fashioned – version. Much remains to be done before the fortunes of these versions in eleventh-century England can be straightened out. Preliminarily (or perhaps superficially), it seems to be the case that the Gallicanum version gets an English foothold in the late tenth century, the Salisbury Psalter (Salisbury Cathedral, MS 150) being apparently the first psalter made in England to contain it; and that it has taken over at Winchester by the middle of the eleventh, in such books as BL Stowe 2, Cotton Tiberius C.vi, Cotton Vitellius E.xviii, and Arundel 60, all probably having some connection with one or another of the scriptoria at Winchester.[26] What is not clear is whether there was at Canterbury a corresponding conservatism about abandoning the older version, for the relevant pieces of evidence are really only two: the Bosworth Psalter (BL Add. MS 37517), virtually contemporary with the path-breaking Salisbury Psalter, and Harley 603, with its suggestions that the Gallicanum is about to break in.

The question is heightened rather than resolved by the text of the Arundel Psalter; for though Eadui wrote it in the Romanum version, he subsequently made extensive corrections to try to bring it into conformity with the Gallicanum. (The full extent of this is a bit hard to see because even more widespread corrections were made in the twelfth century, not at all to our purpose.) Eadui's changes are often over careful and complete erasures: for example, a 'conteruisti' changed to 'contriuisti' (ps. 3.8), 'iniusticia' to 'iniquitate' (ps. 51.3), 'bene nunciate' to 'annunciate' (ps. 95.2), 'potentatibus' to 'virtutibus' (ps. 150.2). The result is far from being a complete Gallicanum text, but the overall effect is of a version that will now, as it were, stand muster in the wider world. Did Eadui try to produce a revised text of this kind because he was asked to do so or because it fell to him, at least in part, to make that kind of decision for the community?

The second respect in which the Arundel Psalter may bear witness to Eadui's stature is in the contents of the calendar which stands at the head of the book. Again, his potential contribution has to be approached cautiously, because there is very little in the way of comparative calendarial material for Christ Church from before or during his time, and because the numerous and complex subsequent additions make it hard to ascertain exactly what the document looked like when it left Eadui's hands. These cautions stated, it does appear possible that the calendar of this psalter represents a stage of

26 See, e.g., the discussion in Brooks, pp. 261-65.

'normalizing' the saints honoured at Christ Church. If this is the case, the intelligence behind such 'normalizing' would almost certainly be that of someone of both perceived stature and future influence.

The primary point of comparison here has to be with the calendar of the Bosworth Psalter, extensively studied by Edmund Bishop and Aidan Gasquet in 1908.[27] It would be too much to claim that Bosworth's calendar was anything like an official Christ Church document of the beginning of the eleventh century,[28] any more than that Arundel's had that character perhaps twenty years later. This is not the place to discuss in detail the comparative tables Bishop provides, but a brief juxtaposition with Bosworth's calendar may tell us something useful about the nature of Eadui's. There are three strong contrasts. First, Bosworth contains many more saints than Arundel – approximately fifty-five more. Secondly, to a striking extent the saints present in Bosworth's calendar but missing from Eadui's are not just obscure persons from Continental martyrologies but English (and British) figures of considerable familiarity: such names as abbot Hadrian, Guthlac, Aldhelm, Botulf, Eadburga (15 June), Aethelburga, Aidan, Paulinus, and Wilfrid, plus a whole group of (arch)bishops of Canterbury – Mellitus, Deusdedit, Honorius, Nothelm, Justus. The relative spareness of Arundel's calendar, especially at the expense of all these figures from the Anglo-Saxon past (between fifteen and twenty in all), is so striking that it misled as great a scholar as Edmund Bishop into regarding the Psalter as post-Conquest and its calendar as a document of the so-called Lanfrancian purge.[29]

Eadui's calendar is in a sense purged, though not by supposed archiepiscopal action; but the contrast with Bosworth's is not solely in the direction of sloughing off excess saints. For the Arundel calendar also includes some thirty names lacking in Bosworth. Only three of these are primarily English, all with Winchester affinities – the translations of Cuthbert and Birinus 4 September, Birinus alone 3 December, and perhaps Judoc on 13 December – together with Ælfheah. The great majority of these additional names are Continental. A few can be connected with relics at Christ Church (for example, Blaise), but the majority imply Continental sacramentary traditions of some complexity: Emerentiana and Macharius (23

27 F. A. Gasquet and E. Bishop, *The Bosworth Psalter* (London, 1908).

28 Two difficulties in so doing would be 1) that Bosworth's calendar has some clear Glastonbury affinities, e.g. its entries at 23 Aug. 'Patricii senioris in Glaestonia' and 25 Sept. 'Ceolfrithi abbatis in Glaestonia'; and 2) that its calendar seems to be somewhat later than the rest of the book, though exactly how much later is not clear. For further complications see M. Korhammer, 'The Origin of the Bosworth Psalter', *ASE*, 2 (1973), 173-87.

29 Gasquet and Bishop, pp. 30-32.

January), Vitus and Modestus (15 July), Pantaleon as well as Sampson (28 July), Symphorian as well as Timothy (22 August).

These details permit us to understand Arundel's calendar. First, there is a general if quite selective awareness of the English past: Alban, Augustine, Oswald, Cuthbert, Boniface, Erkenwald. Secondly, particular attention is paid to observances connected equally with both great Winchester houses.[30] Thirdly, limited but striking awareness is shown of Continental saints, both of early Christian antiquity and of Frankish origin: figures like Vedast and Amand (6 February, with Vedast again, joining Remigius and Germanus, on 1 October), Leodegar (Leger, 2 October), Lambert (17 September). None of these is included in Bosworth's calendar (and none primarily connected with areas where Cnut had his major dealings). The determining intelligence is at once historically and liturgically sophisticated; is it also Eadui's? It may of course belong to someone else entirely, but until a better candidate can be suggested, he would seem to hold the field. At the least, the suggestion is not implausible, nor inconsistent with the other evidence considered.

The very substantial, perhaps pre-eminent, position which the Arundel Psalter suggests that Eadui held by about 1020 may help to explain the nature of his involvement in the third psalter associated with him. This is the Vespasian Psalter, mostly written in the eighth century (in the Romanum version), and with continuous interlinear Old English gloss added in the ninth.[31] It was kept at St Augustine's in the fifteenth century, and there is no reason to think that it was not there in the eleventh. The book is not only splendid but also quite complete. As it stands, it contains the full psalter (plus the extranumeral psalm, added in the ninth century at f. 141), nine canticles, and three hymns. Then comes a new quire, ff. 155-60, containing Te Deum, Quicunque vult, and various prayers, and written by Eadui. This is the work of his which T. A. M. Bishop refers to as 'late and degenerate; mainly deliberate, but in places negligently formed'.[32]

30 Brooks's discussion of these matters on p. 265 is interesting but a bit simplistic in two respects. It is not enough merely to say that 'By the time of the Arundel Psalter, Christ Church had changed to a calendar of Winchester origin', because the 'Winchester' saints reflect both those of the Old Minster (Swithun, Birinus) and the New (Grimbald, Judoc): this is no more a single calendarial tradition than would a mix of Christ Church and St Augustine's be a 'Canterbury' tradition. Nor is it quite accurate to characterize the removal of English saints from Arundel's calendar as 'an apparent attempt in the early 11th century to remove the feasts of saints whose cult has developed in other Kentish houses'; because too many of the 'purged' saints do not fall into that category – Gildas, Maerwynna, Guthlac, Botulf, Aidan, Aldhelm, Rumwold – for that to be the whole story.

31 BL Cotton Vespasian A. i; facsimile edn, D. H. Wright, *The Vespasian Psalter* (Early English Manuscripts in Facsimile 14, Copenhagen 1967).

32 Bishop, *ECM*, p. 22; he notes 'Two forms of the ct-ligature; the frequent hooked e

Three unanswerable questions that arise here begin with one perhaps irrelevant to Eadui: what had happened to the final quire of the original psalter? The second is the most obvious one: why was Eadui asked to supply the gap? And the third is: to what extent is he responsible for the choice of the prayers that follow the Quicunque – especially the first, the 'Oratio Eugenii Toletani episcopi' ('Rex Deus inmense qui constat machina mundi')? We might also ask why the Te Deum and Athanasian Creed have Old English glosses, apparently also in Eadui's hand,[33] whereas the prayers, equally in Latin, do not.

If we simply suppose that Eadui was asked to complete what was clearly regarded as a prize possession because he was known to be an eminent scribe, we still need to consider the issues implied by this. To take one obvious aspect, was he paid for his work? Far-fetched as that possibility may sound, there is some reason to entertain it. Heslop cites the mention in Ælfric Bata's *Colloquia* of the scribes who 'write books and sell them and thence gain for themselves lots of money'.[34] If payment seems unlikely – it is, after all, only six folios – can we rather imagine a friendly exchange of scribes between the two great Canterbury houses, not themselves always on such friendly terms? To prove such an idea we would need to find a Christ Church book similarly supplied by a known St Augustine's scribe, but without proof this must remain hypothetical.

It is more likely that the monks of St Augustine's turned to Eadui because he was known to be an expert on the contents of psalters. If it is true, as Bishop has suggested, that this is a late, let alone degenerate specimen of Eadui's hand, it is more probable that he would be asked to take on this work as one whose knowledge about such matters was worth having rather than because of the beauty of his writing.

There is, however, one further possibility which should be mentioned. This is that the Vespasian psalter was for some reason loaned to Christ Church and that while it was there something – spillage, rats, a small fire – ruined the final gathering: whereupon the monks not of St Augustine's but of Christ Church naturally turned to their eminent master-scribe Eadui Basan to supply the damaged material. This is far-fetched, perhaps, but it does fit the facts of the existing situation.

---

occurs, less frequently, in the scribe's portion of Harl. MS 603.'

33 Ker, *Catalogue*, no. 203, describes the hand as 'a very fine upright hand of s. xi med, apparently an early version of the St Augustine's hand found in Cambridge Corpus Christi College, MS 270 and in other manuscripts: in OE *s* is regularly long and *y* is straight-limbed and dotted: hyphens are on a level with the base-line'.

34 Heslop, p. 177, citing the text in *Early Scholastic Colloquies*, ed. W. H. Stevenson (Oxford, 1929) p. 50.

The kind of eminence here presupposed also explains Eadui's work on Christ Church charters, work which in turn makes his stature much clearer. The most important of these documents is the celebrated confirmation of privileges of Christ Church by Cnut within the period 1017-20, most likely in 1018: an Old English document of thirteen lines written by Eadui on the top half of a blank leaf in an early eleventh-century Gospel book, BL Royal MS 1. D.ix (f. 44v).[35] This is a book whose special donation (because it was believed to have been given by Cnut) and beautiful execution (because it was written largely by the scribe who wrote the Trinity Gospels and the Robert of Jumièges Sacramentary)[36] made it a highly suitable location for the insertion of a document which clinched the resecuring of the *freols* of the monastery – a process begun by a ceremony in which Cnut had himself laid certain charters granted by earlier kings on the high altar at Canterbury. It is the description of this solemn public act which Eadui recorded in the Gospel book: 'Then I myself took the charters of freedom and laid them on Christ's own altar, with the cognizance of the archbishop and of earl Thurkill and of many good men who were with me...'.[37] Thus, as Nicholas Brooks has put it, 'the skill of the outstanding writer at Christ Church reinforced the authority of the royal act by associating it with the holy gospels that were kept upon the most sacred altar in England'.[38]

Equally striking is Eadui's involvement in preserving a bilingual charter linked with Æthelred II and the year 1006, similarly written on blank leaves between the gospels of Luke and John in an even more venerable Gospel book, the late ninth- or early tenth-century continental codex given to Christ Church by King Athelstan before his death in 939.[39] This is a very extensive and important privilege, securing for the cathedral establishment its distinctive status as a monastic community. It is therefore an appropriate text

35 Temple, no. 70; f. 44v is printed and translated in F. E. Harmer, *Anglo-Saxon Writs* (Manchester, 1952; reprint Stamford, 1989), no. 26. Here Ker, *Cat.*, no. 247, notes that 'long and low *s* are initially used indifferently and round *s* initially: high *e* occurs once in the combination *æ*'. The blank leaves are the last two of a quire of eight, and come between the Markan prologue and title page; presumably they were left blank so that his portrait could be placed at the head of a new gathering.

36 Respectively, Cambridge Trinity College MS. B.10.4 and Rouen, Bibl. mun. Y.6. Both were written by the scribe generally known as B in the identification by Bishop, *ECM*. A colleague, Bishop's C, also worked on the Royal Gospels.

37 As translated by Harmer, *Writs*, p. 182.

38 Brooks, p. 288.

39 BL Cotton Tiberius A.ii, from which were detached before 1621 seven leaves which now make up Cotton Claudius A. iii (and four more now in Cotton Faustina B. vi): N. R. Ker, 'Membra Disiecta', *British Museum Quarterly*, 12 (1937-38), 130-31.

to be written by a prominent scribe and preserved in a book of solemn importance, especially since, again in Brooks's words, this 'monastic refoundation charter is in fact a forgery, and it is very possible that it was Eadui Basan himself who both doctored the gospel book to receive it and concocted the text of the charter'.[40]

We know of at least two other charters written by Eadui, and may assume that he wrote more. One is a charter for Cnut dated 1018, the contents of which also concern Christ Church, or at least the archiepiscopal estates, and which was probably granted at the same time as Cnut visited the cathedral to take part in the ceremony of confirming its previous privileges just described.[41] The other is a copy of the confirmation at the Synod of Cloveshoe in 716 of a charter of liberties granted to the religious establishments of Kent by King Wihtred twenty-five years before. This is by far the earliest manuscript of this charter to have survived, probably with a major interpolation in a kind of postscript which threatens dire penalties to anyone who 'tyrannica potestate inflatus ex habitu secularium seu ecclesiasticarum infringere minuere temptauerit auctoritatem archiepiscopi et Christi ecclesie uel libertatem coenobiarum'.[42]

The overall import of Eadui's activity with the Christ Church charters may be summed up by referring once more to Brooks's assessment of the 1018 episode. He finds it likely '1) that prior to Cnut's visit Eadui re-examined the charters of his house and recopied them where necessary; 2) that the Christ Church monks stage-managed the king's elaborate ceremony at the altar of Christ; and 3) that Eadui prepared the text of the royal writ to be sent to the shire-court'.[43] Such an assessment puts us in a position to consider Eadui's impact on his community as a whole.

Three further pieces of evidence are crucial in any attempt to evaluate Eadui's overall importance. The first is the famous illustration on f. 133 of Eadui's own Arundel Psalter (Pl.41).[44] The kneeling monk crouching at the

40 Brooks, p. 257. As to a precise date, he notes that 'the script of the refoundation charter compares rather with the late and somewhat less carefully written work of this scribe, and we have no information about how long he lived. The forgery had certainly been entered into the gospels before another scribe added another series of notes of subsequent bequests to Christ Church apparently early in Edward the Confessor's reign.' He therefore suggests a date in the early part of the second quarter of the century.

41 BL Stowe Charters 38, printed in B. Sanders, ed., *Facsimiles of Anglo-Saxon Manuscripts*, 3 vols (Ordnance Survey, 1878-84), III.39. Cf. Brooks, pp. 277 an 288.

42 BL Stowe Charters 2, printed in Sanders, *Facsimiles*, III.2.

43 Brooks, p. 290.

44 BL Arundel MS 155, f. 133, illustrated in colour in *Golden Age of Anglo-Saxon Art*,

foot of St Benedict and holding a book in his left hand is generally taken to be Eadui, a portrait of the scribe, so to speak – indeed, if Eadui is also the illustrator of this manuscript (a possibility we shall consider presently), a self-portrait. The book he holds is presumably this psalter (the letters 'Lib ps' are evident to the left of where his hand is holding the book); the prostrate monk is in physical contact with the saint (whose footstool he is and whose foot he is kissing); the girdle around his waist is lettered 'zona humilitatis'. His whole figure is coloured, like Benedict's; since the other monks are virtually monochrome, he is clearly the second most important figure in the picture. Is this a piece of mere self-advertisement or a fair reflection of his status in the community? So prominently is he depicted that one would almost prefer that the figure be meant as someone else, but the carrying of the book in his hand makes this all but impossible.

Related to the impression conveyed by this (self-) portrait is a further puzzling question: the meaning of 'cognomento Basan'. Do we best infer from the Hanover Gospels colophon that Basan is a surname in an age when surnames as such were very little known; or that it is what we would more accurately call a nickname; or – the least desirable alternative – that it is a now incomprehensible sign of demarcation in a community where there may have been a number of people with names like Eadui? A search through modern works on personal names in this period has so far drawn a total blank. The only, admittedly far-fetched, possibility I can think of is a corrupt form of the colour adjective *basu*, purple, perhaps related to the Gothic word for berry.[45] This hypothetical question is made chiefly because in the Arundel Psalter illustration just discussed, the face in profile of the kneeling monk whom we have assumed to be Eadui is not only shaded (as is Benedict's) but curiously mottled by nine or so little double marks, like double inverted commas. Can these be meant to represent some sort of disfigurement, like a widespread birthmark? If this should indeed be a self-portrait, it is Eadui who chooses to emphasize this aspect; which would in turn be congruous with the display-letter prominence of 'cognomento BASAN' in the Hanover Gospels colophon, itself the only source we have for this puzzling name.

The second indication of Eadui's overall status in Christ Church is again admittedly conjectural but cannot be ignored. This is a marginal note in a Christ Church manuscript of first importance to the community in the mid-eleventh century – the period, we would suppose, around the time of or just after Eadui's death: BL Cotton Tiberius A. iii, which contains a (the?) Christ Church copy of the *Rule* of Benedict and various supplements, the

pl. xviii.

45 J. Bosworth and T. N. Toller, *An Anglo-Saxon Dictionary* (Oxford, 1882-98), p. 68. I am grateful to Bernard O'Donoghue for discussing this point with me.

Regularis Concordia, the *Colloquy* of Ælfric, and further miscellaneous contents. Most of the items are supplied with interlinear Old English gloss.[46] After Benedict's *Rule* (ff. 118-63v as the manuscript is now constituted) comes a seven-line injunction to observe it (beginning 'Dicebat uero sanctus Fulgentius') and what is here called an 'Epitome of the Rule' but is in fact part ii of Benedict of Aniane's *Memoriale* (ff. 164-68v). As the latter document begins there are in the margin of fol. 164 in a late-eleventh-century hand the words 'Eadwi m[...] me ah' (as read by Ker; we may conjecture *-unuc*, giving 'munuc', in the illegible space). The presumption is that the writer of these words thought that an 'Eadwi' either possessed the book or had obtained the book, or was the author ('owner') of the Benedict of Aniane treatise on the Rule or even the maker of the collection of largely monastic documents that comprise the codex.

Before we turn to the third and most speculative suggestion as to Eadui Basan's stature at Christ Church, we need to notice the possibility of his having been what we would call an artist as well as a scribe. Probably neither of two extreme positions is correct: that all decoration in every book he wrote is by another hand than his, or that he is responsible for most of the illustrative material in the books he wrote – indeed, if the latter were the case Eadui would immediately become the major named artist of his time. A middle-ground position must take seriously the possibility that at the least he did a good deal of the decoration of 'his' psalter, including the somewhat self-advertising depiction at Benedict's feet. The two most recent students of the manuscript both suggest that Eadui had a major hand in the decoration of this book. Brooks says that Eadui 'produced a superbly written and decorated psalter'; while Heslop notes that Arundel 155 and the Hanover Gospels 'are fairly clearly painted by the same hand, and in both books minuscule and capital letters very like Eadui's form an integral part of the visual imagery', and remarks that 'the case for these being Eadui's own paintings and drawings is strong if not yet conclusive'.[47]

The third possible indication of Eadui's importance at Christ Church is connected with the question of how his memory was chiefly preserved there. Was it as a scribe, or as an artist, or as one whose sagacity was vital in preserving (or improving) the house's privileges? There can be little doubt that the primary category was that of scribe, an understood, even dignified position which might extend on one side to the decoration of manuscripts and on the other to controlling the wording of the charters he wrote. And it is as scribe that this final possible clue presents itself as to how lasting his impact may have been.

[46] BL Cotton Tiberius A. iii is analysed at length in Ker, *Cat.*, no. 186. Temple, no. 100.

[47] Brooks, p. 264; Heslop, p. 176.

This has to do with the Leonine hexameter verses around the famous portrait of the monk-scribe on f. 283v of the Eadwine Psalter (Cambridge, Trinity College MS R.17.1/987; pl. 42):

SCRIPTORUM PRINCEPS EGO. NEC OBITURA DEINCEPS
LAUS MEA NEC FAMA. QUIS SIM MEA LITTERA CLAMA.
TE TUA SCRIPTURA QUEM SIGNAT PICTA FIGURA
PREDICAT EADWINUM FAMA PER SECULA VIVUM.
INGENIUM CUIUS LIBRI DECUS INDICAT HUIUS
QUEM TIBI SEQUE DATUM MUNUS DEUS ACCIPE GRATUM.

The curious thing about these often-quoted verses is that the distinguishing characteristic of the verse form as fully developed – the bisyllabic internal rhyme – breaks down at what seems to be the crucial place, the name of the person being honoured. Since as these words stand the whole point of the inscription seems vitiated by the defective rhyme 'Eadwinum/vivum', it is tempting to wonder whether the verses – and, just conceivably, the portrait itself – were not originally meant to refer to someone other than the figure we think of as Eadwine, ostensibly a Canterbury monk-scribe of the twelfth century. And one cannot help noting that 'Eaduiuum' makes a true, if not elegant, rhyme with ('secu)la uiuum'. Of course, Eadui Basan signs himself, in the rustic capitals of the Hanover Gospels colophon, EADUUIUS, not EADUIUUS. But such a name in minuscule script could, by a misreading of the seven vertical strokes which form UUIU as UIUU, be rendered as EADUIUUS: in the accusative case, therefore, not 'Eaduuium' but 'Eaduiuum', which creates the true rhyme for '-la uiuum'.[48]

Clearly this suggestion hovers between plausibility and absurdity, but this may not be an inappropriate posture in which to end this preliminary enquiry. In descending order of likelihood, the following points should be considered. 1) It is highly probable that if Eadui Basan 'signed' one of his books (and that one intended for a recipient whose name he does not seem to have known) he signed others as well. 2) It is certainly possible that one or more such 'signatures' existed in minuscules, giving rise to the possibility of misunderstanding just noticed. 3) It may well be the case that the import of the 'portrait' in the Arundel Psalter was understood for some decades after his death; without question, the book was used in the mid-twelfth century (extensive additions to its calendar, further prayers, numerous hymns, and a concerted effort to make the text conform to the Gallicanum) and also

48 I have broached this question at somewhat greater length in chapter III of M. Gibson, T. A. Heslop, R. W. Pfaff, ed., *The Eadwine Psalter. Text, Image, and Monastic Culture in Twelfth-Century Canterbury* (London and University Park, PA, 1992).

thereafter (further additions to the calendar, even into the fifteenth century). 4) It is conceivable that the memory of Eadui's role in securing Christ Church privileges at the time of a new, foreign dynasty (Cnut's) survived, and was viewed gratefully, in the time of another new and foreign dynasty, that of William. 5) It is not inconceivable that this memory is somehow perpetuated in the Leonine verses of the Eadwine Psalter which (whatever their relevance to Eadui) clearly do not seem to have been composed originally in honour of someone named Eadwine.

As we look over this chain of probabilities, possibilities, and guesses, it seems unwise to discard entirely the figure of Eadui Basan. There can be little doubt that on the basis of what we now know about him he qualifies amply for the sobriquet 'scriptorum princeps'. Whether he was so known at Christ Church either during his lifetime or after his death, and whether the appellation is in some distant way preserved in the Eadwine Psalter inscription with its false rhyme, we can probably never establish with certainty. But there can be no doubt about the importance of his role in English eleventh-century studies.

40. (Pfaff) Hanover Gospels, Eadui Basan's autograph

41. (Pfaff) Arundel Psalter, St Benedict and Eadui Basan

42. (Pfaff) Eadwine Psalter, portrait of *scriptorum princeps*

III

Lanfranc's Supposed Purge of the Anglo-Saxon Calendar

Among the cardinal questions in the relationship between lay and ecclesiastical power in the high middle ages is that of designating which departed members of the body of Christ were to be venerated as saints.[1] The consequences of such veneration are so many and obvious that it is not necessary even to adumbrate them here. The purpose of this essay is to consider one widely-held view about the way this power was exercised at the time of the Norman Conquest of England.

It is a commonplace that among the ecclesiastical effects wrought by the Norman Conquest was a marked diminution in the number of saints venerated in the English church: a diminution which, furthermore, is said to have been the result of a deliberate policy on the part of Lanfranc, from 1070 on William the Conqueror's new (and first Norman) archbishop of Canterbury. Exactly how this notion came to have currency in the modern world is not clear; but the *locus classicus* from which

[1] The general subject of saints and sainthood is one which has been intensively worked on in recent decades. The main thrust of much of this work, summed up in such phrases as 'the role of the holy man in society', is not at all my concern here, which is rather to clear some ground between older liturgical scholarship of e.g. Edmund Bishop and Francis Wormald on one hand and current investigations like those of Susan Ridyard (see nn. 33 and 50) and David Rollason (see n. 48) on the other. Much of the work for this essay was completed before the books of the two last-named scholars were published, though I am glad to see that we are in general agreement.

the idea ultimately arose is without question the passage in Eadmer's *Life of Anselm* which relates the well-known conversation in, it seems, 1079 between the saint (while still abbot of Bec) and the archbishop. The focus of the discussion was one saint only, albeit an important one: Alphege (Ælfheah), the archbishop slaughtered by drunken Danes in 1012.[2] Anselm's defence convinced Lanfranc, who thereupon promised to 'worship and venerate the saint with all my heart', and indeed commissioned Osbern of Canterbury to write a life 'not only in plain prose for reading but also put . . . to music for singing; and Lanfranc himself for the love of the martyr gave it the seal of his eminent approval . . .'[3]

The implication is, of course, that Lanfranc could have withheld his 'eminent approval'; and, had he done so, that Alphege would thenceforth have been out of the calendar of the English church. And the impression given by this implication is intensified by a sentence at the beginning of this chapter of Eadmer's work (c. 30) where the biographer speaks of *quaedam institutiones* which Lanfranc found in England and some of which he changed 'simply by the imposition of his own authority (sola auctoritatis suae deliberatione)'. That this statement is followed immediately by an account of the conversation with Anselm – 'itaque dum illarum mutatione intenderet' – and that the general topic of the conversation *appears* to be that of English saints about whose sanctity he has doubts, seems to have led to a natural conclusion that though Alphege escaped, others were purged. In fact, Eadmer says nothing of the sort; so though it is his account out of which the idea seems to have developed, the notion of a 'Lanfrancian purge' cannot be substantiated from his words. The first question we need to ask is whether it can be substantiated at all.

Modern scholars of generally impeccable reliability have gone on retailing this idea.[4] Among the earliest, and probably the most influential, has been Edmund Bishop, who, in his investigation of the calendar of

[2] Saints' names are generally given in the forms of the main entries in D.H. Farmer (ed.), *The Oxford Dictionary of Saints* (Oxford, 1978).

[3] *Eadmer's Vita Sancti Anselmi*, ed. and trans. R.W. Southern (Edinburgh, 1952), pp. 50–54 especially 54.

[4] For example, F.M. Stenton, *Anglo-Saxon England* (Oxford, 1943), p. 664: 'The revised calendar which he [Lanfranc] imposed on them omitted the names of many saints whose cult had been traditional in that church'.

the Bosworth Psalter (London, British Library, MS Additional 37517) in a book of that name published in 1908, included a section entitled 'The Changes at Canterbury under Lanfranc.'[5] Here he argued, from a comparison between, on the one hand, four Christ Church calendars of the thirteenth to fifteenth centuries (all in the British Library: MSS Cotton Tiberius B. III; Egerton 2867; Additional 6160; and Sloane 3887) and on the other the calendar of the Bosworth book (*c.* 1000), that there had been 'a singular and extensive series of changes'. He found the key document in explaining these changes to be the calendar of the Arundel Psalter (London, British Library, MS Arundel 155).

After characterising Arundel's calendar as 'the post-Conquest calendar of Winchester', he went on to account for its particular nature in this way: 'that during the archiepiscopate of Lanfranc, that great and strenuous prelate abolished the existing and traditional calendar of his church at Canterbury and substituted for it by his authority that of the church of the capital of his master's newly acquired kingdom, Winchester' (p. 31). Bishop then repeated the story of the conversation about Alphege, and cited two other pieces of evidence, a supposed suppression of the feast of the Conception of Mary and a favouring of the Gallican feast day for (the Translation of) Benedict on 11 July over the old English date of 21 March (we shall notice both of these later). His conclusion – for our purposes – was that 'the calendar of Arundel 155 as originally drawn up is a record of the primitive and "rude" phase of Lanfranc's liturgical reformation in the ancient Church of which he was now archbishop' (p. 32).

What Edmund Bishop, superlative scholar though he was in most respects, did not realise is that the Arundel Psalter was written not in the later eleventh century but between 1012 and 1023 by Eadui Basan, the prize monk-scribe of Christ Church in the first quarter or third of the eleventh century.[6] Its calendar was extensively altered in the middle of the twelfth century (and later, in both the thirteenth and the fifteenth centuries), but in the form in which Eadui wrote it – which can be

[5] [F.A. Gasquet and] E. Bishop, *The Bosworth Psalter* (London, 1908), pp. 27–34.

[6] Alphege's martyrdom on 19 April, 1012 is included, his Translation on 8 June, 1023 is not. On this manuscript see E. Temple, *Anglo-Saxon Manuscripts, 900–1066* (London, 1976), no. 66, and J. Backhouse and others, *The Golden Age of Anglo-Saxon Art* (London, 1984), no. 57. The identification of Eadui Basan as the scribe of this and other manuscripts (his hand has been found in at least eleven) was made by T.A.M. Bishop, *English Caroline Minuscule* (Oxford, 1971), p. 22. See now R.W. Pfaff, 'Eadui Basan: *Scriptorum Princeps?*', in *England in the Eleventh Century*. Proceedings of the Harlaxton Conference 1990, ed. C. Hicks (Woodbridge, forthcoming).

ascertained without too much difficulty – it is a document which antedates Lanfranc's time by a good half century.

There seems to be no other relevant anecdotal evidence for any Lanfrancian purge of Anglo-Saxon saints as such.[7] The principal source for what might be termed his liturgical attitudes is his *Monastic Constitutions*,[8] directed ostensibly at the monks of Christ Church but extendible as far as persuasion and influence might stretch: for example, to the newly-established monks at Durham Cathedral *c.* 1083.[9] These Constitutions do not specify any sort of calendar, but some information can be inferred about the feasts deemed most important. Besides the five greatest occasions (Christmas, Easter, Pentecost, Assumption, and the *festivitas loci*), which were celebrated with immense elaboration, there is a list of fifteen others (plus the octaves of Easter and Pentecost) to be kept 'magnifice . . . quamuis non aequaliter'. Of these fifteen, five are feasts of Christ or Mary (Epiphany, Purification, Annunciation, Ascension, Nativity of the Virgin); five are the ancient major solemnities of John the Baptist, Peter and Paul, Michael, All Saints, and Andrew; and five speak directly to Christ Church tradition: Gregory, Augustine of Canterbury, Benedict, Alphege (as a consequence, we assume, of Anselm's eloquent defence), and the Dedication of the church. That Lanfranc is aware of 'Englishness' as a factor here seems to be indicated by his specifying that the feast of Gregory is included among the greatest 'quia nostrae, id est, Anglorum gentis apostolus est' – which Knowles calls 'one of the few recognisable touches of Lanfranc's own hand'.[10]

The fifteen feasts (plus Octave of the Assumption) of the third rank, celebrated a good deal less solemnly, were concerned largely with New Testament figures (Conversion of Paul, Philip and James [the Less], James, Peter's Chains, Bartholomew, Beheading of John the Baptist, Matthew, Simon and Jude, Thomas) or the Cross (Invention, Exaltation). Three of the remaining five are of greater antiquity than most of the

[7] The mid twelfth-century *Vita Lanfranci* attributed to Milo Crispin (see M. Gibson, *Lanfranc of Bec* [Oxford, 1978], pp. 196–97) tells the same story as Eadmer's *Life of Anselm* had but at somewhat greater length, including a comparison between Alphege's sanctity and that of John the Baptist. The text, edited by L. D'Achery in 1648, is available in Migne, PL 150, cols. 56–57.

[8] *Decreta Lanfranci monachis Cantuariensibus transmissa*, ed. and transl. D. Knowles (Edinburgh, 1951); a revised edition by Knowles is in the *Corpus Consuetudinum Monasticarum*, vol. 3 (Siegburg, 1967).

[9] D. Knowles, *The Monastic Order in England* (Cambridge, 2nd edn., 1963), p. 123.

[10] *Decreta* (as n. 8), p. 61.

feasts of the apostles – Vincent, Laurence, Martin. There is also, slightly surprisingly, Augustine of Hippo; and the list closes with a vague 'aliae festiuitates ita celebrari instituantur', which leaves open the possibility that others may be added.

Taken as a whole, these three groups of major feasts have only one striking element about them: the presence of Alphege and of Augustine of Canterbury (and perhaps of Augustine of Hippo). Certainly we would not expect to find any other Anglo-Saxon saints among this select group of two to three dozen (Dunstan is the only possible exception).[11] Equally certainly there is no indication of a systematic exclusion of anyone who might have reminded the Christ Church monks of their English past.

If there is little direct evidence for a Lanfrancian policy of purging Anglo-Saxon saints from the calendar, is there indirect or inferential evidence from the calendars themselves? In trying to answer this question one runs up against a pair of historiographical difficulties. The first is that very few English calendars survive from the last quarter of the eleventh and first quarter of the twelfth centuries: the period during which such a policy, had it existed, would have been reflected most clearly. The other, and related, problem is that though Francis Wormald published a corpus of all the English calendars known to him which dated from before 1100 (for the most part, from before the Conquest),[12] for the period after 1100 he limited his field of collection to localisable Benedictine calendars only – and of them was able to publish only two of three projected volumes.[13] This means that the pre-1100 evidence appears to have a kind of discreteness lacking for that of the later period.

[11] See Gibson, *Lanfranc*, pp. 171–72. Her suggestion that the *festivitas loci* was the feast of Dunstan 'rather than (as we might expect) the feast of the Trinity' deserves consideration, especially in the light of the fact that it is extremely unlikely to have been Trinity Sunday, an observance scarcely known anywhere in Christendom at that time.

[12] *English Kalendars before A.D. 1100* (Henry Bradshaw Society 72, London, 1934). To the twenty there listed may be added Paris, Bibliothèque Nationale, MS latin 7299, but it is not clear whether this distinctly sparse calendar was written in England or merely descends from an English exemplar: see B. Barker-Benfield in *Medieval Learning and Literature: Essays Presented to R.W. Hunt*, ed. J.J.G. Alexander and M.T. Gibson (Oxford, 1976), p. 152. Its entries (for information about which I am indebted to Professor Michael Lapidge and Dr. Patricia Stirnemann) add little to the present argument.

[13] *English Benedictine Kalendars after A.D. 1100* (Henry Bradshaw Society 77 and 81, London, 1939 and 1946). Publication of the third volume has been taken in hand by Dr. N.J. Morgan.

Because the amount of calendarial evidence directly relevant to our enquiry is very limited, it is difficult to compare calendars used in the same places, or at least areas, immediately before and soon after Lanfranc's time. This would be a desirable procedure above all for Christ Church itself: yet to set alongside the Arundel Psalter, clearly designed for that house and almost without question reflecting its traditions between 1012 and 1023,[14] there is no Christ Church document earlier than the mid twelfth century. From this time there survive three witnesses, one of them being the extensively added-to calendar of the Arundel Psalter itself.[15] The resulting gap of roughly sixty years is too wide to permit conclusive argument to be advanced as to calendarial developments in Lanfranc's own house.

Similar problems exist in trying to ascertain the situation in other establishments of primary importance: monastic houses like St. Augustine's, St. Albans, Bury St. Edmunds, Ely, Glastonbury, Westminster, Worcester and the Old and New Minsters at Winchester among monastic churches, and London, Exeter, Salisbury and perhaps Hereford among secular cathedrals. To lay out the whole of even the limited evidence that exists for pre- and post-Conquest calendarial usages at each of these places, with necessary analysis of the manuscripts involved, would far exceed the scope of this essay. All that can be done here it to try to give as accurate a sampling as possible from a cross-section of the available documents.

Before we do that, however, it will be convenient to establish a rough list of the Anglo-Saxon saints who appear in the great majority of surviving Anglo-Saxon calendars. Such a list can itself be divided into three groups. First come seven 'ancient' saints (one, indeed, pre-English): Cuthbert 20 March (with translation, 4 September), Guthlac 11 April, Augustine 26 May, Boniface 5 June, Alban 22 June, Etheldreda 23 June (with a widely-observed translation on 17 October), Oswald 5 August. Then there are three recent martyrs: Edmund 20 November (869), Edward 18 March (978) and Alphege 19 April (1012), who appear almost universally

[14] Cf. N. Brooks, *The Early History of the Church of Canterbury* (Leicester, 1984), p. 265: 'The Arundel calendar . . . marks the beginning of a medieval Benedictine community's jealous reliance upon its own traditions'. But it is not enough to see this calendar, as Brooks does, primarily as a calendar of Winchester origin.

[15] These three – the added-to Arundel Psalter, the Eadwine Psalter (Cambridge, Trinity College, MS R. 17.1), and a now-detached calendar in Oxford, Bodleian Library, MS Additional C.260 – are analyzed in detail in R.W. Pfaff, 'The Calendar', in *The Eadwine Psalter*, ed. M. Gibson, T.A. Heslop, R.W. Pfaff (London, forthcoming).

from the time of their deaths. Finally, among the many saints who had a strong local cult are three or four who stand out because their connections are with places of the greatest importance. One, Dunstan 19 May (d. 988), is from Christ Church (and also Glastonbury); the others represent Winchester Old Minster: Swithun 2 July (d. 862, translated 15 July 971); Birinus, in some sense the first bishop of Winchester, 3 December (d. 650, translated 4 September, 980); and Ethelwold 1 August (d. 984).

Several other figures were widely observed, notably those connected with the New Minster at Winchester (Judoc, whose deposition feast was 13 December and translation 9 January, and Grimbald 8 July); and with Ely (especially Ermengild 13 February, as well as Etheldreda), Lichfield (Chad 2 March), London (Erkenwald 30 April), and York-plus-Rochester (Paulinus 10 October). But let us in caution use as the basis for our comparisons primarily the fourteen persons identified above as almost always present in pre-Conquest calendars, so as to avoid possible skewing by the inclusion of markedly obscure or predominantly local figures.

It would be unnecessarily tedious to lay this comparison out in chart form. By stretching as far as the third quarter of the twelfth century (and in one case to *c.* 1200 and in another to *c.* 1300), we can establish five localisable pairs, which among them represent (the first one listed is pre-, the second is post-Conquest) these places:

Canterbury Christ Church: London, British Library, MS Arundel 155 (1012–23)[16] and Cambridge, Trinity College, MS R.17.1 (987; Eadwine Psalter).[17]

Ely: Rouen, Bibliothèque municipale, MS Y.6 (probably pre-1012)[18] and Milan, Biblioteca Nazionale Braidense, MS AF.XI.9 (pre-1170).[19]

[16] Wormald, *Kalendars before 1100*, no. 13.

[17] Facsimile in *The Canterbury Psalter*, ed. M.R. James (Canterbury, 1935); this is the only one of the three witnesses mentioned above which has not been extensively added to: see the discussion in Pfaff (as n. 15).

[18] *The Missal of Robert of Jumièges*, ed. H.A. Wilson (Henry Bradshaw Society 11, London, 1896); this is not printed in Wormald, *Kalendars before 1100*, though it is listed there.

[19] MS D in Wormald's collation of Ely calendars in *Kalendars after 1100*, vol. 2, pp. 8–19.

Winchester Old Minster (=St. Swithun's): London, British Library, MS Cotton Vitellius E. XVIII (probably 1060s)[20] and Madrid, Biblioteca Nacional, MS Vit. 23–8 (mid twelfth century).[21]

Winchester New Minster (from 1110, Hyde Abbey): London, British Library, MS Cotton Titus D. XXVII (1023–32)[22] and Oxford, Bodleian Library, MS Gough liturg. 8 (*c.* 1300).[23]

Worcester: Cambridge, Corpus Christi College, MS 9 (*c.* 1025–50)[24] and Oxford, Magdalen College, MS 100 (*c.* 1225).[25]

For all of the comparisons the results are similar. From the fourteen figures on our list, those missing from the later calendar of each pair number between one and four, along with an occasional translation feast. The saints lacking from the later calendars are for Ely, Edward the Martyr and Ethelwold; for Winchester Old Minster, Guthlac, Dunstan and Boniface; for Hyde, only Guthlac; for Worcester, Boniface (and Ethelwold, not in the earlier calendar either) and the translations of Swithun, Birinus and Etheldreda. Canterbury alone has lost as many as four: of saints present in the Arundel Psalter calendar, that in the Eadwine Psalter lacks Guthlac, Boniface, Swithun and Birinus, along with the translations of Swithun and of Cuthbert and Birinus (Ethelwold and the Translation of Etheldreda are not present in either calendar).[26]

It must be stressed that these comparisons are not, and from the limitations of the evidence cannot be, either exhaustive or wholly scientific. Nonetheless, it is reasonably clear that there was neither a massive nor a systematic loss of the principal Anglo-Saxon saints – of, that is, those most universally venerated in the pre-Conquest English church. Between

[20] Wormald, *Kalendars before 1100*, no. 12. There is some possibility that the calendar may have originated at the New Minster instead.

[21] The English entries are listed in F. Wormald, 'Liturgical Note', in H. Buchthal, *Miniature Painting in the Latin Kingdom of Jerusalem* (Oxford, 1957), pp. 122–23. Though again it has been suggested that this is a Hyde Abbey calendar, Wormald concludes that 'it was unquestionably written for the Cathedral Priory'.

[22] Wormald, *Kalendars before 1100*, no. 9.

[23] *The Monastic Breviary of Hyde Abbey*, vol. 5, ed. J.B.L. Tolhurst (Henry Bradshaw Society 71, London, 1934).

[24] Wormald, *Kalendars before 1100*, no. 18.

[25] The calendar is printed as column 4 in the table in *The Leofric Collectar*, ed. E.S. Dewick and W.H. Frere (Henry Bradshaw Society 56, London, 1921), pp. 589–600.

[26] The situation at Canterbury was probably unusually complex, and indeed there seem to be three calendarial traditions apparent at Christ Church in the middle of the eleventh century: see Pfaff, 'Calendar' (as n. 15).

ten and thirteen of the fourteen saints who have formed the basis of our comparison were still present in the later documents. Furthermore, had any systematic 'purge' of the kind often alluded to taken place, surely the same saints would have been removed everywhere: say, Guthlac (lost at the two Winchester houses and at Christ Church but kept at both Ely and Worcester) or Edward the Martyr (lost only at Ely).

Almost certainly, however, two things did happen which among them resulted in the loss of quite a number of entries present in many pre-Conquest calendars; it seems likely that between them these two are responsible for much of the widespread if erroneous impression we have been considering. One is the removal of numerous saints, whether Anglo-Saxon or not, who in the age of Early Scholasticism (Lanfranc's period and after) must have seemed hopelessly obscure or confused. A good example is the saints who appear in most pre-Conquest calendars on January 19 (or sometimes 20) either as Mary and Martha or as a family of Persian martyrs called Marius, Martha, Audifax and Abbacuc.[27] Whereas of the twenty pre-1100 calendars printed by Wormald only six lacked an entry of this sort, of a dozen twelfth-century calendars he printed or collated in his later collection, any such commemoration is evident in manuscripts from only two houses, Durham[28] and Ely.[29] Whatever the reason for the dwindling away of this confused commemoration, it cannot have been because the figures involved were Anglo-Saxon. (It is somewhat ironical that the saint who came to be almost universally present on 19 January in English calendars from the early thirteenth century on was the last Anglo-Saxon bishop, Wulfstan of Worcester, canonised in 1203.)

To be sure, among those lost in this process were numerous Anglo-Saxon 'saints'. Some are so obscure as to defy identification: figures like the *Athelmodus confessor* on 9 January in an unlocalised Wessex calendar;[30] or the Othulph whose translation is recorded on 10 October along with Ecgwin's in one mid eleventh-century Worcester calendar[31] but in no others, pre- or post-Conquest. To be sure also, some regional royal or semi-royal personages disappeared as a consequence of both the passage of time and the existence of a national (and Anglo-Norman)

[27] A study of this curious phenomenon by the present author is near completion.

[28] Durham, Cathedral Library, MS Hunter 100 (soon after 1100): *Marii et Marthae* on the 19th; Cambridge, Jesus College, MS Q.B.6 (mid twelfth century), has the same entry on the 20th.

[29] The calendar now in Milan (see n. 19), on the 20th.

[30] London, British Library, MS Cotton Nero A. II.

[31] Oxford, Bodleian Library, MS Hatton 113.

monarchy;[32] though there is evidence that at some places, perhaps most notably at Ely, their memory survived tenaciously.

The other category of observance which seems to have been to a large extent lost after the Norman Conquest – although again there seems no reason to speak of a systematic purge – is that of three or four distinctively if somewhat inexplicably Anglo-Saxon feasts none of which has a logical connection with England. These are the Ordination of Gregory, the Conception of John the Baptist, one of two Translations of Benedict and the Oblation of the Virgin Mary (possibly the feast of the Conception should be included here also).[33] How these come to be distinctive features of Anglo-Saxon calendars is not part of the present investigation. We need to note here only the following facts.

The Ordination of Gregory appears in about three-fifths of pre-Conquest calendars on March 29 (eight of Wormald's twenty) or March 30 (four more). This date, liturgically inconvenient (it will always fall within Lent or Eastertide, and very often within Holy Week or the Paschal octave), apparently derives from the translation of some relics of Gregory's to Soissons in 826.[34] In any case, after the Conquest the feast was widely found in English calendars not in late March but on 3 September, a date both more historically accurate (Gregory seems to have been ordained Bishop of Rome on that day in 590) and more liturgically feasible.[35] That this change can plausibly be ascribed to Lanfranc seems most unlikely. The new date is not to be found in the mid thirteenth-century calendar of Bec,[36] nor in the early thirteenth-century calendar of St. Neots, which was a cell of Bec.[37] It was, however, added

[32] Some of these, particularly those connected with Ely and with Winchester, are studied in detail by S.J. Ridyard in her important book, *The Royal Saints of Anglo-Saxon England* (Cambridge, 1988); but her emphasis is primarily on their character as royal rather than as some among many possibilities for liturgical commemoration.

[33] The two Marian feasts will not be treated here because it is by no means clear that they were feasts of anything like widespread observance in Anglo-Saxon England. The evidence that exists seems to point only to Winchester and Canterbury; see E. Bishop, 'On the Origins of the Feast of the Conception', in his *Liturgica Historica* (Oxford, 1916), pp. 238–59, at 258–59, and R.W. Pfaff, *New Liturgical Feasts in Later Medieval England* (Oxford, 1970), pp. 103–15.

[34] See the account by Odilo of St. Medard's, printed in Migne, PL 132, cols. 579–622.

[35] It seems to remain at 29 March only in a Chester calendar of the late twelfth century, Oxford, Bodleian Library, MS Tanner 169*.

[36] *Missale Beccense*, ed. A. Hughes (Henry Bradshaw Society 94, London 1963).

[37] London, Lambeth Palace, MS 563; collated in Wormald, *Kalendars after 1100*, vol. 2, p. 115.

in an eleventh-century hand to the Glastonbury calendar which forms part of the so-called Leofric Missal,[38] and it was noticed in the very late eleventh-century St. Augustine's mass-book through the insertion, by a hand which has made many contemporary annotations, of the words 'De ordinatione sancti gregorii require in ordinatione sancti martini'.[39]

The situation is similar with the Conception of John the Baptist, except that here it is not a matter of an alternative date. That feast, appearing in all twenty of Wormald's pre-1100 calendars on 24 September, is almost as uniformly absent from those of the early post-Conquest period. Perhaps its earliest (re-)appearance is in three calendars of second half of the twelfth century, from Chester, Ely and Gloucester.[40] At other places where it is known to have been included before the Conquest – notably Christ Church and Worcester – there look to be no traces of it afterwards.[41]

This leaves us with the observance which Edmund Bishop took as the most symptomatic of Lanfrancian purge, that of 'his own patriarch St. Benedict, and his own compatriot too in a sense;' here 'Lanfranc simply trampled under foot the old English tradition of honouring with high observance the feast of 21 March . . . and puts instead of it in the place of honour, among the most "magnificent" feasts of the year, the Gallican feast of St. Benedict, the translation in July' (July 11th).[42] Bishop's 'instead of it' implies that the March feast was done away with: but of course it is not usually the case that a translation feast supplants that of the deposition. Nor was this so with Benedict, though once again the date of the latter, 21 March, put it in danger of being often overshadowed by seasonal observances.

In fact, there was no supplanting whatever. Both feasts are present in all twenty of the pre-1100 witnesses used by Wormald.[43] What changed

[38] Oxford, Bodleian Library, MS 579; ed. F.E. Warren (Oxford, 1883).

[39] *The Missal of St. Augustine's Abbey Canterbury*, ed. M. Rule (Cambridge, 1896), p. 108.

[40] Respectively, Oxford, Bodleian Library, MS Tanner 169*, Milan, Biblioteca Nazionale Braidense, MS AF.XI.19 (but not the other twelfth-century Ely calendars), and Oxford, Jesus College, MS 10.

[41] One later Christ Church calendar does – inexplicably – contain the feast, Paris, Bibliothèque Nationale, Nouvelles acquisitions latins 1670, a psalter of *c.* 1200: Bishop, *Bosworth Psalter*, p. 107.

[42] *Bosworth Psalter*, p. 32.

[43] The Translation is not included in the calendar of the Robert of Jumièges sacramentary (probably from Ely, Rouen, Bibliothèque Municipale, Y.6) but its mass is in the *sanctorale*; the same thing is true of Dunstan.

was rather that a second translation, on 4 December,[44] which is present in thirteen of these documents, seems to disappear almost wholly after the Conquest.[45] The 21 March feast continued with complete regularity. Bishop was right that Lanfranc did not include it in his list of greater feasts, undoubtedly for the commonsense reason noted above; but to speak of 'trampling under foot' an old English tradition of high observance is fanciful to say the least.[46]

It may seem odd to devote attention largely to arguing that something did not happen; a verdict of Not Proven is, even if correct, never very exciting. Though absence of proof can never be as conclusive as proof positive, in this case it seems amply clear that there was no 'Lanfrancian purge' of the Anglo-Saxon calendar. That statement in itself, however, contains the seeds of several large questions which, though they cannot be pursued here, deserve to be laid out.

The first is, was there any meaningful sense in which there was such a thing as 'the Anglo-Saxon calendar' in the years just before the Norman Conquest. Literally, of course, the answer is no; there is no mid eleventh-century equivalent of the position the Use of Sarum came to have in England in the years just before the Reformation. Yet there may be some signs that a kind of Canterbury–Winchester mix (with perhaps a dash of Worcester) was coming to predominate in terms not only of the basically monastic character of the calendar – witness the two translations of Benedict – but also of the presence of an increasingly discrete body of English saints and other observances like the Conception of John the Baptist. It is certainly a question worth pursuing.[47]

[44] The controverted and knotty question of which translations took place on which days, to say nothing of which (if any) were of Benedict's genuine relics, cannot be discussed here. A judicious, if somewhat dated, treatment of the matter is J. McCann, *Saint Benedict* (London, 1937; revised paperback edition 1958), especially pp. 168–69.

[45] It appears, again with no conceivable explanation, in a late fourteenth-century calendar for Dunster Priory, London, British Library, MS Additional 10628: Wormald, *Kalendars after 1100*, vol. 1, p. 160.

[46] Very few of the pre-1100 calendars are graded in anything like the sense we come to encounter with later documents. In those that are there is no preponderance of dignity one way or the other. In perhaps the most noteworthy case (because the one so badly misunderstood by Bishop), Arundel 155 has the March feast graded 'II' but the July one as 'III', among the six highest.

[47] I have not seen the unpublished Ph. D. thesis of V.N. Ortenberg, 'Aspects of Monastic Devotions to the Saints in England, *c.* 950 to *c.* 1100: The Liturgical and Iconographic Evidence' (Cambridge, 1987).

The next such question is, what then happened to account for the fact that English calendars do look somewhat different in, say, the mid twelfth century from the way they looked in the mid eleventh? Some attempt has been made here to indicate partial answers, but it must be admitted that this is a particularly difficult area to treat because of a curious counter-phenomenon to any slimming (though not purging) of late Anglo-Saxon calendars. This is the resurgence, or perhaps better revitalisation, of the tradition of hagiographical writing about English saints which took place in the generation after the Norman Conquest. A mere mention of the names of Goscelin, Osbern and Eadmer – each sometimes called 'of Canterbury' – is sufficient reminder that in a sense the culmination of Anglo-Saxon hagiography (albeit expressed in Latin) lay in the two decades or so on either side of the year 1100.[48] Full appreciation of this phenomenon is to be welcomed, but it may be useful to recall another contemporary development alluded to earlier: that the age of Lanfranc (d. 1089) and Eadmer (d. *c.* 1128) was also that often associated with the phrase Early Scholasticism. The critical mentality involved was inevitably confronted by questions of saints' cults and relics; the kind of attitude expressed by Abelard towards the relics of St. Denis is likely to have crossed the Channel and to have had consequences for the persistence of some of the less well-attested English saints in Anglo-Norman calendars.

'Less well-attested' does not only mean not supported by a Life, preferably one in Latin. It may also mean not supported by a place in the sanctorale of a mass-book. This observation leads to the next open-ended question: what the relationship was between the presence of a saint in a liturgical calendar (especially given the fact that many early liturgical calendars exist in the context not of service books but of *computistica*) and in a liturgical book, most often a mass-book. Too few pre-Conquest mass-books survive for this question to be investigated systematically,[49] but it is a consideration which must be kept in mind in the light of the general (modern) presumption that a saint will be 'culted' in part by having a place in the sanctoral cycle.

[48] On this see above all D. Rollason, *Saints and Relics in Anglo-Saxon England* (Oxford, 1989), especially chap. 9, 'Englishness and the Wider World'.

[49] There are only eight (and two fragmentary ones) in the listing by H. Gneuss, 'Liturgical Books in Anglo-Saxon England and their Old English Terminology', *Learning and Literature in Anglo-Saxon England: Studies Presented to Peter Clemoes*, ed. M. Lapidge and H. Gneuss (Cambridge, 1985), pp. 91–141, at 101–2. Only four of the eight have calendars.

A fourth question, again only to be adumbrated here, is how to account for the undoubted revival of Anglo-Saxon saints, sometimes of considerable obscurity, in the thirteenth century and thereafter. Part of the reason why it is necessary to be so cautious in the comparison of pre- and post-Conquest calendars is that the further one gets from the late eleventh century the likelier one is to encounter Anglo-Saxon saints of less than the greatest visibility: figures like Wenefred, Frideswide and John of Beverley are more prominent in the fifteenth century than at any earlier time.

This is in turn a separable question from our final one, the very large matter of how 'useful' – culturally and politically as well as ecclesiastically – Anglo-Saxon saints were in Anglo-Norman England. The logic of the matter is simple enough: that the more important the saint, the more potentially useful to those running the new ecclesiastical regime; and that, conversely, the saints likeliest to drop by the wayside were those not of the greatest potential import (e.g., an Alphege) but those of the greatest obscurity.[50] As Karl Leyser has put it with typical pithiness: 'It is characteristic of rising dynasties in this period that they sought to acquire and make the *virtus* of especially exalted and martial saints their own'.[51] An Alphege, an Oswald, an Etheldreda or any of the others of the most prominent (though not necessarily martial, save that a martyr is always *miles Christi*) Anglo-Saxon saints fall, of course, into this category.

A full consideration of all the uses the Anglo-Normans may have had for these saints would make for a large and fascinating study in the spiritual as well as political history of England in the late eleventh and twelfth centuries. Such a study should not be hampered by a presupposition that the starting point of Norman action was anything like a deliberate and systematic purging of the Anglo-Saxon calendar.

[50] This point is well supported by the investigations of S.J. Ridyard, especially in her article '*Condigna Veneratio*: Post-Conquest Attitudes to the Saints of the Anglo-Saxons', *Anglo-Norman Studies* 9 (1987), pp. 179–206. She considers each of four literary instances involving apparent Norman scepticism about or disrespect towards English saints, and shows that when an important figure was involved, like Alban, there was no sign of disrespect.

[51] K.J. Leyser, *Rule and Conflict in an Early Medieval Society* (London, 1979), p. 88.

IV

The Hagiographical Peculiarity of Martha's Companion(s)

I

Anglo-Saxon calendars have furnished a convenient, and ostensibly discrete, object of study since at least 1934, when Francis Wormald produced his *English Kalendars before A.D. 1100*.[1] In the succeeding sixty-plus years much work has of course been done on these documents, and many refinements suggested to the often rough datings and localizations assigned by Wormald.[2] Nonetheless, it is possible to use his twenty (of which, inexplicably, he printed

---

[1] Henry Bradshaw Society (=HBS) 49, 1934. Other standard abbreviations used here: *AA. SS.* = the Bollandist *Acta Sanctorum*; AB = *Analecta Bollandiana*; CCSL = Corpus Christianorum, series Latina; *CLA* = E. A. Lowe, *Codices Latini Antiquiores*; *DACL* = *Dictionnaire d'archéologie chrétienne et de liturgie*; MGH = Monumenta Germaniae Historica; *PL* = Migne, *Patrologia Latina*. For manuscript citations the principal libraries have been abbreviated thus: BL = London, British Library; BN = Paris, Bibliothèque Nationale; Bodl. = Oxford, Bodleian Library; Cbg. = Cambridge (where CCC = Corpus Christi College and Trin. = Trinity College); CUL = Cambridge, University Library; Vat. = Rome, Bibliotheca Apostolica Vaticana; B.m. = Bibliothèque municipale (of the place cited). I have inspected only about half of the many MSS mentioned here; for the rest I have had to rely on the trustworthiness of editors. Of course in every case I have tried to supply references to printed editions where these are available.

[2] See especially the prolific work of David Dumville, most notably in 'On the Dating of Some Late Anglo-Saxon Liturgical Manuscripts,' *Trans. Cbg. Bibliog. Soc.* 10 (1991), 40-57, and in his *Liturgy and the Ecclesiastical History of Anglo-Saxon England. Four Studies* (Woodbridge 1992), above all ch. 2: 'The Liturgical Kalendar of Anglo-Saxon Glastonbury: a Chimaera?', pp. 39-65.

the text of only nineteen)[3] as a basis for laying out with some vividness a hagiographical puzzle of more than trivial interest: the appearance on January 19 and/or 20 January of saints - two or four, as it turns out - about whom the only absolutely constant thing is that one is called Martha. Nineteen of these twenty calendars range in date from about 970 to the end of the eleventh century; the remaining one is of the late ninth century and sheds no light on our subject. The majority of them are for our purposes free-standing: that is, the other contents of the books they belong to add no further information. Only in three are the contents clearly relevant; these will be noticed presently. Wormald localized most of these documents rather precisely (though with question marks in three cases), those not so localized being assigned more generally to 'West Country' or 'Wessex'.

We can best begin by arranging the witnesses not in order of date or place but (so to speak) by grammatical constructions.

Wormald no. manuscript	**Wormald localization**	**Wormald Date**
	Marie (or -ae) et Marthe (or -ae)[4] *(Sanctarum)*	
2. Salisbury Cath. 150[5]	West Country	c. 969-78
3. BL Cott. Nero A.ii	Wessex	s.xi
4. Bodl. 579	Glastonbury	c.970
6. CUL Kk.v.32	West Country	s. xi, late
7. BL Cott. Vit. A.xii	Exeter	s.xi, late
14. Cbg., CCC 422	Sherborne	c. 1061
18. Cbg., CCC 9	Worcester?	$s.xi^{2/4}$
15. Rouen, B.m. Y.6	Ely?	s.xi, early
	Sanctorum Marie et Marthe	
11. BL Arundel 60	Winchester	c. 1060
17. Cbg., CCC 391	Worcester	$s.xi^{2}$

[3] See note 6 below.

[4] In general no attempt will be made to indicate the cedilla, which is neither used consistently by medieval scribes nor transcribed consistently by modern editors. Here *Marie* and *Marthe* will be used for those forms with or without cedilla, but the clear spellings *Mariae* and *Marthae* are so indicated.

[5] *Marie* erased.

	Sanctarum Marii et Marthe	
13. BL Arundel 155	Canterbury, Christ Church	1012-23
	Sanctarum Marii et Marthe, Audifax et Abbacuc	
8. BL Cott. Vit. A.xviii	Wells	1061-88
	Sanctorum Marii et Marthe	
16. Bodl. Hatton 113	Evesham?	s.xi^2
19. Vat. Reg. lat. 12	Bury St. Edmunds	c. 1050
	(*No such indication at 19 or 20 January)*	
1. [Bodl. Digby 63	North Country	s.ix]
5. BL Add. 37517	Cant. Christ Church	988-1012
9. BL Cott. Tit. D.xxvi	Winchester New Minster	1023-35
10. Cbg., Trin. R.15.32	Winchester New Minster	c. 1025
12. BL Cott. Vit. E.xviii	Winchester New Minster?	c. 1060
20. Bodl. Douce 296	Croyland	s.xi, med

This listing shows the two main possibilities: Maria (Mary) and Martha or Marius and Martha, the latter with people called Audifax and Abbacuc sometimes appended. Who the latter two or four are (the first two are obviously Mary and Martha of Bethany) is not clear from any of these indications.

In two of these witnesses there seems to be an awareness of both possibilities simultaneously. The Missal of Robert of Jumièges (no. 15; thought most convincingly to be of Ely origin), while having 'Sanctae [sic] Mariae et Marthae' in its calendar, heads the 19 January entry in its sanctorale 'Sanctorum Mariae et Marthae.' The three prayers there given (all used only at this point in the book) refer to the masculine plural 'sanctorum,' and nowhere mention any proper names.[6] And in St Wulfstan's Homiliary (no. 16) the calendar entry had originally begun 'SANCTARUM UIRG. . . .' interlined in green capitals; this was erased, and the full and quite contrary entry 'Sanctorum martyrum Marii et

[6] H. A. Wilson, ed. *The Missal of Robert of Jumièges* (HBS 11, 1896), 10 and 153. Wormald included this calendar in his numbering but did not print it.

Marthe cum filiis eorum Audifax et Abbacuc' written in.[7] It is as though someone had looked over the scribe's shoulder and said, in effect, 'Wrong sex; indeed, wrong saints.' The puzzle thereby implied is what this paper will try to explore.

The list given above comes close to exhausting the Anglo-Saxon calendarial sources as such. There is also an enigmatic group of metrical calendars, the three principal members of which have been studied expertly by Patrick McGurk. Each of the three has on 19 January an entry which is basically Martha and Mary (and nothing relevant on the 20th).[8] The oldest, BL Cott. Galba A.xviii, is a late ninth-century psalter of North French origin which was given to King Athelstan (d. 939) and, according to tradition, by him to Winchester cathedral;[9] in England it received various additions, including a metrical calendar in an early tenth-century hand at the beginning and at the end considerable devotional matter, some of it with Greek affinities. The next, BL Cott. Jul. A.vi, is a monastic hymnary and canticle book of the early eleventh century written perhaps at Christ Church, Canterbury and used at Durham; its metrical calendar is unrelated to the other contents. The same is true of the third, BL Cott. Tib. B.v, written in the second quarter of the eleventh century and again perhaps at Christ Church, a miscellaneous compilation famous for its illustrations. It would be natural to suppose that the younger of the latter two was copied from the older, but the entry of interest to us disproves this possibility. The metrical line in Galba for 19 January is 'Martha Maria simul flores [gap] cont ex vere.' Tiberius's reading, though obviously somewhat related to Galba's, is a little better: 'Martha Maria simul florescunt lege diurna.' But Julius, the middle of the three in age, has a line of a quite different sort: 'Quardecimis mun Martha Maria delazariathelphae.' This seems significant, for what lies behind the splendid nonsense word 'delazariathelphae' must be something like 'de Lazari adelphae' - bad Latin and worse Greek, but they were the sisters of Lazarus.

---

[7] I. Atkins, 'An Investigation of Two Anglo-Saxon Kalendars,' *Archaeologia* 78 (1928), 241. Wormald merely says, 'An erased inscription in green is written above this entry' (p. 198).

[8] P. McGurk, 'The Metrical Calendars of Hampson. A New Edition,' *AB* 104 (1986), 79-125.

[9] On this tradition, see S. Keynes, 'King Athelstan's Books,' in *Learning and Literature in Anglo-Saxon England: studies presented to Peter Clemoes*, ed. M. Lapidge and H. Gneuss (Cambridge 1985), 143-201, at 193-6.

It may be pertinent that a probably related document, Bodl. Junius 27, which is most likely a Canterbury or Winchester production of purely English origin (unlike Galba) and of the early tenth century, has nothing in its calendar - twenty-seven lines of which are metrical - between Marcellus on 16 January and Fabian and Sebastian on the 20th.[10] And while the late ninth-century calendar which is the oldest of Wormald's twenty, Bodl. Digby 63, has saints for most days in the second half of January, there is nothing on the 19th. Nor is there any entry for that date in the early-eighth century Calendar of St Willibrord (the manuscript of which will be discussed shortly). So although, as we shall see, it is clear that Bede knew a martyrological commemoration relevant to our enquiry, we may suspect that the influence reflected in English calendars of the tenth and eleventh centuries is a purely continental one very likely arising from the late Carolingian period. It may thus be wise to begin our consideration with the earliest known continental sources.

II

Recorded awareness of the confusion-causing story seems to date from no earlier than the eighth century, though how much before that time the story arises it is not possible to say. Later passionals contain a lengthy tale of a noble Persian family, Marius (or Maris), his wife Martha, and their sons Audifax and Abbacuc (the spellings of the sons' names vary widely).[11] They come on pilgrimage to Rome in about the year 270, during the persecutions under the emperor Claudius II 'the Goth,' there, having devoted themselves to works of charity in collecting the remains of the recently martyred, they fall into the hands of the authorities and, refusing to renounce their faith, are themselves

[10] In the calendar of Junius 27 the leaf containing January has been badly hacked up; but enough survives to make possible this statement: see D.N. Dumville, *Liturgy and the Ecclesiastical History*... (note 2 above), ch. 1: 'The Kalendar of the Junius Psalter,' 1-38.

[11] Of the very earliest surviving passionals (see G. Philippart, *Les Legendiers latins*, Typologie des Sources du Moyen Age occidental 24-5, Turnhout 1977, p. 31) none of those containing saints-not-apostles, and remotely as old as the martyrology and sacramentary evidence to be considered, includes anything like *passio* for Marius et al. (CLM 3514, CLM 4554, Vienna 1556, St Gall 548, Turin D.v.3). The standard version of the *passio* of Marius and his family is that printed in *AA. SS. Jan.* II (1643), 580-83; it is there intermixed with the *passio* of St. Valentine et al. Earlier printings are listed in *Bibliotheca Hagiographica Latina* (Brussels 1900), no. 5443.

martyred, the males by decapitation and Martha by drowning in a pond some thirteen miles from Rome.[12]

Despite the supposed third-century date for this story, it does not seem to be referred to in any source for several centuries thereafter. To mention merely the two most celebrated possibilities, neither the primitive martyrology included in the work of the Chronographer of 354[13] nor the Carthaginian 'calendar' of the early sixth century (which runs from 19 April to 16 February and has a list of Roman martyrs)[14] contains the names we are looking for.[15] Nor is there any such entry in the so-called calendar (really just a list of occasions) from Luxeuil or Corbie c. 700.[16]

We come to the earliest datable witnesses to the Marius and Martha story only with the oldest manuscripts of the *Martyrologium Hieronymianum*. The form, however, in which mention of the story appears there already hints at the confusion so manifest in the tenth- and eleventh-century English calendars - a confusion which therefore must antedate even the martyrological notices. What its editors take as the oldest surviving manuscript of the *Mart. Hieron.* (BN lat. 10837, Codex Epternacensis) has at 19 January (xiiii Kal.), after mentions of Sebastian and Fabian, 'via Cornelia miliario ab urbe XII Mari et Ambacu.'[17] Note that this manuscript is generally accepted as having been written in an Anglo-Saxon hand of the first half of the eighth century, probably at Epternach by the scribe Laurentius;[18] and that the thirty-two folios of the martyrology are succeeded by the eight of the Calendar of St Willibrord, from almost exactly the

---

12 The oldest passional I am aware of which contains this story is Chartres, B.m. 144, perhaps from S. Denis, Dreux, late tenth century: anon., 'Cat. Cod. Hag. Bibl. Civ. Carnot.,' *AB* 8 (1889), 126. This is the version printed in *AA. SS. Jan.* II (1643), 216-19 (without sections 12-14).

13 Ed. T. Mommsen, MGH *Auctores Antiquissimi* 9.i (1892), 13-196.

14 H. Achelis, *Die Martyrologien ihre Geschichte und ihr Wert* (Abh. königl. Gesells. Göttingen, philol-hist. Kl. n.F. III.3; Berlin 1900), 21.

15 Nor does even the mid-ninth century 'Kalendarium Marmoreum' of Naples, with its full list of commemorations: D. Mallardo, *Il calendario marmoreo di Napoli* (Bibliotheca Ephemerides Liturgicae 18; Rome 1947); cf. V. Brown, 'A New Beneventan Calendar from Naples: the Lost "Kalendarium Tutinianum" Recovered,' *Mediaeval Studies* 46 (1984), 385-449.

16 A. Wilmart in *DACL* III.ii (1914), col. 2927.

17 J. B. de Rossi and L. Duchesne, ed. *Martyrologium Hieronymianum*, *AA. SS. Nov.* II.i (1894), pp. [10]-[11].

18 *CLA* V (1950), no. 605.

same date (perhaps the second decade of the century), which contains no entry for 19 January and only Sebastian on the 20th.[19]

The other two principal early manuscripts of the *Mart. Hieron.* are at once a little fuller and even more confusing in their accounts of the Persian family. In both Bernensis (Bern, B.m. 289, originally at Metz, s.viii^{ex})[20] and the coeval Wissenburgensis (Wolfenbüttel, Wiss. 23, connections with Fontanelle)[21] the entry for 19 January reads, 'Hierusolima Marthe et Mariae sorores Lazari,' and for the 20th, 'in cimiterio Mariae et Marthae Audefax et Abacuc.' As compared with Epternacensis, this entry for the 20th introduces Martha, turns Marius (or Maris) into a woman, and brings in also Audifax (the spelling of his name is thus emended in Bern.), while Ept.'s Ambacu has become the more usually-encountered Ab(b)acuc.[22]

The *Mart. Hieron.* tradition is even more complicated than this, however. The first element making for complication is that at 15 January (xviii Kal. Feb.) the three oldest manuscripts all have 'depositio Ambacu prophetae' (these words prefaced in Bern. and Wiss. with 'et alibi'). Then, at 16 January (xvii Kal. Feb.) Ept. has, after a notice for Marcellus (bishop), 'et via Appia in cymiterio Calesti passio sancti Anani Mari. via Cornelia VIIII mil. in cymiterio aliorum XIII quorum nomina Deus scit;' while for the same date there are in Bern. and Wiss., 'et via Appia in cimiterio Calisti passio sanctae Marthae Audeini martyris. via Corniva in cimiterio mil. VIIII et aliorum tredecim quorum nomina in libro vitae tenentur scripta.' On these thoroughly puzzling entries the great Bollandist Delehaye commented, 'Martyrum turma quae mox sequitur hisce constat nominibus: Marius, Martha, Audifax et Abacuc, quae, collatis codicibus, diebus ian. 15, 16, 20 facile agoscimus. Abacuc praemissus heri. Ananus . . . al Audeinus . . . est pro Audifax.'[23]

---

[19] H. A. Wilson, ed. *The Calendar of St. Willibrord* (HBS 55, 1918). The martyrology and calendar were bound together before the ninth century.

[20] *CLA* VII (1956), no. 861.

[21] *CLA* IX (1959), no. 81 (=23 in *AA. SS.* edn.).

[22] Bern. spells it Abbacuc and Wiss. originally had Abacus, corrected to Abacuc. Awareness of the story in a more accurate version is revealed by the substitution of 'Marii' for 'Mariae' in four other principal manuscripts, and its correction to 'Marii' in a fifth; only the last-named, of the late ninth century, is early enough to be worth noting here (BN N.a.l. 1604, from Sens; the others are late eleventh or twelfth-cent., BN lat. 12410, Lucca. Bibl. Capit. 618, Florence, Bibl. Laur. 151 and Bibl. Laur. Conv. soppr. 331).

[23] H. Delehaye with H. Quentin, *Commentarius perpetuus in Martyrologium Hieronymianum, AA. SS. Nov.* II.ii (1913), p. 43.

With all deference to the greatness of Delehaye, this presupposes rather than explains; in fact, it is far from clear that the four-member Persian family comprise (so to speak) primary data. Especially dubious is the supposition that Ept.'s Ananus and Bern.-Wiss.'s Audeinus are simple variants of Audifax. Delehaye points out that the topographical indication 'miliario XIII' was originally written 'VIIII' in both manuscripts (Bern. and Wiss.), and then corrected in the margin (of which manuscript he does not say) to XIII; and that the scribe (*librarius*) took the XIII to refer to that many additional martyrs whose names, being unknown, are written only in the book of life. So Delehaye's reconstruction of the Ur-form of the notice reads like this: '(item Romae) via Cornelia miliario XIII in cimiterio (eorum) passio sanctorum Marii, Marthae, Audifacis (et Abacuc).' In effect, then (though he does not say this in so many words), Delehaye seems to have thought that the notice for the 20th is a doublet of that for the 16th. One consideration that might argue for this is that two really important saints are also commemorated on the 20th: Sebastian and Fabian. (Of course, their presence on that day could also suggest precisely the opposite: that is, that the commemoration of Marius et al. antedated those of the two better-known saints and so remained, rather like St Anastasia on 25 December, after their days were fixed on the 20th.) There is as well a tiny numerical and topographical hint: that, as Delehaye also pointed out, the notice for the 16th has the milestone-from-Rome indication corrected accurately as 'XIII via Cornelia,' whereas that for the 20th has it as XII.[24]

But this is to ignore the import of the *Mart. Hieron.* entry for 19 January (the one that gives, after a large number of names, 'Hierosolima Marthae et Mariae sororum Lazari'). This Delehaye regards as an interpolation; were it not (he says), there should be a commemoration on that day at Jerusalem or somewhere in the region, whereas there is none. On the contrary, this negative fact can prove only that there was no tradition connected with Martha and Mary on that day in the East, which does not preclude such a tradition's having sprung up independently in the West.

The Greek aspect we can notice very briefly, because it is virtually nonexistent, save in one fascinating peculiarity. Both our Marius and Audifax seem totally unknown, and Abbacuc, insofar as he is rooted in the prophet Habbakuk, is commemorated on 2 December. But a Mary and Martha do appear, along with a boy Lycarion, as martyrs under Decius on 8 or 9 February.

[24] Delehaye, p. 51.

The only witness cited in the *Bibliotheca Hagiographica Graeca* (no. 2257) is an eleventh-century manuscript now in Jerusalem; but the story is included in a Latin passional of the ninth/tenth century which was at Bobbio at least by the fifteenth (Vat. lat. 5771). It is number 87 of 101 items, not in liturgical order; 19 January is specified, but the place is given as a city 'Athens' in Egypt.[25] Nevertheless, 'Licarionis' sounds plausibly close to Lazarus, and one may suspect that the scriptural Mary and Martha combination lies behind this story also.

To summarize the evidence of the *Mart. Hieron.* witnesses: the only thing that seems at all clear in this tangle of manuscripts is that the elements of three commemorations are discernible in the eighth-century codices we have: one for an Ab(b)acuc or Ambacu(c) who is presumably meant to be the Old Testament prophet Habbakuk; one for Mary and Martha, the sisters of Lazarus; and one for from two to four 'Persian' martyrs, a Marius and an Ab(b)acuc (or Ambacu), with perhaps a Martha and an even more shadowy Audifax. Questions of the ultimate origins of these commemorations, as of the historicity of the persons in the last group, probably cannot be solved - though a brief hypothesis will be offered later.

Instead, we need to go on to notice that the confusion among them persists in the various martyrologies of the eighth and ninth centuries. The earliest of these, Bede's (completed by 725) is indeed as old as the oldest *Mart. Hieron.* manuscript (Ept.). If the principal manuscript of Bede's Martyrology, St Gall 451 (no older than the mid-ninth century), reflects without any interpolation what he wrote,[26] he witnesses to only the third of our three commemorations - but for, and as the sole notice on, 19 January rather than 20 (which is devoted entirely to Fabian and Sebastian):

> Natale ss. mm. Marii et Marthae cum filiis suis Audifax et Abacuc, nobilium de Persida, qui ad orationem venerant Romam, tempore Claudii principis: e quibus post toleratos fustes, equuleum, ignes,

---

[25] A. Poncelet, *Cat. Cod Hag. Lat. Vat.* (Brussels 1910), 506-8.

[26] A. Bruckner, *Scriptoria medii aevi helvetica* III (Geneva 1938), 105. Cf. H. Quentin, *Les Martyrologes historiques du Moyen Age* (Paris 1908), 19. M. L. W. Laistner, *A Handlist of Bede Manuscripts* (Ithaca 1943), 92, points out that the correct date is mid-ninth century.

> ungues, manuum praecisiones, Martha in nympha necata, ceteri decollati, et cetera sunt omnia incensa.[27]

In this Bede is followed in the ninth century by the martyrologies of Florus of Lyon (in the first recension) and of Ado, but in Florus on 19 and in Ado on 20 January. Both also have what Bede lacked: at 15 January, 'Abbacuc et Michaeae prophetarum, quorum corpora sub Archadio imperatore divina revelatione reperta sunt,'[28] although, like Bede, neither mentions the Mary and Martha commemoration.[29] On the other hand, Rabanus Maurus (also ninth century) has that element - 'Hierosolyma natale Marthae et Mariae, sororum Lazari' - on 19 January and the four Persians back on the 20th, following Fabian and Sebastian, as well as Ab(b)acuc (with Micheas) on the 15th.[30] The fourth ninth-century martyrologist, Usuard (whose martyrology is the principal basis for the *Martryologium Romanum* of 1584), has Ab(b)acuc and Micheas (in the form used by Florus and Ado) on 15 January, no Mary and Martha, and the Persian family, on the 20th, in virtually the same words as Bede's.[31]

The evidence provided by the early martyrologies may be summed up as follows. The Hieronymian tradition knows Ab(b)acuc (without Micheas) on 15 January, Mary and Martha on the 19th, and on the 20th either Marius (Maris?) and Ambacu(c) as in Ept. or Maria (sic), Martha, Audifax, and Abacuc as in Bern. and Wiss.; it also knows, uniquely, the commemoration on the 16th of 'Passio sancti Anani Mari via Cornelia' (Bern. and Wiss.). A second main tradition, Bede's, knows only Marius and Martha and their sons, on 19 January. A third, which may be called in general that of the continental followers of Bede, introduces Ab(b)acuc and Micheas on 15 January (Florus, Ado, Rabanus, Usuard) and has Marius and Martha et al. either on the 19th (Florus) or 20th

---

[27] J. Dubois and G. Renaud, eds. *Edition pratique des martyrologes de Bede, de l'Anonyme Lyonnais et de Florus* (Paris 1976), 16.

[28] Ibid., p. 161.

[29] J. Dubois and G. Renaud, eds., *Le Martyrologe d'Adon. Ses deux familles, ses trois recensions. Texte et commentaire* (Paris 1984), 63: the second family of MSS of Ado's work contains also the Mary and Martha notice, at Jan. 19th. Of this entry the editors remark, 'Il s'agit d'une confusion des homonymes.'

[30] J. McCulloh, ed. *Rabani Mauri Martyrologium* (Corpus Christianorum Continuatio Mediaevalis 44, 1979), 14-15.

[31] J. Dubois, ed. *Le Martyrologe d'Usuard. Text et commentaire* (Subsidia hagiographica 40, 1965), 164-5; there are three slight textual changes, and Usuard adds 'Via Cornelia.'

(Ado, Rabanus, Usuard); of the ninth-century martyrologies in this tradition only Rabanus mentions Mary and Martha also, on the 19th.[32]

Roman topographical sources are less helpful than we might expect from the details given in martyrologies. The oldest evidence of this kind seems to be that of the itinerary 'De locis sanctis martyrum quae sunt foris civitatis Romae,' existing in three manuscripts of the late ninth or tenth centuries. It begins with an account of the saints venerated on the Via Cornelia. First comes, at the Vatican, Peter; then 'Iuxta eandem quoque viam, sancta Rufina, sancta Secunda [there should apparently be a break here], sancta Maria, sanctus Marius, sanctus Ambacu, sanctus Audafax, et alii quamplurimi sancti iacent.'[33] It may be noteworthy that Maria is named first, and that Ambacu is so spelled. It is also perhaps significant that an earlier itinerary (probably compiled originally by the mid-seventh century), the 'Notitia ecclesiarum urbis Romae,' had no indication for anything along that way after St Peter's.[34] There was at Rome in the twelfth century a church on the Via Cornelia dedicated to (or at least thought to hold the remains of) Marius et al.: William of Malmesbury knew of it, and in 1158 Adrian IV granted to the canons of St. Peter's a number of Roman churches, including 'ecclesiam Sanctorum Marii et Marthae;' this may be the church referred to ('ecclesia sanctorum martirum Marii et Marthae [et] filiorum eorum') in 854 as having been given by Pope Leo IV to St. Martin's monastery in Rome. But William also records resting places beyond the Appian gate of a number of saints, including Mary and Martha![35]

Nor does the ostensible translation of the relics of the four Persians to the monastery of St Médard at Soissons in 828 help; for the account of this event,

---

[32] The briefly-expressed poetical martyrology of Wandalbert of Prüm has no Maria/us-Martha commemoration; only the one for the 15th, 'Bisque novenam Abacuc simul et Micheas honorant;' ed. E. Dümmler, MGH *Poetae latini aevi* II (1884), 579.

[33] R. Valentini and G. Zucchetti, *Codice topografico della citta di Roma*, II (Rome 1942), 106-7.

[34] Ibid., p. 69.

[35] William of Malmesbury, *Gesta Regum* iv. no. 452, ed. W. Stubbs (Rolls Series 90, 1880), II 404 and 407. Adrian's grant is printed in PL 188. 1559. On the ninth-century church, see L. Schiaparelli, 'Le carte antiche dell' archivio Capit. di S. Petro in Vat.,' *Arch. Soc. Rom. di Stor. Patr.* 24 (1901), 435. J. P. Kirsch, 'Le memorie dei martiri sulle vie Aurelia et Cornelia,' *Misc. Fr. Ehrle* II (Studi e Testi 38, Rome 1924), 63-100, devotes three pages (96-98) to our subject; he seems to have been determined to tidy up all the confusions and repetitions, e.g., simply equating the puzzling 'Mariae' in the Gelasian heading (see next section) with 'Marii.' The three witnesses referred to above are printed in parallel columns in G. B. de Rossi, *La Roma sotteranea cristiana*, I (Rome 1864), 182.

which was long ascribed to Odilo, an early tenth-century monk of that house, was shown by its nineteenth-century editor to be an eleventh-century forgery based on Einhard's 'Translatio et miracula Sanctorum Marcellini et Petri.'[36] Odilo apparently had written an account of the translation of St Sebastian, which is of some interest because of Sebastian's sharing of 20 January with the Persian martyrs in some witnesses. The relics of Tiburtius, Marcellinus, and Peter are the forger's principal interest; Marius et al. seem simply to have been thrown in for good measure.

III

Virtually as early as the tradition of the martyrologies (both Hieronymian and Bedan), and only slightly less confused, is that of the Gelasian sacramentaries. In dealing with this kind of evidence we have to take into account not only questions of filiation and cross-influence but also the existence of two elements, the heading or *titulus* for the observance in question and the prayers supplied for it (when, in later liturgical texts, there comes to be a calendar, the entry in that will form a third element). These considerations need to be kept in mind as we look at a number of individual liturgical texts. It is one thing, and a true one, to say that the observance we are tracing is roughly Gelasian and not Gregorian in transmission; it is another, and grossly erroneous, to suppose that there is anything like a unified Gelasian witness.[37]

With the principal, and oldest (c. 750), manuscript of the 'Old Gelasian' tradition, Vat. Reg. lat. 316 (henceforth Vat.) we are already squarely in the middle of our problem. That manuscript reads at 20 January, in the heading, 'IN NATALI SANCTORUM MARTYRUM SEBASTIANI MARIAE MARTAE AUDIFAX ET ABACUC XIII Kal. Februaris.'[38] But the latest

---

[36] O. Holder-Egger, MGH *Scriptores* XV.1 (1887), 391-5, who printed this as an appendix to Odilo's account of the translation of St Sebastian. The MSS are Vat. Reg. Lat. 1864 and Vat. Ottob. 811 pt. ii.

[37] A useful conspectus of information about the principal Gelasian sacramentary MSS, both 'Old' and 'Young' (or 'Eighth-Century') is to be found in the Appendix (pp. 175-205) to M. S. Moreton, *The Eighth-Century Gelasian Sacramentary, A Study in Tradition* (Oxford 1976).

[38] L. C. Mohlberg, ed. *Liber Sacramentorum Romanae Aeclesiae Ordinis Anni Circuli* (Rerum Ecclesiasticarum Documenta ser. maior 4; Rome 1960), 131; cf. the edition of H.

editor has pointed out that the AE of MARIAE is of a different color (brown) from the rest of the word and above the line, while the date is a later marginal addition, also in brown. Even more noteworthy is that of the four prayers given, only the first applies to the Persian family, and in terms so general as to be applicable to any plural martyrs: 'Concede, quaesumus omnipotens Deus, ut sanctorum martyrum tuorum celebramus victorias, participemur et praemiis.' The other three prayers, which form a complete mass set of collect (or *oratio*), secret, and postcommunion, refer to Sebastian only. This is doubly strange in that in the heading Sebastian is listed first, then the four family members; but the prayer applicable to them comes before those relevant to him. Before leaving this book we should notice also that there are no commemorations between Marcellus on the 16th (nor anything on the 15th) and those on the 20th.

The other 'Old Gelasian' manuscript which survives in a complete enough form to be a witness here is the so-called Prague Sacramentary (Prague, Metropolitni Kapitoly O.83), from Upper Bavaria in the later eighth century.[39] There something else odd has happened. Immediately after Marcellus on 16 January comes Sebastian, but on the 17th (xvi Kal.) rather than the 20th (xiv Kal.) with no others mentioned. And of the three prayers specified for Sebastian the first is that which Vat. used for the Persians - that is, the one which, cast as it is in the plural, cannot possibly apply to Sebastian (the secret and postcommunion are the proper ones for him, as in Vat.). Here, therefore, we must be dealing with a compiler who knew a text like that of Vat. and who had no use for the Persian family. Desiring to separate Sebastian from Fabian (widely commemorated on the 20th) he moved the former to the 17th, but in copying the prayers for Sebastian he took the first of the prayers in the Vat.(-like) set, not noticing its irrelevance once the Persians were omitted.[40]

A small step towards clarity may be seen in the fragmentary 'Index of St. Thierry' - a bifolium of the later eighth century which is a contents-list for a sacramentary very much like Vat. - where the pertinent entry has straightened out the sex of Marius: 'in natale sanctorum sebastiani mari marthe audifax et

---

A. Wilson, *The Gelasian Sacramentary* (Oxford 1894), 163, and the color facsimile ed. L.M. Tocci and B. Neunheuser in the Codices Vaticani Selecti series, 2 vols (Rome 1975).

[39] A. Dold and L. Eizenhöfer, ed. *Das Prager Sakramentar* (Texte und Arbeiten 38/42; Beuron 1949), 12*.

[40] Cf. Moreton, p. 205: 'Though some "Gregorianizing" of the mass-sets has taken place, in that they are cut down uniformly to single collect sets, the collect given is nearly always the first of the pair in Reg. 316.'

abacu(c) XIII kl feb.'[41] Fabian is given on 20 January as well as in this entry. This fragment, offering as it does a third testimony, witnesses to what may be regarded as a fixed, if unclear, Old Gelasian tradition about the Persian family.

It would not be possible here even to begin to delve into the vast complexities of the various fragments of the 'Young Gelasian' sacramentaries. Four or five of the best known witnesses to that tradition will serve our purposes well enough. Of these the most celebrated and perhaps oldest is probably the Gellone Sacramentary (BN lat. 12048), dating from the second half, and more likely the last quarter, of the eighth century. In its somewhat full sanctorale Pope Marcellus comes on 15 January, Marcellus martyr on the 17th, Prisca on the 18th; then on the 19th (under the curious spelling XIIII Kl. Phebr.) comes 'Natale Marie et Marte,' followed by Fabian and Sebastian both (but separately) on the 20th.[42] Four prayers are given for the feast of Mary and Martha. The first three, a coherent mass set, refer merely to 'sanctorum tuorum,'[43] with no names mentioned; it is merely the first of several sets 'In natali plurimorum sanctorum' in the Gelasian tradition, Old and Young. The fourth, after the proper postcommunion and not specified as to function, is in fact another postcommunion prayer, but for the festival of a single saint: 'Quaesumus domine salutaribus repleti misteriis, ut cuius solemnia celebramus eius orationibus adiuuemur' - indeed, that is the proper postcommunion of the set for St. Prisca on the previous day (which however ends 'adiobemur' for 'adiuuemur'), and may simply have been repeated by inadvertence. Even with this observance being clearly devoted to Mary and Martha, confusion remains.[44] Further confusion is reflected in the abbreviated martyrology which follows the sacramentary proper: the entry for 19 January reads (after four unrelated saints)

---

[41] A. Wilmart, 'L'Index liturgique de Saint Thierry,' *Revue Bénédictine* 30 (1913), 437-50; cf. Mohlberg, *Liber Sacr.* [Vat. Reg. lat. 316], pp. 267-75.

[42] A. Dumas, ed. *Liber Sacramentorum Gellonensis* (CCSL 159-159A, 1981), 19; cf. *CLA* V (1950) no. 618.

[43] It may be that these words, in the masculine plural, are themselves testimony to our confusion; to match the two female saints they should of course be 'sanctarum tuarum.' But the casting of plurals into the generalizing masculine is common enough that too much weight should not be put on the grammatical peculiarity here.

[44] Cf. the passing mention by P. de Puniet, *Le Sacramentaire romain de Gellone* (Bibliotheca Ephemerides Liturgicae 4; Rome 1938--also published as articles in *Eph. Lit.* 1934-8), 44, that Marius and Martha are among six saints or groups of saints who are honored in extra-mural cemeteries outside Rome. He wholly ignores the confusion caused by the change of Marius to Maria.

'Hierusol(imis) Marte et Marie;' that for the 20th, 'Rom(ae) Fabiani, Sebastiani mar(tyris), Mariae, Adafex.'[45]

The St Gall Sacramentary (St Gall lat. 348) of c. 800 agrees with the Gellone in the dating and naming of Mary and Martha on 19 January (and with Fabian and Sebastian, separately, on the 20th); but the puzzling extra (singular-form) postcommunion has gone.[46] The same is true of the Rheinau Sacramentary (Zurich, Zentralbibl. Rheinau 30), although Sebastian is apparently - but perhaps only by oversight - meant to be observed on the 19th also and Fabian is missing entirely.[47] It is true also of the Gelasian stratum of the early eleventh century Sacramentarium Triplex (Zurich, Zentralbibl. C.43).[48]

But with the Angoulême Sacramentary (BN lat. 816), also c. 800, we find the same awareness of the tradition about the Persian family as was reflected in the Old Gelasian Vat.; for at 19 January, in place of the simple Mary and Martha of the *Junggelasiana* we have just noticed there is, 'In nt. beatorum Mariae et Marte, Audifax et Abbacuc.' (Fabian and Sebastian, in that order and separately, are on the 20th.) Of the four prayers there supplied, the last three are as for Mary and Martha in the Gellone and St Gall books; but the first is the old Gelasian collect 'Concede, quesumus omnipotens Deus, ut sanctorum martyrum tuorum, quorum celebramus victorias, participemur et praemiis' - the one applicable to the four Persian martyrs on the 20th as opposed to the proper one for Sebastian.[48bis] This development is carried one step further in the Fulda Sacramentary of the late tenth century (Göttingen Theol. 231) where at 19 January we find 'Nat. Sanctorum Marii et Marthae,' followed by the same three Mary-and-Martha prayers as in the Young Gelasians.[49] But the Fulda book belongs to what is generally called the mixed Gelasian-Gregorian tradition - one

---

[45] Ed. cit., p. 492. The same information is contained in the Sacramentary of Autun (alias Phillipps [1667] sacramentary), where the final Persian figure is rendered as Adaflex: O. Heiming, ed. *Liber Sacramentorum Augustodunensis* (CCSL 159B, 1984), 20.

[46] C. ('K.') Mohlberg, ed. *Das fränkische Sacramentarium Gelasianum in alamannischer Überlieferung* (Liturgiegesch. Quellen 1/2; Münster-i-W. 1918), 20.

[47] A Hänggi and A. Schönherr, eds. *Sacramentarium Rhenaugiense* (Spicilegium Friburgense 15; Fribourg 1970), 190.

[48] O. Heiming, ed. *Corpus Ambrosiano-Liturgicum* I: *Sacramentarium Triplex* (Liturgiewissenschaftliche Quellen und Forschungen 49, 1968), 36-7.

[48 bis] P. Saint-Roch, ed. *Liber Sacramentorum Engolismensis* (CCSL 159C, 1987), p. 147.

[49] G. Richter and A. Schönfelder, ed. *Sacramentarium Fuldense saeculi X* (Fulda 1912; repr. as HBS 101, 1982), 20.

that, as far as the Gregorian element is concerned, can be dealt with more summarily.

The plain fact is that there is no mention of any Marius- or Mary-and-Martha feasts (nor of the prophet Habbacuc) in any of the 'pure' Gregorian sacramentaries, whether those of extant texts or of proposed reconstructions.[50] The Gregorian sanctorale for the part of January that concerns us is as follows: on the 14th Felix 'in pincis,' 15th vacant, 16th Marcellus pope, 17th vacant, 18th Prisca, 19th vacant, 20th Fabian and (separately) Sebastian, 21st Agnes. With sacramentaries 'contaminated' by Gelasian influence the picture is different, though not uniformly so. Only a small sampling can, or need, be mentioned here.

This can be laid out simply, without regard for the elaborate classification systems developed by Klaus Gamber[51] and others. The St Eligius Sacramentary (BN lat. 12051), a Corbie book of the second half of the ninth century, celebrated because Hugo Ménard in the seventeenth century thought it was *the* Gregorian Sacramentary,[52] lacks the observance entirely. The Rodradus Sacramentary (BN lat. 12050), written around 853 for Corbie, includes in its largely Gelasian supplement prayers for a mass 'XIII Kal. Feb. Natalis Sanctae Mariae et Marthae.'[53] In a late ninth-century Senlis sacramentary (Paris, Ste-Genèviève lat. 111, olim BB 20), written around 880 under Bishop Hadbert, the calendar, somewhat martyrological in form, gives for XIII Kal. 'Hierosolima Marthe et Mariae sororum Lazari.'[54] (The well-known Drogo Sacramentary of 826-55, BN lat. 9248, is of no relevance because it contains masses for only the major feasts.)

It does not seem to be until the tenth century that books of this kind, whether called 'mixed sacramentaries' or by some other term, allow Marius and his

---

50 There would be no point in listing here all the editions and attempts at reconstruction which provide merely negative evidence; there are many lists available, including a summary one in my *Medieval Latin Liturgy: a Select Bibliography* (Toronto Medieval Bibliographies 8; Toronto 1982), 76-8.

51 *Sakramentartypen* (Texte und Arbeiten 49/50; Beuron 1958) and *Codices Liturgici Latini Antiquiores*, 2nd edn (Spicilegii Friburgensis Subsidia I.i-ii; Fribourg 1968).

52 And therefore printed it in his edition of the works of Gregory the Great, 1642, whence it eventually showed up in *PL* 78.

53 *DACL* III.ii (1914), 2935.

54 L. Delisle, *Mémoire sur d'anciens sacramentaires* (Méms. Acad. Inscrs. et Belles-Lettres 32.i; Paris 1886), 314. There is no such indication in a ninth century St Denis sacramentary, BN lat. 2290, otherwise very close to the Senlis (ibid. n. 8).

family to creep in. The most striking arrangement here is that of BN lat. 9432, a sacramentary from Amiens dated by Bernhard Bischoff to the tenth century (though by Delisle to the later ninth). Here the calendar has some metrical entries; that at XIII Kal. Feb. reads

> Tredecimas Sebastianus tenuisse probatur
> Et Fabiani, Mari et Marthe, Audifax et Abac,

but the Proper of Saints has for that day (as well as Fabian and Sebastian) 'Natale Marie et Marthe.'[55] A similar inconsistency is found in the Ratold Sacramentary (Corbie/St Vaast; BN lat. 12052), written 972-86, with a very full calendar of a martyrological sort which gives

(15th) XVIII Kal. Feb...Abbacuc et Micheae prophetarum
(19th) XIIII " " Hierosolimis, Marthae et Mariae
(20th) XIII " " Et Sanctorum Marii, Marthae, Audifax et Abbacuc.[56]

But again the masses for saints' days, intercalated with those for Sundays, include only Mary and Martha on 19 January.[57]

From the same general region and time comes the sacramentary component which in the eleventh century was joined with a (probably) Glastonbury calendar and other English matter to make up what is known as the Leofric Missal (Bodl., Bodley 579). Here the calendar entry (as was noted in tabular form at the beginning of this paper) reads, for 19 January, 'Natale Sancte Marie et Marthae.' That seems clear enough, but the sanctorale (Lotharingian rather than English) reflects confusion; its heading reads 'Sanctorum Mariae et Marthae,' and the prayers given are those in the Young Gelasians (Gellone, St Gall, etc.) for Mary and Martha; but while the collect uses the masculine plural *sanctorum*, both secret and postcommunion change that form to feminine (*tuarum sanctarum*).[58]

---

[55] Delisle, p. 326; H. Netzer, *L'Introduction de la messe romaine en France sous les Carolingiens* (Paris 1910), 104. Bischoff's dating is mentioned by Gamber (presumably expressed in a letter) in *CLLA* (see above, n. 50), no. 910.

[56] Delisle, p. 246.

[57] *DACL* III.ii (1914), 2939.

[58] F. E. Warren, ed. *The Leofric Missal* (Oxford 1883), 135.

The masculine plural form is restored in the early eleventh-century English book, perhaps c. 1010, called the Missal of Robert of Jumièges (Rouen, B.M. Y.6). Here (with the calendar reading 'Sanctorum Mariae et Marthae') the observance in the proper of saints is, as was noticed earlier, again headed 'Sanctorum Mariae et Marthae' but all three mass prayers are in the masculine plural, as though for Marius et al.[59] Since the same book uses *sanctarum tuarum* in the Secret for Perpetua and Felicity on 7 March (that section is missing in the Leofric Missal), it may be assumed that the feminine plural was not eliminated as a matter of consistency, and therefore that the confusion of gender persists until at least the time of the Norman Conquest in England.[60]

IV

This brings us back to the overall confusion of English calendars with which we began, and the discrete nature and number of which furnish the justification for isolating them among various possible witnesses. To try to isolate a similar number of contemporary calendars from Germany or France or Italy would very possibly be as instructive.[61] One factor, however, is likely to make the English evidence somewhat tidier than that from the continent: the growth in England of the cult of Wulfstan of Worcester, who died on 19 (or 20) January 1095.[62]

---

[59] H. A. Wilson, ed. *The Missal of Robert of Jumièges* (HBS 11, 1896), 153.

[60] The only other clearly pre-Conquest English mass book which could be adduced, the Red Book of Darley, Cbg. CCC 422, has no Proper of Saints; its calendar, assigned by Wormald to Sherborne, has at 19 January 'Sanctarum Marie et Marthe.' Cf. Warren, *Leofric Missal*, pp. 271-5. In the sanctorale of the sacramentary connected with Giso, the Lotharingian bishop of Wells 1061-88 (BL Cott. Vit. A.xviii), the prayers are those of the Gelasian tradition, uniformly in the masculine, although the calendar entry reads 'Sanctarum Marii et Marthae Audifax et Abbacuc.'

[61] Particularly instructive are the St Gall calendars of the ninth to eleventh centuries collected and studied by E. Munding, *Die Kalendarien von St Gallen* (Texte und Arbeiten 36-7, 1948-51), esp. I.37-8 and II.28. The evidence is too complex to be laid out here, but it should be noted that the earliest calendar printed (St Gall 914, c. A.D. 800) has the unusual form Adaflex. See also Munding's *Das Verzeichnis der St Galler Heiligenleben und ihrer Handschriften in Codex Sangall. 566* (Texte und Arbeiten 3/4, 1918). But the St Gall material seems to advance our particular purposes no further.

[62] See R. R. Darlington's introduction to his edition of *The Vita Wulfstani of William of Malmesbury* (Camden Soc. 40; London 1928), xliii.

But Wulfstan was canonized only in 1203, so there is no reason why his death should have scotched previously existing observances for 19 January. Yet, whereas of the twenty pre-1100 calendars printed by Wormald only six lacked Mary- or Marius and Martha, of a dozen twelfth-century calendars he printed or collated,[63] any such commemoration is evident in manuscripts from just two houses, and these witnesses themselves serve only to deepen the confusion. A Durham calendar of soon after 1100 (Durham Cath. Lib., Hunter 100) gives 'Marii et Marthae' at 19 January, while another (Cbg., Jesus Q.B.6) of the mid-twelfth has 'Marii et Marthe' on the 20th after Fabian and Sebastian.[64] The only other twelfth-century English witness of this sort seems to be from Ely: a pre-1170 calendar now in Milan (Bibl. Naz. Braidense AF.xi.9) has the entry on the 20th as in the Jesus College Cambridge MS above, with the 19th blank also.[65] But at Christ Church Canterbury (where 'Marii et Marthe' was at the 19th in BL Arundel 155, datable 1012-23), neither the calendar of the Eadwine Psalter (Cbg. Trin. R. 17.1) nor another mid-twelfth century calendar (Bodl. Add. C.260) has anything for the 19th.[66] Nor does any of the other houses represented by one surviving twelfth-century calendar each: Chester, Crowland, Gloucester, or St Albans.[67]

In short, it looks as though there is a break in English calendars after which there seems to be no awareness of a Mary and Martha observance, while of the Marius and Martha one there are hints only at Durham and Ely. This break does not appear to be a result of the Conquest as such - certainly not as part of any alleged purging by Lanfranc of Anglo-Saxon elements in English calendars, since there seems no conceivable way that our observance could have been

---

[63] *English Benedictine Kalendars after A.D. 1100*, I: *Abbotsbury-Durham* (HBS 77, 1939) and II: *Ely-St Neots* (HBS 81, 1946).

[64] BL Harl. 1804, a Durham calendar which dates from after 1494, has the entry as in Q.B.6, minus Marthe.

[65] Wormald, *Post-1100 Kals.* II, no. 1; the text he prints is of BL Harl. 547, s.xiii; by collation the Milan MS agrees with his, as does also BL Arundel 377, c. 1200; the calendar in the 'Liber Eliensis,' Cbg. Trin. 0.2.1, has no entries from the 14th through the 20th.

[66] R.W. Pfaff, 'The Calendar,' in *The Eadwine Psalter. Text, Image, and Monastic Community in Twelfth-Century Canterbury*, ed. M. Gibson, T.A. Heslop, and R.W. Pfaff (London and University Park, PA 1992), 80.

[67] Gloucester (Oxford, Jesus 10, pre-1170) has the Breton saint Launomar at the 19th, uniquely. A Westminster calendar in BL Roy. 1.A.xxii of c. 1200 has what may be the earliest surviving mention of Wulfstan at 19 January. In both calendars Fabian and Sebastian remain on the 20th.

construed as Anglo-Saxon.[68] To speculate why and how observances of this sort were removed, however, is even more difficult (and probably fruitless) than to try to establish how and why they were included.

We may seem to have arrived at a dead end. The present investigation may nonetheless be brought to a close with a little pure speculation - no more than that - as to how the confusion we have been tracing arose. The primary elements to our story seem to be martyrs, among whom is a Marius; Persia as a place of origin; and a pairing with Martha. Though even speculative explanations for some of the secondary elements (Audifax" name, for example) are not possible, the following points may have relevance. First, the names Marius and Martha are found together as far back as the second century A.D., in Plutarch's report that the Roman dictator Marius carried about with him on campaign a Syrian prophetess called Martha (*Marius*, xvii). Secondly, there was a confessor at Rome named Maris or Marius who is mentioned in a letter of Lucian of Carthage to Celerinus which is often included among the letters of Cyprian; a Maria is mentioned in the same letter, but among the other eight names are nothing like Martha, Audifax, or Abbacuc.[69] There is an historical Persian figure named Maris (Latinized as Marius?), the bishop of Hardascir who attended the Council of Ephesus in 431 and was addressed by Ibas of Edessa in a celebrated letter written in 433 which a century later was condemned by Justinian in the episode of the Three Chapters.[70] Though there is no suggestion that this Persian Maris was either a martyr or a confessor, a sixth- or seventh-century Western view of him as oppressed by Justinian's condemnation might conceivably result in his having been seen in that light. Finally, if either of the above Maris's should have been honorifically promoted into the category of martyr, an unclearly written 'Marii mart.' might have been expanded into 'Marius (et) Mart(ha)' or even, by a reader unfamiliar with either the Carthaginian or the Persian Maris, as 'Maria Mart(ha)' or the genitive-case equivalent.

---

[68] See R.W. Pfaff, 'Lanfranc's Supposed Purge of the Anglo-Saxon Calendar,' in *Warriors and Churchmen in the High Middle Ages: Essays presented to Karl Leyser*, ed. T. Reuter (London 1992), 89-102.

[69] Ep. 21 in the old numbering, 22 in the new, as ed. W. Hartel, Corpus Script. Eccles. Lat. 3.ii (Vienna 1871), 533. On the letter see E. W. Benson, *Cyprian* (London 1897), 70-74.

[70] L. Duchesne, *The Early History of the Christian Church*, III (1910; Eng. tr. London 1924), 273, citing Mansi, *Concilia* VII.241.

It may be objected that to search for such explanations is in itself wrong-headed, and that the tradition of four Persians called Mari(u)s, Martha, Audifax, and Abbacuc martyred under Claudius II should best be accepted at its face value. But in the realm of conjecture that which stands on one leg may be preferable to the wholly unsubstantiated. In this case to place much reliance on a tradition which is mentioned in no source earlier than the eighth century witnesses of the *Mart. Hieron.*manuscripts and Bede's Martyrology is close to leaning on the unsubstantiated. It looks as though the story was confected, out of such strands as have been noted above woven together with a blend of historical and linguistic misunderstandings, between the late fifth and late seventh centuries. That a *passio* should have been constructed from such misunderstandings in, say, the age of Gregory of Tours (who does not himself seem to know the story) is surely not inconceivable; clearly Bede's lucid summary and the garbled entries in the *Mart. Hieron.* must have come from somewhere.

Whatever whole cloth they did come from, or whatever kernel of historical truth there may be to the story of Marius and family, the appearance of the *dramatis personae* as Mary and Martha may represent simply an understandable instinct for comprehensibility, for known as opposed to hopelessly obscure figures. And whatever the case there, the obscurity of the Marius et al. story clearly militated against its retaining any widespread currency, while the notion of a Mary and Martha observance was to be overshadowed by the growth of the high medieval cult of Mary Magdalen (identified in tradition with Mary of Bethany).[71]

There is a tiny after-history to both observances. The Marius and Martha story survived at 19 January, probably because of its Roman topographical associations, into the later middle ages, and was, as we saw, incorporated into

[71] This paper was virtually complete before Dr Veronica Ortenberg called to my attention the conclusions, in some respects similar, reached by Victor Saxer in his influential work, *Le Culte de Marie Madeleine en occident des origines à la fin du moyen age* (Auxerre and Paris 1959), esp. pp. 35-9. He has been over a good deal of the same ground, primarily with an eye to tracing the 'false start' of a Mary and Martha feast on 19 January prior to the eleventh century, when the 22 July feast of Mary Magdalen begins to become a major saint's day. Having no intrinsic interest in the Mary and Martha tradition, he spends little time on that, and maintains without qualification (p. 39) that the Mary and Martha observance arises (perhaps in Frankia in the late sixth century) out of a confusion with the Persian family, whose existence he takes as primary data. It does not seem to me possible to be that certain.

the *Martyrologium Romanum* of 1584. Mary and Martha, on the other hand, were separated owing to the immense popularity of the former (when understood as Mary Magdalen) from the eleventh century on, and Martha came to be commemorated, if at all, only on her supposed sister's octave day, 29 July. She survives in the current Roman Catholic calendar (1979), but Marius et al. no longer have a place.

The questions raised by the pursuit of the puzzle of Martha's companion(s) on 19/20 January, and the bearing these questions have on a variety of hagiographical and liturgical matters, have seemed to justify devoting a certain amount of attention to it. Nonetheless,it is frustrating that no clear solution has emerged. At present, anyhow, it looks at though we shall have to accept the ambiguity manifest in the deep and tangled roots of the twofold tradition about Martha's hagiographical companion(s): a first-century sister or a third-century husband and sons.

V

The "Abbreviatio Amalarii" of William of Malmesbury

Among the minor works of William of Malmesbury his *Abbreviatio Amalarii* has been long known and frequently referred to, but has never received more than a passing page or so of attention [1], and has not been published. This is unfortunate, because the *Abbreviatio* adds considerable light to our knowledge of William, by showing us something of how he responded to, and worked with, materials from the past which were not primarily historical. It also provides a certain amount of information about the liturgy in early twelfth century England, and about how the liturgy was understood — information which is so scanty for that period that any supplement is most welcome.

William's *Abbreviatio* survives in (at least) five manuscripts. They are :

O : *Oxford, All Souls College 28*, fols. 123-137; a twelfth-century collection of liturgical and canonical treatises (Isidore, Rupert of Deutz, William, 'Ivo of Chartres'). No indication of provenance; given to All Souls by Henry VI [2].

1. The principal notices are those by William STUBBS in his preface to the *Rolls Series* edition of William's *Gesta Regum* (I, 1887), pp. cxxviii-cxxx, where there are printed William's preface, note at the end of book II, and conclusion; R. MÖNCHEMEIER, *Amalar von Metz* (Münster i.W. 1893), 204-205 (and on 256-258, capitula from the Wolfenbüttel MS, see below); Max MANITIUS, *Geschichte der lateinischen Literatur des Mittelalters* III (Munich 1931), 469-470; J. M. HANSSENS, Introduction to *Amalarii Episcopi Opera liturgica omnia* I (*Studi e Testi* 138; Vatican City 1948), 171-173; and Hugh FARMER, the leading modern authority on William (to whom I am indebted for advice), in *William of Malmesbury's Life and Works*, in *Journal of Ecclesiastical History* 13 (1962) esp. pp. 50-51.

2. H. O. COXE, *Catalogus Codicum Manuscriptorum qui in Collegiis Aulisque Oxoniensibus hodie adservantur* II (Oxford 1853) 7. Dr. N. R. Ker kindly informs me that he would date the MS to the third quarter, or perhaps early in the last quarter, of the century.

L: *London, Lambeth Palace 380*, fols. 171-195v; a collection of
* liturgical treaties in two volumes, William's abridgement being in the second. Written in two (?) twelfth-century hands; this part of the MS comes from Lanthony ('secunda': Gloucestershire)[3].

L2: *London, Lambeth Palace 363*, fols. 38-60; thirteenth or perhaps late twelfth century, the same collection of liturgical treatises as in MS *380*, followed by Anselm, *Cur deus homo* and other unrelated items. Perhaps also from Lanthony 'secunda'[4].

W: *Wolfenbüttel, Herzog-August-Bibliothek Lat. 1205 (Helmst. 1098)*, fols. 3-45; a miscellany of several apparently unrelated items in different hands, of which the first (fols. 2-45) is a thirteenth-century copy of the *Abbreviatio*. Provenance unknown, but formerly owned by M. Flacius (1520-75)[5].

C: *Cambridge, Corpus Christi College 68*, fols. 111-120v; dated 1432, written by Tielman Kerver. Cassiodorus and liturgical treatises, originally forming one volume with *King's College 9.ii.* Belonged to Cambridge University library in the fifteenth century[6].

Of these, *O* appears to be the earliest (though it is not in William's hand)[7]; it has no particular claim to distinction as the 'best' manuscript, and the text presented here has been constructed with the help of *L*, *L2*, and *W* as well as that of *O*. (Selected collations from *C* suggested that this codex was not worth including in the apparatus). Minor variations in spelling and word order have mostly been ignored.

Simple and obvious editorial principles have been employed. The orthography of *O* has generally been followed, but with 'v' used for consonantal 'u'. Very often 'c' and 't' are virtually indistinguishable, and the transcription of these letters is by no means consistent. Punctation and capitalization have been largely

3. M. R. JAMES, *A Descriptive Catalogue of the Manuscripts in the Library of Lambeth Palace* (Cambridge 1930-32) 523-525.

4. *Ibid.*, 491-493; not attributed to Lanthony in N. R. KER, *Medieval Libraries of Great Britain*, 2nd edn. (London 1964) 112.

5. O. VON HEINEMANN et al., *Die Handschriften der Herzoglichen Bibliothek zu Wolfenbüttel* III (Wolfenbüttel 1888) 53.

6. M. R. JAMES, *A Descriptive Catalogue of the Manuscripts in the Library of Corpus Christi College, Cambridge* I (Cambridge 1909) 146.

7. As identified by N. R. KER, *The Handwriting of William of Malmesbury*, in *English Historical Review* 59 (1944) 371-376.

* **treaties** ***should read*** **treatises**

normalized. In general cardinal numbers below ten have been spelled out, and those above ten printed as Roman numerals. Psalms are cited in the Vulgate numbering. Patristic references have mostly been taken, after being verified, from the exhaustive citations in J.M. Hanssens's definitive edition of the liturgical works of Amalarius (*Studi e Testi* 138-140; Vatican City 1948-50).

I am grateful to the Warden and Fellows of All Souls College, Oxford, for permission to use their MS for the establishment of the text, and to the other libraries involved for supplying microfilms of their MSS.

* * *

In the preface to book I William explains the occasion of his work, and sets it in a rather charming context. William and his friend Robert, to whom the preface is addressed, are sitting 'in our library' (presumably that at Malmesbury) turning over books; Robert comes across the *Liber Officialis*, or *De ecclesiasticis officiis*, of Amalarius. The full work proves too much for Robert — a feeling we can easily sympathize with — and he asks William to abridge it for him. William explains that he has expended considerable labor on the project, and now presents his abbreviated Amalarius, whose 'catholic way' of interpreting the liturgy is commended to Robert, especially in contrast to that of Rabanus Maurus, to whose scholarship and theology alike William takes violent exception [8].

Some light on a possible date for the work may be shed by trying to identify the friend Robert. William's conclusion to the whole work, which in most of the manuscripts begins 'Videor michi amice', reads in one the manuscripts 'Videor michi, domine

8. Why William feels so fierce an animus against Rabanus is beyond the scope of this enquiry, but it should at least be noted that Rabanus was a strong opponent of Paschasius Radbertus, whose commentary on Lamentations William used as the basis of his own: see Hugh FARMER, *William of Malmesbury's Commentary on Lamentations*, in *Studia Monastica* 4 (1962) 283-311. As Farmer points out, William's preface to that work describes a similar stimulus, the request of a friend to abbreviate a long and verbose commentary. This coincidence does not, however, compel us to regard the two prefaces of William as mere literary conventions.

antistes'[9]. If we can suppose that we infer correctly from this witness that the friend for whom William undertook the work was a (monk?) Robert who became a bishop, the likeliest choice seems to be the Robert who was bishop of Bath from 1136 to 1166[10], with alternate possibilities being Robert Warelwast, Exeter 1138-55[11] or Robert de Béthune, Hereford 1131-48[12].

It would appear that the copy of Amalarius's *Liber Officialis* (*L.O.*) which William used is no longer extant, but we can learn something about it both from William's work and from similar MSS which do survive. William's copy was almost certainly of the type which is called the first edition of the *L.O.* — that in three books (as opposed to the second, third, and possibly fourth editions, in four books), issued by Amalarius somewhere between 820 and 822[13]. Of this first type, some sixteen MSS have been traced and identified by Hanssens in his magisterial work on the text of Amalarius[14]. Unfortunately, none of these MSS is English by present location or, apparently, by provenance. Two of the MSS of Hanssens's sub-group I*, with affinities to I but containing four books, are English : *Cambridge*, *Corpus Christi 416* and *Cambridge*,

9. This MS, *Wolfenbüttel Helms. 1098*, contains no preface, and it is possible that the bishop referred to in the conclusion has no connection with William at all; furthermore, all the verb-forms are changed from the second person singular (as in the other MSS) to the second person plural (which might, of course, still be used in writing to a dignitary no matter how well one knew him).

10. F. M. POWICKE and E. B. FRYDE, *Handbook of British Chronology*, 2nd edn. (London 1961) 205. But this Robert was a monk of Lewes (Cluniac) : D. KNOWLES, *The Monastic Order in England*, 2nd. edn. (Cambridge 1963) 709.

11. If we were to assume that William's attack on Rabanus (see n. 8, above) could be taken to indicate that the *Abbreviatio Amalarii* was written after the Commentary on Lamentations (which is not earlier than 1138 : see FARMER, *Stud. Mon.* 4 [1962] 288-289)), then, if the 'Robertus amicus' of the preface is the 'Domine antistes' of the Wolfenbüttel MS, probably only Robert Warelwast could qualify. But he is the least likely in terms of monastic or religious affinity.

12. Robert de Béthune had been prior of the Augustinian house at Llanthony ('Prima' : Monmouthshire); William spoke of him, in the *Gesta Pontificum*, as 'religiosissimum, in victu et vestitu abstemium' (ed. HAMILTON, *Rolls Series*, 1870, p. 304).

13. Following the argument of Allen CABANISS, *Amalarius of Metz* (Amsterdam, 1954) 52 and 111-112, against Hanssens' dating of some time after April 823.

14. Initially in a series of articles in *Ephemerides liturgicae* 47-49 (1933-35) collected and published separately as *Le Texte du 'Liber officialis' d'Amalaire* (Rome 1935); subsequently summarized in the introduction to his edition of Amalarius, *op. cit.* I, 120 ff.

Pembroke 44. Two further English MSS are noted by Hanssens as containing excerpts of the *L.O.* : *Cambridge*, *Corpus Christi 265* and *British Library*, *Cott. Vesp. D.xv*. Finally (for our purposes) Hanssens noted two English MSS of the type he terms 'Retractatio I', a fixed set of selections compiled (by someone other than Amalarius) in northern France or thereabouts, and passing into England either via Brittany (*Cambridge*, *Corpus Christi 192*) or directly (*Cambridge*, *Trinity 241*). (William's *Abbreviatio*, four MSS of which are mentioned by Hanssens, constitutes 'Retractatio V').

Of these English MSS the oldest is *Cambridge*, *Corpus Christi 192*, written at Landévennec in Brittany in 952[15], and in the library at Christ Church, Canterbury by 1170 at the latest; M.R. James assumed it had been brought there before the Norman Conquest, but without giving reasons for this assumption[16]. The next oldest are *Cambridge*, *Trinity 241*, in an English hand of the 11th century, one of the books given by bishop Leofric (d. 1072) to Exeter[17]; and the celebrated *Cambridge*, *Corpus Christi 265* (containing only miscellaneous excerpts from Amalarius), from Worcester and dateable chiefly to the late 11th century[18]. The two 'complete' MSS of the *L.O.* surviving in England, *Pembroke 44* and *Corpus 416*, are contemporary with William of Malmesbury and come from, respectively, Bury St. Edmunds and Ely[19]. So there were texts of the *L.O.*, in one form or another, in a least four of the greatest English monastic libraries — Canterbury Christ Church, Worcester,

15. M.R. James, *CCC Cat.* I (1909) 465-466.

16. M.R. James, *The Ancient Libraries of Canterbury and Dover* (Cambridge 1903) xxviii and 11. Hanssens, *Eph. liturg.* 47 (1933) 246-248, discusses the MS and notes that another Landévennec MS of 'Retractatio I', *Paris Nat. nouv. acq. lat. 1983*, went to Beauvais in probably the 12th or 13th century. The Anglo-Saxon glosses he thought he had discovered in these two MSS are (as James had realized) Breton: L. Fleuriot, *Nouvelles Gloses vieilles-bretonnes à Amalarius*, in *Études celtiques* 11 (1964-67) 415-464.

17. M.R. James, *The Western Manuscripts in the Library of Trinity College, Cambridge* I (Cambridge 1900) 327-328; N.R. Ker, *Catalogue of MSS containing Anglo-Saxon* (Oxford 1957) 129. *Brit. Lib. Cott. Vesp. D.xv*, listed by Hanssens as containing excerpts of the *L.O.*, also probably comes, at least in part, from Exeter. Fols. 2-67 are a pontifical of the twelfth century ascribed to Exeter with a query by Ker (*Med. Libs. Gt. Brit.* 82); fols. 68-101 a treatise on penance in Anglo-Saxon which Ker (*Cat.*, pp. 277-278) dates mid-tenth century but gives no provenance for.

18. James, *CCC Cat.* II (1912) 14; Ker, *Cat.* 94.

19. M.R. James, *A Descriptive Catalogue of the MSS in the Library of Pembroke College, Cambridge* (Cambridge 1905) 43; *CCC Cat.* II, 308-309.

Bury, and Ely — and at Exeter, by William's day. It would seem that Malmesbury had one as well, and we can conjecture that other important libraries were similarly equipped.

I

Book I of William's *Abbreviatio* corresponds principally to Amalarius's book I, which deals with the liturgical year, beginning at Septuagesima. The first fourteen of William's nineteen chapters cover roughly the material in the first thirty or forty chapters of Amalarius; thereafter William's cap. xv deals with the Ember Days (= AMAL. II.ii), xvi with Advent (= AMAL. III.xl), xvii with Holy Innocents' day (= AMAL. I.xli), xviii with Candlemas (= AMAL. III.xliii), and the last chapter, xix, with masses for the dead (= AMAL. III.xliv).

The long chapter on Septuagesima which begins both works gives a pretty clear indication of how William's work will come to have a much more original character than the simple abridgement he admits to. Where Amalarius starts with two brief sentences on the computation of Septuagesima and then strings together thirteen scriptural references, two quotations from Jerome, and one from Bede, William devotes a good part of his chapter to the historical background. It was, he remarks, a custom of apostolic antiquity to fast for six weeks before Easter, the thirty-six days (Sundays being of course excluded) equalling a tithe of the year [20]. However, Pope Thelesphorus (William has now skipped to sect. 18 of Amalarius's chapter), wanting to make the fast imitate the Lord's forty days in the wilderness, lengthened it to seven weeks, which minus Sundays left forty-two days (the odd two days being, William suggests, for good measure) — hence the term Quinquagesima for the Sunday at the head of the seven weeks. Later Pope Melchiades decided that Thursday was unsuitable as a fast day, which involved stretching the period to eight weeks, the fifty-six days minus the sixteen Sundays and Thursdays leaving exactly the desired forty. This gives us Sexagesima Sunday — not, William

20. On the Lenten fast as a tithe of the year, see G. CONSTABLE, *Monastic Tithes from their Origins to the Twelfth Century* (Cambridge 1964) 18.

remarks rather blandly, because it is sixty days before Easter but because it is the next capital number after Quinquagesima!

It may be well to analyze fairly closely for this first chapter how much of this material William takes from Amalarius. Of the historical facts William includes — the 'apostolic' fast of six weeks, its lengthening by Thelesphorus, the exclusion of Thursday by Melchiades, and the subsequent further extending of the fast — only the second is found in Amalarius[21]. The others he seems to have supplied himself, perhaps from his own reading of the *Liber Pontificalis* for Melchiades[22]. For figurative interpretations William follows his model more closely, but by no means slavishly. Of course the seventy days (from Septuagesima through the Saturday after Easter) 'imitate' the seventy years of the Babylonian Captivity. The significance of sixty days is not so straightforward; here William seems either not to have understood Amalarius or to have 'improved' upon his model's admittedly complicated exposition.

AMALARIUS (I.i.14)	WILLIAM
... per hunc numerum viduae quae in magna tribulatione sunt, designantur. Quam tribulationem et afflictionem monstrat compotus digitorum, qui memoratum numerum exprimit indice superposito pollici.	Quia vero sexagenarius numerus significat viduarum sanctarum continentiam sicut in compoto digitorum probatur; sexaginta isti dies significant viduitatem ecclesie qua peregrinatur a sponso suo qui eam corporaliter reliquit.

The primary relation of widows to the number sixty is, of course, the prescription in *I Tim.* 5.9 that a widow must be sixty years old to be enrolled as such. William has discarded Amalarius's reference, borrowed from Jerome[23], to widows 'in the great tribulation', retained the mention of the 'compotus digitorum', and added on his own the widowhood of the church, whose spouse has bodily left her. This elaboration continues in the three remaining days (i.e. from nine weeks minus sixty days: the 'triduum sacrum'): for Amalarius they signify the three day fast proclaimed by the Ninevites after the preaching of Jonah (*Jon.* 3.4, but only, as

21. Who refers to Thelesphorus also in his *Ep. ad Hilduinum*, cap. 34; ed. HANSSENS I, 347.

22. William certainly had access to the *Liber Pontificalis*: W. LEVISON, *Englische Handschriften des Liber Pontificalis*, in *Neues Archiv* 35 (1910) 333-431.

23. JEROME, *Adv. Iovin.* 1.3 (PL 23.223).

Amalarius points out, in the Septuagint), but for William this repentance is combined with a bewailing of the sojourning (?: 'incolatum') of our widowhood. It would appear that William is fully a match for his model in inventing figurative explanations. Moreover, the six week-days of the Easter octave, William adds, signify the good works of our whole lives, i.e. the six ages of man, which are then enumerated. Adding touches like this is, we may think, a curious way of going about an abridgement of an already too long work.

In the actual liturgical details for Septuagesima William and Amalarius agree entirely. As well as specifying the omission of Alleluia and the Gloria in excelsis, Amalarius refers specifically to the introit, collect, epistle, and gradual. William, at the end of his long chapter, gives incipits or characteristic tags for these forms, all coinciding with those of Amalarius, and for the Gospel, offertory chant, and communion chant as well (all the latter agreeing with those in the later Roman missal of Pius V).

William's numerological ingenuity is continued in the next chapter, on Sexagesima: ten times sixty is the commandments which we should observe through all the six ages of man. Amalarius had arrived at the desired number by a multiplication of the six days of creation by the ten-fold reward of works (from keeping the Decalogue, presumably). His only mention of an 'age' is that the fourth day, the Wednesday in Easter week, corresponds to the fourth age, in which David and Solomon reigned. William has only partially understood, or accepted, this; for him these two kingdoms signify the two kingdoms of Christ, one in the church, the other in the life everlasting, the first 'laboriosum', the second 'pacificum'. William then picks up Amalarius' explanation of sixty, repeating it almost verbatim. The only abridging William accomplishes here is by eliminating all the patristic references of Amalarius and some of the scriptural citations. As in the previous chapter the liturgical details — tags from the various mass propers — are identical, in both authors being specified through the Gospel. William concludes with the curious, rather cryptic remark 'Sic de ceteris potest studiosus lector intelligere quod constitutor officiorum nostrorum nichil otiosum in eis voluit constituere'.

Amalarius' whole discussion of the pre-Lent and Lenten liturgy is structured, one might say, around the twin ideas of the 'varietates' of the liturgy (by this he means chiefly differences in rite) and of the homiletic or allegorical value to be found within the 'officia', chiefly the mass propers, of the various days. So William incorporates, in his discussion of the propers for Quinquagesima, a distinction suggested by Amalarius of the 'tres gradus... trium officiorum' of the day: the first, our complaint that we are 'sub dominis vitiorum' (AMAL.) or 'sub crudelissima damnatione peccatorum' (WM.), this referring to the mention in the collect of the 'peccatorum vinculis'; the second, our 'voluntatem fugae' (AMAL.) or 'meditationem fuge' (WM.) while ('dummodo') the Lord wishes to come to our aid — this with reference probably to the gradual, 'liberasti in brachio tuo populum tuum'; the third the actual plan of flight in William ('consilium fugiendi') or of defense in Amalarius ('consilium... quomodo se muniat'), looking back to the introit, 'Esto mihi in Deum protectorem'. These three are then related, at great length by Amalarius and abruptly by William, to the three 'returns' from the captivity in Babylon. In this section it is again not at all certain that William has understood his model; if he has, his abridgement at this point makes obscure what Amalarius' prolixity had rendered tolerably clear.

In the following chapter, on Quadragesima, the first Sunday in Lent, this extreme terseness is abandoned, and the result is a more intelligible abridgement. For the first time William includes passages from some of Amalarius's long patristic quotations: from Augustine's *De consensu evangelistarum* (from *L.O.* I.iv, 'De quadragesima'), and, at the end of the chapter, from Augustine's *Ep.* 55, *Ad Januarium* (from *L.O.* I.v-vi, brief appendices to the main chapter). Even when following Amalarius as closely as in this chapter, however, William adds new interpretations and observations of his own: in this case, equating Good Friday and Holy Saturday (as being 'left over' after forty days have been exhausted of the forty-two — the number of generations in the Lord's genealogy — days in the six full weeks of Lent) with the commandments of love of God and love of neighbour.

William's peculiarly inconsistent notion of abridgement — not only shortening some sections and omitting others but also adding or expanding material considerably — can be even more clearly seen in the brief chapter on Ash Wednesday. William diverges from Amalarius' inclusion of Augustine's etymological-numerical explanation of the name Adam in connection with the forty-six days, counting Sundays, from Ash Wednesday to Easter (the letters Αδάμ having the numerical equivalent of forty-six in Greek) into a detailed description, adapted directly from Augustine[24], of how the human embryo is formed (I.v.):

> Primis enim diebus sex semen lac est, deinde sequentibus novem convertitur in sanguinem, inde duodecim solidatur. Reliquis decem et octo formatur in omnibus liniamentis. Sex autem et novem et duodecim et decem et octo faciunt xlv. Quibus si addas illum diem quo post perfecta liniamenta incipit corpus crescere fiunt xlvi. Quapropter convenit ut corpus nostrum castigetur ieiuniis in caritate matris ecclesie quot diebus formatur utero in matris sue.

William has also 'looked up' the reference to Gregory the Great which Amalarius makes in passing, and has identified it as the homily on the Gospel 'Ductus Ihesus in desertum' (for the first Sunday in Lent, as in matins for that day)[25]; but he has left out all mention of the liturgical forms for Ash Wednesday.

William follows Amalarius faithfully in singling out one weekday in Lent for commentary in a chapter to itself: the Wednesday in the fourth week of Lent (fifth Wednesday in Lent), called 'In apertione aurium', after the ancient custom of touching the nostrils and ears of catechumens on that day and delivering to them the creed which they were to recite on Easter Eve. This day, one of those to which the term 'Mediana' was anciently applied[26], was distinguished (as it continued to be in the subsequent Roman missal) by two prophetic lessons before the Gospel. Amalarius himself seems to regard the ceremony of touching the catechumens as something of a rarity (though he describes it in the present tense): 'Memorata quarta

24. AUGUSTINE, *De diversis quaest.* 56 (PL 40.39), a passage which, according to Hanssens, is not cited by Amal., whose discussion of the forty-six days is taken from *In Ioan.* 10.

25. *The Monastic Breviary of Hyde Abbey, Winchester*, ed. J. B. L. TOLHURST, I (HBS 69, 1932), fol. 70.

26. For some idea of the controversy surrounding this term and its application see G. G. WILLIS, *What is Mediana Week* in his *Studies in Early Roman Liturgy* (*Alcuin Club Collections* 46, 1964), 101-104, and *Mediana Week*, in *Downside Review* 87 (1969) 50-53.

feria apud cultores ecclesiae in apertione aurium dicitur' (I.viii.2). Hanssens glosses the phrase 'cultores ecclesiae' as 'viri rerum liturgicarum periti'[27]; but it would seem to have rather the sense of 'liturgical founders', like the 'constitutor officii' so often mentioned by Amalarius, than of 'liturgical experts'. For William, certainly, the custom is one of the past: 'more antiquo tangebatur illa die * nares et aures caticuminorum' — though again it is impossible to say unequivocally whether for him 'antiquo' is used from the standpoint of the twelfth century or of the ninth.

An even clearer instance of the ambiguity of William's time-perspective, taking in as it must his own age as well as that of Amalarius, is offered by the next chapter, on the Saturday before Palm Sunday. Amalarius' chapter (I.ix) begins 'Varietas tertia est sabbato ante palmas. Haec est varietas eius. Praetitulature in sacramentario nostro et in antiphonario: "Sabbato vacat. Dominus papa elemosinam dat"', and goes on to explain why this day should be specially singled out, namely because according to John's gospel[28] that was the day on which Mary washed the feet of Jesus at Bethany (the moral is then drawn out by a quotation from Augustine). Amalarius concludes on an exhortatory note, 'Hoc preciosissimum exemplum sequitur apostolicus. Utinam et nos sequamur; ubicumque officium romanae ecclesiae agitur, haec fama personat'. William, having given the gist of the passage from Augustine, concludes his chapter, 'Ad imitationem igitur Marie illa die apostolicus elemosinam donat et etiam in sacramentariis ascribi patitur ut ceteros per orbem ad suam imitationem trahat. Hoc et sabbato ante xl facit et elemosina ieiunium precedat'. This raises obvious questions: is it in sacramentaries William has seen that the pope has allowed his charitable practice to be included as an edifying example to all, or is William just embroidering slightly on Amalarius' somewhat bald statement? More importantly, is it true that the Saturday before Palm Sunday — and also, as

27. 'Index verborum philologus' in his edn. of Amal. III (*Studi e Testi* 140) 382; this is the only instance of the phrase which he finds.

28. William changes Amal's. 'Iohannes synmista' (spelled five different ways in the various MSS: see Hanssens' apparatus *ad* I.viii.2) to 'Iohannes evangelista', though 'symmista' (companion) is attested for England in 790, the eleventh century, and c. 1125: R. E. LATHAM, *Revised Medieval Latin Word-List* (London 1965) 472.

*** tangebatur *should read* tangebantur**

William adds, that before Quadragesima — is still 'vacat' in twelfth century England[29]?

About Palm Sunday itself William, like Amalarius, has very little to say; but ignoring Amalarius' remarks, which are almost wholly confined to two quotations from Bede, William 'abridges' by explaining the significance of the palms, an aspect totally ignored by his original : that they signify the victory of Christ over the devil, as victors (in games) were crowned with them. William notes, as Amalarius had not, that the Passion is read on that day.

One more 'varietas' of the Lenten liturgy has to be discussed before the extensive ceremonies of the 'triduum sacrum' are reached. This is the Wednesday in Holy Week, made noteworthy by an additional prophetic lesson and responsory, as well as by the continued reading of the Passion. Here William has suppressed a good deal, especially the stipulation, from the Ordo Romanus which Amalarius used, of the solemn prayers which are to be said before the 'publicum officium' (in this case, mass) just as on Good Friday, i.e., the Bidding Prayers. But he adds a ceremony which Amalarius does not mention, of the cutting ('scinditur') of the veil which has hung throughout Lent 'inter nos et altare'. It is clear that here the rite William knew differed from that described by Amalarius[30].

II

William's chapter on the rites of Maundy Thursday (I.x) is, like his model's, one of the longest in the work. Amalarius' chapter (I.xii) is composed of some fifty-four sections; William has not only boiled these down very considerably, but has also again introduced a certain amount of information not found in the *L.O.*

29. It is not 'vacat' in the early eleventh century missal of Robert of Jumièges (ed. H.A. WILSON, HBS 11, 1896), nor in the thirteenth century Bec Missal (ed. A. HUGHES, HBS 94, 1963). A missal presumably very close to what William would have known, that of the New Minster, Winchester (late eleventh century; ed. D.H. TURNER, HBS 93, 1962) lacks the temporale before Easter.

30. This veil is ordered removed ('cortina deponatur') after Compline in the *Monastic Constitutions of Lanfranc*, ed. D. KNOWLES (London 1951) 27; it had been hung after Compline on the first Sunday in Lent (*ibid.*, p. 19), 'inter chorum et altare', to be pulled back only during feasts of twelve lessons. There is no mention of this custom in the *Regularis Concordia*, c. 970.

William's description of the 'multae varietates' of the day — a term he takes over from Amalarius — begins by mentioning the omission of the *Venite*, *Glora Patri*, and the sounding of bells. These items are not included in the *L.O.* account of the day; William either supplied them on his own, or took them from other works of Amalarius (or even from other writers on the liturgy). Amalarius mentions the omission of bells only in his letter to Hilduin, and of the *Gloria Patri* (at all the daily offices) and *Venite* ('Invitatorium' at Matins) only in the fourth book of the *L.O.*, which, as we have seen, William's exemplar did not contain. Next William passes to a discussion of the twenty-four candles on the altar at *Tenebrae*, again a subject treated by Amalarius not in the chapter in book I of the *L.O.* which William is abridging, but briefly in book IV (cap. xxii) and at greater length in cap. xliv of the *Liber de ordine antiphonarii.* Neither passage contains William's explanation that of the twenty-four candles, twelve represent the twelve apostles and the other twelve stand for the relatively less important seventy-two disciples.

In the following sections, on the blessing of oils, William returns more directly to his immediate source. Giving only cursory attention to Amalarius's disquisition on the symbolism of oil in general, William passes to the first of the three consecrations, that of the 'oleum infirmorum'. This oil is blessed at the consecration of bread and wine at the mass, which William, following Amalarius, explains by juxtaposing the New Testament witness about the anointing (*Jas.* 5.14-15) with the warning from the epistle for the day (*I Cor.* 11.30) about maladies which befall those who communicate unworthily. The second blessing of oil, that of chrism, takes place at the giving of the Pax (which, apparently on his own invention, William justifies by explaining that the word 'crisma' is derived from 'Christ', who has made peace between God and men!). Here William seems to diverge a good deal from Amalarius, who has explained that the *Ordo Romanus* he chiefly refers to prescribes that acolytes should hold the *ampullae* of chrism veiled until the bishop, having breathed thrice on the chrism (William adds 'in the form of a cross', a note omitted by Amalarius)[31], blesses it, where-

31. But it must be remembered that the liturgy described by Amalarius, himself a bishop, assumes as normal an episcopal presence; whereas for William, as for

upon it is 'exposed' for 'salutation' by all. At this point Amalarius goes into one of his more far-fetched allegorical explanations; William, however, comments soberly that the 'lector prudens' will understand a relationship between the chrism and the Lord, full of both divinity and the Holy Spirit, as is indicated by three scriptural verses (not cited by Amalarius).

Another section largely original to William follows his brief mention of the third kind of oil to be blessed, that of exorcism. In this section William puts together what begins like a very short homily on the necessity of the three different kinds of oil, with proof-texts drawn from six New Testament passages, and continues as a quite substantial rationale of the symbolism of anointing. Here again the title 'abbreviatio' is hardly justified, for William has if anything expanded Amalarius rather than the contrary. Amalarius writes (I.xii.18):

> Tres memoratae consecrationes ex una atque eadem substantia fiunt, id est olei liquore. Sic namque spiritus sancti substantia una, qui tamen dividitur multiformiter per gratiam donorum suorum: alii datur sermo sapientiae, alii sermo scientiae, alii fides, alii gratia sanitatum, et reliqua (*I Cor.* 12.8-9). Haec videntur nobis habilia esse ad dilucidandas consecrationes nostras;

and goes on to exemplify each of these gifts of the Spirit. William follows the general outline, but leans both to different explanations and to different supporting texts, as can be seen from the following comparison:

AMALARIUS	WILLIAM
Sermo sapientiae bonam conversationem tenet (then *Col.* 3.1-2 and *I Cor.* 15.10a).	Alii enim secundum apostolum datur sapientia id est ut christiane vivat quod est summa sapientia (then *Prov.* 1.7).
Ecce habes oleum. Addatur sermo scientiae. Scientia ad doctrinam pertinet... (*I Cor.* 15.10b). Habes et balsamum. Ubi haec duo coniuncta fuerint, perfectum faciunt servientem.	Ecce oleum crismatis, sed ut addatur balsamum datur sermo scientiae ut bene vivat et bene loqui et intelligere sciat.
Sequitur: alii fides. Fidem in promptu ad duo opera introducimus: ad ex-	Sed quia sunt plerique qui simplici fide contempti sunt additur alii fides.

the *Regularis Concordia* and even for Lanfranc, it is rather the absence of a bishop which is presupposed.

pulsionem videlicet (then *I Cor.* 13.2) ... et ad munimen (then *Eph.* 6.16). Habes exorcismum olei, ut ipsa verba testatur discendo (then quotation from prayer for blessing of oil of exorcism).
Sequitur : alii gratia sanitatum. Habes oleum pro infirma. Verba huius orationis demonstrat, non solum necessarium esse medicinam corporalem, sed potius spiritualem....

Et alibi (then *Rom.* 1.17). Ecce oleum exorcizatum. Alii gratia sanitatum. Ecce oleum infirmorum (then *I Cor.* 12.11). Et quidem ista sua karismata posset sine visibili oleo spiritus sanctus largiri sed per visibilia nos ammonet ut ad invisibilium amorem rapiamur. Posset etiam dominus nos baptizare invisibiliter spiritu sancto sed aquam addi voluit ut sicut aqua foris abluit ita intelligere debeamus spiritum sanctum intus operari.

Clearly William did not set himself a simple boiling-down of the prolixities of Amalarius; he is, rather, providing a work of both liturgical instruction and spiritual edification, both aims to be pursued with a contemporary twelfth-century audience in view.

On matters where Amalarius is in doubt which of two usages to present as the basis for his allegorizing commentary, William simply cites the practice he himself is familiar with. He allows for no ambiguity in the matter of the candles at *Tenebrae*, which was noticed earlier, where Amalarius had reported both the Roman usage and the Frankish. Again, Amalarius finds conflicting practices about the reservation of the Host on Maundy Thursday: he knows of an *Ordo Romanus* which specifies that the Host shall be reserved (sect. 34), and of another which apparently (it has not been found) prescribed the contrary (sect. 1) [32]. Amalarius himself is not impressed by the practice ('Quod superfluum esse compertum est' : sect. 34). Of this disagreement there is no trace in William, who says without any hesitation, 'Ab ipsa die servatur corpus domini usque in crastinum'. Reservation of the Host was an essential part of the Maundy Thursday rites as known to William, and there was no point in including information to the contrary which might simply confuse. Furthermore, he uses the proof-text adduced by Amalarius against the practice (*Mt.* 26.29) to precisely the opposite effect!

William also appears to indicate a different usage from that contained in Amalarius when he discusses, somewhat more briefly, the two remaining ceremonies of Maundy Thursday, the stripping and washing of altars, and the pedilavium. William states that the

32. See HANSSENS' note *ad L.O.* I.xii.1.

walls and floors are washed, as well as the altars, in most churches ('apud plerasque ecclesias'), whereas Amalarius had indicated only that the floors were washed (he does not speak of the altar's being washed, but only stripped). What interests both writers at this point is the opportunity to expand a symbolic gesture into a social model of the church. Here the comparative passages are worth looking at because William again uses Amalarius only as a springboard for his own striking originality:

AMALARIUS (I.xii.36 and 39)	WILLIAM
Parietes domus vocabulum habent ecclesiae, quia continent ecclesiam; non sunt ipsi ecclesiae (there follows etymological explanation from Bede's commentary on Luke)... Pavimentum ecclesiae auditores magistrorum significat. Lavatio domus, quae nuncupative ecclesia dicitur, signum est lavationis pedum fratrum; lavatio pedum fratrum signum est remissionis peccatorum....	Ligna autem et lapides non sunt ecclesia sed sancte fidelium anime.... Altare potest significare sacerdotes et clerum qui ei deserviunt. Parietes potentes laicos quorum protectione defenduntur populi. Pavimentum humile vulgus. Omne itaque hominum Christianorum genus debet lavari per penitentiam ad sanctam resurrectionem suscipiendam.... Et hoc in cena domini quia eo die lavit pedes discipulorum suorum. Ad quod imitandum lavamus nostros pedes et pauperum.

This leads William naturally into a brief discussion of the pedilavium. Amalarius does not seem to know the custom in the form of giving a meal to poor men and then washing their feet, and he connects the pedilavium primarily with the symbolism of the forgiveness of sins. Though William may well have known the 'double' pedilavium (as described in the *Regularis Concordia* and the *Constitutions of Lanfranc*: poor men in the morning, monastic brethren in the evening), he refers only to the washing of the feet of the poor. He concludes his chapter on the observances of the day by providing a commonsensical, English reason why, although the Lord dined first and then instituted the Last Supper, the monks have mass first and then eat: 'Nos ante mensam deo sacrificiamus quia supplicatur attentius et liberius oratur castius et mundius cum cibis corporalis non gravatur stomachus'.

The Good Friday rites are for the most part treated much more briefly: the fore-mass culminating in the reading of the Passion, during which two deacons strip away the linen altar-cloth 'quasi furantes' (so William; Amalarius says 'in modo furantis'); the solemn prayers of intercession — those for the Jews said standing, because the Jews bent the knee to Christ in mockery: a similar reason, the kiss of Judas, is offered to explain why the kiss of peace is omitted during the 'triduum'; and the veneration of the cross, which William deals with almost summarily compared to Amalarius's lengthy disqusition, with this rather stern comment:

> Plura vero de crucis laude subnectit Amalarius, que mihi non videntur necessarium hic attexere. Id enim solummodo suscepti operis exposcit necessitas ut ea que dixit de significationibus ecclesiasticorum officiorum breviter defloremus; omissis omnibus testimoniis que ille tantis involvit anfractibus ut quid velit dicere vix intelligamus.

The fierce opposition which Amalarius displays towards communion from the reserved sacrament on Good Friday reflects a difference in usage even within the city of Rome (see AMALARIUS I.xv.1-2) which had long been a dead issue by William's time. William simply remarks that the reserved host is brought in (from the Altar of Repose), wine is consecrated by immixture, and the elements are consumed ('sumuntur': he does not indicate how general the communion was) without the 'Pax domini' being said.

William's treatment of Holy Saturday — that is, of the rites of Easter Eve through the first mass of Easter — is notable for the severity of its abridgement of Amalarius, for an unusually clear illustration of William's working methods, and for some substantial divergences of interpretation, if not of detail, from his model. William omits completely Amalarius' long discussion of the baptismal ceremonies of the day, from the oil of unction (I.xxiii) through the clothing of the newly baptized in their white garments (I.xxix): well over half the treatment of Holy Saturday in the *L.O.* The reason William gives for this extensive omission is extremely interesting:

> De cuius sacramentis (i.e., baptism), Amalarius plura volvit et revolvit que hic pretermittimus, ne ego et ille quem defloro rideamur in comparatione Carnotensis episcopi Ivonis, qui talia nobilissime prosecutus est in sermone de sacramentis neophitorum.

Perhaps William really felt that Ivo's sermon[33] was the last word on the matter, rendering Amalarius' discussion obsolete; but more likely it is the meaninglessness of the idea of adult Easter Eve baptisms in a twelfth century monastic context which indicates that even a drastic abridgement of Amalarius would not be worth the space required.

Even the sections on Holy Saturday which are retained are not abridged entirely consecutively. It is clear from this chapter of William's that he read a whole section of Amalarius through and then re-organized the subject matter somewhat as well as shortening it. William's chapter, 'De Sabbato Sancto', divided into seven sections, corresponds to chapters xvi-xxxiii of book I of the *L.O.* Of these, xxiii-xxix are mostly omitted as noticed above, and William's abridgement represents the remainder in the following order: xvi (only very loosely); xvii; xviii sections 1, 2, 5, 1 again, 6, 1 again, 6 again, 11, 16, 4, 5 again, 6 again, 9, 11 again, 16; xxi; xxii; (omission of xxiii-xxix); xx; xxxi (xxx, of three lines, also omitted); xxix sections 7 and 11. William completely reorganizes Amalarius' long chapter xviii, which is an application of the 'four senses' of scripture to the lessons and canticles of the Easter vigil. Where Amalarius ponderously takes up one sense at a time, with the corresponding example from the vigil, William culls four disconnected sections of his model to provide a consecutive summary of the four senses, and then relates them quickly to the vigil readings. And with the tightening up of the organization goes a considerable overall shortening: the section on why the lessons are read without announcing the names of the books from which they are taken occupies seventy-five words in Amalarius' version as against twenty-four in William's, to take a not untypical example.

As well as shortening his original considerably, William feels free to suggest variant interpretations when these suit him. Both alleluia and tract are sung at the first mass of Easter because, according to Amalarius, 'Ex uno precepto pendent alleluia et tractus qui sequitur, hoc est ut neofyti offerant Deo sacrificium laudis', but William, for whom Easter Eve baptisms are scarcely pertinent, has a much more ingenious explanation: 'Alleluia et

33. *Sermo* i: PL 162.505.

tractus ideo dicuntur quia et leticia iam inchoat, et aliquid tristicie restat'. Ingenuity is one thing, far-fetchedness is another; and where Amalarius explains that the offertory chant is also omitted 'Reducendo ad memoriam silentium et sacrificium mulierum, in tempore sacrificii silent cantores', William's explanation comes down squarely to practical considerations: 'Offerenda ideo dimittur propter eandem rationem quam superius dixi de introitu' — which was in turn that 'officii longitudo exigit ut aliquid omittatur'!

III

After such full treatment of the rites of the 'triduum sacrum', Easter itself and its octave are treated rather summarily, and largely from the standpoint of the neophytes. This is a bit awkward for William, who has understandably de-emphasized the (in his milieu largely meaningless) Easter catechumens; and so it is not surprising that this is perhaps the most consistently 'allegorizing' of William's chapters: the significance of the seventh day as against the eighth, of the responsory as against the alleluia (responsory signifies the active life, alleluia the contemplative), of the seventy days before Easter as against the fifty after it. This section gives the impression of being almost mechanical 'potting', and William comes to life only in his discussion of Amalarius' explanation of why the Alleluia precedes the tract on Easter eve:

> Dicit sane Amalarius ergo in sabbato ante pascha alleluia ante tractum cantari, quia alleluia nomen hebreum est et hebrea lingua mater est linguarum omnium. Idem autem est alleluia ebraice quod laudate dominum latine. Decet igitur ut propter dignitatem lingue prius laudemus deum hebraice deinde latine.

This a bit more than Amalarius actually does say (I.xxxii.3), and indeed William has then to explain that during most of the year the responsory is said, priority of languages notwithstanding, before the alleluia, as the active cares signified by the responsory are prior in time to the happiness of future joys foreshadowed by the Alleluia.

The remaining chapters of book I treat, much more briefly, other occasions in the liturgical year at which there are special ceremonies, or special points to be observed, at mass: the vigil of

Pentecost, the Ember Days, Advent, Holy Innocents, Candlemas, and masses for the dead. In arranging his matter this way, William has to take from both books II and III of Amalarius so that, as he explains in the supplementary paragraph which concludes the first book of his abridgement[34], 'Totus primus liber de varietatibus misse totius anni absolveretur'. The chapters of Amalarius he draws on for this section are I.xxxviii; II. ii, i, ii again, iii, i again; III. xl-xlii (and perhaps xxxviii); I.xli; III. xxxix; III. xliii; III. xliv — a skipping around which indicates that William had his plan firmly in mind before he began to abbreviate.

William's version of the ceremonies of Whitsun Eve differs from Amalarius's in two notable respects: he knows five lessons and canticles, whereas the *L.O.* mentions only four; and his silence about any baptisms during the vigil reminds us that in his time and milieu that sacrament was no longer part of the rites of Pentecost. It is interesting, though perhaps not surprising, that William omits entirely Amalarius' intriguing if enigmatic mention of his 'allegorical' captivity at Constantinople while still a catechumen.

Amalarius' diffuse discussion of the Ember Days and the ordination ceremonies is much shortened by William, but without any substantial differences of detail or interpretation. Curiously, William's treatment ends with the statement with which Amalarius' had begun:

AMALARIUS (II.i.1)	WILLIAM (I.xv)
Sex lectiones ab antiquis Romanis grece et latine legebantur; qui mos apud Constantinopolim hodieque servatur, ni fallor, propterea duas causas: unam, quia aderant Greci, quibus incognita erat latine lingue, aderantque Latini quibus incognita erat greca; alteram, propter unanimitatem utriusque populi.	Vocantur vero ista sabbato in duodecim lectionibus quia grece et latine solebant legi Rome sicut apud Constantinopolim leguntur hodieque.

— though it is much to be doubted whether William thought the lessons were still being read in Latin as well as Greek in Constantinople in the twelfth century, the 'unanimitas utriusque populi' being long a thing of the past. Here, as elsewhere, it is difficult to

34. Printed PL 179.1773.

tell whether by a word like 'hodie' William means in his own day or is just repeating Amalarius.

In one chapter, however, William makes it perfectly clear that usage has reversed direction since Amalarius' day. On the feast of the Holy Innocents, Amalarius had explained, the *Gloria in excelsis* and *Alleluia* were not sung, because of the sadness of the occasion. For William that is purely historical information: a custom 'prisco tempore', which he contrasts with 'modernus usus' which omits neither,. 'rationabilius iudicans gaudere pro martirum gloria quam flere pro pena' [35].

Though it is Amalarius who, of all medieval exegetes of the liturgy, is most famous, or notorious, for the fecundity of his allegorical interpretations, not even he is more given to explanations involving the ages of man, or of the world, than William. In the chapter on Advent, for instance, William supplies his own four 'ages' to correspond to the four 'offices' (in this case, sets of chants) for Advent: from before circumcision to Abraham, under circumcision to Moses, under the law to David, and under the prophets.

Also in the chapter on Advent, William shows some rare signs of confusion (as he admitted in his concluding paragraph to book I, he abridged Amalarius 'quantumque potui intelligere'), by including mention not only of the time of the Christmas masses — two, not three, are mentioned — but also of the feast of John the Baptist and of the 'canonical' times for celebrating mass. For the first, he apparently fails to understand that there were formerly two masses on the Nativity of St. John, as well as a vigil [36]; from the six lines of explanation which comprise Amalarius' chapter on the subject (III.xxxviii), William has gathered only that there used to be ('solebat et olim') a dawn mass on St. John's day. The problem of a proper dawn mass on another feast day than Christmas seems to have led William to the next chapter but three of his exemplar (III.xlii), where the symbolic suitability of the third, sixth, and

35. For some idea of the various liturgical attitudes towards Holy Innocents' day before William's time, see C. CALLEWAERT, *Feestdag der HH. Onnozele Kinderen*, in his collected papers *Sacris Erudiri* (Steenbrugge 1940) 419-434.

36. As in the Gregorian Sacramentary; cf. K. A. H. KELLNER, *Heortology* (Eng. tr.; London 1908) 222; P. JOUNEL in *L'Eglise en prière*, ed. A. G. MARTIMORT, 3rd edn. (Paris 1965) 801 n. 5.

ninth hours for mass is balanced by a general excuse for those who celebrate outside the hours 'pro necessitate vel devotione'. Similarly, it is either confusion or a momentary passion for completeness which leads William to conclude his chapter on the feast of the Innocents (from *L.O.* I.xli) with a somewhat distorted summary of what Amalarius says about the repetition of whole phrases in the offertory chant 'Vir erat in terra' for the twenty-first Sunday after Pentecost. Amalarius' explanation is, to be sure, itself ludicrous (that it is not the 'historical' words which are repeated but only the words of Job, who as sick and short of breath was likely to repeat himself!), but William seems to have compounded it by providing a three-fold reason — 'causa magni gaudii, devocionis, magni doloris' — with examples for what was to Amalarius just an isolated case.

We have seen that several of the MSS containing William's abridgement also include the *De ecclesiasticis officiis* of Isidore, and it is interesting that William's chapter on the Purification begins by mentioning that Isidore's work says nothing about the feast because it had not yet been established. William ascribes its promulgation initially (and quite correctly) to Justinian, though he seems not to have realized that Isidore lived well after Justinian; and, in the West, to Pope Sergius. Rather than repeating the long quotation from Bede which forms most of Amalarius' treatment of the subject, William relies on his knowledge of Virgil to make the beeswax candles carried in the Candlemas procession signify the 'virgin flesh' of Christ, 'nam et apes (sic: here singular) sine coitu generatur' [37].

Theological considerations are seldom factors in William's divergences from his exemplar, but in the last chapter of book I, on masses for the dead, there is perhaps a hint of the influence of Anselm's theory of the atonement on the next generation, which was William's. Whereas Amalarius has said that the Pax is not given at requiem masses because the offices for the dead imitate those of the death of Christ (III.xliv. 2), William's reason for the withholding of the Pax is 'quia mors peccati vindicta est et ubi ultio exigitur pax non datur'.

37. This appears to be an echo of *Georgics* IV. 197-199.

IV

William's book II follows in general both contents and order of Amalarius' book III; but the abridgement here, of the thirty-six chapters of the original into twenty brief ones, is much more drastic than in the first book. Book II (AMAL. III) is an explanation of the various parts of the mass, prefaced by chapters on the 'site' of the church, on bells, and on the cantors.

William takes up the question of the site or position of the church — by which he means only a few general remarks on the names by which the building is called and on the arrangement of the worshippers — at the very beginning of his book rather than, as does his model, after the discussion of the bells which summon the congregation (about which William is restrained where Amalarius is highly fanciful). William remarks that there has been much comment on the site and building and dedication of the church, especially the recent work of Ivo of Chartres[38]. In view of this, he implies, he has really only two points to make, both taken from his exemplar but each considerably altered. The first is etymological. The word 'church', 'kirica', means 'dominica casa': 'est enim grece kirius dominus'. So much Amalarius had said (as also, subsequently, that 'basilica' means 'regia': 'Grece enim basileus, rex latine', says William), in explanation of the Germanic word with which he was clearly already familiar. William may have been puzzled by this, and so adds, 'Quo nomine angli et cetere illius gentes consuete utuntur'. The second point William makes in this chapter has to do with the separation of men and women during services. Here one would expect that William, whose liturgical life was carried out in a monastic choir with no women visible, would simply follow Amalarius; but instead we find him providing quite different explanations for why men and women must stand on the north and south sides of the building respectively: *

AMALARIUS (III.ii.10)	WILLIAM
Masculi stant in australi parte et feminae in boreali, ut ostendatur per fortiorem sexum firmiores sanctos semper constitui in maioribus temp-	... femine stare debent ad aquilonem significantes quia per feminam venit malum super filios hominum. Unde dicitur (then *Jer.* 1.14). Itemque ad

38. Probably *Sermo* iv ('De sacramentis dedicationis'): PL 162.527.

* **north and south *should read* south and north**

tationibus aestus huius mundi, et per fragiliorem sexum infirmiores in aptiores loco ....

conversos (then *Joel* 2.20). At contra masculi stare debent ad austrum significantes se illius sequaces esse et per illum redemptos (then *Ps.* 125.4).

None of the three scriptural texts William employs here is used by Amalarius; William has gone out of his way not only to give a markedly misogynistic twist to his explanation but to buttress it with proof-texts as well. Likewise, at the conclusion of the chapter William adds a reason for the prescription ascribed to Pope Linus and quoted by Amalarius from the *Liber Pontificalis*, that women's heads should be veiled in church: 'Propter hanc confusionem quia prevaricatio per feminam venit, velat caput suum ...'.

William's chapter iii, on cantors (combining Amalarius III.iii 'De choro cantorum' and iv 'De vestimento cantorum') is given over largely to a brief summary of Amalarius' symbolic explanation, borrowed in turn from Augustine, of the eight-fold instruments of praise in *Ps.* 150; the rather perfunctory air of this section is indicated by William's concluding remark, 'Hec non ex nobis (he presumably means himself here, though he might mean himself and Amalarius as well, or even the latter alone), sed ex beati Augustini in extremum psalmum expositione dicimus'.

Not only drastic abridgement — six sections as opposed to his model's thirty-four — but also a certain change in emphasis marks William's chapter (II.iv) on the introit of the mass. Amalarius' chapter (III.v) is headed 'De introitu episcopi ad missam', and, derived largely from an *Ordo Romanus*, presupposes an episcopal celebrant at mass. For William this is not the usual kind of mass but a special form, in modern terms a pontifical mass. William gives a fairly curt summary of the ceremonial instructions, then goes on to the allegorical significance of all these actions. In general his explanations follow those of Amalarius, but selectively and with occasional divergences. The most important of these are several references which William introduces to the Jews, whom Amalarius has mentioned in his symbolic explanations less often, and much more sympathetically. Compare their exposition on the following points:

a) *the bishop's giving the kiss of peace to those on his left and right:*

AMALARIUS (sect. 21)	WILLIAM
In ipsa inclinatione dat pacem ministris qui a dextris levaque sunt. Ipse est enim pax per quam reconciliatur ecclesia Deo, sive de novo testamento, sive de veteri.	Dat pacem a dextris et sinistris quia Christus ad amicitiam suam admisit credentes tam de sinagoga quam de gentibus.

b) *the bishop's kissing of the altar and gospel-book:*

(sect. 29)	
Osculatur altare, ut ostendat adventum Christi fuisse Hierusalem; osculatur evangelium, in quo duo populi ad pacem redeunt, ut et nos eos diligamus qui disiuncti erant a nobis ... sicut Christus his se offert ultro, quibus dicit: Missus sum ad oves quae perierant domus Israhel, sic se episcopus altari, per quod recolimus Hierusalem.	Altare designat gentem Iudeam, que habebat altare dei. Huic pacem optulit, cum dixit, Non sum missus nisi ad oves que perierant domus Israel. Evangelium significat gentes que illud gratanter susceperunt.

c) *the placing of the gospel-book:*

(sect. 31)	
Remanet evangelium in altari ab initio officii, usque dum a ministro assumatur ad legendum, quia ab initio adventus Christi evangelica doctrina resonuit in Hierusalem....	Evangelium remanet in altari donec lecturus tollat, quia verbum dei permansit apud Iudeos, donec predicatum est in gentibus.

d) *the movement of the bishop for the collect:*

(sect. 32)	
Dein transit episcopus ad dexteram altaris. Liquet omnibus quod semper Christus egit dexteram vitam, postquam resurrexit a mortuis.	Transit ad dextram altaris quia Christus a Iudeis transivit ad gentes.

e) *the disposition of the ministers around the altar:*

(sect. 33)	
Ad insinuandum nobis libere vetus testamentum legere et tenere... aliqua pars ministrorum in sinistra parte stat, per quam temporalis benedictio designatur.	Minor pars ministrorum stat a sinistris, maior a dextris, quia minus crediderunt in Christum de Iudeis quam de gentibus, vel quia minoris dignitatis sunt que promittuntur in veteri testamento, quamque in novo.

At every point William's statement is harsher and less eirenic.

William's chapter on the *Kyrie* (II.v) is an abridgement of two chapters of Amalarius, III.vi 'De kyrie eleison' and vii 'De cereis'. Despite its heading, William's fairly brief chapter is largely concerned with the symbolism of setting the candles down during (after? : *tunc*) the threefold chant. William here curiously ascribes to Amalarius, as a sensible statement, something which that author does not appear to have said:

> Dicit sane Amalarius quod non minus quam tria debent esse candelabra quia nichil boni habent homines nisi per Christi gratiam qui lumen est verum, vel per imitationem sanctorum patrum utriusque testamento de quibus dicitur in propheta, Isti sunt duo olive et due candelabra.

It may be speculated that William is here quoting from memory another author and confusing him with Amalarius.

In treating the *Gloria in excelsis* William (ch. vi) is principally interested in the explanation of why the celebrant turns to the east at that point, and especially in the question of the exact location of the spot from which the angels sang the first *Gloria*. Amalarius identifies it thus: 'Angeli ad orientem cecinerunt. De quo statu dicit Micha, Et tu turris gregis nebulosa filiae Sion, usque ad te venient (for Vulgate veniet). Turris quippe gregis, quae ebraice dicitur turris ader, mille circiter passibus a civitate Bethleem ad orientem distat'. William's caution here is worth noting: 'Nam et locus in quo angeli illum cecinerunt cantum ad orientem est non longe est a Behleem'. * The question of the symbolism of turning to the east is continued in the brief chapter on the collect (II.vii 'De prima oratione', corresponding to AMAL. II.ix).

A possible reflection of William's own time is contained in his amplifying of Augustine's explanation of the word 'episcopus' (from *Enarr. in ps.* 126, as quoted by Amalarius in the chapter 'De sessione episcopi'):

AUG./AMAL. (III.x.5)	WILLIAM (II.viii)
Nam ideo altior locus positus est episcopis, ut ipsi superintendant et tamquam custodiant populum. Nam et grece quod dicitur episcopus, hoc latine superintentor interpretatur, quia superintendat, quia desuper videt.	Quamquam et superior sedes nomini conveniat episcopi qui superintendens interpretatur luiturus graviter si vertit ad pompam seculi quod ei conceditur pro dignitate officii.

* **Behleem *should read* Bethleem**

It seems not unlikely that William is referring to one of the princely English bishops of his time, like the notorious Roger le Poer of Sarum, who would have been William's bishop from 1107 to 1139, or Henry of Blois, who as bishop of Winchester from 1129 paved the way for the accession of his brother Stephen and who was therefore the enemy of the monks at Malmesbury, whose patron was Stephen's principal opponent Robert of Gloucester.

William combines into one chapter the four in which Amalarius deals with the lesson and subsequent chant and alleluia. Here William has pruned intensively, omitting matter which must have been tempting, like references to Boethius' *De musica* and a fine Amalarian passage comparing one who listens to the lesson to a cow. But again, even in the midst of this severe abridgement William's originality is discernible. In addition to introducing three scriptural allusions where his model does not have them, he alters interestingly the wording of Amalarius' comparison of the difference between lesson and responsory to that 'inter elementa et artes ipsas':

AMALARIUS (III.xi.8)	WILLIAM (II.ix)
Ars quoque musica habet elementa sua, et geometrica ab elementis incipit linearum, et dialectica atque medicina habent YSAGOGA sua.	Elementa grammatice sunt littere, elementa geometrie et arithemetice sunt puncti et linee, elementa dialectice et medicine sunt isagoge.

Substantial differences in the celebration of the liturgy, and consequently in its understanding, appear in William's chapter (again combining two of his model's) 'De casulis diaconorum et subdiaconorum et tabulis et sequentia'. There are three problems here. On the vesture of deacons and subdeacons, Amalarius says simply, 'Ministri casula se exuunt, quando lectoris sive cantoris officium assumunt', adding later that this is done 'quando prudenter et strenue agit contra oblectamenta mundi', but without indicating any particular season for the observance. William limits this practice to Lent and Advent (which is very likely what Amalarius meant anyhow), and specifies that while the subdeacon takes his chasuble off altogether, the deacon merely throws his over his shoulder (the so-called 'folded chasuble' or 'planeta plicata')[39]. Secondly, for Amalarius it is customary for the cantors to sing the chants

39. Cf. *Regularis Concordia*, ed. T. SYMONS (London 1953), sect. 34.

before the Gospel from books bound in bone, called 'Tabulae' or 'Cantatoria'. By William's time these have been replaced by more modern chant books, so that he describes the practice of Amalarius' day as 'antiquo more'[40]. Finally, the sequence, which is well known by William, is only beginning in the ninth century. Amalarius calls it 'iubilatio', or prolongation of the last syllable of the *Alleluia* in an elaborate *melisma*; this, the beginning stage of the sequence before words were customarily added, he refers to the higher — that is, wordless — praise of God. Again this is difficult for William, who seems confused as to whether such wordless sequences are still current:

> Cantus quem vocant sequentiam, quem sine ullis verbis quondam ubique nunc in aliquibus ecclesiis post alleluia solent canere, illam laudem figurat qua in futura vita sancti deum laudabunt, magis conscientie puritate quam sono articulato.

The chapter on the reading of the Gospel exemplifies points of comparison between William and his model which we have seen several times: differences in rite or ceremony, differences in interpretation, omission, amplification, and an original choice of biblical texts. For the first, where Amalarius (III.xviii.4) has the bishop putting incense into the thurible, William assigns this task to the deacon. In providing a symbolic interpretation for the action, William once more shows a heightened feeling towards the Jews: for him the altar (here) stands for the Jewish people, rather than for Jerusalem as in his exemplar. Much of Amalarius' symbolic explanation is, however, omitted, like the figure that the deacon who carries the Gospel is the foot of Christ, and that the left arm in which he carries it symbolizes the earthly life. On the other hand, William has no hesitation in adding touches of his own, like the commonsense instruction that the people are to lay aside anything they have in their hands or on their heads before signing themselves with the cross. Finally, William supplies *Acts* 13.46 and *Gal.* 6.14 to buttress his comments, though neither is used by Amalarius in the whole of the *L.O.*

Even where William is faced with abbreviating a very long passage as in the next chapter, on the Offertory — Amalarius' chapter

40. Presumably the elaborately bound 'cantatoria' of Carolingian and Ottonian times have given way to more modestly covered chant books.

(III.xix) has thirty-six paragraphs plus two on the secret — he will introduce material of his own. Two examples show this clearly. Where Amalarius explains that (xix.20) 'Panis, quem offert, et vinum exprimit omnia desideria pia intrinsecus latentia, sive sint pro immolatione seu pro hostia viva', William returns to the idea of the model of the church which we have noticed earlier:

> Sicut enim panis multis granis, et vinum ex multis acinis confit, ita catholica ecclesia, que verum deo sacrificium offert, ex multis gentibus, gradibus, conditionibus, etatibus congregatur.

And just before this, when discussing the return of the celebrant to the altar after washing his hands, William interpolates a devotional passage which smacks very much of his own century:

> Redit ad altare episcopus, et Christus in ierusalem ivit, ubi erat altare dei, ut se ipsum sacrificaret deo patri. Ante quod factum et patri preces fudit, et hominibus memoriam suam commendavit. Secrete deinde peregit misterium passionis, quia homines et demones et nescio an angeli passionem quidem videbant, sed ad quantum bonum perventura esset ignorabant. Sed hoc misterium duraturum esse per omnia secula seculorum clarificavit in resurrectione sua, ammonens in ascensione sua ut sursum corda haberent discipuli, quo eum ascendere videbant.

In places like this William's originality lifts the level of his work far above that of a simple abridgement.

Again, both liturgical change and William's own interest in the Bible cause him, in his chapter on the Preface, to depart from his model. Amalarius has said that during the Preface 'Stant interim episcopi, sive sacerdotes, seu diaconi post pontificem; subdiaconi vero in facie eius'. This implies that the celebrant is behind the altar, i.e. 'facing the people'. William either does not realize what was the general custom in earlier centuries, or (this is just possible) is aware that the solemn papal mass continues to be celebrated in that way. In either case he calls the practice a 'Roman custom'. And in amplifying the role of the subdeacons, he adds to Amalarius' mention of Joseph of Arimathea also Nicodemus, to make more accurate the biblical reference (i.e. by considering verse 39 as well as *John* 18.38 which Amalarius had cited) to 'hidden disciples' who, like the subdeacons, 'tempore passionis ante eum fuerunt'.

The heart of Amalarius' work is of course the exposition of the central action of the mass, the canon. The great length with which he treats this part presents a severe challenge to the abridger. Amalarius' exposition is divided into five sections: xxiii, 'De Te igitur'; xxiv, 'De institutione dominica in conficiendo corpus et sanguinem' (i.e. on the prayer 'Quam oblationem' and the Words of Institution); xxv, 'De ascensione Christi in crucem' (on the prayers 'Unde et memores', 'Supra quae', and 'Supplices'); xxvi, 'De corpore domini post emissum spiritum in cruce et nostra mortificatione in idipsum' (on the prayers 'Nobis quoque', 'Per quem', and 'Per ipsum'); and xxvii, 'De praesentatione patenae'. William largely ignores the final section and divides his discussion into four extremely brief chapters (xiv-xvii), headed simply first, second, third, and fourth parts of the canon. Frequently he does little more than simply sum up the elaborate expositions of his model. In severely abridging these long sections William may also have been working somewhat hastily. For instance, in the chapter on the first part of the canon he ascribes to Amalarius the statement that 'Hec dona' refers to the bread, 'Hec munera' to the wine, and 'Hec sancta sacrificia' to both: a misunderstanding which could conceivably result from a too cursory reading of xxiii.15-17. Secondly, William states that concerning the number of signings with the cross Amalarius 'nullam certam traditionem se accepisse dicit', whether one, two, three, or five — in fact, Amalarius in the next chapter (xxiv) discusses the diversity in the number of signings and clearly favors only one.

The second part of the canon, containing the words of consecration, begins for William with the prayer 'Hanc igitur', which Amalarius includes in the preceding section. In this chapter especially William is terse where his model is verbose. Of the consecration of the elements itself William says simply 'In hac fit panis vinumque corpus et sanguis domini per verba eiusdem'; and, further, 'In hac oratione significat sacerdos ipsum Christum, qui carnem et sanguinem suum tradidit persecutoribus'. The third part of the canon, from 'Unde et nos' to 'Nobis quoque', is treated almost equally briefly, but William here includes, rather parenthetically, a point of considerable importance. After quoting the beginning of the 'Unde et memores' (through 'tam beate passionis' which would then continue 'necnon et ab inferis resurrectionis, sed in caelos gloriosae ascensionis'), he observes 'nam quod adorande nativatis in nostris codicibus habetur, non est autenticum'. There is no mention of this in Amalarius. William seems to be talking about a variant text of the canon, i.e. one in which the 'Unde et memores' is interpolated with the phrase 'adorande nativitatis'. This is a tantalizing roference: he has seen, or knows of, manuscripts, presumably English ('nostris codicibus') with the interpolated phrase; but he neither gives a hint as to what these codices are nor tells us on what grounds he so clearly rejects the addition as 'non autenticum'[41].

William's critical sense is also operative, but in an archaeological rather than literary way, in the following chapter, on the fourth and final part of the canon. In discussing the chalice which the deacon covers at the end of the canon Amalarius specifies 'ab aure ad aurem': a phrase which William clarifies by adding 'quia calices antiqui ansas habebant, et forsitan adhuc alicubi habent' — though clearly he himself is used only to the handleless chalice[42].

In general the concluding chapters of William's abridgement — the last three in book II and all those in book III — show some signs of haste: the condensing is much more business-like, many tempting points of interpretation are passed up in silence, and William adds less of his own than in earlier parts. Also, at the end of book II William is working more rapidly in terms of the units he covers in a single chapter of his. His chapter xviii, on the Lord's Prayer, summarizes three of his model's (xxviii-xxx); and chapter xix, on the *Agnus Dei*, no fewer than five in the *L.O.*

41. It is known that this phrase, or a similar one, is found in three Frankish mass-books of the ninth and tenth centuries (B. Botte, *Le Canon de la Messe romaine* [Louvain 1935] 40); and has been added in the eleventh century to the Lorsch Sacramentary (A. Ebner, *Quellen und Forschungen zur Gesch. und Kunstgesch. des Missale Romanum*... [Graz 1896] 247-248). J.A. Jungmann (*The Mass of the Roman Rite*, Eng. tr. I [New York 1951] 221 n. 21) is not quite accurate in saying that Amal. reads the 'nativitas' into the text: what Amal. does say (III.xxv) is that the Nativity is included in the total remembrance of the 'Haec quotiescumque feceritis'. William may have been following the attack made on this interpolation in the *Micrologus* (PL 151.985). The phrase is not included in the canons of the Missal of Robert of Jumièges (see above, n. 29), nor in that of the Lesnes Missal (early thirteenth century; ed. P. Jebb, HBS 95, 1964). The 'Missals' of the New Minster Winchester and of Bec contain no canons.

42. The handles or 'ears' had been a feature of the large 'calix ministerialis' when communion in both kinds was the rule; by William's time there is no longer a need for such a big chalice.

(xxxi-xxxv). The final chapter of book II, 'De ultima benedictione', corresponds to a section which is in the middle of Amalarius' book III; the remaining chapters, on such things as the masses of Holy Innocents and the Purification, are treated by William (if at all) at the end of book I.

Only a few points in these final chapters require mention. Three are in chapter xix. First, William says that Pope Sergius ordered the *Agnus Dei* to be sung thrice, where Amalarius, quoting from the *Liber Pontificalis*, specifies no fixed number of times. Here William is reflecting the practice of his own day, though ascribing it back to the seventh century; the threefold recitation seems only to have become common in the eleventh century[43]. Secondly, William calls the following chant by its modern name, 'Communio' — 'antiphona quam communionem vocamus' — where Amalarius has called it simply 'antiphona sequens'. Thirdly, there seems to be a confusion in the way the word 'eukaristia' (as the MSS of William spell it) is understood by the two writers. Amalarius in III.xxxiv uses it to mean communion: 'Eucharistia sumenda est post osculum pacis'. For William it means the part of the Host which is reserved: 'Pars corporis domini qui in sepulchro quod nos eukaristiam vocamus'. William points out that this particle is only to be taken from the 'sepulchre' (aumbry?) 'pro magna necessitate', until the eighth day, when it is presumably to be renewed; there is no section corresponding to this in Amalarius. And in the last chapter of book II, William shows himself aware of two 'concluding' phrases, the 'Ite missa est', which his model of course knows (William ignores the discussion of the etymology of the word 'mass'), and also 'Benedicamus domino' for ordinary week days: this latter formula came into use only in the eleventh century.

V

William's third book, which largely corresponds to the second of Amalarius, is abridged with greater dispatch than the first two. In dealing with the various orders of clergy and their respective vestments there is somewhat less room for edifying comment than in

43. JUNGMANN II (Eng. tr.), 338.

discussing the central mysteries of the mass. In the chapters on the minor orders — doorkeepers, lectors, exorcists, and acolytes — William follows Amalarius without significant departure. This section is little more than precis-making. William's interest is aroused, however, by one of the vessels which Amalarius says are given to subdeacons as their distinctive 'instruments': as well as chalice and paten and 'urceolum ad ministrandum vinum', the 'aquamanile cum manutergio'. Of the latter William remarks, 'Est autem aquamanile vas quod ita vulgo dicitur apud Italos, a quo funditur aqua in manus'. It is curious that William finds it necessary to explain, as his model had not done, the 'aquamanile' (but not the 'urceolus', the cruet from which the wine was poured into the chalice), as though the term, if not the thing, was unknown in England[44].

The following three chapters, on the major orders, are likewise little more than summaries of Amalarius. Again we see William silently omitting any mention of a controversy which is no longer relevant in his day: this time, Amalarius' indignation at the direction in the *Ordo Romanus* ('Antiquus') that only the bishop (to the exclusion of the attending priests) should lay his hands on the new deacon at the time of ordination. Perhaps more surprisingly, William skips also the remark of Amalarius, noteworthy for the historical sense it displays, that the deacon's ministry of reading the Gospel was added later, 'Quod in primo tempore non legebatur. Quando Stephanus fuit factus diaconus, ut opinor, nondum erant evangelia scripta'. Likewise in the chapter on priests William omits Amalarius' discussion of the supposed presbyteral ordination at Alexandria (II.xiii.9-11), which one might have thought would be of interest; though he does summarize his model's long exposition of the original identity of priests and bishops and their subsequent separation into two orders, and in doing so implies a view of early church history which is not quite derived from that of Amalarius: 'Sed postquam ambitio cepit inolescere ad sanandam contentionem unum electum qui ceteris in hoc tantum preponeretur, quod solus ordines daret. Ipsum vocatum episcopum'.

An even more surprising omission, and one which may be taken

44. In fact the aquamanile seems to have been the basin or plate into which the water was poured: see W. HENRY in *DACL* I (1907) 2647.

as showing how self-denying William is in this last book, occurs in the chapter on the bishop: he ignores the exception which Amalarius had cited to the rule of episcopal consecration by more than one bishop, that of Augustine of Canterbury who was allowed by Gregory the Great to consecrate English bishops (at least one) by himself. This privilege is not mentioned by William in his *Gesta Pontificum*, though it is included by Bede in his account of the 'responsiones' of Gregory, and it is curious that William passes it up a second time here in Amalarius (who does not cite Bede for this passage).

In the second half of the book, on the sacred vestments, there is a significant difference in the order in which the two authors take them up. Though both begin by treating of the amice and alb (William closing his chapter rather waspishly, 'Preter ista duo indumenta primi quatuor ordines non usurpant alia'), Amalarius discusses the chasuble (xix), stole, dalmatic, 'tonica quam sacerdos induit super camisam', pallium, sudarium, and sandals, while William considers them strictly in the sequence of the order to which they belong, tunic(le) and maniple, dalmatic, chasuble, and the various pontificalia. The basic reason for this change is of course that for Amalarius the chasuble is still the 'generale indumentum sacrorum ducum... (quae) pertinet generaliter ad omnes clericos', while by William's time it has become the distinctive vestment of the (celebrating) priest.

William's treatment is distinctly the more systematic. For one thing, Amalarius does not deal with the maniple at all (deliberately: 'De vestimento pedum et manuum reticetur', xxii.3), so William has to concoct an 'Amalarian' explanation of it: 'Manipulum unde nichil dixit Amalarius, que duplicatum in leva portatur potest significare labores in hac vita anime et corporis'. For another, Amalarius' terminology is not very clear — understandably so, since he is living in a period of evolution in liturgical vestments and their nomenclature. He still calls the alb the 'camisa'; it is complemented by the chasuble proper ('casula') which was formerly — until about the eighth century — worn by all the ministers at the altar; the distinctive vestment of the celebrant (as far as there is one) he calls the 'tonica', though he speakes also of two 'tunics', meaning presumably our modern chasuble and dalmatic ('Si quis voluerit uti duabus tonicis, ostendit se esse diaconum et sacerdotem', xxii.3). In the face of such confusion William has consistently used the terminology of his own century, even where this means departing from his model. For him 'tunica' means 'tunicle', and is the subdeacon's distinctive vestment, handed to him at ordination along with the maniple. To the deacon is added the dalmatic, along with the stole. His description of the dalmatic follows Amalarius' fairly closely, though with some variation as to the possible number and placing of the tassels; but for William the deacon must wear the dalmatic, whereas this has not been the case for Amalarius, who says 'Diaconus qui non est indutus dalmatica, casula legit circumcinctus', as though it were a matter of relative indifference. In similar fashion Amalarius is much less definite about the stole. He simply indicates that it goes about the deacon's neck and hangs down to the knees, where William specifies the modern fashion of the crossed stole, resting on the left shoulder and tied under the right arm (again William has to come up with an explanation for this: 'quia presentis vite pacienter portatus labor, in futuro victoriam promeretur'). In dealing with the chasuble William, perhaps because of the confusion of his model's usage, departs a good deal from the explanations Amalarius offers. Amalarius' statement that the chasuble is common also to deacons and subdeacons seems to be construed by William in the light of the practice of Advent and Lent: 'Ideo autem diaconi et subdiaconi in quadragesima et adventu casulis induuntur, quia cum semper tum maxime his diebus, debet virtutibus studere clericus'. William supplies a different list of the good works which the chasuble signifies, and is in almost every phrase inclined to alter rather than reproduce the ideas expressed by Amalarius.

As is the case with the discussion of vestments in general, William's treatment of the pontificalia is more systematic than his model's (though he ignores Amalarius' chapter on the sudarium, or liturgical handkerchief, which is no longer in use in the twelfth century). William mentions, if only summarily, ring, staff, crosier — the distinction in practice between these two is not clear, except that the latter has the curved end — mitre, and sandals, followed by the archbishop's pallium. Of these Amalarius considers only the sandals and the pallium. Much of what Amalarius has to say about sandals, especially the four different kinds for the four higher orders and the elaborate word-play about tongues of sandals and tongues of preachers, is passed over by William, who however adds a rather grotesque note of his own: 'Solee de mortuis animalibus facte monent ut non suas inventiones, sed patrum precedentium doctrinas predicet'!

The degree of William's independence of Amalarius, even when he is abridging fairly straitly, can be seen in brief in the summary with which the two writers conclude this book (III in WM., II in AMAL.). This summary forms a separate chapter (xxvi), 'Recapitulatio vestimentorum', in Amalarius, but William tacks his corresponding passage on the significance of the vestments onto the end of his chapter on the pontificalia. (In the following columns the order of William's items has been rearranged to match that of Amalarius).

AMALARIUS	WILLIAM
Amictus est castigatio vocis	Amictus ... sermonum discretionem
Alba ceterorum inferiorum sensuum	alba virtutes apertas
Sandalia ornatus iter praedicatoris	(in sandaliis predicationis instantiam)
Secunda tonica opera mentis	tunica occultas.
Casula opera corporis pia	casula communiter omnis
Stola iugum Christi	stola humilitatem
Dalmatica ... cura proximorum	dalmatica fraternam compassionem
Pallium torques devotissimae praedicationis.	in pallio puritatis et scientie prerogativam et eternam coronam.

(William adds, in further summary, 'manipulos labores terrenas, cingulum castitatem... anulus fidei prestantiam, virga severitatem et misericordiam, mitra spem divini auxilii').

This is, quite clearly, a curious kind of abridgement.

* * *

William's 'abbreviatio' is without doubt an important document: to a slight extent, for the light it sheds on the transmission and continued popularity of Amalarius; to a greater extent, for the glimpses it offers of twelfth century attitudes towards the liturgy; but above all for the added insight it gives us into William's mind, and for the fresh dimension it provides to his total accomplishment. Not that this point should be exaggerated. There are in the work no startling observations or opinions which reveal William as more than we otherwise already knew him to be: an intelligent, observant, and generally sympathetic monk, working in a rich cultural context which the word 'renaissance' has often been employed to characterize. That our total picture of William is deepened by a knowledge of his work does not, however, mean that we can do what it would be most desirable to do: to speak with some confidence of his 'liturgical sensibility'. Disentangling William from Amalarius is too precarious for that to be done. Still, it is fair to claim that we now have some idea of William as a religious whose life inevitably centered on liturgical worship to set beside our ideas of William as biblical commentator, antiquarian, biographer, political partisan, and historian.

The "Abbreviatio Amalarii" of William of Malmesbury*

TEXT

Sigla

O: *Oxford, All Souls College MS 28*
L: *London, Lambeth Palace MS 380.*
L2: *London, Lambeth Palace MS 363.*
W: *Wolfenbüttel, Herzog-August-Bibliothek Lat. 1205.*

* * *

Incipit prefatio Willelmi in abreviatione Amalarii[a]

In historicis nos narrationibus occupatos detorsit a proposito tua, Rodberte amice, voluntas. Nuper enim cum in bibliotheca nostra sederemus et quisque pro[b] studio libros evolveret, impegisti in Amalarium De ecclesiasticis officiis. Cuius cum materiam ex prima statim tituli fronte cognosceres[c], amplexus es occasionem qua rudimenta nove professionis animares, sed quia confestim animi tui alacritatem turbavit testimoniorum perplexitas et sermonum asperitas, rogasti ut eum abreviarem. Ego autem qui semel proposuerim deferre tibi ut homini dilectissimo munus iniunctum non aspernanter accepi. In quo experiare licebit quantum propter faciliorem intellectum in deiciendo sermone laboravi qui cultius fortassis loqui potui. Est enim res de qua tractatur pernecessaria et cuius ignorantia sit cunctis sacerdotibus pudenda. Interea te ammonitum volo ut unum ex his qui de talibus disputaverunt fugiendum scias, Rabanum nomino, qui in[d] libro De officiis ecclesiasticis[1] dicit sacramenta altaris proficere ad saginam corporis ac per hoc corruptioni vel morbo vel etate vel secessu vel postremo morte obnoxia. Que de domini corpore dicere credere scribere quanti sit periculi vides; preterea libri eius per se parum conferunt scientie, minimum accomodant doctrine, de aliorum

* Cf. *Rech. Théol. anc. méd.* 47 (1980) 77-113.

a. No preface W *b.* suo *add. L2* *c.* cognosceris *L2* *d.* in *om. L*

1. Cf. Rabanus, *De inst. cler.* 1.31 (PL 107.316-321).

quippe laboribus aut ad litteram aut ad sententiam omnino usurpati. Denique duo libri voluminis illius quod supra dixi ex Isidoro et tercius ex Augustino De doctrina Christiana et Pastorali Gregorii ad verbum sunt transcripti. In libro porro De natura rerum quid dicit aliud quam Isidorus Ethimologiarum; vel in illo De compoto, quid nisi quod Beda De temporibus preter quedam allegoriam commenta? Fuit enim vir ille huic vicio peculiariter[e] assiduus quasi prorsus desperaret lectores suos memoriam non habere qua possent eius furta deprehendere. Enimvero sicut aliquanta verba dissimulata prudentia a maioribus mutuari datur glorie, ita totas sententias aperta impudentia furari deputatur audacie. Illo ergo repulso in Amalarium qui catholice de talibus scripsit animum intende.

EXPLICIT PROLOGUS. INCIPIUNT CAPITULA[f]

De septuagesima
De sexagesima
De quinquagesima
De quadragesima
De quarta feria cinerum
De quarta feria in apertione aurium
De sabbato ante palmas
De dominica palmarum
De quarta feria ante cenam domini
De cena domini
De parasceve[g]
De sabbato sancto
De octo diebus albatorum[h]
De vigilia pentecostes
De quatuor temporibus anni[i]
De adventu domini
De natali innocentum
De purificatione sancte Marie
De missa mortuorum

EXPLICIUNT CAPITULA. INCIPIT LIBER WILLELMI IN ABBREVIATIONE AMALARII[j]

I. DE SEPTUAGESIMA[k]

Antiquus ecclesie mos fuit iam inde ab apostolorum servatus temporibus ut sex ebdomade ante pascha ieiunaretur[l], ut[m] decime dierum totius anni

e. pecalariter *O* *f. Chapters numbered L, L2*; Incipiunt capitula libri primi quatuor temporum *W* *h. After* de parasceve *W* *i.* anni *om. W* *j.* Incipit libri primi Willelmi de officiis ecclesiasticis. *W* *k. om. O, L, L2* *l. ieiunarentur L2* *m.* et *W* deo consecrarentur. Habet enim annus ccclxv dies quorum decime sunt xxxvi dies; quos invenies si de sex septimanis sex dominicas subraxeris que non ieiunantur. Sunt enim in sex septimanis xlii dies. Quapropter dominica dies que est huius ieiunii caput vocabatur quadragesima. At vero Thelesphorus papa nonus post beatum Petrum volens ut christiani Christum dominum suum xl dierum sequerentur ieiunio precepit ut septem septimanis ante pascha ieiunaretur[2]. Si enim de septem septimanis septem dominicas subtraxeris remanent xlii dies ad ieiunandum. Quadraginta ergo in exemplo domini ieiunantur, duo autem qui supersunt cene domini et sabbato paschali deputantur, qui quamvis a fidelibus pro continuatione abstinentie ieiunetur, sunt tamen pro sanctitate sua ab omni ieiunio liberi. Dominica autem dies que est eius ieiunii caput quinquagesima vocatur, sive quia ab ea usque ad pascha quinquaginta uno excepto dies sunt, sive quia quinquagesimus numerus proximus est numerus post quadragesimum.

Intercedentibus annis Melchiades[3] papa xxxiiii^{us} post Petrum constituit ut nunquam feria quinta ieiunaretur quia in ea cenavit dominus cum discipulis, et in ea ascendit ad celos. Propterea constitutum est ut octo septimanis ante pascha ieiunaretur. Si enim de octo septimanis primam et quintam feriam subtraxeris secundum Melchiadis pape iussum, remanent dies xlii ad ieiunandum. Dominica vero dies que est harum septimanarum caput vocatur sexagesima, non quod inde usque ad pascha sint[n] lx dies sed quod sexagesimus numerus proximus est capitalis numerus post quinquagesimum et ante septuagesimum.

Quem numerum mox placuit in ieiunio observari ad imitationem annorum septuaginta quibus israeliticus populus in Babilone servivit. Est ergo septuagesima novem septimanis ante pascha; nec ideo dicitur septuagesima quod lxx dies sint usque ad pascha sed quia septuagesimus numerus proximus est capitalis post sexagesimum. Terminantur autem isti lxx dies in sabbato septimane pasche a quo die usque ad pentecosten frequentius et celebrius cantitatur alleluia. Sunt ergo a dominica septuagesime usque ad quartam feriam ante cenam domini lx dies. Quia vero sexagenarius numerus significat viduarum sanctarum continentiam sicut in compoto digitorum probatur, sexaginta isti dies significant viduitatem ecclesie qua peregrinatur a sponso suo qui eam corporaliter reliquit. Tres dies qui supersunt ad pascha innuunt ninivitarum triduanum ieiunium. Quibus omnibus et viduitatis nostre incolatum deflere et superne ire comminationem exemplo ninivitarum per ieiunium debemus avertere. Sex reliqui ad sabbatum paschalis ebdomade dies, in quibus iam alleluia cantare id est deum laudare incipimus, significant bona opera quibus deum laudando insistere debemus vel totius seculi tempore, quod sex etatibus volvitur vel tota vita nostra que sex etatibus, infantia,

n. sunt *W*

2. *Liber pontificalis* 9, ed. L. DUCHESNE, 1 (Paris 1886), p. 129 (hereafter cited as *LP*).

3. (Miltiades) *LP* 33; 1.168.

pueritia, adolescentia, iuventute, senectute, senio peragitur, ut mereamur pervenire ad sabbatum, quod intelligitur septima etas mundi quando plenam requiem habebimus et perfecte deum laudabimus. Quod significat quia licet ante alleluia cantaverimus tunc plenius canimus adeo ut paucissimas antiphonas nisi tantum alleluia canamus. De illis sex diebus quibus iam spe future vite haurimus gaudia, dicit psalmus *In convertendo dominus captivitatem sion facti sumus sicut consolati*[4]. Dum enim dicit Sicut consolati, ostendit quod in hac vita multum pleni solacii deest sanctis quamdiu impedimenta carnis obstant, quo minus spiritum sanctum paraclitum id est consolatorem habeant. Quem nobis in septimo die perfecte infundi in eodem psalmo precamur dicentes, *Converte, domine, captivitatem nostram sicut torrens in austro*[5]; per austrum septiformis spiritus intelligitur qui flores id est virtutum aromata facit flagrare in anima. Hinc dicit sponsa in canticis, *Surge aquilo* quod est Discede diabole, et *veni auster* spiritus sancte *perfla ortum meum et fluant aromata illius*[6]. Sex ergo dies nos erigunt post penitentiam ad consolationem, septimus nos perducit ad requiem. LXX proinde diebus vel peccata nostra deflemus vel plenam leticiam non habemus ad imitationem ut dixi plebis Israhelitice que lxx annis servivit in Babilone. Diemque pro anno mutuamur quia tanto propiores ipsi[o] sumus ad salutem quanto baptismus circumcisione prestat, quantoque ieiunium nostrum voluntarium illorum ingratitudinem superat. Illi annis lxx canticum domini non cantaverunt dicente ad eos Ieremia propheta, *Cessare*[p] *faciam a vobis vocem gaudii et leticie*[7]. Et ipsi in psalmo *Quomodo cantabimus canticum domini in terra aliena*[8], proinde nos nec Alleluia nec Gloria in excelsis deo cantamus que sunt cantica angelorum qui superne Ierusalem cives sunt. Nam et Iohannes in Apocalipsi dicit se audisse angelos cantantes Alleluia[9] et in nativitate Gloria in excelsis[10] cantaverunt ipsi. Dicimus autem tractum illud[q] nos significantes fecisse quod increpat propheta dicens, *Ve qui trahitis mendacium in funiculis vanitatis*[11]. Qui ergo mendacium in funiculis vanitatis peccando traximus, bene est ut cantum in gemitu cordis penitendo trahamus. Hinc pene omnes tractus gemitum et tribulationem sonant, ut *De profundis*[12], *Commovisti*[13]. Pauci post peractam penitentiam gaudium, ut *Iubilate*[14],

o. ipsis *W* *p*. cessare *in all MSS, as in LO 1.1.16; Vulgate* quiescere
q. illus *L2*

4. *Ps*. 125.1
5. *Ps*. 125.4.
6. *Cant*. 4.16.
7. *Jer*. 7.34.
8. *Ps*. 136.4.
9. *Apoc*. 19.1.
10. *Lk*. 2.14.
11. *Isa*. 5.18.
12. *Ps*. 129.1.
13. *Ps*. 59.4.
14. *Ps*. 99.1.

Qui confidunt[15]. Ita et introitus septuagesime tribulationem innuit, *Circumdederunt me gemitus mortis*[r][16]. Collecta, Ut qui pro peccatis nostris iuste affligimur. Responsorium, Adiutor in oportunitatibus in tribulatione. Epistola, labores in huius stadio vite[17]. Evangelium, in vinea ecclesie[18]. Offerenda, *Bonum est confiteri*[s][19]. Communio, *Illumina*[t][20]. A quo die, ut dixi, ad pascha novem septimane sunt et lxiiii dies. De quibus si tres omni septimana[u] id est dominicam et feriam quintam et sabbatum propter dominicam requiem in sepulchro subtraxeris, remanebunt xxxvi qui sunt decime anni nostri. Ita si septimanas sex ieiunaverimus subtrahentes dominicas vel si de novem septimanis tres semper, ut dixi, abstulerimus dies, decimam anni nostri deo dabimus. Vel si abstractis dominicis de septem septimanis cena domini et sancto sabbato vel si de octo septimanis feria prima et feria quinta sublatis reliquos ieiunaverimus, ieiunium domini quadragenarium imitabimur.

II. De sexagesima

Sexagesima pertendit[v] usque ad feriam quartam paschalis ebdomade. Sexies autem[w] decem sunt lx. Decem significant legis decalogum quem sex[x] etatibus nostris tota scilicet vita observare debemus ut ad illud regnum perveniamus ad quod nos introitus quarte ferie paschalis invitat dicens, *Venite benedicti patris mei, percipite regnum*[21]. Hoc regnum quatuor evangelia predicant. Sunt autem duo regna Christi, unum in ecclesia, alterum in vita eterna, significata per regna David et Salomonis, qui quarta etate seculi regnaverunt: primum laboriosum propter labores ecclesie, secundum pacificum propter pacem requiei eterne. Ad hoc regnum per sexagesimam veniemus. Est enim senarius numerus perfectus et in eo fecit deus omnia opera sua. Senarius autem per denarium ductus surgit in sexaginta. Denarius ad mercedem operum pertinet. Si quis ergo per senariam perfectionem operum requirit mercedem ipse perveniet ad regnum, ad quod nos introitus quarte ferie paschalis invitat. In sexagesima vero sicut et in septuagesima tribulationibus premimur. Unde et introitus est *Exurge quare obdormis domine*[22]. Oratio,

r. mortis *om.* W *s.* confessionem peccatorum *add. O, L, L2 after* confiteri
t. serenitatem misericordie dei pretendunt *add. O, L, L2 after* Illumina *u. corr. L2*
v. pretendit *O* *w.* atque *L2* *x.* quod *W*

15. *Ps.* 124.1.
16. *Ps.* 17.5.
17. *I Cor.* 9.24-10.5.
18. *Mt.* 20.1-16.
19. *Ps.* 91.2.
20. *Ps.* 30.17.
21. *Mt.* 25.34.
22. *Ps.* 43.23.

Deus qui conspicis, quia ex nulla nostra virtute subsistimus[y]. In epistola bonus athleta nos hortatur exemplo qui tribulationes patienter sufferre[23]. In gradali contra demones tribulatores nostros imprecamur, *Sciant gentes quoniam nomen tibi dominus*[24]. *Deus meus pone illos ut rotam*[25]. Tractatus, *Commovisit*[26]. Et qui in evangelio septuagesime missi sumus in vineam domini, in evangelio ammonemur sexagesime[z] ut simus boni agricole tale semen iaciendo quod afferat fructum in patientia[27]. Sic de ceteris potest studiosus lector intelligere quod constitutor officiorum nostrorum nichil otiosum in eis voluit constituere.

III. De quinquagesima

Quinquagesima pertendit ad diem dominice resurrectionis. Sicut sexagenarius numerus significat perfectionem, ita quinquagenarius monstrat perfectam penitentiam quia quinquagesimus psalmus in penitentia est decantatus. Quinquies decem quinquaginta. Qui ergo perfectam penitentiam fecerit de omnibus peccatis que per quinque sensus transgrediendo decalogum legis commisit, digne santum pascha celebrare poterit. In quinquagesima iam aliquantulum spei percipimus, iam deum protectorem nostrum esse confidimus. Inde est introitus, *Esto mihi in deum protectorem*[28]. Gradalis, *Tu es deus qui facis mirabilia, liberasti in brachio tuo populum*[a 29]. In tractu iubilamus deo quod habemus spem misericordie[30]. In epistola nos hortatur Paulus ad caritatem[31], in evangelio cecus ad fidem[32], ut per hec evadamus tribulationem. Notanda autem distinctio horum trium officiorum. Primum continet planctum nostrum, quod simus sub crudelissima damnatione peccatorum. Secundum meditationem fuge ab eis dummodo velit dominus ad auxilium[b] nostrum exurgere. Tertium agit consilium fugiendi presumens de susceptione. Hec significaverunt tres egressiones Israehelis de Babilone. Prima sub Zorobabel, secunda sub Ezra, tertia sub Neemia quando et muri Ierusalem extructi sunt.

y. subsistimus *om. L2* *z*. sexagesime ammonemur *W* *a*. populum *om. L2*
b. aulium *L2*

---

23. *II Cor*. 11.19ff.
24. *Ps*. 82.19.
25. *Ps*. 82.14.
26. *Ps*. 59.4.
27. *Lk*. 8.4-15.
28. *Ps*. 30.3.
29. *Ps*. 76.15-16.
30. *Ps*. 99.1-2.
31. *I Cor*. 13.
32. *Lk*. 18.31-43.

IIII. De quadragesima

Quadragesimam nobis ipsius domini consecravit ieiunium. Numerus autem iste ut verbis Augustini in libro secundo De consensu evangelistarum loquar illud tempus significat, quo in seculo nos oportet regi a Christo secundum disciplinam laboriosam, qua *flagellat omnem filium quem recipit*[33]. Dimicamus ergo his diebus contra diabolum ieiunantes xl diebus ieiunium quod per se Christus et per Moisen et Heliam id est prophetas et legem consecravit. Quid aliud prefigurans quam per omne huius seculi tempus temptationem nostram quam in sua carne de nostra mortalitate assumpsit[34]. Quadraginta ergo dies sunt usque[c] cenam domini. Duo superstites significant duo precepta dilectionis dei[d] et proximi, que qui perfecte servaverit et perfecte ab omnibus viciis ieiunaverit feliciter pascha videbit, de morte scilicet ad vitam transibit. Pascha quippe transitus interpretatur. Merito vero xlii dies ieiunamus pro Christo qui xlii[a] generatione pro nobis in mundum[e] ieiunaturus teste Matheo[35] venit. Quadraginta etiam duas mansiones Israhelite in heremo habuere antequam terram repromissionis potuissent introire. Quorum imitatione nos xlii diebus ieiunamus ut ad veram patriam quam Christus nobis promisit perveniamus. Cur autem inquit idem doctor[36] Iste numerus temporalem vitam significet illa interim causa occurrit de proximo, quia et tempora annorum quadripartitis vicibus currunt et mundus iste quatuor terminatur partibus. Quadraginta autem quatuor habent decem. Porro ipsa decem ab uno usque ad quatuor progrediente numero consumantur. Quod autem illud ieiunium ipso anni tempore congruenter observetur quod est contiguum dominice passioni in qua significatur hec vita laboriosa cui opus continentia est, ut ieiunetur ab huius mundi amicitia, dicit idem in libro ad Ianuarium[37]. In quadragesima omnis continentia officii propiciationem nobis divinam promittit. In introitu invocamus[f] et exaudimur[38], in epistola similiter tempore accepto exaudimur[g][39], in responsorio angeli domini custodiunt nos[40], in tractu habitamus in adiutorio altissimi[41] ut diabolum vincamus cum domino in evangelio[42].

c. ad *add. L2* *d.* dei *om. W* *e.* mundus *W* *f.* invocamur *W* *g.* in epistola... exaudimur *om. W*

33. *Heb.* 12.6.
34. Cf. Aug., *De cons. evang.* 2.4.9 (PL 34.1075).
35. *Mt.* 1.17.
36. *De cons. evang.* (as above).
37. Aug., *Ep.* 55.15.28 (CSEL 34.201).
38. *Ps.* 90.15.
39. *II Cor.* 6.1ff.
40. *Ps.* 90.11.
41. *Ps.* 90.1ff.
42. *Mt.* 4.1-11.

V. De quarta feria cinerum

Ante dominicam quadragesime quarta feria ieiunare incipimus et cinerem super capita nostra mittimus significantes quia sicut in principali corporis nostri cinerem spargimus, ita in principali anime nostre, id est ratione, nos morituros et in cinerem redigendos intelligamus. Hanc diem[h] et tres sequentes quidam post tempus sancti Gregorii additos putant ad explendum numerum quadragenarium quia ipse in evangelii expositione, Ductus est Ihesus in desertum, dicit non esse nisi xxxvi dies usque ad pascha in quibus oporteat ieiunare[43]. sed est alia secretior ratio quam dicemus. Ab illa feria quarta usque in sabbatum ante pascha sunt xlvi dies. Totidem annis templum Ierosolimitanum[i] fabricatum est, totidem diebus verum dei templum in utero virginali factum est sed et corpus[j] humanum totidem diebus in utero matris compingitur. Primis[k] enim diebus sex semen lac est, deinde sequentibus novem convertitur in sanguinem, inde duodecim[l] diebus[m] solidatur. Reliquis decem et octo formatur in omnibus liniamentis. Sex autem et novem et duodecim et decem et octo faciunt xlv. Quibus si addas illum diem quo post perfecta liniamenta incipit corpus crescere, fiunt xlvi. Quapropter convenit ut corpus nostrum castigetur ieiuniis in caritate matris ecclesie quot diebus formatur in utero matris sue. Nam et littere nominis Adam a quo omnes nascimur eundem numerum habent apud Grecos.

VI. De quarta feria in apertione aurium

Quarta feria quarte quadragesimalis ebdomade vocatur In apertione aurium, quia more antiquo tangebantur illa die nares et aures catecuminorum et tradebatur eis simbolum quod redderent sabbato pasche et fiebat scrutinium, id est scrutabantur presbiteri quid crederent et docebant eos quomodo vivere et quid credere deberent. Ideo illa die sunt due lectiones et duo responsoria. In priore lectione de fide et baptismo agitur, *Tollam* inquit *vos de gentibus et congregabo vos de universis terris*, quod intelligimus de errorum varietatibus, *et adducam vos in terram vestram* ad fidem scilicet et[n] in[o] eam ad quam habendam creati estis et *effundam super vos aquam mundam*[44] baptismi. Nec minus in responsorio vocantur ad fidem, *Venite filii, audite me*[45]. Item *Accedite ad eum, et illuminamini*[46]. Secunda lectio de moribus agit, *Quiescite agere perverse*, *discite benefacere*[47] et cetera. Item,

h. idem *W* *i.* Ierosolimitatum *W* *j.* corpusque *W* *k.* primus *ut vid. O*: primi *W* *l.* duodecim: diebus *add. L*, *W* *m.* diebus *om. O* *n.* et *om. L2* *o.* in *om. W*

43. Greg. Mag., *Hom. in evang.* 1.16.5 (PL 76.1137).
44. *Ezek.* 36.24-25 (Tollam ... mundam)
45. *Ps.* 33.12.
46. *Ps.* 33.6.
47. *Isa.* 1.16-17.

responsorium de fide, *Beata gens cuius est dominus deus eius*[48]. Versus de virtutibus morum quas baptizandi per deum habituri sunt, *Verbo domini celi firmati sunt et spiritu oris eius omnis virtus eorum*[49]. De baptismo agitur in evangelio pro lotione ceci nati, dicente Augustino, Lavit ergo oculos in ea piscina, que interpretatur missus, baptizatusque est in Christo[50]. Si ergo quando eum illuminavit tunc baptizavit, quando inunxit[p] fortasse catecuminum fecit. Ratio ergo est quare due lectiones leguntur, quia teste eodem doctore in libro De fide et moribus, Audiant baptizandi non solum quid credere debeant sed etiam quemadmodum se ab hoc seculo pravo eripiant[51]. Hec autem ideo fiunt quarta feria quarte septimane quia vocantur illi ad doctrinam quatuor evangeliorum que cum frequenter[q] ab initio seculi tum[r] manifestius prefigurata est in quarta etate in qua et David regnavit et ceteri prophete fuerunt.

VII. De sabbato ante palmas

Sabbato ante palmas vacat quia domnus papa elemosinam dat. Ipsa die ante sex dies pasche dicit Iohannes evangelista dominum Bethaniam venisse ibique sibi cena facta, lavisse[s] Mariam pedes eius unguento et tersisse capillis. Quod quid significet Augustinus in expositione eiusdem evangelii docet, Quecumque anima fidelis vis esse Maria unge pedes domini precioso unguento[52]. Illud unguentum iusticia fuit ideo libra fuit. Et post pauca, Unge pedes Ihesu bene vivendo, domi eius sectare vestigia. Si habes superflua, da pauperibus et domini pedes tersisti. Capilli enim superfluunt corpori[53]. Ad imitationem igitur Marie illa die apostolicus elemosinam donat et etiam in sacramentariis ascribi patitur ut ceteros per orbem ad suam imitationem trahat. Hoc et sabbato ante quadragesima facit ut elemosina ieiunium precedat.

VIII. De dominica palmarum

Dominica in crastino secundum evangelistam Iohannem procedimus cum palmis et puerorum cantibus ad imitationem Hebreorum. Palma, que immarcescibiliter frondibus vestitur, significat victoriam Christi de diabolo, quia victores ea coronari solebant. Victoriam Christi et Hebrei pretinuere[t] venturam et nos[u] gaudemus impletam. Ipsa die passio domini legitur quia

p. iniunxit *O* *q.* frequentes *W* *r.* vel tamen *suprasc. W* *s. corr. L2*
t. pretinuerunt *W*, *suprascrip*, *L*, *L2* *u.* nos *om. W*

---

48. *Ps.* 32.12.
49. *Ps.* 32.6.
50. Aug., *In Ioan.* 44.2 (CCL 36.382).
51. Aug., *De fide et operibus* 8 (CSEL 41.50).
52. Aug., *In Ioan.* 50.6 (CCL 36.435).
53. *Ibid.*

ea die ad passionem ultro Ierosolimam venit. Sicut enim decima die mensis primi iussus est legalis agnus domum immolandus introduci, ita et decima die mensis eiusdem dominus immolandus dignatus est Ierosolimam ingredi [54].

IX. De quarta feria ante cenam domini

Quarta feria ante cenam domini passio iterum legitur quia ipsa die consilium fecerunt Iudei ut eum dolo tenerent et occiderent. In introitu eiusdem diei ubi apostolus ait, *In nomine* domini *Iesu omne genu flectatur celestium terrestrium et infernorum* [55], constitutor officii pretermisit, *Et omnis lingua confiteatur*, ut significaret malignam linguam Iudeorum que illum confiteri noluit sed dampnare presumpsit. Due illa die leguntur lectiones de passione Christi, quia simpla mors corporis eius destruxit duplicem nostram anime et corporis. Caro enim eius, ut ait Ambrosius [v], pro salute corporis [w] immolata est [x], sanguis vero pro salute anime est effusus [56]. Primam lectionem sequitur responsorium cum versu, quia non nisi duobus modis peccamus in anima, cogitatione et consensu. Secundam sequitur tractus cum quinque versibus quia in corpore peccamus quinque sensibus. Que omnia peccata et corporis [y] et anime passio Christi destruxit. Ea die scinditur [z] velum quod tota quadragesima fuit inter nos et altare ad significandum illud quod dicit propheta, *Peccata vestra separant inter vos et deum* [57]. Causa scissionis, ut sicut ea die Iudei se obstinatione sua paraverunt ad eius passionem implendam, ita nos confessione peccatorum preparemus nos ad eandem digna veneratione suscipiendam.

X. De cena domini

In cena domini multe sunt varietates. Quarum prima est quod dimittimus Venite exultemus domine et Gloria patri [a] et campanarum sonitum. Que omnia quia videntur ad quandam dei gloriam et nostram pertinere leticiam, merito illis [b] diebus omittimus quibus ipse humiliatus est ad mortem crucis et sancti apostoli magno merore deiecti.

Altera quod ad [c] matutinas xxiv et unam excelsiorem accendimus candelas. Duodecim significant apostolos et altere duodecim septuaginta duos discipulos qui quia minoris dignitatis erant quam apostoli non suo significantur per candelas numero sed apostolorum quodam modo decrescendo medium tenent numerum. Una que est excelsior significat ipsum dominum *qui illuminat omnem*

v. ut ait Ambrosius *om. W* *w*. nostri *add. W* *x*. immolata est *om. O, L, L2*
y. corporisque *W* *z*. scindunt *L* *a*. *om. L* *b*. illius *O* *c*. ad *om. W*

54. Cf. Bede. *In Marc.* 3.11 (CCL 120.576).
55. *Phil.* 2.10-11.
56. Ambrose, *Comm. in 1 Cor.* 11, apud Rabanus Maurus, *Enarr. in ep. Pauli* 11 (PL 112.103).
57. Cf. *Isa.* 59.2.

hominem venientem in hunc mundum[58] et illos etiam quibus ipse dixit, *Vos estis lux mundi*[59]. Appropinquante autem passione domini paulatim deficiebat et extinguebatur lumen fidei eorum ita ut fugerent donec eo crucifixo et extincto quicquid in eis erat credulitatis[d] omnino deficeret. Quod mihi videntur significare ille candele que non[e] repente sed paulatim extinguntur. Hinc est quod ea nocte et duabus sequentibus benedictiones non petuntur ut timor apostolorum significetur qui tutius ducebant a societate magistri sui fugere quam ab eo benedictionem[f] expetere.

Tercia est varietas quod oleum ipso die tripliciter benedicitur. Oleum significat gratiam spiritus sancti sive quia ab arbore pacis profluit, neque enim sine gratia eius pacem cum deo habere possumus; sive quia lassa membra reficit quia est ipse paraclitus et *sanat contritos corde et alligat contritionem eorum*[g][60]; sive quia omnibus excellit liquoribus, ipse enim in initio ferebatur super aquas; sive quia ministrat lucem, spiritus enim est vera lux mentium.

Oleum infirmorum consecratur in ipsa consecratione corporis et sanguinis domini ut ostendatur quod qui iuxta epistolam eiusdem diei infirmus est in anima quia indigne sumit corpus domini[61], unguatur oleo secundum Iacobum apostolum, In nomine domini, peccata scilicet deo confitens accipiat remissionem per gratiam spiritus sancti et sic digne ad communionem accedat[62]. Inde est quod super hanc consecrationem invocatur paraclitus quia ipse est consolator infirmorum.

Crisma[h] consecrat sacerdos in eo loco ubi dicitur Pax domini sit semper vobiscum[i], ut ostendat Christum, a quo crisma dicitur, pacem fecisse inter deum et homines. Nos quoque a Christo vocamur Christiani. Crismate liniuntur baptizati cui balsamum aromaticus scilicet liquor adicitur ut significet Christianum bonarum virtutum odore debere fragrare[j] iuxta apostolum dicentem, *Christi bonus odor sumus deo*[63]. Sed et illud, quod precipitur in ordine Romano ut cum ampulla crismatis ad aram defertur, partim sit cooperta, partim non, post benedictionem autem omnino cooperta salutetur ab omnibus, ita potest exponi. Ampullam cum crismate ipsum dominum divinitate plenum et spiritu sancto potest intelligere lector prudens. Unde per prophetam dicit, *Spiritus domini super me eo quod unxerit me*[64]. Et ad

d. crudelitas *W* *e.* non *om. W* *f.* benedictione *W* *g.* sive quia lassa... a.c.e. *om. W. W* *h.* risma *W* *i.* sit semper vobiscum : super vos *W* *j. mg. note in anr. hand*: Fla facit ardorem fla reddit mihi odorem *O*

58. *Jn.* 1.9.
59. *Mt.* 5.14.
60. *Ps.* 146.3.
61. *I Cor.* 11.27.
62. Cf. *Jas.* 5.13-15.
63. *II Cor.* 2.15.
64. *Isa.* 61.1.

eum psalmista, *Unxit te deus deus tuus oleo leticie*[65]. Quod exponens apostolus Petrus ait, *Quomodo unxerit*[k] *eum deus virtute et spiritu sancto*[66]. Dominus ergo antequam super aram crucis immolaretur partim videbatur radiantibus foris miraculis sed abscondebatur intus sempiterna eius virtus et divinitas[l]; post crucem autem tota eius divinitas et humanitas latent sed tamen per totum orbem adoratur ut deus. Halatio pontificis in ampullam ter in modum crucis invitationem spiritus sancti significat qui non aliter venit nisi per fidem sancte trinitatis et fidem sante crucis.

Sequitur exorcismus olei quo unguntur caticumini ad fidem invitandi ut diabolus ab eis discedat, sicut in ipsa benedictione dicitur. Nullus spiritualibus nequitiis locus, nulla refugis spiritibus sit facultas.

Fiunt autem[m] hee benedictiones olei inter ipsam corporis dominici[n] consecrationem quia unum sine altero non provehit[o] hominem ad vitam eternam. Nam idem qui dixit *Nisi manducaveritis carnem filii hominis et biberitis eius sanguinem non habebitis vitam in vobis*[67], alibi dixit *Nisi quis renatus fuerit ex aqua et spiritu sancto non potest introire in regnum*[68] celorum. Quod pertinet ad crisma quia sine crismate baptisma non fit. Item non posse ad vitam eternam perveniri sine fide testatur apostolus dicens, *Sine fide impossibile est placere deo*[69]. Quod rescipit ad oleum exorcizatum quo unguntur catecumini ut vocentur ad fidem. Non posse autem ad vitam eternam perveniri sine remissione delictorum, remissionem porro peccatorum non esse sine penitentia certissimum est. Unde ipse dominus, *Penitentiam agite : appropinquabit enim regnum celorum*[70]. Et apostolus Petrus, *Penitemini et convertimini ut deleantur vestra peccata*[71]. Quod pertinet ad oleum infirmorum quo unguntur infirmi ut habeant remissionem peccatorum dicente Iacobo, *Infirmatur quis in vobis? Inducat presbiteros ecclesie et unguant*[p] *eum in nomine domini et si in peccatis sit dimittentur ei*[72].

Fiunt autem ista in feria quinta cene domini quia et in fine quinte etatis seculi veniens dominus in mundum vespere etiam istius ferie quinte, cassatis[q] legis veteris sacrificiis, novum testamentum in suo dedicavit sanguine dicens, *Hic est calix sanguinis*[r] *mei novi et eterni testamenti*[73]. Unde sacerdos in prima collecta misse dicit, Ita nobis ablato vetustatis errore resurrectionis

k. unxit *L2* *l*. divitas *W* *m*. autem *om. W* *n*. domini *W* *o*. unguatur *W* *p*. oleo *add. L2* *q*. cessatis *O* *r*. dicens hic est calix sanguinis: mei calix *W*

65. *Ps*. 44.8.
66. *Acts* 10.38.
67. *Jn*. 6.54.
68. *Jn*. 3.5.
69. *Heb*. 11.6.
70. *Mt*. 3.2.
71. *Acts* 3.19.
72. Cf. *Jas*. 5.14-15.
73. Cf. *Lk*. 22.20ff.

sue gratiam largiatur. Dedicavit etiam dominus ipso die per sacramentum corporis sui et ablutionem pedum discipulorum suorum et remissionem peccatorum et fidem et fidei sacramentum, que tria diximus significari per triplicem consecrationem olei. Que consecratio in una quidem olei materia sed ad diversos fit respectus quia una quidem est spiritus sancti substantia sed diversa munera. *Alii* enim secundum apostolum[s] *datur sapientia*[74] id est ut Christiane vivat quod est summa sapientia. *Principium* enim *sapientie timor domini*[75]. Ecce oleum crismatis, sed ut addatur[t] balsamum datur sermo scientie ut bene vivat et bene loqui et intelligere sciat. Sed quia sunt plerique qui simplici fide contenti[u] sunt additur alii fides. Et alibi, *Iustus autem ex fide vivit*[76]. Ecce oleum exorcizatum. *Alii gratia sanitatum*[77]. Ecce oleum infirmorum. *Hec autem omnia operatur unus atque idem spiritus dividens singulis prout vult*[78]. Et quidem ista sua karismata posset sine visibili oleo spiritus sanctus largiri sed per visibilia nos ammonet ut ad invisibilium amorem rapiamur. Posset etiam dominus nos baptizare invisibiliter spiritu sancto sed aquam addi voluit ut sicut aqua foris abluit ita intelligere debeamus spiritum sanctum intus operari. Ab ipsa die servatur corpus domini usque in crastinum nec celebratur consecratio illius sacramenti a cena domini usque in resurrectionem quia officium quod celebratur die sabbati de nocte resurrectionis est. Hoc ideo quia dominus in ultima cena dixit discipulis suis, *Non bibam de hoc genimine vitis usque in diem illum quo bibam illud in regno patris mei*[79], regnum dei resurrectionem suam vocans per quam et pater et ipse clarificatus est in mundo. Expoliatio[v] quoque altaris usque in officium resurrectionis fugam apostolorum significat. Altare enim in hoc loco Christum significat quia per oblationes[w] quas ei facimus[x] ad misericordiam dei patris pervenimus; ipse altare, ipse sacerdos, ipse sacrificium. Hoc altare apostoli quasi vestimenta ornabant cum eius lateri obambularent. Sed ablati sunt ab eo per timorem quando tempore passionis relicto eo omnes fugere. De his dicit Innocentius papa, Constat apostolos biduo[y] isto in tristicia et merore fuisse et propter metum Iudeorum se occuluisse[80]. Quod utique in tantum non est dubium eos ieiunasse biduo memorato ut tradicio ecclesie habeat isto[z] biduo sacramenta penitus non celebrari[a].

Ipso die lavantur altaria et apud plerasque ecclesias parietes et pavimenta ecclesie. Ligna autem et lapides non sunt ecclesia sed sancte fidelium anime.

s. apostoli *O* *t.* datur *W* *u.* contempti *O* *v.* expolatio *L2* *w.* ablationes *O* *x.* facinus *O* *y.* Iudeo *O* *z.* isto *om.* *W* *a.* celebrare *W*

---

74. *I Cor.* 12.8 et rel : *Sermo scientie*, etc.
75. *Prov.* 1.7.
76. *Rom.* 1.17.
77. *I Cor.* 12.9.
78. *I Cor.* 12.11.
79. *Mt.* 26.29.
80. Inn. I, *Ep.* 25.4.7 (PL 20.555-556).

Ideo autem hec foris fiunt in manu factis ut ostendatur quid fieri debeat in nobis. Altare potest significare sacerdotes et clerum qui ei deserviunt. Parietes potentes laicos quorum protectione defenduntur populi. Pavimentum humile vulgus. Omne itaque hominum[b] Christianorum genus debet lavari per penitentiam ad sanctam resurrectionem suscipiendam; lavari autem et aqua et vino per credulitatem[c] videlicet passionis domini ex cuius latere effluxit sanguis[d] et aqua. Et hoc in cena domini quia eo die lavit pedes discipulorum suorum. Ad quod imitandum[e] lavamus nostros pedes et pauperum; pauperum ad humilitatis eius imitationem, nostros ad significationem. Unde dominus dicit, *Qui lotus est non indiget nisi ut pedes lavet*[81], quasi diceret, Qui lotus est baptismo non indiget iterum[f] lavari eo nisi ut terrena opera[g] per penitentiam tergat que ipsi adherent dum in hac vita pulverulenta ambulat. Inde Augustinus[h], Cotidie lavat pedes nobis qui interpellat pro nobis. Et cotidie opus habemus ut pedes lavemus[82], id est ut vias spiritualium gressuum dirigamus.

Die ipsa cenatur et inde pedes pauperum abluuntur et sic refectioni plene servitur quia dominus primo cenavit et a[i] cena pedes discipulorum abluturus surrexit et iterum recubuit. Quare autem dominus corporis sui misterium consecravit post cenam, quod nos cotidie exequimur ante mensam, hec est ratio: ille ut ostenderet veteris legis completum esse sacrificium in fine antiqui pasce induxit novum; nos ante mensam deo sacrificamus quia supplicatur attentius et liberius oratur castius et mundius cum cibis corporalibus non gravatur stomachus.

XI. De parasceve

Sexta feria passionis domini vocatur Grece parasceve in qua deus hominem quem sexta die fecerat redemit; parasceve autem dicitur quod interpretatur preparatio quia eo die precipue preparamus corda et corpora nostra deo. Ea die leguntur due lectiones propter eandem rationem quam in quarta feria dixi. Primam lectionem sequitur tractus quatuor versuum[j] quia per passionem quam lectio presignavit deus totum mundum qui quatuor dividitur partibus et quatuor constat elementis redemit. In secunda lectione resurrectio domini cita et nostra tarda predicitur. Tractus qui eam sequitur longus est quia quod in illo scimus cito completum, in nobis diu expectamus complendum. Hoc autem secundum ecclesie Romane morem dictum[k] est[l]. Ceterum in nostris ecclesiis prima lectio est de Osee, secunda de Moyse; hoc vero quod dicitur in primo tractu *in medio duorum animalium cognosceris*[83], constitutor

b. omnium *O* *c*. crudelitatem *W* *d*. sanguinis *O*, sanguinem *W* *e*. mutandum *O* *f*. utrum *W* *g*. corpora *L2* *h*. Augustus *O*, *L*, *L2* *i*. ad *O* *j*. versum *O* *k*. *corr*. *L* *l*. sit *O*, *L*, *L2*

81. *Jn*. 13.10.
82. Aug., *In Ioan*. 56.4 (CCL 36.468).
83. *Hab*. 3.2 (animalium *vice* annorum).

officii in medio duorum latronum intellexit, quamvis hanc opinionem vulgarem esse beatus Ieronimus dicat[84]. Inde legitur passio ut re vera audiamus quod figurate in lectionibus audieramus. Tunc more Romano duo diaconi sindonem super altare positam quasi furantes[m] surripiunt. Altare significat Christum in quo nostras oblationes offerimus deo. Vestimenta significant apostolos ut predixi[n]. Sublato ergo evangelio id est dedito Christo in manus Iudeorum, vestimenta eius scilicet apostoli more furum fugerunt. Post hec per orationes que dicuntur, ad memoriam nobis reducitur pro omnibus amicis et inimicis orandum esse illo presertim die quo dominus in cruce pro inimicis suis oravit. Quod autem ad solam orationem pro Iudeis genua non flectimus, hoc innuit quia eorum derisionem qua salvatori genua flexere execramur, et quod ipsi simulate domino nostro fecerunt, nos pro ipsis vere facere non debemus. Hinc est quod his tribus diebus pacem non damus, vitantes perfidiam Iude qui deum osculo tradidit, eiusque factum et opere et verbo[o] non sequentes. Sequitur veneratio crucis quatinus sicut dominus noster ea die humiliatus est in ea usque ad mortem, ita nos ea die humiliemur ante eam usque ad terram. Plura vero de crucis laude subnectit Amalarius que mihi non videntur necessaria[p] hic attexere. Id enim solummodo suscepti operis exposcit necessitas ut ea que dixit de significationibus ecclesiasticorum officiorum breviter defloremus, omissis omnibus testimoniis que ille tantis involvit anfractibus ut quid velit dicere vix intelligamus.

In eadem die post adorationem sancte crucis afferunt presbiteri corpus domini quod pridie remansit cum vino non consecrato. Calix pridie consumptus potest significare sacrificia legis veteris consummata que maxime fiebant in sanguine quamvis et pro cautela possit servari mos iste quia vinum citius labitur quam panis amittitur. Sanctificatur autem vinum non consecratum per panem sanctificatum. Sumuntur autem sine pronuntiatione pacis domini pro causa quam superius dixi.

XII. De sabbato sancto

In sabbato sancto agunt Romani vigilias ad mediam noctem resurrectionis ut vigiliantes sanctam resurrectionem inveniant. Ipsa nocte baptizant caticuminos significantes illud apostoli, *Quicunque in Christo baptizati sumus in morte ipsius baptizati sumus*[85]. Et iterum, *Consepulti sumus cum ipso per baptismum in mortem ut cum ipso*[q] *resurgamus in vitam*[86]. De cera faciunt agnos oleumque immiscent dantque populo in octavis pasche ad facienda lumina in domibus suis. Cera significat virgineam domini carnem, lumen divinitatem. De cera fiunt agni significantes agnum dei qui tulit peccata

m. furentes *O*   *n*. prediximus *O*   *o*. animo *W*   *p*. necessarium *O*, *L*, *L2*
q. per baptismum... cum ipso *om*. *W*

84. Cf. Jerome, *Comm. in Abacuc* 2 (PL 25.1309).
85. *Rom*. 6.3.
86. *Rom*. 6.4.

mundi. Miscentur agni oleo quia plenus ille fuit spiritu sancto. Precepit autem papa Zosimus ut in aliis ecclesiis benediceretur cereus in similitudinem[r] columne que precessit filios Israhel repromissionis terram ingressuros. Columna ista significat Christum qui precedit caticuminos nostros primum ad baptismum et postea baptizatos ad regnum. Quod autem illa columna hunc significet cereum intelligitur dum in benedictione dicitur, sed iam columne huius preconia novimus. Quod a diacono benedicitur mos est Romanus.

Lectionum ordo multo aliter Rome quam apud nos agitur. Proinde secundum significationes Romanas dicamus ac primo ut facilior sit intellectus quedam premittamus. Quatuor modis intelligitur sacra scriptura. Per historiam cum res aliqua plano sermone refertur quomodo facta vel dicta sit. Per allegoriam cum verbis sive rebus misticis presentia Christi et ecclesie sacramenta signantur. Per tropologiam id est moralem locutionem que ad institutionem et correctionem morum apertis aut figuratis sermonibus profertur. Per anagogen id est sensum superiorem qui de premiis celestibus planis seu figuratis sermonibus procedit. Isti modi scripturarum in lectionibus et canticis illius diei proferuntur ut intelligant plene catecumini ad quid vocantur. Prima lectio est *In principio fecit deus celum et terram*[87]. Secunda plano sermone refert quomodo filii Israhel egressi sunt de terra Egipti[88]. Utraque pertinet ad historiam. Ideo unum eas complectitur canticum quia una refert quomodo fecerit deus hominem, altera quomodo liberaverit servientem. Post lectiones sequuntur orationes in quibus rogat sacerdos spiritualiter in nobis complendum quod lector dixit corporaliter factum. Tercia lectio est *Apprehendent septem mulieres virum unum*[89]. Hec pertinet ad allegoriam quia figuratis verbis Christi et ecclesie sacramenta pronuntiat. *Apprehendent septem mulieres*, id est septem dona spiritus sancti, virum unum Christum. Cum *abluerit dominus sordem*[s] *filiarum Syon in spiritu ardoris*[90], abluet[t] spiritus sancti igne peccata frigentium animarum ut sint filie celestis speculationis. Sequitur canticum *Vinea facta est*[91], quod de spiritualibus nuptiis Christi et sinagoge que fient in fine mundi loquitur. Et quia in lectione de ecclesia in cantico narratur de sinagoga, dicit sacerdos in oratione, Deus qui nos ad celebrandum paschale misterium utriusque testamenti paginis instruis.

Quarta lectio est de moribus instituendis: *Inclinate aurem vestram et venite ad me; audite et vivet anima vestra*[92], et cetera, quibus moralis doctrina exprimitur. Quod et canticum sequens ostendit, *Audite celi que loquor*[93].

r. similitudine *W* *s.* sordes *L2* *t.* enim *add. L, L2*

87. *Gen.* 1.1.
88. *Ex.* 14.24ff.
89. *Isa.* 4.1.
90. *Isa.* 4.4.
91. *Isa.* 5.1.
92. *Isa.* 55.3.
93. *Deut.* 32.1.

Quartum canticum pertinet ad anagogen id est ad supernorum misteriorum desiderium: *Sicut cervus desiderat ad fontes aquarum ita desiderat anima mea ad te deus*[94].

Lectiones autem ideo sine nominibus librorum de quibus sumpte sunt proferuntur, quia frustra caticuminis profertur auctor incognitus quibus firmissima[u] auctoritas potest vilescere per ignorantiam. Subsequitur canticum quia in proximo futuri sunt caticumini de illorum numero qui cantant in Apocalipsi canticum novum[95]. Prebet ergo lectio speciem magistrorum, canticum benivolentiam auditorum, oratio preces ecclesie ut in his que docti sunt possint perseverare. Quare autem illa die fiat baptismus superius dictum. De cuius sacramentis Amalarius plura volvit et revolvit[96] que hic pretermittimus ne ego et ille, quem defloro, rideamur in comparatione Carnotensis episcopi Ivonis, qui talia nobilissime prosecutus est in sermone de sacramentis neophitorum[97]. Sufficiat ergo de varietatibus que fiunt in missa illius diei dicere[v].

Precipitur in ordine Romano ut alter cereus accendatur post primum ut primus significet Christum, secundus apostolos et apostolicos viros quibus ille dicit, *Vos estis lux mundi*[98]. Ambo precedunt baptizandos.

Missa sine introitu incipitur quia et ante Celestinum papam similiter toto anno fiebat et officii longitudo exigit ut aliquid omittatur. Ad evangelium portatur timiamaterium solum sine cereo quia timiamata portabant qui Christum resurrexisse non credebant. Offerenda ideo dimittitur propter eandem rationem quam superius dixi de introitu. Alleluia et tractus ideo dicuntur quia et leticia iam inchoat et aliquid tristicie restat. Sanctus qui est cantus angelorum dicitur quia angeli resurrectionem Christi annunciaverunt[w], sed agnus dei non dicitur quia mulieres illum surrexisse et resurrectione sua mundi peccata tulisse non credebant.

Hic dicit Amalarius intelligi posse quod septuagesima et sexagesima[x] et quinquagesima possunt referri ad illud tempus quo filii Israhel tribulabantur in Egipto sub persecutione pharaonis, quia in istis diebus semper pene cantatur de tribulatione. Quadragesima autem in qua cantatur *Invocavit me et ego exaudiam eum*[99] ad illud tempus potest reputari quo iam exauditi de Egipto educti sunt et in rubro mari baptizati; hinc fuisse xlii mansiones in deserto, hinc[y] esse totidem dies usque ad baptismum; tempus autem quo illi fuerunt in deserto antequam ingrederuntur terram promissionis significare totum tempus quo hic vivitur post baptismum, quod etiam significant octo dies neophitorum de quibus iam dicendum.

u. firmissa *W* *v*. discere *O* *w*. anciaverunt *L* *x*. quadragesima *W* *y*. hic. *L*, *L2*

94. *Ps*. 41.2.
95. *Apoc*. 5.9.
96. See *LO* 1.25, 1.27.
97. Ivo, *De sacramentis neophytorum sermo* (PL 162.505-512).
98. *Mt*. 5.14.
99. *Ps*. 90.15.

XIII. De octo diebus albatorum

Qui baptizandi sunt induuntur vestibus albis quas octavo die deponunt. Albe vestes significant bona opera, de quibus dicit Salomon, *Omni tempore sint vestimenta tua candida*[100]. Has septem diebus quibus tota vita nostra volvitur portare debemus usque finito mundo perveniamus ad requiem, que per octavum diem quod est sabbatum significatur. Item septem dies pertinent ad vetus testamentum propter sabbatum, octo ad novum propter domini resurrectionem. Septem ergo diebus spiritualiter observare debemus quod in veteri testamento preceptum est, ut in octavo perveniamus ad id quod promissum est in novo. Item, septem sunt dona spiritus sancti et octo beatitudines. Septem igitur dona nobis in baptismo collata immaculata toto tempore servare debemus, ut octo beatitudines consequamur. A sabbato usque ad sabbatum portande sunt vestes, id est ex qua die spiritus pignus accepimus usque perfectam requiem accipiamus; duplicia solent esse vestimenta quia duplex remuneratio, id est beatitudo anime et corporis, promittitur nobis. Sabbatum ergo ante pascha, quo[z] baptismus datur, significat principium bonorum operum, sabbatum post pascha, quo albe deponuntur, consumpnationem. Ideo in isto sabbato et in sequentibus sex diebus dicuntur responsorium et alleluia, in sabbato autem post pascha duo alleluia. Responsorium dicit significare negociosos actus huius seculi in quibus sibi concordant et quasi respondent anxietates corporis et anime. Alleluia significat leticiam futuri seculi. In septem ergo diebus dicimus responsorium et alleluia, quia in[a] tota vita ista habemus anxietates duplices in re, leticiam unam in spe. In octava autem die id est in futura vita duplex alleluia cantamus quia duplicem leticiam[b] anime et corporis habebimus. Similiter in dominicis usque ad pentecosten duo dicimus alleluia, recolentes perfectam leticiam quam habebimus in resurrectione. In nataliciis quoque sanctorum duo dicimus alleluia quia ipsi perfecta fruuntur leticia, anime in re, corporis in spe; in septimana unum quia tota vita nunquam plena gaudebimus leticia. Responsorium autem per sex dies non secundum ordinem versuum psalmi sed secundum congruentiam dierum cantari. Hoc est indicium[c] quod post aliquos posteriores versus feria sexta cantatur, *lapidem quem*[d] *reprobaverunt edificantes*[1]. Sexta enim feria lapis Christus a Iudeis reprobatus est et cruci affixus quasi edificationi legis eorum non aptus. Dicit sane Amalarius ideo in sabbato ante pascha alleluia ante tractum cantari, quia alleluia nomen Hebreum est et Hebrea lingua mater est linguarum omnium. Idem autem est alleluia Ebraice quod laudate dominum Latine. Decet igitur ut propter dignitatem lingue prius laudemus deum Hebraice deinde[e] Latine. Ideo autem toto anno prius[f] responsorium dicimus quam alleluia, quia ut dixi

z. corr. O. *a.* in *om. W* *b.* leticia *O* *c.* iudicium *O* *d.* quam *O*
e. dein *L* *f.* prius *om. W*

100. *Eccles.* 9.8.
1. *Ps.* 117.22.

responsorium significat curam actionum secularium, alleluia leticiam futurorum; et nos dum in hoc mundo sumus prius, hoc est frequentius, pro transitoriis[g] quam pro celestibus oramus. Item, responsorium significat activam vitam, alleluia contemplativam. Activa vita est elemosinas omnibus modis impendere, contemplativa soli deo intendere. Nos autem toto anno preter a pascha in pentecosten et a septuagesima usque in pascha responsorium et alleluia cantamus, quia semper utrique vite studere debemus. Septuagesima autem significat tempus penitencie quo ab alleluia cessare debemus quia non est speciosa laus in ore peccatoris. Septem vero septimane que sunt inter pascha et pentecosten significant vitam futuri seculi in quibus responsorium non cantamus sed duplex alleluia, quia ibi activa vita necessaria non erit, ubi nullus elemosina indigebit, sed sola ibi erit vite contemplative leticia dupliciter in corpore et in anima. Septies enim septem sunt xlix. Quibus si unum addas fiunt quinquaginta. Iste numerus significat futuram vitam in qua sicut in iubileo, id est in quinquagesimo anno, perfecte iubilabimus erimusque septies, hoc est perfectissime septeno divini spiritus munere pleni et hoc complente trinitatis unitate.

XIV. De[h] vigilia pentecosten

In vigilia pentecostes legitur prima lectio quomodo factus est homo qui peccavit. In secunda legitur quomodo temptatus est Abraham et deo placuit. Ibi audit homo quid caveat, hic discit quid faciat. Tercia[i] sequitur lectio et canticum in quibus intelligitur que premia sperare debeat qui bene et que supplicia qui male operatur. Est autem lectio, *Scripsit Moyses canticum*[2]. Quarta est lectio de Isaia propheta, *Apprehendent septem mulieres virum unum*[3], ut intelligant Christiani eas virtutes ad quas vocantur in Christo capite suo se percepisse. Quinta lectio est de Ieremia propheta ubi dicens, *Disce ubi sit sapientia ubi virtus ubi prudentia*[4] vocat nos ut ad celestem patriam, in qua omnes iste virtutes certius quam in ista vita reperiuntur, tendamus. Unde sequitur canticum, *Sicut cervus desiderat ad fontes aquarum ita desiderat anima mea ad te deus*[5]. Quare autem tota ebdomada pentecostes genua non flectamus hec ratio est. Alleluia non omittimus, ieiunia repetimus. Sancti spiritus septiformis est gratia, ideo eius adventus septem diebus celebratur. Ieiunia repetuntur ut digniores eius adventu habeamur. Stantes oramus pro gaudio festivitatis. Similiter pro eadem ratione illi qui post baptismum ab episcopo crismate liniuntur septem diebus et crisma et vestem conservare debent.

g. transoriis *O* *h.* in *W* *i.* terciam *L*, *L2*, *W*

---

2. *Deut.* 31.22.
3. *Isa.* 4.1.
4. *Bar.* 3.14.
5. *Ps.* 41.2.

XV. De quatuor temporibus anni

Quatuor temporibus anni, vere, estate, autumpno, hieme singula ieiunia[j] celebramus diebus tribus, de singulis mensibus unum diem dicantes sancte trinitati. Sed quia cotidiana peccata gravant, non sufficit unius diei ieiunium per menses singulos, quos dies ut dixi per quatuor tempora congregamus. Facimus ergo ieiunium quadragesimale ut totum nostrum tempus dicemus deo. Quatuor sunt tempora anni, quatuor partes mundi, quatuor evangelia. Que per denarium numerum observamus cum deo creatori servientes nos in eius servitio per eius gratiam custodimus. Tria enim que sunt in decem significant sanctam trinitatem; septem ea que sunt in homine cuius anima habet rationem, memoriam, intellectum; corpus ex quatuor humoribus constat. Sed redeamus ad ieiunia quatuor temporum in quibus sacri ordines dantur. A dominica die primi mensis qui est apud nos tercius usque ad quartam feriam decimi mensis sunt septimane quadraginta due. Totidem generationes sunt in genealogia Christi. Primum ieiunium et prima ordinatio in vere. Hec pertinent ad Abraham qui fuit tercia etate mundi et ad terciam etatem hominis in qua sanguis hominis incipit calere quia et ab Abraham cepit populus dei augescere et in vere flores incipiunt aperiri. Secunda ordinatio et ieiunium sunt in estate que calida est. Hec pertinent ad iuventutem, quartam etatem hominis que calida est et apta bellis, et ad David qui fuit quarta etate mundi, sub quo populus dei preliis et victoriis crevit. Tercia ordinatio et ieiunium sunt in autumpno quando flores cadunt. Hec pertinent ad senectutem, quintam etatem hominis quando paulatim deficit sanguis, et ad Iechoniam qui fuit quinta etate mundi quando populus dei multum labefactatus est. Quarta ordinatio et ieiunium sunt in hieme quando frigus dominatur. Sic in sexta etate hominis que vocatur senium omnino debilis est homo, et sexta etate mundi quando Christus venit populus dei omnino deficit. Semper autem ab una ordinatione usque aliam sunt xiiii septimane, sed ab illa que est in septimo mense usque ad illam que est in decimo sunt aliquando xiii aliquando xiiii. Similiter ab Abraham usque David sunt generationes xiiii, et a David usque Iechoniam xiiii, a Iechonia usque ad Christum si bis numeretur Iechonias xiiii sunt generationes, si semel xiii. Nunquam sane invenitur quod aliquis apostolicus fecerit ordinationem nisi in Decembri mense, credo, propter proximam nativitatem domini[k]. Primus Simplicius[6] a beato Petro quadragesimus nonus sacravit in Februario mense. Debent ergo hi qui consecrandi sunt deo devovere et ab Abraham fidem, a David humilitatem, a Iechonia patientiam, a Christo virtutes omnes addiscere. Sabbato vero fiunt ordinationes, quia sabbatum sanctificavit deus. Episcopi[l] autem ordinatio differtur in dominicum pro excellentia dominice resurrectionis et episcopalis ordinis. Istis diebus ieiunatur feria quarta quia in eo dies consiliati sunt Iudei Christum crucifigere. Sexta feria quia in ea

j. ieiunia *om. W*   *k.* pro proxima nativitate *W*   *l.* Epistoli *W*

---

6. *LP* 49; 1.249.

crucifixus dominus, sabbato quia ea die iacuit in sepulchro. Leguntur feria quarta due lectiones ut habeat ordinandus noticiam legis et prophecie que quarta etate mundi precipue viguerunt. Sexta feria legitur una ut sciat illa duo adimpleri evangelio quod sexta etate seculi predicatum est. Sabbato sex; quatuor significant quatuor ordines benedicentium [m] deo ad imitationem illorum qui benedicendi sunt ad ordines. De his ordinibus David dicit et Augustinus [7] exponit *Benedicat domus Israel dominum*, hoc est communiter populus Christianus, *Benedicat domus Aaron*, hoc est prelati ecclesie. *Benedicat domus Levi*, hoc est ministri ecclesie. Qui de ceteris nationibus timetis dominum vel adhuc catecumini estis, benedicite dominum. Hos quatuor ordines debet discernere qui [n] ordinandus est et ideo quatuor lectiones leguntur. Quinta legitur de tribus pueris qui in fornacem missi non cessaverunt benedicere dominum, ut ordinandus tali ammonitus exemplo in tribulationibus roboretur. Ideo autem non flectimus genua nec in quadragesima ad orationem que hanc lectionem sequitur, ut discernatur nostra [o] adoratio ab illorum genuflexione quos Nabugodonosor compellebat adorare statuam auream quam fecerat. Sexta est lectio de apostolo, sequente evangelio, ut sciat qui ordinandus est nichil se boni posse perficere sine apostolica et evangelica doctrina. Vocantur vero ista sabbata in xii lectionibus, quia Grece et Latine solebant legi Rome sicut apud Constantinopolim leguntur [p] hodieque.

XVI. De adventu domini

Nunc de adventu domini et de quibusdam aliis dicendum. Constitutor officii constituit quinque dominicis ante natale domini officia in missali, significans per quinque etates mundi Christi adventum fuisse figuratum, vel quod his quinque septimanis expurgare debemus quicquid per quinque sensus deliquimus. In gradali autem et in antiphonario quatuor constituit officia, significans Christi adventum fuisse prefiguratum per quatuor tempora : ante circumcisionem usque Abraham, sub circumcisione usque Moysen, sub lege usque David, sub prophetis deinceps; vel quod corpora nostra que constant ex quatuor elementis ad eius nativitatem suscipiendam castigare debemus. Dimittuntur autem dalmatice et alia solempnia ornamenta ut letius [q] in nativitate domini [r] resumantur. Hinc etiam Gloria in excelsis non cantamus ut in nocte nativitatis qua [s] illud angeli cantaverunt solempnius reincipiamus. Ipsa nocte cantantur misse ex precepto Thelesphori pape [8] quia in ipsa natus est dominus. Similiter et in luce quia exortum est in tenebris lumen quod *illuminat omnem hominem venientem in hunc* [t] *mundum* [9]. Solebat et olim in die

m. benedicium *W* *n*. qui *om. W* *o*. nostra *om. L2* *p*. reguntur *W*
q. levius *W* *r*. domini *om. W* *s*. quia *O* *t*. huc *O*

7. Cf. *Ps*. 134.19 and Aug., *Enarr. in ps*. 134.25 (CCL 40.1956).
8. *LP* 9; 1.129.
9. *Jn*. 1.9.

nativitatis Iohannis Baptiste prima luce missa cantari quia natus est qui fuit lucerna ardens et lucens. Ceteris temporibus ex precepto eiusdem pape[10] cantatur missa vel ad terciam quia in ea ductus est Christus ad crucem[u], vel ad sextam quia in ea crucifixus est, vel ad nonam quia in ea emisit spiritum; nec tamen qui ante vel post pro necessitate vel devotione cantat inprobandus est.

XVII. De natali innocentium[v]

Prisco tempore in natali Innocentium[w] non dicebatur Gloria in excelsis nec alleluia ut animos devotarum feminarum ecclesiasticus cantor immitaretur de quibus scriptum est, *Vox in Rama audita est ploratus et ululatus*[11] et cetera. Sed nunc modernus usus neutrum dimittit, rationabilius iudicans[x] gaudere pro martirum gloria quam flere pro pena. Hic adiciendum est quod Amalarius dicit de repeticionibus que fiunt in cantibus. Repetuntur enim verba in ecclesiasticis cantibus non ociose sed cause magni gaudii, ut *Iubilate deo omnis terra, iubilate deo omnis terra*[12], vel cause devocionis, ut precatus est Moyses in conspectu domini dei sui, precatus est Moyses in conspectu domini dei sui[13], vel cause magni doloris ut illa que tociens repetuntur in offerenda *Vir erat in terra*[14]. Ita enim egrotans sepe conatur verba sua exprimere nec valet.

XVIII. De purificatione sanctae Marie

De purificatione domine sancte Marie nichil sanctus Isidorus in libro de[y] ecclesiasticis officiis dixit, quia eius tempore illa solempnitas constituta non erat. Hanc apud Grecos tempore Iustiniani imperatoris pro mortalitate que in Constantinopoli seviebat accipimus inchoatam statimque mortalitatem cessasse. Vocant eam Greci Ipapanti[z] quia ea die Symeon et Anna Christo in templo obviaverunt. Ipanthee[a] enim Grece obviare dicitur. Post vero multum tempus Sergius[15] papa iussit eam apud Latinos celebrari. Presentamus autem ea die lumina in templo ad imitationem presentationis Christi per ceram significantes eius carnem virgineam, de virgine matre sine coitu editam. Nam et apes sine coitu generatur. Per lumen vero intelligimus divinitatem que ut diximus *illuminat omnem hominem venientem in hunc mundum*[16].

u. est *add. O* *v.* Innocentum *O, L, L2* *w.* innocentum *O, L, L2* *x.* iudi *W*
y. de *om. W* *z.* ὑπαπαντή *a.* ὑπαπαντάω

10. *LP* 9; 1.129.
11. *Mt.* 2.18.
12. *Ps.* 99.2.
13. *Tract for Pentecost XII.*
14. *Job* 1.1.
15. *LP* 86; 1.376.
16. *Jn.* 1.9.

XIX. De missa mortuorum

Missa mortuorum in hoc a ceteris differt quod in ea nec alleluia nec Gloria in excelsis dicitur, quia nulla leticia convenit ubi sunt presentes mortuorum exequie vel ubi celebrantur eorum memorie. Pax non datur quia mors peccati vindicta est et ubi ultio exigitur pax non datur. Prima et anniversaria dies eorum agitur ut quicquid toto vite deliquerunt tempore quod per dies et annos transcursum est eis condonetur. Similiter et tricesima quia mensis constat triginta diebus, vel quia transgrediendo fidem trinitatis et decalogum legis homo peccavit, vel quia sanctos viros Moysen et Aaron triginta diebus defletos legimus. Apud quosdam etiam celebratur dies tercia et septima; tercia propter peccata anime, septima propter peccata corporis. Constat enim homo ex tribus virtutibus in anima, ex quatuor humoribus in corpore.

Hucusque quanta[b] potui brevitate quantumque potui intelligere librum primum Amalarii defloravi, coniungens primo libro quedam capitula secundi et tercii, ut totus primus liber de varietatibus misse totius anni absolveretur. Quare conveniens putavi ut tercium librum Amalarii hic secundum facerem, ut post varietatem officiorum totius anni statim significationes sequerentur[c] usus cotidiani. Tercium autem librum posui quem ipse secundum ut post explanationem ministeriorum diceretur de gradibus et vestibus ministeriorum.

Explicit liber primus abbreviationis Amalarii. Incipiunt capitula secundi[d].

b. quantum *W*   *c.* sequarentur *W*   *d.* libri *add. W*

De oratione dominica
De agnus dei
De ultima benedictione

EXPLICIUNT CAPITULA. INCIPIT LIBER SECUNDUS.

I. DE SITU ECCLESIE

De situ et structura et dedicatione ecclesie abunde plures doctores et nuperrimo tempore Ivo Carnotensis episcopus significationes dixere. Sufficiat igitur hic dicere quod ecclesia est congregatio fidelium. Et ideo per metaforam domus dicitur ecclesia que continet congregationem fidelium. Ipsa dicitur kirica[e] id est dominica casa. Est enim Grece kirius dominus. Quo nomine Angli et cetere illius lingue gentes consuete utuntur. Ipsa est et basilica id est regia. Grece enim basileus, rex Latine. In ea masculi seorsum, femine stant seorsum, et ad cautelam castitatis et observantiam antique legis femine stare debent ad aquilonem significantes quia per feminam venit malum super filios hominum. Unde dicitur *Ab aquilone pandetur malum super omnes habitatores terre*[17]. Itemque ad conversos, *Eum qui ab aquilone est longe faciam a vobis*[18]. At contra masculi stare debent ad austrum significantes se illius sequaces esse et per illum redemptos, *qui convertit captivitatem nostram sicut torrens in austro*[19]. Propter hanc confusionem quia prevaricatio per feminam venit, velat caput suum cum stat in ecclesia ex precepto Lini pape per beatum Petrum apostolum[20].

II. DE SIGNIS

In veteri lege preceptum est fieri tubas[f] argenteas quibus sacerdotes convocarent populum. Tuba significat predicationem sacerdotis, que debet esse clara et nitida ut convocet unanimes habitare in domo domini. In novo autem testamento fiunt vasa ex ere que congregant populum. Es quod est sonorius et durabilius argento significat predicationem novi testamenti quod *in omnem terram exivit*[21]. Nam in veteri *notus in Iudea deus tantum*[22]. Illud finem accepit in novo, istud durabit perpetuo. Vas ergo significat predicatores, plectrum ferreum linguam eorum que pro merito peccata delinquentium tundit. Vinculum quod tenet plectrum discretionem significat, sine qua bonus doctor nunquam predicat. Funis qui ligno coniungitur sacram scripturam que maxime in laude crucis versatur designat. Scriptura enim mentem et linguam

e. kiricus *W* *f*. tubulas *W*

17. *Jer*. 1.14.
18. *Joel* 2.20.
19. *Ps*. 125.4.
20. *LP* 2; 1.121.
21. *Ps*. 18.5.
22. *Ps*. 75.2.

predicatoris movet ut sonent et laudent Christum[g] qui nos redemit per lignum.

III. De cantoribus

Chorus est, ut Isidorus ait, multitudo in sacris collecta dictus, quod[h] initio in modum corone cantores stabant[23]. In choro diversitas vocum concorditer sonat. Ammonet ergo chorus cantorum ut diversi auditores una fide, una morum congruentia deo deserviant. Chori primus auctor David. Eius cantores, sicut in novissimo psalmo dicit, *Laudabant dominum in tuba, psalterio, cithara, timpano, choro, cordis, organo, cimbalis*[24]. Nichil horum nostri cantores corporaliter faciunt sed ipsi spiritualiter sunt omnia. Ipsi tuba propter claritatem predicationis. Ipsi psalterium propter observationem decalogi, habet enim psalterium decem cordas. Ipsi cithara propter mortificationem viciorum quia corde que sonant in cithara ex mortuo fiunt animali, que quanto plus fuerint tense sonant acutius quia sancti in maioribus tribulationibus deum laudant studiosus. Ipsi timpanum pro eadem re. In timpano quippe corium siccum resonat. Ipsi chorus pro concordia. Ipsi corde propter pressuras. Ipsi organum pro communione[i] omnium virtutum. Organum siquidem est commune omnium instrumentorum nomen et abusive presumitur in solis his que follibus urgentur. Ipsi cimbala invicem sibi in caritate respondentia. Hec non ex nobis, sed ex beati Augustini in extremum psalmum expositione diximus[25].

Cantores antiqui bisso vestiebantur, nostri lino. Bissus et linum viridia ex terra oriuntur, sed multis pressuris ad candorem perducuntur. Sic oportet ut caro nostra multis abstinentiarum laboribus ad nitorem castitatis perveniat. Linee ergo vestes et albe castitatem quam[j] debent habere cantores significant, ut ostendatur exterius quales dei laudatores debent esse interius.

IIII. De introitu

Celestinus papa constituit ut antiphonatim canerentur psalmi David in missa, quia ipse primus cantor fuit. Antea enim lectio apostoli erat principium misse. Ingreditur episcopus ad missam et precedunt eum tres ordines, diaconi, subiaconi, acoliti, ceroferarii, et timiama (*sic*) in medio. Numerus eorum est vel septem vel quinque vel tres vel unus. Diaconus ferens evangelium iuxta episcopum est. Ingreditur episcopus ad Gloria patri. Stat inclinatus usque post confessionem. Erectus dat pacem his qui sunt a dextris et sinistris et his qui retro. Deinde vadit ad altare, et osculatur altare et evangelium, idemque faciunt in latere ministri eius. Evangelium autem non aufertur ab altari donec

g. Christi *O*   *h.* in *add. L, L2, W*   *i.* communitione *W*   *j.* qua *L*

---

23. Cf. Isid. *Orig.* 6.19.5 (PL 82.252).
24. *Ps.* 150.3-5.
25. Cf. Aug., *Enarr. in ps.* 150.5-8 (CCL 40.2195-6).

lecturus tollat. Indeque transit ad dexteram altaris. Diaconorum maior pars stat a dextris, alia a sinistris. Episcopus rite non sedet usque post primam orationem. Interim stant acoliti et tenent luminaria usque Kyrrieleison.

Horum omnium significationem breviter dicemus. Episcopus ingrediens ad missam significat Christum ad passionem venientem in mundum. Precesserunt eum tres ordines, quos ipse dixit se misisse et missurum esse : *Ecce ego inquid mitto ad vos prophetas, sapientes et scribas*[26]. Diaconi sunt in loco prophetarum, qui ex evangelio annuntiant vitam futuram. Subdiaconi in loco sapientum, qui sapienter disponunt vasa domini. Acoliti ceroferarii in loco scribarum, qui per sanctas scripturas accendunt corda fidelium ad dei amorem. Inter hos portatur timiama, quia omnes isti bonus odor Christi sunt sive in vita sive in morte. Hi precesserunt Christum quia omnes eum venturum prophetaverunt. Sed et numerus ministrorum significat scripturas novi et veteris testamenti que famulantur adventui Christi vel in spe vel in re; quasque semper episcopus debet in promptu habere.

Si septem sunt, designant quod tribus modis intelligitur utrumque testamentum, historice, allegorice, moraliter. Vetus historice, sicut genesis. Allegorice, sicut prophete. Moraliter ut[k] libri Salomonis. Item novum historice, sicut Actus apostolorum. Allegorice, sicut Apocalipsis. Moraliter, sicut epistole Pauli. Ecce sex ministri. Septimus est diaconus evangelium portans quique proximus est episcopo[l], quia familiare est evangelium Christo et familiare debet esse episcopo. Quinque ministri designant quod duo sunt que docet[m] utrumque testamentum, dilectio dei et dilectio proximi. Ecce quatuor ministri; quintus est evangelium quod quia dignius[n] est in medio est.

Tres ministri designant quod ipse dominus divisit legem veterem in tria dicens, *Que scripta sunt in lege et prophetis et psalmis de me*[27]. Item novum testamentum divisit in trinitatis credulitatem, dicens *Euntes docete omnes gentes baptizantes eos in nomine patris et filii et spiritus sancti*[28].

Unus minister significat quod utrumque testamentum unum deum insinuat : vetus, ut *Audi Israel dominus deus tuus deus unus est*[29]; novum, ut *Hec est vita eterna ut cognoscant te et quem misisti Jhesum Christum solum verum deum*[30].

His comitibus ingreditur episcopus ad Gloria patri et Christus in mundum veniens gloriam que soli patri in Iudea reddebatur toto trinitati predicari fecit. Stat inclinatus ad confessionem et Christus humiliavit se in carne et dixit patri, *Confiteor tibi pater celi et terre*[31]. Dat pacem a dextris et sinistris

k. sicut *L, L2, W* *l.* Christo *O, L, L2* *m.* docent *O, L, L2* *n.* dignus *O*

26. *Mt.* 23.34.
27. *Lk.* 24.44.
28. *Mt.* 28.19.
29. *Dt.* 6.4.
30. *Jn.* 17.3.
31. *Mt.* 11.25.

quia Christus ad amicitiam suam admisit credentes tam de sinagoga quam de gentibus. Dat et his qui retro sunt, quia Christus dicit, *Pacem meam do vobis, pacem relinquo vobis*[32] — presentibus do, absentibus adhuc non credentibus relinquo. Idem significat quod osculatur altare et evangelium. Altare designat gentem Iudeam, que habebat altare dei. Huic pacem optulit, cum dixit, *Non sum missus nisi ad oves que perierunt domus Israel*[33]. Evangelium significat gentes que illud gratanter susceperunt. His osculum misit cum dixit, *Euntes docete omnes gentes*[34]. Idem faciunt ministri eius non a fronte sed latere, quia Christus potestate predicavit evangelium et miracula fecit, ministri autem eius non ita. Necessitate enim ut apostolus dicit evangelizant et gratia non potestate, quasi non fronte sed a latere, miracula faciunt. Inde ad episcopum redeunt quia quicquid sancti boni faciunt, ad Christum referunt. Evangelium remanet in altari donec lecturus tollat, quia verbum dei permansit apud Iudeos, donec predicatum est in gentibus. Transit ad dextram altaris quia Christus a Iudeis transivit ad gentes. Minor pars ministrorum stat a sinistris, maior a dextris, quia minus crediderunt in Christum de Iudeis quam de gentibus, vel quia minoris dignitatis sunt que promittuntur in veteri testamento, quam que in novo. Ceroferarii interius stant, quia doctor in manibus doctrinam debet habere, ut magis opere quam verbis predicet. Episcopus non sedet donec compleat orationem, quia donec Christus orasset post cenam pro amicis et in cruce pro inimicis, non sedit ad dexteram patris.

V. De kyrie[o]

Post hec dicuntur supplicationes kyrieleison, ter ad sanctam trinitatem, orantque cantores pro se et pro sacerdote ut misereatur eis deus et indulgeat omnia peccata cogitationis, locutionis, operis, quatinus ipsi digni sint ministri ipseque dignus vicarius Christi. Que supplicationes etiam dicuntur ad oras ante orationem dominicam quatinus sancta trinitas emundet nos ad illa digne suscipienda que oratio complectitur dominica. Tunc et cerei deponuntur quia quandocumque vel pro nostris vel pro aliorum peccatis oramus; ita si qua bona vel per dei gratiam vel per nostram industriam fecimus, contempnere et humiliare debemus quasi nunquam ea fecissemus. Parvi pendere ergo et quasi deponere bona nostra debemus maxime in oratione ut nos exaltet qui *superbis resistit humilibus autem dat gratiam*[35]. Dicit sane Amalarius quod non minus quam tria debent esse candelabra quia nichil boni habent homines nisi per Christi gratiam qui lumen est verum, vel per imitationem sanctorum patrum utriusque testamenti de quibus dicitur in

o. kirrieleison *L*; kirieleison *W*

---

32. *Jn*. 14.27.
33. *Mt*. 15.24.
34. *Mt*. 28.19.
35. *Jas*. 4.6.

propheta, *Isti sunt due olive et due candelabra*[36]. Candelabrum ergo medium significat Christum, a quo alia illuminantur. Nec excedere debent numerum septenarium, quia septiformi spiritu illuminatur omnis ecclesia. Disponuntur autem cerei lineatim[p]; quia licet diversa sint munera gratiarum, unus tamen est spiritus largitor eorum.

VI. De gloria in excelsis deo

Quia dictum est quod per pacem quam episcopus dat significatur pax illa quam Christus resurgens a mortuis annuntiavit iuxta apostolum, *his qui prope et his qui longe*[37], sequitur ut intentionem ascensionis significanter exprimat. Quod tunc facit quando versus ad orientem dicit Gloria in excelsis deo, designans eum qui ascendit super celos celorum ad orientem. Magna enim tunc gloria fuit in celis quando ipse[q] ascendit. Nam et locus in quo angeli illum cecinerunt cantum ad orientem est non longe[r] a Bethleem. Constituit autem Thelesforus papa nonus ut hic hymnus cantaretur ad missam, et Simmachus xlv^{tus} ut omni die dominico et nataliciis martirum diceretur precepit.

VII. De prima oratione

Nec minus oratio illa quam consequenter sacerdos dicit designat benedictionem qua dominus ascensurus in celum benedixit discipulis suis. Ille enim pro potestate benedixit, iste pro humana conditione suppliciter[s] orat. Utraque tamen et benedictio et oratio pro hominum salute fuerunt et fiunt. Hinc est quod sacerdos orientem spectat, non quod ibi magis deum putet esse quam in ceteris mundi partibus, sed quod ab eo speret opem, qui ascendit ad orientem, idemque omnes fideles versus orientem orantes[38]. Vertitur autem sacerdos ad populum quando dicit Dominus vobiscum vel Pax vobis, ut excitet animos eorum secum ad deum. Ante prefationem solummodo non vertitur, quia inhonestum esset ut tergum veteret ad sacra que iam in altari sunt posita.

VIII. De sessione episcopi[t]

Post orationem ascendit episcopus ad sedem suam et post benedictionem ascendit Christus ad celum. Sedent presbiteri et ordines ceteri in suis sedibus, quia sicut dicit apostolus, *Ascendens in altum Christus*, *alios dedit evangelistas, alios prophetas*[39], et ordines ceteros quibus commisit ecclesiam. Quod quidam

p. liniatim *O* *q.* ipse *om. W* *r.* est *add. O* *s.* suspliciter *O* *t. caption lacking; space left for it L2*

36. *Apoc.* 11.4.
37. *Eph.* 2.17.
38. Cf. Aug., *De serm. Dom. in monte* 2.5.18 (CCL 35.108).
39. *Eph.* 4.8,11.

ascendunt cum episcopo, hoc est quod Christus ait, *Volo ut ubi ego sum ibi sit et minister meus*[40]. Quidam sedent quia pars membrorum Christi iam cum eo requiescit. Quidam stant quia adhuc quidam in hac carne laborant. Sedet ipse superius quia nulla sanctitas[u] hominum potest Christo comparari. Quamquam et superior sedes nomini conveniat episcopi[v] qui superintendens interpretatur luiturus graviter si vertit[w] ad pompam seculi quod ei conceditur pro dignitate officii. Hic finiuntur significationes introitus ut dicit Amalarius.

IX. De lectione et responsorio et alleluia et tractu

Lectio sequitur et responsorium. Hec significant duo lectionem legis et prophetarum que omni sabbato legebantur apud Iudeos sicut actus apostolorum testantur. Ideo interim sedemus sicut Iudeis sedere mos erat, quod in evangelio comprobatur ubi dicitur dominum surrexisse in sabbato, in sinagoga ut legeret[41]. Lectio significat legem, cantus prophetiam; que ideo post legem prolata est ut qui ad legem audiendam obsurduerant illo cantu excitarentur. Item lectio significat vetus testamentum quod non multum clare auditum est dum tantum *in iudea notus deus*[42]. Responsorium designat novum testamentum, *cuius sonus exivit in omnem terram*[43]. Sicut cantus dulcior est auditu quam lectio, ita evangelium quod promittit vitam eternam dulcius est lege que promittit felicitatem caducam. Item hoc interest inter lectionem et cantum quod est inter elementa artium et ipsas artes. Elementa grammatice sunt littere, elementa geometrie et arithmetrice sunt puncti[x] et linee, elementa dialectice et medicine sunt isagoge. Similiter de ceteris. Sic etiam per vetus testamentum religiosi[y] animi eruditur infantia; ut ad clarionem evangelii tubam paulatim assurgat. Quod ideo responsorium dicitur, quia respondet et consonat veteri legi, ut impleat spiritualiter quod illa carnaliter prefigurabat. Habet et versum, quia omnis bonus predicator postquam aliis predicaverit ad mentem suam convertitur, ne cum aliis[z] predicat ipse reprobus inveniatur[44]. In lectione ergo discimus, in responsorio aliis predicamus, in versu ad nos versi, nos ipsos castigamus. Dicit autem Ysidorus quod responsorium Itali tradiderunt[45] quod ideo ita vocatur quia uno desinente alter respondet.

Responsorium cui respondetur significat vitam activam que multos cooperatores habet, sicut et columba[a] que gregatim gemit. Tractus cui nullus respondet designat vitam contemplativam, que paucos sectatores habet, sicut et

u. sanitas *W* *v*. episcopum *W* *w*. verterit *W* *x*. puncta *W* *y*. regiosi *L2* *z*. predicaverit ... aliis *om*. *W* *a*. columbam *O*

40. *Jn*. 12.26.
41. *Lk*. 4.16.
42. *Ps*. 75.2.
43. *Ps*. 19.5.
44. Cf. *I Cor*. 9.27.
45. Isid. *Orig*. 6.19.8 (PL 82.252).

turtur solivagus gemit. Hec autem vita quia vel sua et aliena peccata deflet vel spe future leticie gaudet, ideo aliqui tractus lamentantur ut *De profundis*[46], vel letantur, ut *Iubilate deo*[47]. Alleluia vero significat gaudium future vite non in spe sed in re. Distat inter alleluia et tractum quod tractus aliquando de leticia, aliquando de tristicia loquitur, alleluia semper leticiam sonat. Pulcherrimus ergo ordo, ut qui in lectione didicimus, in responsorio docuimus, in versu teneamus disciplinam, in alleluia pro talibus studiis perpetuam habeamus leticiam. Quod ideo repetitur, quia duplex leticia erit ibi anime et corporis.

X. De casulis diaconorum et subdiaconorum et tabulis et sequentia

Subdiaconus et diaconus lecturi exuunt se in quadragesima et adventu casulis, subdiaconus omnino, alter super humeros, significantes predicatorem debere exui negotiis ·secularibus, et vel nichil vel parum debere involvi mundi impedimentis.

Cantores antiquo more tenebant osseas tabulas ad nullam necessitatem, set ut Beda in tractatu Hesdre dicit ad significationem, per manus opera, per osseas tabulas bonorum[b] figuratur[c] perpetuitas[48]. Tenent ergo cantores tabulas, ut ammoneantur[d] non solum voce canere sed etiam sensum cantus voce explere.

Cantus quem vocant sequentiam, quem sine ullis verbis quondam ubique, nunc in aliquibus ecclesiis post alleluia, solent canere, illam laudem figurat qua in futura vita sancti deum laudabunt, magis conscientie puritate quam sono articulato. Hic finitur secunda divisio vel sicut Amalarius dicit[49] periocha significationum misse.

XI. De evangelio

Diaconus sumit ab altari evangelium, data sibi ab episcopo benedictione. Mittit thimiama in turibulum. Precedunt eum in pulpitum duo cerei et thimiamaterium. Ex precepto Anastasii pape non sedetur ad evangelium sed statur inclinato capite propter reverentiam verborum vel gestorum dei. Populus quod habebat in manibus seu in capite deponit et signat sibi frontem. Evangelio lecto, extinguuntur cerei.

Altare populum Iudeorum ut dixi significat, in quo erat dei veri altare. Ab hoc evangeliste sumpserunt verbum dei, et tulerunt ad gentes cum dixerunt, *Vobis oportebat primum loqui verbum dei sed quia repellitis illud,*

b. operum *add. L2* *c.* fuguratur *O*, *L*, *L2* *d.* ammoveantur *O*

46. *Ps.* 129.1.
47. *Ps.* 99.2.
48. Bede, *In Esdram* 1.4 (PL 91.838).
49. *LO* 3.16.3.

ecce convertimur ad gentes[50]. Episcopus vice Christi dat evangeliste benedictionem ut constanter predicet. Hoc[e] Christum super apostolos fecisse, nulli dubium. Turibulum significat corpus Christi, ex quo per ignem passionis salutifer odor credentibus emanavit. In hoc diaconus mittit thimiama quia predicatores et fide catholica et recta vita et sacra facundia evangelium Christi quodammodo condiunt. Duo cerei precedentes eum sunt lex et prophetia que precesserunt evangelium. Thimiamaterium est bonus odor Christi, qui ut ait apostolus, *aliis est odor vite in vitam, aliis odor mortis in mortem*[51]. Quod diaconus et ceteri lectores et cantores ascendunt in pulpitum, ex veteri lege sumptum est. Fecit enim Salomon basim eneam et Hesdras gradum ligneum super que stantes populo loquerentur vel legerent. Sive ergo basis sive pulpitum sive gradus vocetur idem est. Sive vero fiat eneum, sicut a Salomone, sive ligneum sicut ab Esdra sive saxeum sicut a nobis, idem significat, id est credulitatem[f] Christi super quam omnis predicator inniti debet. Enea propter perpetuitatem, lignea propter crucem, saxea propter soliditatem, *petra enim erat Christus*[52]. Predicantibus evangelistis populus gentilis ad reverentiam assurexit et statim a se proiecit, quicquid perversum erat quod gravabat opera quasi manus, vel quod pompaticum gerebat in mente sicut thiaram in capite. Quin et frontes signo munierunt. In fronte signum verecundie est. *Est autem crux Christi verecundia Iudeis et scandalum*[53]. De hoc ergo quod illis est verecundia et quod est nobis gloria, credentes signant frontes suas in quibus, ut dixi, est sedes pudoris, dicentes[g] *Nobis absit gloriari, nisi in cruce domini nostri Ihesu Christi*[54]. Lecto evangelio, extinguuntur[h] cerei, quia finita predicatione evangelii, lex et prophetia cessaverunt. Tercia divisio misse secundum Amalarium desinit.

XII. De offertorio

Quarta incipit ab eo ubi post evangelium sacerdos salutat populum, et finitur ibi ubi post secretam excelsa voce dicit Per omnia secula seculorum. Offert populus panem et vinum. Interim expandit diaconus super altare sindonem, quam corporalem vocamus, et cantores cantant in choro offerendam. Lavat sacerdos manus, et revertitur ad altare. Mittit diaconus in calice vinum, et mittit eum in medio altaris, et sudarium in dextra parte. Sacerdos thurificat, et post orationem ad deum vertit se ad populum, rogans pro se orari. Utrumque enim convenit sacerdoti, ut et dei auxilio et populi orationibus mundetur. Postea secrete incipit orationem, quam secretam excelse finiens salutat populum et monet ut sursum corda habeant ad deum.

e. ergo *add. W* *f*. crudelitatem *O* *g*. dicentis *W* *h*. nisi ... extinguuntur *om. W*

50. *Acts* 13.46.
51. *II Cor.* 2.16.
52. *I Cor.* 10.4.
53. *I Cor.* 1.23.
54. *Gal.* 16.14.

Hec partim allegorice, partim moraliter exponit Amalarius. Allegorice ita. Sacerdos salutans populum intelligitur Christus descendens de monte oliveti, et ad passionem pergens. Qui populum sibi[i] occurentem salutasse non dubitatur, pro more[j] Iudeorum, quem ipsi populo frequentissimum esse, Augustinus in expositione psalmi *Sepe expugnaverunt me* protestatur[55]. Oblationes populi designant laudes quas ille[k] populus Christo optulit. Lavat manus sacerdos, quia sicut Beda dicit in expositione tabernaculi, Constat Christum aqua lavacri priusquam ad altare oblaturus intraret esse lotum, quia priusquam thimiama sui sacrosancti corporis propter salutem nostram incenderet in ara crucis pro nostro amore etiam lacrimas fudit in resuscitatione Lazari[56], et in agonia sudorem sanguinis. Redit ad altare episcopus, et Christus in Ierusalem ivit, ubi erat altare dei, ut se ipsum sacrificaret deo patri. Ante quod factum et patri preces fudit, et hominibus memoriam suam commendavit. Secrete deinde peregit misterium passionis, quia homines et demones et nescio an[l] angeli passionem quidem videbant, sed ad quantum bonum perventura esset ignorabant. Sed hoc misterium duraturum esse per omnia secula seculorum clarificavit in resurrectione sua, ammonens in ascensione sua ut sursum corda haberent discipuli, quo eum ascendere videbant.

Moraliter ita. Sacerdos salutans populum ammonet ut non solum dignas oblationes deo, sed et se ipsos sacrificent in *odorem suavitatis*[57]. Hoc et cantores laborant adeo impetrare, cantantes interim dum ipsi offerunt. Hoc et significat diaconus, expandens interim sindonem super altare, ut sicut lintheum illud castigatum est ab omni humore, ita sit mens offerentium pura ab omni carnis delectatione. Oblatio populi est significativa. Sicut enim panis ex multis granis, et vinum ex multis[m] acinis confit, ita catholica ecclesia, que verum deo sacrificium offert, ex multis gentibus, gradibus, conditionibus, etatibus congregatur[58]. Suscipiunt oblationem populi altaris ministri, ut significent unam sibi et concordem mentem esse cum populo in Christi sacrificio. Cur autem vino aqua misceatur, plures rationes attulit beatus Cyprianus[59], sed est maior rationibus cunctis evangelica auctoritas quia de latere Christi fluxit sanguis et aqua. Ablutio manuum episcopi ostendit exterius, quantum se mundare debeat interius. In medio altaris calix ponitur, quia precipua debet esse observantia dominice passionis in ecclesia, que verum dei altare est. Ideoque a dextris sudarium episcopi ponitur, ut maxima sit ei cura quicquid ab eo luxus mundani exsudat per confessionem extergere. Incensum adolet super sacrificium, ut non solum peccata per confessionem abluere aut extergere, sed etiam virtutibus studeat flagrare[n]. Post preces ad

i. sibi *om. W* *j.* morte *O* *k.* ipse *W* *l.* an *om. W* *m.* granis ... multis *om. W* *n.* fragrare *W*

55. Cf. AUG., *Enarr. in Ps.* 128.13 (CCL 40.1888).
56. BEDE, *De tabern. et vasis eius* 3.14 (PL 91.497).
57. *Phil.* 4.18.
58. Cf. CYP. *Ep.* 63.13 (CSEL 3/2.711).
59. *Ibid.*

deum et amonitionem pro se orandi ad populum, secrete facit orationem, quia sui tantummodo est officii sacrificium consecrare, populi vero est consecrationi favere. Cuius ut favor comprobetur, in fine orationis vocem exaltat, et deo respondente rogat ut sursum ad deum cor habeat.

XIII. De prefatione

Quinta est divisio misse que incipit ad ymno quem nos prefationem vocamus, usque ad finem imni quem Sanctus dicimus. Hec nobis cenam domini allegorice introducit. Dominus in cenaculum cum discipulis ascendit, et sacerdos ad ascensionem cordis suos invitat dicens, Sursum corda. Altare in hoc loco significat mensam, in qua dominus convivabatur. Calix hic calicem illum, panis panem, sindonis lintheum quo precinctus est, sudarium laborem quem habebat humanitas de perfidia Jude. Quod secundum Romanam consuetudinem diaconi et presbiteri stant retro episcopum, et subdiaconi ante faciem eius, ipse vero in medio, hoc est quod Christus in eadem cena ait, *Qui maior est in vobis*, *fiat sicut iunior*[o], *et qui precessor est*, *sicut ministrator*[p], et *ego in medio vestrum sum*, *sicut qui ministrat*[60]. Necnon et illud, quod qui maiori[q] dignitate apud eum creverant ut apostoli retro eum fuerunt, quia relicto eo fugerunt. Qui autem minoris dignitatis quia occulti discipuli, tempore passionis ante eum fuerunt, quia Ioseph ab Arimathia et Nichodemus eum sepelierunt. Omnes autem stant inclinati usque post orationem dominicam dicatur Libera nos a malo, quia omnes timore sunt deiecti, quousque resurrectio domini eos a timoris malo liberaret.

Moraliter autem altare significat ipsius sacerdotis animum, in quo debet offerre deo hostiam vivam, sanctam deo placentem. Sindonis mundiciam castitatis eius. Sudarium laborem sanctorum angelorum quem pro nobis habent, quos et ibi adesse non dubium est. Nam et sacerdos, ut ostendat quanta sit reverentia presentis sacrificii, angelorum et hominum ordines invitat. Et quidem per quinque ordines angelicos, scilicet angelos, dominationes, potestates, virtutes, seraphin, quos nominat, quatuor residuos subinnuit. Per angelos enim intelligimus archangelos, per dominationes principatus, per seraphin cherubin, quia illis intelligentia nominum sunt affines; per celos intelligimus thronos, quia celi dicti sunt scabellum pedum dei. Decimus inde hominum ordo introducitur, cum dicitur Cum quibus et nostras voces ut admitti iubeas deprecamur. Idemque significat himnus sequens, qui est cantus angelorum, usque ad[r] Osanna in excelsis. Reliquum cantavit Iudeorum populus in laudem domini. Hunc autem himnum precepit Sixtus[s][61] papa cantari. Inclinatio ministrorum designat reverentiam, statio maiorum retro humilitatem.

o. minor *W* *p*. et qui ... ministrator *om*. *W* *q*. *corr*. *O* *r*. ad *om*. *O*
s. Christus *W*

60. *Lk*. 22.26-27.
61. *LP* 8; 1.128.

XIV. DE PRIMA PARTE CANONIS

Post hec incipiunt misteria, que canonem vocamus. Prima pars est a Te igitur usque Hanc igitur oblationem. In hac facit sacerdos tres orationes, pro universali ecclesia, pro spiritualibus fratribus, pro choro sacerdotum, commemorans quod post cenam Christus ante traditionem suam ter oravit ad patrem. In his orationibus designat altare ipsum dominum qui tradebatur, sindonis puritatem ipsius qui innocenter patiebatur, sudarium laborem de quo in Luca scriptum est, *Et factus in agonia prolixius orabat, et factus est sudor eius sicut gutte sanguinis decurrentis in terram*[62].

Ideo autem in silentio fit consecratio, quia sicut beatus Cyprianus dicit, modesta et verecunda debet esse Christiani oratio, que non in clamore sed in puritate cordis se sciat exaudiri[63]. Quod sacerdos dicit Hec dona, ad panem refert Amalarius[64], Hec munera ad calicem, Hec sancta sacrificia ad utrumque. De numero autem signaculorum[t] nullam certam traditionem se accepisse dicit. Sed si semel signatur, significat quia semel passus est dominus[u]. Si bis[v], pro duabus populis. Si ter, in nomine sancte trinitatis. Si quinquies, propter quinque Christi vulnera.

XV. DE SECUNDA[w]

Altera pars canonis est ab Hanc igitur[x] oblationes usque Unde et nos memores domine. Hec introducit nobis memoriam oblationis qua Christus se ipsum sponte persecutoribus optulit, postquam ad patrem oraverat. In hac fit panis vinumque corpus et sanguis domini per verba eiusdem. Offert ergo sacerdos corpus et sanguinem domini in sacrificium patri, sicut ipse se optulit dicens, *Calicem quem dedit michi pater non bibam illum*[65]. In hac oratione significat sacerdos ipsum Christum, qui carnem et sanguinem suum tradidit persecutoribus. Altare constantiam divinitatis, sindonis nitorem innocentie, sudarium laborem humanitatis.

XVI. DE TERTIA[y]

Tercia pars canonis est ab Unde et nos domine usque Nobis quoque peccatoribus. Hec introducit nobis memoriam crucifixionis Christi, unde et eam nominat primo sacerdos dicens, Unde et memores domine nos servi tui sed et plebs tua sancta eiusdem Christi filii dei[z] domini[a] nostri tam beate passionis. Nam quod adorande nativitatis in nostris codicibus habetur, non

t. singulorum *W* *u*. Christus *L2* *v*. quia *add. W* *w*. *No caption W*
x. igitur *om. L2* *y*. DE SECUNDA PARTE *W* (SECUNDA *rubbed out*). *z*. tui *W*
a. dei *add. W*

62. *Lk*. 22.43-44.
63. Cf. CYP., *Liber de oratione domin.* 4 (CSEL 3/1.268-9).
64. *LO* 3.23.16.
65. *Jn*. 18.11.

est autenticum. In ista parte sacerdos se ante altare inclinans, significat Christum in ara crucis inclinato capite commendantem deo patri spiritum, sicut sacerdos inclinatus commendat deo patri sacrificium. Merito in hac parte commemoratio fit in Christo quiescentium pro quibus ipse mortuus est. Quod in hac parte dicitur Hostiam puram, panem intelligit Amalarius; Hostiam sanctam, vinum; Hostiam immaculatam, utrumque. De tuis donis ac datis ita intelligit, dona sunt eterna in re, data in temporali opere. Hic intelligitur altare crux. Cetera ut supra.

XVII. De quarta[b]

Quarta pars canonis est ab Nobis quoque usque Per omnia secula seculorum. In hac sacerdos extollit vocem parumper dicens Nobis quoque peccatoribus, et tundens pectus suum. Subdiaconi eriguntur et stant usque Per omnia secula seculorum, et tunc recedunt ceteris interim retro sacerdotem inclinatis. Diaconus qui in superiori parte ad inclinationem sacerdotis manus laverat, ut ostenderet omnium criminum ablutionem in Christi morte fuisse, hic, inquam, diaconus cooperit calicem sindone, ut dicit Amalarius[66], ab aure ad aurem, quia calices antiqui ansas habebant, et forsitan adhuc alicubi habent. Sacerdos elevat oblatam, et deponit. Subdiaconi satagunt circa corpus domini cum patenis.

Hec ita exponuntur allegorice. Altare crucem presentat. Sindonis, sindonem qua involutus[c] est dominus; sudarium, sudarium quod fuit super caput eius. Panis et calix et sunt et significant corpus et sanguinem eius. Sacerdos qui tundit pectus et exaltat vocem significat eos qui in passione domini tundebant pectora, et exaltabant vocem dicentes, *Vere filius dei erat iste*[67]. Subdiaconi qui eriguntur et stant significant notos eius et mulieres que a longe stabant. Hi recedunt usque post septem peticiones dominice orationis, et tunc redeunt cum patenis circa corpus domini, et mulieres recesserunt usque ad[d] sabbatum, et tunc redierunt ad corpus domini requirendum. Ceteri interim inclinati significant apostolos timore inclines et abditos. Diaconus representat[e] nobis Ioseph ab arimathia qui similiter sicut apostoli occultus erat propter metum Iudeorum, sed tempore passionis audaciter involvit corpus domini sindone[68]. Sacerdos designat Nichodemum, qui cum Ioseph deposuit corpus domini de cruce.

Moraliter ita. Sacerdos more penitentium elevat vocem sicut debet omnis penitens facere, in luctu et gemitu. Altare significat cor penitentium, quia sacrificium est deo spiritus contribulatus, cor contritum[69]. Sindonis est ipsa castigatio corporis. Ille autem in sindone munda involvit Ihesum, qui eum

b. Canonis de quarta parte *W* *c.* immolatus *ud vid. L2* *d.* in *W* *e.* representet *O*

66. *LO* 3.26.9.
67. *Mt.* 27.54.
68. *Lk.* 23.53.
69. Cf. *Ps.* 50.19.

pura mente susceperit. Sudarium est ipsa intentio penitentie. Inclinati dignioris gradus viri significant sanctos doctores, qui quanto altius misterium passionis Christi intelligunt, tanto humilius venerantur. Subdiaconi peccatores sed penitentes, qui non erubescunt in faciem sacerdotum peccata sua confiteri, et ultro ab ecclesia recedere, donec per penitentiam emendatiores redeant.

XVIII. De oratione dominica

His actis dicitur dominica oratio excelse, quia communiter ad omnes pertinet Christianos, et ideo communi favore debet dici. Neque enim dicitur Pater meus, qui es in celis, aut Libera me a malo, sed communiter Pater noster et Libera nos. Usque ad hanc septimam petitionem qua dicit sacerdos Libera nos a malo, inclinati sunt ministri, sed tunc eriguntur; quia usque post sabbatum discipuli fuerunt in timore, sed tunc propter resurrectionis gaudium liberati sunt a malo timoris. In ista parte canonis extrema sunt tres articuli significant triduanam sepulturam, in qua discipuli domini fuerunt timore inclines. Patena quam acolitus dat subdiacono, subdiaconus diacono, diaconus sacerdoti, significat[f] latitudinem amoris et gaudii quod habuerunt sancte mulieres in resurrectione domini; que patena sicut ab inferioribus gradibus datur superioribus, ita resurrectio domini ab infirmiori sexu annuntiata est apostolis.

XIX. De agno[g] dei

Post hec dicit sacerdos Pax vobis, et veniunt subdiaconi cum patenis, et in eis ponuntur oblate. Postquam enim Christus salutatione sua letificavit corda discipulorum, vota feminarum completa sunt percepto gaudio resurrectionis. Dividitur oblata in tres partes, quia trifarie dicitur corpus domini: unum quod ipse vexit in celum de virgine sumptum; alterum quod adhuc laborat in terris; tercium quod iam in pace quiescit. Una portiuncula facit crucem sacerdos super quatuor latera calicis ut ostendat quatuor climata mundi per crucem in unitate[h] fidei congregata. Eadem particula mittitur in calicem ut monstretur quod sanguis Christi pro nostra fusus anima et caro eius pro nostro corpore mortua redierunt in unam substantiam in resurrectione. Inde est quod tunc sacerdos dicit Pax domini sit semper vobiscum, quia hanc vocem Christus suis exhibuit discipulis primam resurgens. Hanc significat populus, in mutua blande et caste concurrens oscula.

Ex precepto Sergii pape[70] dicunt cantores ter Agnus dei, ut qui tercia die resurgens tulit peccata mundi, tollat peccata populi. Sequitur antiphona quam communionem vocamus, que ipso nomine denuntiat vinculum pacis, ius fraternitatis. Horum tipum gerebant illi duo, qui Emaus euntes optabant

f. figurat *L* *g.* Agnus *O*, *L*, *L2* *h.* unitatem *W*

70. *LP* 86; 1.376.

agnum dei tercia die resurgere, et peccata mundi tollere. At vero cognito domino redeuntes communicaverunt fratribus que viderant, et ipsi vicissim ab eis communionem maioris acceperunt scientie.

Pars corporis domini, que in sepulchro quod nos eukaristiam vocamus ponitur nec inde nisi pro magna necessitate ante octavum diem aufertur, significat[i] sanctorum corpora toto isto tempore, quod septem diebus rotatur, in sepulchris requiescentia futuro tempore quasi die octavo resurrectura.

XX. De ultima benedictione

Ultima benedictio, quam postcommunionem dicimus, designat benedictionem extremam quam dominus ascendens dedit discipulis. Que ideo in quadragesima geminatur, quia in maiori lucta maiori opus est tutela. In quadragesima enim intentius contra diabolum armamur, et ut eum vincamus humiliare capita nostra deo a diacono monemur. Qui etiam cotidianis diebus dicens, Benedicamus domino, iubet ut ei benedicamus, a quo bona et re et sacramento accepimus. Diebus feriatis dicens Ite missa est, reducit ad memoriam illud quod dominus ascendens dixit discipulis[j] Euntes in mundum, predicate evangelium, et *Ecce ego vobiscum sum usque ad consummationem seculi*[71]. *Que sursum sunt querite*[72], ubi me videtis ascendere, quod hic minus habetis, ibi habituri expectate.

Tercium librum Amalarii excerptum loco secundo posui, ut post diversitates officiorum tocius anni, quas[k] liber primus continet sequerentur significationes missarum cotidianarum. Dictis ergo officiorum significationibus, sequentur officialium et vestes et gradus.

Explicit liber secundus[l]. Incipit capitula libri tercii.

De generale nomine clericorum.
De sacris ordinibus.
De hostiario.
De lectore.
De exorcista.
De acolito.
De subdiacono.
De diacono.
De presbitero.
De pontifice.
De sacris vestibus.
De amictu et alba et cingulo.

i. designat *W* *j.* suis *add. W* *k.* quam *W* *l.* primus *W*

71. *Mt.* 28.20.
72. *Col.* 3.1.

De tunica et manipulo.
De dalmatica et stola.
De casula.
De ornamentis episcopi. EXPLICIUNT CAPITULA

INCIPIT LIBER TERCIUS WILLELMI DE ABBREVIATIONE AMALARII

I. DE GENERALI NOMINE CLERICORUM[m]

Clericus generale nomen est omnium ministrorum ecclesie. Clerus autem Grece, Latine sors dicitur. Propterea ergo vocantur clerici, quia de sorte sunt domini, vel quia dominus ipse est sors eorum[73]. Clerici autem in principali corporis, id est capite raduntur. Sunt vero capilli superflua corporis. Capilli ergo in capite sunt superflue cogitationes in mente. Due autem sunt partes animi, superior et inferior. A superiori que tendit ad celestia, debet clericus resecare superfluas omnes cogitationes. Ab inferiori vero qui tendit ad necessaria corporis, non potest resecare superflua, quin etiam aliquando cum facere intendit necessaria, surrepunt et in facto et in cogitatione superflua. Quapropter capilli in inferiore capitis parte dimittuntur. Circulus vero capillorum virtutem equalitatis rationi undique consentientem designat. Tunc enim bene reguntur res temporales, si rationi conveniant. Sepe igitur radunt clerici superiorem partem capitis, cum sedulo superflua et ab actibus et a cogitationibus suis secant. In inferiori coronam portant, cum temporales necessitates concordia rationis exequant. Ideo cavent ne capilli aures vel oculos operiant quia vitare debent ne superflua terrenorum aures cordis obturent, vel oculos cordis obcecent. Propterea vero penitentes barbam et capillos nutriunt, et peracta penitentia recidunt, ut ostendant se multa superflua fecisse sed per penitentiam velle recidere.

II. DE SACRIS ORDINIBUS

Ordines sacri non tot in principio fuerunt ecclesie, quot modo sunt. Quod inde conicitur, quia Paulus apostolos solos sacerdotes et diaconos nominat sine quibus immolatio altaris non rite fit. Sed ecclesia crescente crevit officium ecclesiasticum, ut in officiis inferiores sint superiorum adiutores. Quod Ambrosius in expositione epistole ad Timotheum testatur, dicens quod inferiores ordines non dantes ante altare[74]. Cuius dictum Amalarius ita vult intelligi, ut quando episcopus prosternitur ante altare, aliquos ordinaturus, nullus ex ordinandis cum eo prosternatur, nisi ad diaconatum vel presbiteratum provehendus.

m. No heading O, L, L2, W

73. JEROME, *Ep.* 52.5 (CSEL 54.421).
74. AMB. *In 1 Tim.* apud RAB. MAUR., *Enarr. in ep. Pauli* 23 (PL 112.607).

III. De hostiario

Hostiarios fuisse in veteri lege manifestum est legenti Paralipomenon[75] librum, qui eos ianitores appellat. His ordinandis dantur hostium et claves, diciturque ab episcopo, Ita agite, ac si rationem possitis reddere, pro rebus que his continentur clavibus. Hoc officium continetur in dono gratie, quod enumerat apostolus dicens, *Alii fides in eodem spiritu*[76]. Hostiarius aperit hostium ecclesie. Ecclesia Christi populus est. Si quis per fidem aliquem introduxerit in ecclesiam, spiritualis hostiarius est.

IV. De lectore[n]

Lectores fuisse in veteri lege qui librum Hesdre[77] legit intelligit. Is quippe legit super gradum ligneum stans, distincte et aperte. Hoc orat episcopus super eos, quos lectores ordinat, et assiduitate, inquit, Lectionum sint apti pronunciare verba vite et vocis distinctione populo monstrare intelligibilia. Hoc officium continetur in dono gratie, de quo dicit Paulus, *Alii sermo scientie*[78]. Nos enim spiritualiter lectores sumus, quando de moribus instruimus aliquem.

V. De exorcista

Refert[o] Iosephus Salomonem excogitasse[79] quosdam exorcismos adversus demones, quod qui agebant exorciste vocabantur. Ii ordinandi accipiunt librum exorcismi ab episcopo, et potestatem imponendi manum super inerguminum. Hoc officium pertinet ad augmentum fidei, quale desiderabant apostoli, dicentes domino, *Auge in nobis fidem*. De qua ipse dicit, *Si habueritis fidem sicut granum sinapis, dicetis huic monti tollere, et mittere in mare, et fiet*[80]. Si quis autem vicium diabolicum expulerit ab homine, spiritualis exorcista est.

VI. De acolito

Acolitorum ordinatio ab Aaron et filiis eius sumpsit initium, quibus in lege dicitur de lucerna, *Et collocabunt eam Aaron et filii eius*[81]. Acolitus Grece, Latine ceroferarius. Is cum ordinatur, accipit ceroferarium ab archidiacono. Hoc donum ad prophetiam pertinet. Duo sunt autem officia prophete unum ut scripturas dilucidet, alterum ut futura revelet. Ille autem est spiritualiter

n. de lectore *om. L2*　　*o.* Defert *L2*

75. Cf. *II Par.* 9.24-28.
76. *I Cor.* 12.9.
77. Cf. *II Esdr.* 8.1-8.
78. *I Cor.* 12.8.
79. Bede, *Super act. apost.* 19 (PL 92.982).
80. *Lk.* 17.5,6.
81. *Ex.* 27.21.

acolitus qui verbi celestis ignem in corde auditoris accendit. Hi ergo gradus spiritualiter intellecti geminantur et augmentum capiunt. Hostiarius incredulum per fidem in ecclesiam introducit, lector iam credentem rationabiliter instruit. Exorcista maiori fidei augmento vitia expellit, acolitus in corde illius qui mundatus est divini amoris flammam incendit.

VII. De subdiacono

Subdiaconi apud Grecos ipodiaconi, apud Hebreos nathinnei, id est in humilitate servientes dicuntur. Serviunt enim diacono, et ideo quando ordinantur, accipiunt ab episcopo patenam et calicem, ab archidiacono urceolum ad ministrandum vinum, et aquamanile cum manutergio. Est autem aquamanile vas quod ita vulgo dicitur apud Italos, a quo funditur aqua in manus. Dicit Amalarius mirari se cur hic mos in nostris ecclesiis inoleverit ut subdiaconi legant epistolas, cum subdiaconorum sit officium tantum diacono circa ministeria vasorum domini ministrare, lectorum autem sit lectiones legere.

VIII. De diacono

Diaconorum officium demonstrat liber numerorum, qui dicit filios Caath et filios Gerson subditos esse debere filiis Aaron[82], et debere omnia custodire, que pertinent ad cultum tabernaculi. Quare autem in novo testamento constituti sint, actus apostolorum docent qui dicunt ideo eos constitutos ut apostolis verbo dei vacantibus, ipsi servirent mensis viduarum et pauperum[83]. Palam ergo est officium eorum spiritualiter commutatum, ut oblationes fidelium ad celeste convivium in altaris mensa disponant. Secundum eorundem apostolorum institutionem super eos ordinandos imponit episcopus manus. Per manus opera, per digitorum discretionem, discretionem[p] munerum spiritus sancti intelligimus. Optat ergo eis episcopus bona opera cum dono et discretione spiritus sancti. Legunt ipsi evangelium, quia ministri sunt verbi dei. Diaconus enim minister interpretatur. Quod[q] nomen non debet vile putare, nisi qui maior vult esse illo qui dixit, *Non veni ministrari sed ministrare*[84].

IX. De presbitero

Presbiteri sunt in loco filiorum Aaron de quibus dicitur *hec nomina filiorum Aaron*[r] *qui uncti sunt*[85]. Sic et episcopi nostri ungunt manus presbiterorum ut sint munde ad sacrificandum et large ad donandum.

p. discretionem *om. W* *q.* autem *add. W* *r.* de quibus ... Aaron *om. W*

---

82. *Num.* 4.
83. *Acts* 6.1-2.
84. *Mt.* 20.28.
85. *Num.* 3.3.

Utrumque enim designatur per oleum, et gratia curationis et caritas dilectionis. Pluribus autem exemplis docet Amalarius eosdem temporibus apostolorum dictos et presbiteros et episcopos dum communi caritate disponebant plures ecclesiam; sed postquam ambitio cepit inolescere, ad sanandam contentionem unum electum qui ceteris in hoc tantum preponeretur, quod solus ordines daret, ipsum vocatum episcopum.

X. De pontifice

Loco Aaron summi quondam pontificis sunt episcopi nostri. Qui hoc maius habent quam ceteri in consecratione, quod unguntur oleo in capite, quod accipiunt virgam, anulum, mitram, sandalia. Sed de ceteris posterius dicendum, nunc de oleo. Episcopus Christi vicarius est. Caput nostrum Christus, qui unctus est oleo spiritus sancti pre[s] participibus suis. Pontifex ergo in capite unguitur quia caput suum sequi debet, ut sicut Christus totam regit ecclesiam, ita episcopus pro modo suo regat sibi commissam. Vel sicut beatus Gregorius dicit oleum in capite caritas in mente est[86]. Non ordinatur nisi duo vel tres conveniant, quia, ut idem Gregorius ait, decet ut quando homo deo coniungitur[87] tales conveniant, qui de eius profectibus gaudeant, vel pro eo deo preces fundant[t], aut[u] Innocentius papa dixit, ne videatur furtiva surreptio[88]. Quod autem hoc tempore tenetur evangelium super caput episcopi ordinandi, nec autenticum nec antiquam esse dicit Amalarius, posse tamen significare ut meminerit episcopus semper se subditum esse debere iugo evangelii, de quo ipse dominus dicit, *Tollite iugum meum super vos et cetera eiusdem loci*[89].

XI. De sacris vestibus

Antequam de sacris vestibus dicatur hoc prelibandum, quia[v] non licet ulli laico eis uti, sed nec clericis nisi in ecclesia. Quod et[w] Stephanus papa noscitur prohibuisse et honestas compellit officii[90]. Nec minus est spiritualis ratio, ut clericus cum sacris vestibus non procedat ad vulgus, quia sunt multa sancte ecclesie secreta que populo non debent exponi, ne detecta et minus profanis mentibus intellecta vilescant.

XII. De amictu et alba et cingulo

Amictus vocatur quia illo collum circumamicitur. Quia ergo ex collo vox

s. pro *W* *t.* vel ... fundant *om. W* *u.* aut *om. W* *v.* quod *W* *w.* et *om. W*

86. Greg., *Moralia in Iob* 2.52.82 (PL 75.595).
87. Greg., *Ep.* 64 (PL 77.1191-2).
88. Inn., *Decr.* 9 (in *Coll. Dion.*) (PL 67.242).
89. *Mt.* 11.29.
90. *LP* 24; 1.154.

procedit, castigatio vocis per amictum exprimitur, quia nichil magis convenit clerico, quam ut discrete taceat[x], discrete loquatur.

Ordine procedente alba ita ex colore dicta castitatem clerici significat. Hec in veteri lege astricta erat corpori, ut expedito motu circa sacrificia minister versaretur. Nos autem laxam habemus, quia Iudei acceperunt spiritum servitutis in timore, nos autem per libertatem deo servimus, qua libertate Christus nos liberavit. Libertatem tamen cingulo restringimus, quia non servili sed filiali timore deo servimus. Hec vestis ad pedes descendit, quia motus omnes corporis casti debent esse in clerico. Vel ita vestis significat bona opera, cingulum castitatem, sicut dominus ait, *Sint lumbi vestri precincti, et lucerne ardentes in manibus vestris*[91]. Preter ista duo indumenta primi quatuor ordines non usurpant alia.

XIII. De tunica et manipulo

Subdiaconi induuntur tunica et accipiunt manipulum. Tunica que in veteri lege solebat fieri iacinctina, designat bona clerici opera, que soli sunt deo cognita. Iacinctus enim aerii est coloris. Debet enim clericus, quanto superior est ordine, preter virtutes apertas que significantur per albam, etiam occultas exercere, ut orationes, ut ieiunia. Manipulum unde nichil dixit Amalarius, quod duplicatum in leva portatur, potest significare labores in hac vita anime et corporis. Qui inter se duplicantur, quia[y] vix aut nunquam dolet corpus quod non dolet anima, et e converso. Quod ideo clericus portat, quia quanto magis eos intelligit, tanto magis dolet. Unde Salomon : *Qui apponit scientiam, apponit et laborem*[92].

XIV. De dalmatica et stola[z]

Diacono addicitur dalmatica, ita dicta quia tempore Silvestri pape quidam episcopus a Dalmatia Romam veniens eius formam attulit. Hec candida est significans candorem religionis in diacono. *Religio enim munda et immaculata est visitare viduas et orphanos*[93]. Ad hoc autem ministerium ab apostolis diaconi constituti sunt. Ideo dalmatica, vestis eorum, habet duas lineas coccineas ante et retro, designans ut ipsi addiscant ex veteri et novo testamento fervorem dilectionis dei et proximi. Coccus enim lignei[a] coloris est. Et quia caritas utraque precepta complectitur, fimbrie ex lineis procedunt et eas complectuntur. Quindecim fimbrie sunt[b] ante et quindecim retro, quia quindecim ramos karitatis enumerat Paulus, *Paciens est, benigna est, non inflatur, non agit perperam, non emulatur, non est ambitiosa, non querit que sua sunt, non irritatur, non cogitat malum, non gaudet super iniquitate,*

x. discrete taceat *om. W* *y*. qua *W* *z*. De diacono *O, L, L2, W* *a*. ignei *L2* *b*. et *add. O*

91. *Lk*. 12.35.
92. *Eccles*. 1.18.
93. *Jas*. 1.27.

congaudet autem[c] *veritati, omnia credit, omnia suffert, omnia sperat, omnia sustinet*[94]. In humero sinistro sunt fimbrie, non in dextro, quia in hac vita[d], non in futura, sunt necessaria opera caritative compassionis.

Adicitur[e] et stola diacono quod significat iugum quia lecturus evangelium debet portare iugum evangelii, de quo dicitur, *Iugum meum suave est*[95]. Super humerum autem sinistrum diaconi mittitur stola et dextro subicitur, quia presentis vite pacienter portatus labor, in futuro[f] victoriam promeretur. Procedit usque ad pedes, quia tota vita debet portari iugum domini. Quod autem stola presbiteri collum constringit hoc designat quod dicitur, *Quanto magnus es, humilia te in omnibus*[96].

XV. De casula[g]

Hec omnia indumenta preter tunicam et dalmaticam[h] habet presbiter, et additur[i] ei casula, per diminutionem a casa[j] dicta, quod totum hominem circumtegat. Hec quia commune est indumentum diaconorum et subdiaconorum significat communes virtutes, sine quibus recte clericus esse non potest, ut est assiduitas lectionis, continentia cibi et potus, honestas in sermone et opere. Hec in pectore et humeris duplex esse consuevit, ut firma sit constantia cogitationum bonarum et operum. Per humeros opera, per pectora cogitationes accipe. In operibus sit duplicatio, ut hominibus sic ostendantur, ut tamen inde gratie deo agantur. In cogitationibus veritas ad deum, doctrina ad homines. Ideo autem diaconi et subdiaconi in quadragesima et adventu casulis induuntur, quia cum semper tum maxime his diebus[k] debet virtutibus studere clericus.

XVI. De ornamentis episcopi[l]

Pontifex accipit anulum, quia pre ceteris in eo debet esse fidei signaculum. Virgam qua exterreat superbos et sustentet[m] infirmos et non minus sue fragilitatis conscius sit. Ideo denique curvatura baculi in se ipsam complicatur, ut cum alios pontifex pro meritis vel consolatur vel increpat, quid in se ipso castigandum, quid laudandum sit intelligat. Mitram ut spe divini auxilii hec[n] se posse intelligat, si capitis sui Christi vestigia imitari non negligat. Sandalia ut ad predicationis iter gressus firmos habeat, que ideo ligantur ut constantiam intentionis significent. Solee de mortuis animalibus facte monent ut non suas inventiones, sed patrum precedentium doctrinas predicet. Iam vero pallium archiepiscoporum hortatur eos ut sint vita et

c. autem *om. L2* *d.* vita *om. W* *e.* DICITUR *W* (*display capital not added*)
f. futura *W* *g.* de presbitero *O*, *L*, *L2*, *W* *h.* et dalmaticam *om. W*
i. addicitur *W* *j.* fasa *W* *k.* his diebus *om. W* *l.* De pontifice *O*, *L*, *L2*, *W*
m. sustentat *O* *n.* hec *om. O*

94. *I Cor.* 13.4-7.
95. *Mt.* 11.29.
96. *Ecclus.* 3.20.

scientia ceteris insigniores, maiore quippe gloria in futuro coronandi. Linee candide a pectore et a tergo; hec nitorem doctrine, illa mundiciam vite designat. Torques circa collum, celestis corone premium. Nichil ergo vacat a significatione in habitu clerici, quia amictus significat sermonum discretionem, alba virtutes apertas, tunica occultas, casula communiter omnes, manipulus[o] labores terrenos, cingulum castitatem, stola humilitatem, dalmatica fraternam compassionem. In episcopo qui maioris dignitatis est, anulus notat fidei prestantiam, in virga [*sic*] severitatem et misericordiam, in mitra [*sic*] spem divini auxilii, in sandaliis [*sic*] predicationis instantiam, in pallio [*sic*] puritatis et scientie prerogativam et eternam postremo coronam.

* * *

Videor michi amice[p] satisfecisse iussioni tue[q], ut Amalarium breviarem[r]. Si excidi voto per imperitiam, dabis[s] veniam. Si quid commode et apposite dixi, referes[t] gratias *patri luminum*[97], a quo est largicio omnium bonorum. Sane moneo ut si de compendio vis[u] scire significationes misse, legas[v] versus Hildeberti prius Cenomannensis episcopi, postea Turonensis archiepiscopi[98], si significationes sacrarum vestium et ceterorum id genus, sermones Ivonis Carnotensis episcopi[99]. Hi enim viri talia videntur intellixisse perspicatius et texuisse pulchrius. Ceterum de varietatibus officiorum alium frustra desiderabis[w] quam Amalarium. Fuerit fortassis aliquis qui inde scripserit disertius, nemo certe peritius.

o. manipulos *O* *p*. domine antistes *W* *q*. vestre *W* *r*. breviatem *O*
s. dabitis *W* *t*. referitis *W* *u*. vultis *W* *v*. legatis *W* *w*. desiderabitis *W*

97. *Jas*. 1.17.
98. PL 171.1177-1196.
99. PL 162.505-610.

VI

Why Do Medieval Psalters Have Calendars?

Students of medieval manuscripts are familiar with the notion that a standard component of the book called the psalter (*psalterium*) is a liturgical calendar. For example, Victor Leroquais, whose conspectus of psalters in the public libraries of France is the fullest collection of information about such books that we possess, speaks simply of 'the calendar written at the head of most psalters,'[1] and Henry Thurston (in an article in the old *Catholic Encyclopedia* much referred to by, among others, art historians) remarks that 'from the ninth century onward a calendar was a common adjunct to most of the different classes of service books, for example, sacramentaries, psalters, antiphonaries, and even pontificals.'[2] These general statements turn out to be, as generalizations, true; but when we learn, as we shall do shortly, that books called psalters had been made for at least three centuries before they come to be integrally equipped with calendars, we may wonder why, on the face of it, a calendar should be attached to a psalter at all.

What we call *psalterium* is basically nothing more than a separately written and bound copy of the psalms, arranged with respect to the order in which they are to be recited. The precise relationship between the evolution of the round of daily liturgical services cumulatively called the Divine Office and the earliest books used as this round developed can probably never be worked out at all

1 V. Leroquais, *Les Psautiers manuscrits latins des bibliothèques publiques de France*. 3 vols (Macon, 1940-41), I, lxiii.

2 H. Thurston, 'Calendar,' *Catholic Enclycopedia* III (1908), 164.

fully;[3] but common sense suggests that heavy daily use of the canonical psalms in anything like a *cursus*-fashion - that is, involving more than those that could reasonably be memorized by ordinary monks and clergy - would necessitate a text containing them and (eventually, anyhow) whatever else was required for the services of the hours, in which they predominated.

The oldest psalters which survive as independent books appear to be two Old Latin codices of the sixth century, customarily called the Verona[4] and the St Germain;[5] neither has a calendar. The Verona, which contains canticles as well as the psalms, was added to in the ninth and tenth centuries,[6] but no calendar was supplied at those times.[7] Nor does any of the earliest Romanum psalters - the Vespasian, Salaberga, Montpellier, Morgan, and Echternach[8] - contain a calendar.

The position is the same with regard to the earliest Gallicanum and Hebraicum psalters, which must be considered alongside the phenomenon of the multiple version (duplex or triplex) psalter. Thus, though the earliest Gallicanum text in a psalter appears to stand by itself - the so-called Cathach of St Columba[9] - the two next oldest witness to both Gallicanum and Hebraicum versions: the Psalter of Count Everard,[10] a Gallicanum-Hebraicum duplex, and the Corbie Psalter now in St Petersburg,[11] which contains Old Latin as well as Hebraicum and Gallicanum texts. Then come three solely Gallicanum books from the late eighth or early ninth century, all of great importance artistically or textually, and all probably to be connected with Charlemagne: the Dagulf Psalter,[12] the so-called Charlemagne Psalter,[13] and the Amiens Psalter, early at

---

3 A recent, exhaustive treatment of part of the subject is Jonathan G. Black, 'The Daily Cursus, the Week, and the Psalter in the Divine Office and in Carolingian Devotion,' (Univ. Toronto Ph. D. thesis, 1987).

4 Verona, Bibl. cap. I(1), Greek and Old Latin texts facing; E.A. Lowe, ed. *Codices Latini Antiquiores*, 12 vols (Oxford 1934-72) [henceforth CLA], no. 472.

5 Paris, BN lat. 11947, an Old Latin `Codex Purpureus; 'CLA no. 616.

6 S. Jellicoe, *The Septuagint and Modern Study* (Oxford 1968), 203.

7 Another prime early witness, BN Coislin 186 (CLA no. 520), a Greek and Latin psalter of the seventh century, survives for only Pss. 18.13 to 72.10.

8 Respectively, BL Cott. Vesp. A.1; Berlin, Hamilton 553; Montpellier, Fac. Méd. 409; New York, Pierpont Morgan Library 776; and Stuttgart, Cod. Bibl. Fol. 12.

9 Dublin, Royal Irish Academy, s.n.; s. vi. The possibly even earlier book, Lyons, B.m. 425 (351) plus BN N.a.l. 1585, is too fragmentary to be offered as evidence.

10 Vat. Reg. lat. 11; s. viii.

11 St Petersburg, F.v.I no. 5; also s. viii.

12 Vienna, Lat. 1861 (Theol. 652), datable to 783-95.

Corbie if not made there;[14] and one of even greater pictorial importance, the slightly later Utrecht Psalter.[15] To none of these is a calendar attached.

This admittedly tedious list of psalters without calendars can be concluded quickly. There is no such feature in either of the two surviving ninth-century St Gall Psalters,[16] nor in the duplex (Gallicanum-Hebraicum) St Ebrulf Psalter with strong Irish connections,[17] nor in a Hebraicum psalter from Tours of about 820.[18] Finally, and most notably, no calendar is found in the very elaborate triplex (of the henceforth standard kind, Gallicanum-Romanum-Hebraicum) from Reichenau, datable to the mid-ninth century.[19]

Whatever the roots of the idea that a psalter should fittingly be equipped with a calendar, then, it is an idea not evident in psalters made up to at least the middle of the ninth century. We shall need to turn elsewhere in our search.

Logically, we might expect to find calendars developing out of sacramentaries, and therefore first attached to them. There is after all a calendar implicit in all the oldest sacramentaries we have, the so-called Leonine (in its present form extant from April on)[20] and the old Gelasian[21] as well as in the younger- and mixed-Gelasian forms. But in none of those, nor in any Gregorian sacramentary of the ninth century known to me, is a calendar to be found as an integral part of the book.

The best-known early free-standing liturgical calendar hints at a different direction. This is the calendar of St Willibrord, probably written in the first ten or fifteen years of the eighth century and very likely by the Anglo-Saxon missionary bishop himself.[22] It is not the calendar of any particular church and, as is attested by both the obit-type entries and the long autobiographical note

---

13 BN lat. 13159, datable to 795-800.

14 Amiens, B.m. 18, post-800 (the emperor is mentioned in the litany).

15 Utrecht, Univ. 32 (Theol. 484), probably around 820.

16 St Gall 20, Gallicanum; St Gall 19, Hebraicum.

17 Rouen, B.m. 24.

18 BL Harl. 2793.

19 Karlsruhe, Landesbibl. Aug. XXXVIII. The same thing is true of the triplex made at Würzburg c. 840, Bodl. Laud lat. 35.

20 L.C. Mohlberg et al., ed., *Sacramentarium Veronense*, Rerum ecclesiasticarum documenta, series maior 1 (Rome 1956).

21 L.C. Mohlberg, ed., *Liber sacramentorum Romanae aeclesiae ordini anni circuli*, RED, series maior 4 (Rome 1960).

22 H.A. Wilson, ed. *The Calendar of St Willibrord*, Henry Bradshaw Society [henceforth HBS] 55 (1918).

concerning Willibrord's consecration as bishop, must be regarded as primarily a personal document. In physical form it is part way towards having the characteristics we associate with a liturgical calendar. Each month's page has at the extreme left a column of *litterae lunares*, which refer to the age of the moon on any particular day;[23] then a column of repeated numbers (i-vii), which function somewhat as do the Sunday letters of later calendars; next the Roman dating-system indications; and finally the names of those commemorated. It was, however, joined by the mid-eighth century to an English-derived copy of the *Martyrologium Hieronymianum*. This suggests that the calendar was at that point viewed as more closely related to the genre of martyrology than to either of two alternative genres, those of the sacramentary or (despite its physical form) of computistical matter. Just as a calendar can be inferred from any early sacramentary, so one can be inferred from any martyrology, but it will be as a calendar unsatisfactory, because of the multiplicity of entries on most days. Though in a calendar we sometimes see two or even three entries of saints on a given day, this is a far cry from the half-dozen or more commemorated on most days in the martyrologies.

In some relation to the martyrologies stands a scanty group of metrical calendars, recently studied most helpfully by Patrick McGurk.[24] He distinguishes a main tradition, now represented in four English manuscripts of the tenth and eleventh centuries, from that both of a versified calendar of the later eighth century which comes, according to André Wilmart, from York,[25] and of the mid ninth-century *Martyrologium Poeticum* compiled by Wandelbert of Prüm.[26] But in all these cases the demands of the metre, useful though that may be as a mnemonic device, mean that the resulting calendar cannot function like the practical liturgical calendars we are pursuing.

An intriguingly-named Mysterious Latin calendar of Sinai turns out to be just that: interesting but not conclusive. This document is a codicologically integral part of a psalter found in 1950 at St Catherine's monastery on Mount Sinai.[27]

---

23 Ibid. p. xi n.2.

24 P. McGurk, 'The Metrical Calendar of Hampson. A New Edition,' *Analecta Bollandiana* 104 (1986), 79-125.

25 A. Wilmart, 'Un témoin anglo-saxon du calendrier métrique d'York,' *Revue Bénédictine* 46 (1934), 41-69.

26 J. Dubois, Le martyrologe métrique de Wandelbert ..., *Anal. Boll.* 79 (1961), 257-93.

27 Sinai, St. Catherine's Monastery, Slav. 5; ed. M. Altbauer, *Psalterium Latinum Hierosolymitanum. Ein frühmittelalterlich HS, Sinai MS 5* (Vienna 1978).

The book appears to be an Old Latin text of the psalms (just over half survive) with canticles attached in the manner of the Verona or Count Everard Psalters. Lowe assigned it to the ninth century, and it seems likeliest to be of North African origin.[28] But the physical form of the calendar shows how far removed it is from what we normally understand a liturgical calendar to be. It is closer in fact to a list of selected saints arranged by months, and within months by the days on which they were commemorated. To call this list, as does its editor, Jean Gribomont, 'the sanctoral of its church at the moment of the Arab invasion of Africa,' is to say more than the form really allows us to infer.[29]

Back, then, to the pursuit of practical calendars: that is, capable of being used as a guide to the sanctoral cycle in the liturgical year. These *are* found at an early date, albeit to a limited extent, in the context of computistical works. It may be that the oldest extant one of these, again of English origin, is Bodl. Digby 63 (SC 1664), dating from the mid or late ninth century, in which a calendar forms the middle part of a large amount of computistical material.[30] We see something similar in BL Cott. Tit. D. xxvii, the collection of devotional and computistic material put together for the deacon Aelfwine at the New Minster, Winchester c. 1012-35 (in the years before he became abbot there), where the original placing of the calendar (ff. 3-8v) is noteworthy:[31] not among the material for the liturgical year but preceded by instruction about the suitability of days of the month for bleeding (ff. 1-2) and followed by many folios of computus matter and by Aelfric's version of Bede's *De temporibus*.[32] Other examples include a second Winchester New Minster calendar, c. 1025, set in a great mass of computus matter in a volume of Hyginus and Martianus Capella *De astrologia*;[33] and a late eleventh-century English West Country calendar, again with much computus matter, in a Boethius *De arithmetica*.[34] There is a similar context for a calendar of the late tenth century, but a metrical

28 E.A. Lowe, 'An Unknown Latin Psalter on Mount Sinai,' *Scriptorium* 9 (1955), 177-99.

29 J. Gribomont, 'An Unknown Latin Psalter on Mount Sinai,' *Anal. Boll.* 75 (1957), 105-34.

30 The calendar in Bodl. Digby 63 is printed, but without the obits, in F. Wormald, *English Kalendars before A.D. 1100*, HBS 72 (1934), no. 1.

31 B. Günzel, ed. *Ælfwine's Prayer Book*, HBS 108 (1993), 89-107.

32 This work comprises two present-day codices, BL Cott. Titus D.xxvi, xxvii, of which xxvii seems originally to have preceded xxvi. Much of the material mentioned above is also printed in W. deG. Birch, ed., *Liber Vitae: Register and Martyrology of New Minster and Hyde Abbey, Winchester* (London 1892), the calendar in Wormald, ut sup, no. 9.

33 Cbg., Trin. Coll. R.15.32; printed Wormald, no. 10.

34 Cbg., Univ. Lib. Kk.v.32; printed Wormald, no. 6.

one, found in a computistical miscellany of the early twelfth century from Thorney Abbey, now St John's College, Oxford MS 17.[35] Again, it must be stressed that this is not a liturgical calendar; it contains lines only for those days on which a saint is to be commemorated, so that for example only six days in October are included. This reminds us that, whatever the main purpose of a metrical calendar is thought to be - a mnemonic aid or a bit of virtuosic versification - it is not primarily liturgical: that is, it cannot be used as an aid in deciding what the entire month looks like liturgically.

It is clear enough that practical liturgical calendars existed in some profusion in eleventh-century England. Next we have to look for the affixing of a truly liturgical calendar to a psalter-book. It seems that this search should again cenre on England. Two well-known books deserve attention initially. The first is the Bosworth Psalter.[36] Its calendar, written on parchment of a different size and quality than the rest of the book, should almost certainly be dated between 988 and 1012 (or even 1008). The text of the psalter has sometimes been said to be slightly earlier, but it seems likely that the two were pricked together and indeed that the calendar is an original feature of this book, which we must be content with dating to a dozen years or so on either side of A.D. 1000.[37]

For somewhat greater certainty we turn to a slightly earlier book, the so-called Salisbury Psalter, which dates probably from between 969 and 987.[38] It is often said to have come from Shaftesbury, but the nunnery at Wilton has also been suggested as a place of origin, or at least original ownership (with

35 Edited by M. Lapidge, 'A Tenth Century Metrical Calendar from Ramsey,' *Revue Bénédictine* 94 (1984), 326-69.

36 BL Add. 37517, s. x^{ex} ; printed Wormald, no. 5.

37 In the uneven division of labor between F.A. Gasquet and Edmund Bishop in their ostensibly joint volume, *The Bosworth Psalter* (London, 1908), Gasquet (to whom the physical description of the MS fell) noted merely that the two folios on which the calendar is written are 'of a date somewhat later than the rest of the volume' (p. 3); while Bishop, whose examination of the calendar takes up the greatest part of the work, surprisingly failed to pursue the point. P.M. Korhammer, 'The Origin of the Bosworth Psalter,' *Anglo-Saxon England* 2 (1973), 173-87, repeating that the calendar is slightly later than the body of the book, pays no further attention to the fact beyond remarking that it is 'a fair assumption' that the body of the manuscript had a common origin with the calendar (p. 180); his argument for a possible connection with Westminster need not detain us here. Nor is the point considered seriously in John M. Makothakat, 'The Bosworth Psalter. A Critical Edition' (Ph. D. diss., Univ. of Ottawa, 1972).

38 Salisbury Cathedral 150; ed. C. and K. Sisam, *The Salisbury Psalter*, Early English Text Society o.s. 242 (1959). On p. 11 they suggest c. 975 'as a convenient rough date.'

Sherborne much less likely than either).[39] Here the calendar, prefixed by two pages of computus material, is clearly an integral part of the book. Elzbieta Temple's suggestion that 'there are indications that the scribe was also his own illuminator and that, copying page by page from a model, he designed each initial as it came at the head of each psalm and canticle, subsequently inscribing the text round it,' would not necessarily apply to the calendar pages, and does not therefore entitle us to infer that the model was a calendar with a psalter attached.[40] Nothing in the contents of this book - the standard contents we expect to find in a psalter, the psalms themselves, canticles, and a litany (later, in this case) - suggests a rationale for the prefixing of a calendar; but we might note that this is apparently the oldest Gallicanum psalm-text to be produced in England in a service book.[41] The Gallicanum text was not unknown in England, having been introduced prominently in, for example, the late Carolingian psalter which came to England in the early tenth century and was traditionally supposed to have been given by King Athelstan to Winchester cathedral;[42] but that book has only a metrical calendar, of the kind mentioned earlier. Lest it be supposed, incidentally, that the practice we are tracing might in some way be connected with the spread of the Gallicanum text, it should be stressed that the Bosworth text is Romanum, as was also originally another prime witness of ten to twenty years later (1012-23), the Arundel Psalter.[43]

We are, then, confronted with the necessity of trying to guess where the model used by the Salisbury Psalter's scribe came from and, specifically, whether it might have been a Continental psalter itself containing a calendar. Almost certainly if such a model did ever exist it is now lost, but the plausibility even of supposition about its existence would be enhanced if it were clear that a continental psalter earlier than the (English) Salisbury 150 was equipped in its original state with a calendar.

---

39 Daphne I. Stroud, 'The Provenance of the Salisbury Psalter,' *The Library* 6th ser. 1 (1979), 225-35.

40 E. Temple, *Anglo-Saxon Manuscripts 900-1066*, Survey of Manuscripts Illuminated in the British Isles 2 (London, 1976), no. 18.

41 Sisam and Sisam (1959), v.

42 BL Cott. Galba A.xviii. On the likelihood of Athelstan's involvement see S. Keynes, 'King Athelstan's Books,' in *Learning and Literature in Anglo-Saxon England*, ed. M. Lapidge and H. Gneuss (Cambridge, 1985), 143-201.

43 BL Arundel 155.

At least one such book might appear to qualify: the psalter of St Maximin, Trier, of the late ninth/early tenth century, now in Manchester.[44] This seems to be the earliest psalter, by three quarters of a century or so, discovered so far which looks to have a calendar integrally attached. But the following considerations must give rise to some doubt about assigning to the Trier book this degree of priority. First, it is possible that the calendar is in fact somewhat later than the rest of the book. It occupies a separate gathering (of eight leaves, the first now missing), and is in a hand somewhat smaller than, albeit looking contemporary with, that of the main text.[45] But the colours of the calendar seem not to be quite the same as in the rest of the codex, and - oddly - coloured intials have been filled in for every line, regardless of whether there is a saint for that day or not: a red/orange N (or, especially in May, NT) for Natale, O(ctabas), E(piphania or Exaltatio), and several times I(n). This last form of entry, always preceding a place name, appears with some frequency, suggesting that a martyrology is the, or a, source here - for example, at 5 January, 'In Antiochia Symonis monachi.' Overall, the calendar seems to be a document incorporating several strands beyond what one would expect from its time and place. One strand is very early: Projectus before Conversion of Paul (25 January), Hermes before Augustine (28 August), Cesarius before All Saints (1 November). Another is the presence of several Old Testament worthies, Ezekiel (10 April), Jeremiah (1 May, after Philip and James), Elijah (14 June), Daniel (21 July), Samuel (20 August). A third, perhaps telling, strand is that there are strong insular characteristics: Patrick, Cuthbert, *Augustini episcopi in Cantia, primi Anglorum episcopi*, and possibly the two Ewalds, while the commemoration of Babillas and the Three Boys (24 January) had an enduring if inexplicable popularity in the North of England. Taken together, these peculiarities make it seem doubtful that we are dealing here with a practical liturgical calendar, and suggest a verdict of, at best, 'perhaps' in terms of this psalter's being the first to have a calendar attached integrally to it. That point of junction, and certainly the explanation for it, seems still to seek.

Before we come to the stage at which there will be a plethora of psalters with calendars attached, we need to consider the obvious question which might have provided an alternative approach for this enquiry: whether, rather than dealing

44 Manchester, John Rylands Univ. Lib. lat. 116 (Crawford 133). M.R. James, *Descriptive Cat. of the MSS in John Rylands Lib., Manchester* (Manchester 1921), I.211-17.

45 James, 212. Cf. the supplementary notes added by Frank Taylor to the 1980 reprint of the Rylands Catalogue, 39*.

with the phenomenon summed up by the present title, we should be devoting our attention to an even larger one, the emergence of the fully-developed liturgical calendar and its consequent attachment to liturgical books of whatever kind. In fact, the only kind of such book besides the psalter against which this question can be tested is the sacramentary - from which, as we noted, a rudimentary calendar can always be inferred. Here the surprising truth is that of the roughly thirty sacramentaries from the eighth to the thirteenth centuries that I have checked - Continental as well as Insular, Young Gelasian, Gregorian, mixed, Anglo-Saxon, and miscellaneous - none has a calendar attached integrally until within a couple of decades on either side of the year 1000. In addition, the first two books apparently to be so equipped have a strongly English flavour. One is the so-called Leofric Missal.[46] Here, to a late ninth-century Gregorian sacramentary of Lotharingian origin has been added a calendar seemingly of the late tenth (possibly from Glastonbury) as well as other matter, the supplemented book was given by Bishop Leofric to his new cathedral at Exeter.[47] The other is the equally so-called Missal of Robert of Jumièges, a book from perhaps Ely, perhaps Peterborough, of the early eleventh century, which belonged to its eponymous prelate while he was bishop of London 1044-51.[48]

It seems, then, that about the time the Salisbury Psalter was being written with a calendar as an integral part, the Leofric Missal (to stick to the conventional nicknames) was also being supplied with a calendar; and that by the time a calendar had become a part of both the Bosworth Psalter and (as unquestionably an original feature) the Arundel Psalter datable to 1012-23,[49] a calendar was also included integrally in the Robert of Jumièges missal. And in both the Leofric and Robert books the calendars are found in the context of extensive computistical matter.

This brings us to the turn of the millenium. Looking forward, we become aware that in the course of the eleventh century a large number of psalters do come to be equipped with calendars; so that Thurston's remark about calendars

46 Bodl. MS Bodl. 579, ed. F.E. Warren (Oxford 1883).

47 Of much recent literature on the Leofric Missal, see especially D.N. Dumville, *Liturgy and the Ecclesiastical History of Anglo-Saxon England* (Woodbridge 1992) and *English Caroline Script and Monastic History* (Woodbridge 1993), and P.W. Conner, *Anglo-Saxon Exeter* (Woodbridge 1993).

48 Rouen, B.m. Y.6, ed. H.A. Wilson, HBS 11 (1896).

49 BL Arundel 155.

as a common adjunct of psalters 'from the ninth century onwards' holds true if we reverse IX to XI. Of numerous eleventh-century books from a variety of places which either contain psalters integrally or had them soon added, a handful of Continental witnesses will have to suffice: codices originally from Heidelberg,[50] St Gall,[51] Cremona,[52] St Denis - a psalter of which of about the year 1000[53] lacks a calendar entirely, whereas a roughly contemporary book from the same house has had one supplied in an early eleventh century hand.[54] An elaborate triple psalter made almost certainly at Reims before 1049 and modelled closely on the calendar-less Karlsruhe triplex noticed above, now has a calendar.[55] A new trend is clearly discernible.

In England, certainly, the presence of a calendar as an integral feature of a psalter seems to become the rule rather than the exception in the eleventh century. This statement has to be hedged with a 'seems' because there are several psalters of this period which lack calendars now but may well have had them originally. Notable among these are a pair of Winchester-related books of the third quarter of the century, the Tiberius[56] and Stowe[57] Psalters. The existence of the splendid cycle of pictures still at the beginning of Tiberius suggests strongly that there was other prefactory material as well and makes the existence of a calendar highly likely. It is possible that Stowe originally had a calendar also; in its present form it begins abruptly with Psalm 1, with no prefatory matter whatever. A similar possibility exists for the Romanum psalter with complete Old English gloss now in Paris, of which the first leaf (introduction to Psalm 1) is clearly missing and more may be as well.[58]

In fairness, there should be noted two books that might, along the lines of our current rumination, have been expected to contain a calendar and do not. (I exclude here a psalter sometimes ascribed to Ramsey but recently, and more

50 Vat. pal. lat. 39.

51 Manchester, John Rylands Univ. Lib., lat. 125.

52 Bodl. Canon. pat. lat. 88.

53 Paris, Bibl. Ste. Geneviève 1186.

54 BN lat. 103.

55 Reims, B.m. 15; though the original calendar is largely erased, having been supplanted by one of the fifteenth century: Leroquais (note 1) II.166.

56 BL Cott. Tib. C.vi; E. Temple, *Anglo-Saxon Manuscripts 900-1066* (note 40), no. 98.

57 BL Stowe 2; Temple, no. 99.

58 BN lat. 8824; as for the two previous MSS, see the summary descriptions in P. Pulsiano, 'Psalters,' in *The Liturgical Books of Anglo-Saxon England*, ed. R.W. Pfaff. Old English Newsletter Subsidia 23 (Kalamazoo 1995), 61-85 at 64-6.

convincingly, to Winchester,[59] which from the evidence of its litany[60] seems to be pre-980, or at least pre-1006, and is thus almost contemporary with what still looks to be the innovator, Salisbury 150.) One is the Lambeth Psalter, which does seem to retain its preliminary matter; its lack of a calendar is simply puzzling.[61] The other, sometimes called the Leofric Psalter, has a late twelfth-century calendar added to its mid eleventh-century text in a separate first gathering.[62] Since this gathering contains also a list of the relics at Exeter, it is a reasonable supposition that the present calendar may have replaced an earlier one.

Otherwise, all the well-known psalters one thinks of as postcard-worthy contain calendars: those associated with Christ Church Canterbury (Arundel 155, mentioned earlier), Bury St Edmunds,[63] Crowland,[64] and probably Winchester[65] - to which should be added Worcester, the St Wulfstan Portiforium connected with it being really an expanded psalter, and containing a calendar.[66]

This means that we have a pattern of psalters-with-calendars which are associated with major monastic houses, and raises the obvious question whether the development we are tracing is a by-product of the tenth-century Monastic Reform movement. Unfortunately, the question has to be dropped as soon as it is raised, for a simple reason: that we really do not have comparable data from major, firmly non-monastic establishments - though, in the context of c. 970-1070, that phrase would tend to include meaningfully only Hereford and London (with Exeter, Ramsbury/Salisbury, and Wells for just the last twenty years or so of the period). Certainly what seem to be the key books, the Bosworth and Salisbury Psalters, are monastic in origin; more along these lines we cannot say.

The evidence that has here been mustered seems to point towards England in the late tenth and early eleventh centuries as being a place and time in which the

---

59 BL Harl. 2904; 'Ramsey ?' in N.R. Ker, *Medieval Libraries of Great Britain*, 2nd edn (London 1964), 154; Winchester is suggested in Temple, no. 41.

60 M. Lapidge, ed. *Anglo-Saxon Litanies of the Saints*. HBS 106 (1991), no. XXIV.

61 Lambeth Palace 427.

62 BL Harl. 863.

63 Vat. Reg. lat. 12.

64 Bodl. Douce 296.

65 BL Arundel 60 and Cott. Vit. E.xviii.

66 Cbg., Corpus Christi 391; ed. Anselm Hughes, *The Portiforium of St Wulfstan*, 2 vols, HBS 89-90 (1958-60).

phenomenon we are trying to trace becomes common. But we still want an explanation of how, and if possible why, this development came about. In addition, if we put to the side the St Maximin, Trier psalter of c. 900 on the grounds that its calendar is not clearly one designed for liturgical use, we must next ask ourselves whether there is likelier to have been a single psalter (extant or not is immaterial) with which this practice began and from the influence of which it spread, or whether a complex of factors can be postulated which would among them help to explain the new development.

The former possibility seems probable only if the single book in question was for one reason or another extraordinarily influential. Given our overall time-frame, such a book is likeliest, it seems to me, to have been connected with Charlemagne, or at least with the Carolingian or post-Carolingian court. In this regard it is striking that there is no calendar attached to any of the three Carolingian psalters mentioned above (Dagulf, 'Charlemagne,' or Amiens), nor in the somewhat later and incomparably grand Utrecht, nor to another sumptuous (purple) psalter made at Reims about the middle of the ninth century.[67] From this survey of negative facts it seems reasonable to suppose that the concept of *Psalterium cum calendario* does not arise in circles that could be roughly termed Carolingian.

Nor - as a perhaps related point - is it to be attributed to the culturally most influential of ninth-century monastic houses, as is again shown by the negative evidence adduced above: Corbie, St Gall, Tours, Reichenau all possessed notable ninth-century psalters without calendars. It looks therefore as if we must turn to the less palpable notion of a set of factors which came together by, probably, some time in the tenth century to make the practice of adding a calendar to a psalter comprehensible (if never quite logical). There seem to be three such factors, a very brief survey of which will bring us near to the point where we can ponder an hypothesis.

The first is, without question, the distinctively Christian interest in computistics, related in the first instance to the dating of Easter. Not only is it true that (as we have seen) some of the earliest liturgical calendars are in compilations of computistical and other scientific or mathematical works: it is also the case that all of the few pre-eleventh century calendars - whether affixed to psalters or not - seem to be set in a context of computistical matter. By

67 Bodl. Douce 59.

contrast, calendars in psalters of the twelfth century and later are often placed without any related material on either side (for example, in a separate quire[68]).

A second factor has to do with the possible influence of martyrologies. Although martyrologies are structured according to the days of the calendar (mostly beginning with 25 December), there is nothing computistical about them; each day is given its Roman-system name (xvi Kal. Julii or whatever), and that is that. This aspect has to be considered because it is possible that some calendars affixed to psalters in the eleventh century are fuller in the number of saints included than might be deduced from a sacramentary of roughly the same time and place; and if this is so, another source for the additional saints needs to be postulated. I put this so cautiously because it is difficult to find 'sets' - psalters containing a calendar and mass books from the same place and of roughly the same date - on which to test this hypothesis. One of the few such sets may be provided by a pair of psalters probably to be connected with the New Minster, Winchester, BL Cott. Vit. E.xviii and Arundel 60, the contents of which can be put against those in the mass book of that house from the same period (roughly 1050-75).[69] The calendars in the psalters, though themselves not agreeing in every detail, both contain entries for several saints - Haedde, Kenelm, Eadburga, Wulmar, Praxedis, and Cristina - which the sanctorale of the mass book lacks.[70] These are saints who may well have arrived through martyrologies. While the distinction insisted on by Edmund Bishop between 'sacramentary' and 'martyrology' saints is too rigid to be more than partially useful, some kind of source has to be posited beyond local cultus for what can generically be termed the non-sacramentary saints.[71] Martyrologies are an obvious source for such information, and the ninth century is probably the most fertile period for the production of martyrologies.

The final possible factor, though admittedly it may sound far-fetched, relates to the first two as well as bringing in a distinctively English note - and we have seen that the practice of attaching a calendar to a psalter gets, at the least, an

68 As in the Eadwine Psalter, Cbg. Trin. Coll. R.17.1; see R.W. Pfaff, 'The Calendar,' in *The Eadwine Psalter. Text, Image, and Monastic Culture in Twelfth-Century Canterbury*, ed. M. Gibson, T.A. Heslop, and R.W. Pfaff (London and University Park 1992), 62-87.

69 Le Havre, B.m. 330; ed. D. H. Turner, *The Missal of the New Minster, Winchester*. HBS 93 (1962).

70 Vit. also includes Wandregisilus and Mary Magdalen, while Arundel 60 has Margaret and Samson.

71 *The Bosworth Psalter* (note 37), 19.

early foothold in England. This factor is some degree of awareness, however vague, of the work of Bede. Bede, coming as he does from a milieu of the most intense interest in both aspects, the reckoning of time and a strong concern with the commemorations of saints, is of course the best-known figure to whom both extensive computistical writings and a martyrology can be attached. Furthermore, there was connected with him some of the sort of prefatory material which, in addition to Jerome's own prefaces, came to precede the text of the psalms in many psalters. Indeed, in the St Maximin Psalter there comes, after a good deal of Hieronymian material, the preface which begins 'David filius Iesse,' which in the middle ages went under Bede's name;[72] and this is very often found in subsequent books. It is also through Bede that two of the principal series of psalm *tituli*, those associated with Columba and with Cassiodorus,[73] were mediated into the sorts of psalters we have been considering, though again it would be hard to say with precision how overt the connection with him was thought to have been. But Bede's seems to have been a palpable presence in several respects in the evolution of what we think of as a complete medieval psalter.

Connected with this point is the possibility that a calendar may have been part of one or two very early sacramentaries of Anglo-Saxon origin or descent. A leaf containing May and June, for a long time at Ilmmünster and then Munich but lost since World War II, was written, it seems, between 721 and 755 in Northumbrian majuscule either in England or in an Anglo-Saxon-influenced centre on the Continent; its sources go back as far as King Osric of Northumbria (d. 634).[74] A similar fragment (two leaves, containing July to December) is thought by Klaus Gamber likely to have been part of the Boniface Sacramentary now in Regensburg;[75] and it is possible that the Ilmmünster leaf was part of a sacramentary also. The physical form of the calendars in both fragments is like that of the calendar of St Willibrord but slightly less advanced in having *litterae lunares* but not the column of Sunday-letter equivalents. It is,

---

72 F. Stegmüller, *Repertorium biblicum medii aevi*, 9 vols (Madrid 1950-80), no. 1665. The `true' and complicated authorial history of this preface is irrelevant for our purposes.

73 Pierre Salmon, *Les 'Tituli Psalmorum' des manuscrits latins*, Collectanea Biblica Latina XII (Rome 1959), Series I and VI respectively.

74 K. Gamber, *Das Bonifatius-Sakramentar und weitere frühe Liturgiebucher aus Regensburg*, Textus Patristici et Liturgici 12 (Regensburg 1975), 49-52.

75 Op. cit. pp. 53-9: Schloss Hauzenstein (bei Regensburg), Gräfl. Walderdorffsche Bibliothek (o.N.).

then, just conceivable that the connecting of calendars to liturgical books goes back as far as the eighth century in Northumbria or in areas influenced therefrom. But these fragments are very slim evidence indeed, and the possibility must be reckoned a remote one.

It is time now to offer an hypothesis as to what may have happened. The process traced here strikes me as having had four stages, of which the first three do not have to have been consecutive. First, there is the development of the calendar form itself out of a core of computistical material and Easter tables - so that the matter we are accustomed to looking *past* when when peruse a medieval calendar (or even that of the Book of Common Prayer) while we see which saint is entered on a given day is in fact the matter at the heart of what is being looked *for*. Secondly, there is the existence of lists of names of saints, especially the two lists which from at least the fifth century form part of the Roman mass canon, *Communicantes* and *Nobis quoque*. The names in these lists were, however, arranged not in calendar order but in groups, like later litanies of saints: apostles, martyrs, confessors, virgins. Thirdly, there is the emergence of the martyrology as a physical artifact, from at the latest the time of the earliest manuscripts (seventh century) of the *Martyrologium Hieronymianum*, which made available a model for remembering large numbers of saints on all days of the year. And, without question, the self-consciousness about the sanctoral cycle as a consequence of the intersection of Roman with Frankish mass books in late Merovingian and Carolingian times must have increased the importance of having a comprehensive and comprehensible way of organizing saints' days in the liturgical year.

The fourth stage I am positing is, in some relation to the first three, simply the evolution of what might be called the all-purpose liturgical calendar: one that would serve equally well for all books keyed to the liturgical year. It is only as such calendars have evolved that they become attached to psalters, liturgical books to which (as was noted at the beginning) they are not strictly relevant. So it may have been in something like the coming together of these factors - interest in computistics, popularity of martyrologies, and perhaps some awareness of Bede not only in these two areas but also in the provision of the sort of devotional material which came to be prefixed (as well as a calendar) to many psalters - that there emerged the notion that a liturgical calendar could be a desirable adjunct to a psalter-book.

VII

SOME ANGLO-SAXON SOURCES FOR THE "THEOLOGICAL WINDOWS" AT CANTERBURY CATHEDRAL

The Theological (or, more accurately, Typological) Windows at Canterbury are those put into the western half of the east end of the cathedral in the course of the great rebuilding that followed the fire of 1174.[1] Most likely these windows occupied locations in the north choir aisle, north-east transept, and one bay of presbytery beyond that, and in the corresponding bay of presbytery on the south, the south-east transept, and south choir aisle (Fig. 1).[2] It is probable that these windows began to be painted around 1180, and that they were complete within twenty years or so. The number of these windows has always been thought of as twelve, but this is specified only in the three literary sources we have as to the contents of the windows. There may be reason to think that fourteen windows were originally envisaged as being involved in this plan, and — or — that the extreme easternmost windows of the Corona, perhaps somewhat later than the other typological windows, is in some unclear way related to the main scheme.[3]

The primary evidence for these windows is that portion of them which survives: much of window II and some of III *in situ*, and some scenes from IV and VI placed in II and III by later restoration. In all, roughly a sixth of the total number of scenes survives. Evidence about the entire program is available through the three literary sources mentioned above: four leaves of the later thirteenth century attached to a chronicle to which it is otherwise unrelated in Cambridge, Corpus Christi MS 400; a roll of the early fourteenth century apparently hung up at the entrance to the north choir aisle, perhaps as a guide for viewers of the windows (Canterbury Cathedral MS C.246); and a fifteenth-century account appended to the Canterbury chronicle of William Glastynbury (Oxford, Corpus Christi MS 256).[4] These sources do not

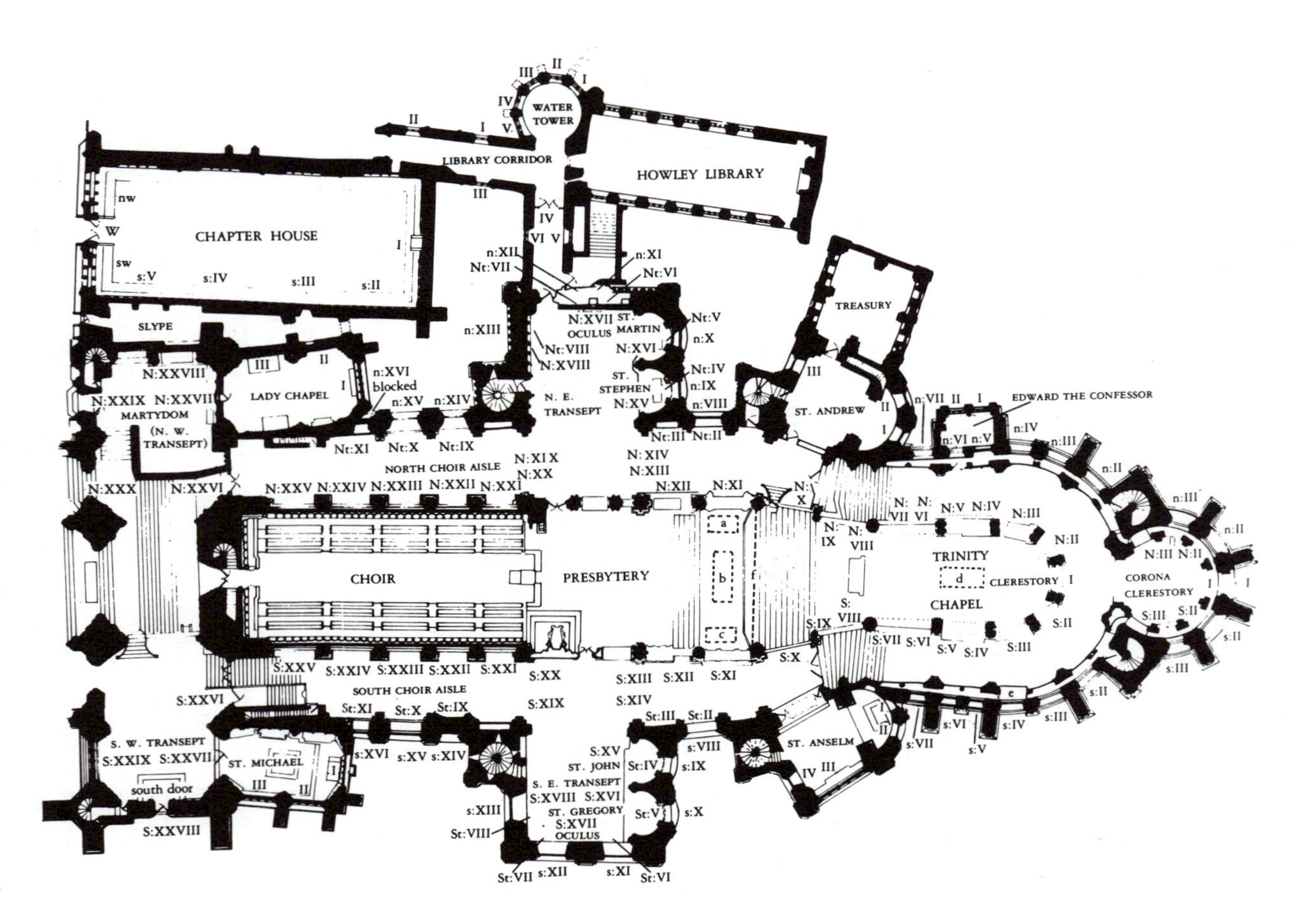
WATER TOWER
LIBRARY CORRIDOR
HOWLEY LIBRARY
CHAPTER HOUSE
TREASURY
SLYPE
ST. MARTIN
OCULUS
ST. STEPHEN
N. E. TRANSEPT
LADY CHAPEL
blocked
MARTYDOM
(N. W. TRANSEPT)
ST. ANDREW
EDWARD THE CONFESSOR
NORTH CHOIR AISLE
CHOIR
PRESBYTERY
TRINITY
CLERESTORY
CHAPEL
CORONA
CLERESTORY
SOUTH CHOIR AISLE
S. W. TRANSEPT
ST. MICHAEL
south door
ST. JOHN
S. E. TRANSEPT
ST. GREGORY
OCULUS
ST. ANSELM

Figure 1.

agree perfectly among themselves, and the Oxford MS diverges quite notably from the other two, especially in a confusion of numbering towards the end which results in an account of only eleven windows instead of the twelve indicated. The two other sources contain obvious errors as well; the writer of the Canterbury roll was characterized by M. R. James as "either a careless or a stupid man."[5] So though these MSS are the *sine qua non* for any reconstruction of the contents of the windows, they also create serious obstacles to that reconstruction.

The surviving scenes and the literary accounts between them permit us to speak confidently of certain things. The basic structure of the program was typological, but not always in the strict sense in which that term is normally understood. Not all the types are drawn from the Old Testament by any means; some are taken from the New Testament and some from other sources, the latter being the most instructive for my purposes. Around the scenes were (and are, in most of the extant ones) Latin verse inscriptions, with a few exceptions in couplets and most often couplets of the Leonine hexameter variety. The MSS give headings for the scenes as well, but these headings seem on the whole not to have appeared in the windows themselves (though occasionally characters carry scrolls or are identified in something like a caption). In the vast majority of the windows there are no verses for the antitypes; where this is not the case it is therefore a subject for remark. Finally, the antitypes are generally arranged vertically, to be read top to bottom, flanked by their types; but the exact disposition of types and antitypes depends on the armatures of the individual windows, which fortunately do survive and have been studied carefully by Professor Caviness.

These preliminary facts already enable us to ask certain basic questions. Is it likely that what was finally glazed represents a single program? Who would have drawn up such a program, and what would have been the extent of contributions made to it by the artists and by the designers of the armatures (assuming that these were different people)? Who composed the verses? Does variation in the verses, say in meter or number of lines, indicate a plurality of authors? What is the relation between the author or authors of the verses and the person (or persons) who drew up the final scheme? Indeed, what is the relation between this final scheme — the one from which artists and glaziers worked — and possible preliminary versions? Is there (here is the focus of my particular concern) someone we can conceive of predominantly as a library figure rather than as a design figure? In short, to what extent is a literary intelligence perceptible behind the various elements that were finally brought together in the Canterbury typological windows as they have now been reconstructed?

It will be convenient to prescind from some of these questions and speak here of "the compiler of the program" as though he were a single figure — though with the caution that we do not thereby regard his compilation as necessarily forming in a strict sense a single program. This caution is all the more necessary as we notice comparable pictorial schemes. Parallels to many of the antitypes and some of the types of the first three windows and of the last one or two exist in the stall paintings that were recorded as noteworthy features of the choir of Peterborough Abbey (and which seem discernible still in the Peterborough Psalter of c. 1300 now at Brussels, Roy. Lib. MS 9961-2);[6] in some lost paintings in the chapter house at Worcester (recoverable, like those at Peterborough, from a literary source), and on some related leaves of a MS now at Eton (177);[7] in three English twelfth-century ciboria;[8] and above all in the ambitious compendium of types and antitypes drawn up towards the end of that century under the title *Pictor in carmine.*[9] Detailed study of these parallels yields a certain amount of information for our purposes; but parallels are not necessarily sources, and there is no reason to think that the Canterbury compiler had to have relied on any of these productions in making his selections. The likeliest of these as a "source" would seem to be Peterborough, but even there the argument smacks strongly of *similis huic ergo propter hoc.* In any case, it is in the subjects and verses that have no, or only partial, parallels in these other schemes that we may be able to get closest to our compiler.

Scenes from three windows can serve to illustrate these complexities. Let us start with the only one of the three to survive, the scene of Julian and Maurice (Fig. 2) originally in window VI (n: XI), now in window II (n: XV). That they are to be understood as the last Roman emperors of those names is quite clear from the name-bar behind them and from the crowns they wear. What is far from certain is why they should be depicted as conspicuously rich, *locupletes*:

Figure 2.

Isti spinosi locupletes deliciosi
Nil fructus referunt quoniam terrestria querunt.

Indeed, in the case of Julian this would seem positively misleading, because Julian's reputation is as a "philosopher" — one who sat lightly to earthly riches — as well as an apostate from Christianity. Whatever Julian might be a type of, it should not be a rich man.

But a misunderstanding of an Old English homily can turn Julian into a figure laden with wealth. The story of Julian's being bested by Mary's intervention, which comes to form part of the Miracles of the Virgin collection[10] and which again gives no hint that Julian is conspicuous for his wealth, is rooted in the section of the patristic homily on Mary's Assumption concerning Julian's quarrel with St. Basil.[11] In Aelfric's Old English adaptation of this homily the story is told in a self-contained section "concerning the end of the impious adversary of God, Julian." Basil, having in an exchange of taunts offended the emperor, tries to avert Julian's threatened destruction of Basil's city by purchasing his goodwill. The bishop says (the translation is Thrope's): *

> Hwaet ða Basilius cydde his ceastergewarum ðaes reðan caseres ðeowrace, and him selost raedbora waerð, þus cweðende, "Mine gebroðra, bringað eowre sceattas, and uton cunnian, gif we magon, ðone reðan wiðersacan on his genancyrre gegladian." Hi ða mid glaedum mode him to brohton goldes, and seolfres, and deorwurtðra gimma ungerime hypan. Se bisceop ða underfeng ða madmas. . . .

> Hereupon Basilius made known to his fellow-citizens the cruel emperor's threat, and was a most excellent counsellor to them, thus saying, "My brothers, bring your treasures, and let us endeavour, if we can, to gladden the cruel apostate on his return." Then they with glad mind brought to him of gold, and silver, and precious gems in immense heap. Thereupon the bishop received the treasures. . . . [12]

* Thrope *should read* Thorpe

The story continues, rather inconsecutively, with Mary's effecting the emperor's assassination through the long-distance agency of the spear of St. Mercurius, who was buried in Basil's city. But a literal-minded reader of the Old English homily might well – especially if his command of that vernacular were shaky – have taken the antecedent of "him" in "mid gladum mode him to brohton goldes . . . " to be not Basil but the immediately preceding personal noun "wiðersaca," apostate. On this (mis-) reading the Christians would then have brought to Julian "gold, silver, and precious gems in an immense heap" – like the heap the Canterbury scene shows – even though the subsequent syntax makes it plain that it is bishop Basil who receives the money.

Knowledge of Aelfric's homilies was of course widely available in twelfth-century England. At least ten extant MSS contain this (first) homily on Mary's Assumption, one of which (London, British Library Cotton Vespasian D. xiv) is from either Canterbury or Rochester.[13]

As for Maurice, no reason can be adduced for his inclusion save the obvious, though far from strong, one: that (as Caviness has noticed) he was coupled with Julian by Gregory the Great in a letter denouncing the imperial policy of forbidding soldiers to become monks.[14] Again, there is a Canterbury MS of the register of Gregory's letters that would have been available to the confector of the Maurice and Julian scene (Cambridge, University Library Ii.3.33).[15]

Evidence along the same lines, but less suppositious, is provided by the case of Drusiana, who appears in window VI (n: XI), with a title that reads in the MSS, "Drusiana vestit et pascit egenos." According to Caviness's reconstruction, at the top of the window was a scene of Jesus casting out a devil (Legion?), flanked slightly lower down by a two-panel type of an angel casting out a (the?) devil. The next central scene down, a roundel, showed Mary Magdalen washing Christ's feet, again flanked by a single type split into two scenes, Drusiana feeding the poor on the (observer's) left and clothing the poor on the right.[16] This reconstruction follows the Oxford MS in distributing the four verses given to this type into two couplets:

> Curam languenti victum qui prebet egenti.
> Seque reum plangit Christi vestigia tangit (on the left);

and Illa quod unguendo facit hec sua distribuendo.
Dum quod de pleno superest largitur egeno (on the right).

Drusiana is a character in the apocryphal Acts of John, where she is mentioned in three passages: first, a mere notice as being among various Christians who accompanied John to Ephesus; secondly, the long story of the illicit passion entertained for her by Callimachus, who attempts to violate her corpse following her death but who is converted after she is raised from the dead; and finally, another brief mention that she with all the brethren followed John when he departed from Ephesus.[17] Nowhere is there any mention of her as succoring the poor. How, and how much, of this apocryphal work passes into the West makes no difference here, because not even in the fullest form of the Greek *Acta* does Drusiana appear in the character that the Canterbury window gives her.

The established iconography[18] for Drusiana reflects almost exclusively the incidents just summarized. A key to the iconographic puzzle furnished by the Canterbury window may, however, be available once more through an Old English homily, also by Aelfric, this time the one for the Assumption of St. John (= St. John's day, 27 December). This reads, at the point where the saint meets the bier holding the widow's corpse:

> Heo waes swiðe gelyfed and aelmesgeorn, and þa ðearfan, ðe heo mid cystigum mode eallunga afedde, dreorige mid wope ðam lice folgodon.
>
> She was much beloved and zealous in alms, and the poor, whom she had bountifully [and] entirely fed, sad with weeping, followed the corpse.[19]

It is even easier to imagine what has happened here than with the case of Julian: that our compiler's rusty knowledge of Old English has led him to take the appositive phrase "dreorige mid wope" to refer not to the poor but to Drusiana.

Since nowhere else in the iconography of Drusiana is there any indication of her weeping (nor, as noted above, of succoring the poor) it seems almost incontrovertible that the source of this Canterbury scene is, at least ultimately, Aelfric's homily. Again, several extant monastic

MSS contain the homily in question (which is from a different series than the homily on Mary's Assumption), though none of the surviving ones seems to be from Canterbury. But we know that even in the fourteenth century the Canterbury library included three volumes of Old English homilies, at least one (no. 309 in Eastry's catalogue) being almost certainly those of Aelfric.[20] What seems decisive for Canterbury is the combination of the weeping with the almsgiving in the homily and in the Canterbury verses – in which, be it noted, Drusiana is not named. At the most cautious extreme one would have to posit some stage at which the Magdalen's weeping suggested the highly improbable name of Drusiana: who then, once she had become a type for Mary Magdalen, is shifted (or misunderstood) by the author of the verses to be primarily not a weeper but a benefactor ("Illa quod unguendo facit hec sua distribuendo"). The loss of the window itself makes such a degree of caution necessary – since we do not after all know how Drusiana was depicted – but even so the connection with the Anglo-Saxon source would seem clearly established.

Thirdly, we turn to the type of "monks washing the feet of the poor" ("monachi lavant pedes pauperum") in the seventh window (n: VIII). One would expect this as a type of Christ washing the apostles' feet at the Last Supper; but that scene, placed in window XI, has as types Laban washing camels' feet and Abraham washing angels' feet; and the monastic footwashing in window VII is placed, improbably, as a type of Jesus setting a child in the midst of the apostles (the other type is "Kings obey Peter and Paul.") Window VII appears to be a highly confused composition, with such scenes as Jesus going to Jerusalem and the Crucifixion used as *types,* the latter twice. It would seem that humility is the theme common to this set of scenes: that, in the words of the summary titles, "Statuit Ihesus parvulum in medio discipulorum" is flanked by "Monachi lavant pedes pauperum" and "Reges inclinantur doctrine Petri et Pauli." But whereas the title indicates the poor as those whose feet are being washed, the verses speak of travellers:

> Hoc informantur exemplo qui monachantur
> Ne dedignentur peregrinis si famulentur.

"By this example" would more logically seem to refer to the footwashing at the Last Supper; but leaving that aside (if humility is indeed the theme), the discrepancy between the poor and travellers as objects of this exercise remains striking.

Here there is a partial, but illuminatingly false, parallel with the Peterborough scheme. As a type of the dominical footwashing there was at Peterborough, along with both Abraham and Laban, a scene of St. Benedict washing the feet of the poor. The verses, as recorded in the Peterborough Psalter, formed an elegiac couplet:

> Prebuilt exemplum monachis sanctus benedictus
> Ut fiant humiles pauperibusque pares.[21]

The Peterborough couplet stresses St. Benedict, the obvious monastic regulator, as the giver of the example; whereas the Canterbury verses cast the footwashing in the passive voice, without specifying who is or are performing the action. Furthermore, the Peterborough verses suggest, like the Canterbury title, that it is the poor whose feet are being washed (by which action the monks become humble and equal to the poor, i.e., in spirit, whose is the kingdom of heaven) while in the Canterbury verses travellers are the beneficiaries. In short, though Canterbury and Peterborough are depicting basically the same scene, the verses are totally variant, only Peterborough names Benedict, and there is a discrepancy within the Canterbury accounts between the title (which like Peterborough specifies the poor) and the verses (which mention travellers).

Both late Anglo-Saxon and reformed Anglo-Norman monastic customs contain provisions for foot-washing, in the *Regularis Concordia*[22] and the *Monastic Constitutions of Lanfranc,*[23] respectively. Lanfranc, whose prescriptions would seem of course most immediately relevant for Canterbury, gives directions for the Maundy Thursday *pedilavium* of the poor (fol. 108) and then of the monks (fol. 110), and alludes to an ordinary Saturday Maundy. The *Regularis Concordia* of c. 970 contains specific provisions for the Maundy Thursday and weekly footwashing, but also a daily Maundy for three poor men (sect. 62). And in the following section (63) the same treatment (i.e., of the Maundy, presumably including footwashing) is commanded for poor travellers also: "De cetero, superuenientibus peregrinis pauperibus abbas cum fratribus quos elegerit, secundum regulae praeceptum, Mandati exhibeat."

Given this slight variation between Lanfranc's monastic regime, which would have been generally in force at Canterbury throughout the twelfth century,[24] and that of the *Regularis Concordia*, it does not seem fanciful to suggest that the mention of travellers in the Canterbury verses (as opposed to the poor in the Peterborough couplet) may show an awareness of the tenth-century document. Happily, strong evidence for such awareness exists. The two surviving MSS of the *Regularis Concordia* both come from Christ Church Canterbury. One, British Library Cotton Tiberius A.iii, contains four important monastic texts, with almost continuous Old English glosses of the first three, including the *Regularis*.

Here, once more, the possibility that suggests itself is of a monastic scholar, with an interest in the Anglo-Saxon past and some knowledge of Old English, drawing from his studies in the Canterbury library elements of the program of the windows. Nor are the three examples adduced the only indications of that kind of intelligence at work (it is almost certain, for example, that the MS just mentioned, Cotton Tiberius A.iii, was open when the stories of the three dominical raisings were being drawn on for window X [s: XII]).[25] Whatever the other sources and models employed – and certainly there are relationships to be explored further not only with English but also with continental analogues – it seems clear that an awareness of the Anglo-Saxon vernacular heritage, an awareness perhaps somewhat antiquarian in nature and certainly striking more than a century after the Norman conquest, bulks large in the evolution of these windows which must have formed one of the great monuments of late twelfth-century art.

NOTES

1. This paper, in a slightly different form, was read at one of the sessions on "British Art and Architecture 1100-1450" sponsored by the International Center for Medieval Art, at the Sixteenth Congress on Medieval Studies at Kalamazoo, May 1981. Professor Madeline Harrison Caviness, who chaired the session, was then extraordinarily generous in allowing me to use proofs of the relevant sections of her Corpus Vitreaum Medii Aevi volume, *The Windows of Christ Church Cathedral, Canterbury,* published in the summer of 1981. Her work there and in *The Early Stained Glass of Canterbury Cathedral* (Princeton, 1977) is definitive for most aspects of the Canterbury glass. But she has expicitly not undertaken a full investigation of the sources of the verses or of all the iconographic ideas; and it is this sort *

* Vitreaum *should read* Vitrearum

of investigation that is attempted here. The older name for the windows here dealt with has been retained in my title to point up continuities with earlier work (see n. 4).

2. The Typological Windows will here be referred to by simple Roman numerals, I-XII, with the numbering of the Corpus Vitrearum in parentheses. By this new numbering the Typological Windows are reckoned as n: XVI, n: XV, n: XIV, n: XIII, n: XII, n: XI, n: VIII, s: VIII, s: XI, s: XII, s: XIV, and s: XV in Caviness's reconstruction. But in order to stress the possibility that this assignment of windows may have to be revised, and to emphasize that my concern is chiefly with what existed by c. 1200 rather than with what now survives, I prefer to use the consecutive numeration.

3. I hope to expand on this and other matters in a subsequent study.

4. The Canterbury roll was published by M. R. James, *The Verses Formerly Inscribed on Twelve Windows in the Choir of Canterbury Cathedral,* Cambridge Antiquarian Society Octavo Pubs. 34 (Cambridge, 1901); the fifteenth-century account, from a transcript by W. A. Pantin, in C. E. Woodruff, "The Chronicle of William Glastynbury," *Archaeologia Cantiana,* 37 (1925), 121-51, esp. 138-51. Divergences between the Cambridge MS and the Canterbury roll are noted in Caviness (1981).

5. James (1901), p. 3.

6. Lucy Freeman Sandler, "Peterborough Abbey and the Peterborough Psalter in Brussels," *Journal of the British Archaeological Association* 3rd ser. 33 (1970), 38-49; and her *The Peterborough Psalter and other Fenland Manuscripts* (London and New York, 1974). But for important corrections see Alison Stones's review of the latter in *Zeitschrift für Kuntsgeschichte,* 43 (1980), 211-18.

7. The Worcester verses are printed in M. R. James, "On Two Series of Paintings formerly at Worcester Priory," *Proceedings of the Cambridge Antiquarian Society,* 10 (1904) 99-110. The Eton MS is described in James's *Catalogue of MSS at Eton College* (Cambridge, 1895), 95-104; a little additional information is given in N. R. Ker, *Medieval Manuscripts in British Libraries,* II (Oxford, 1977), 772. See also J. M. Wilson, "Some Twelfth Century Paintings on the Vaulted Roof of the Chapter House at Worcester,"* *Association Architectural Societies Reports and Papers,* 32 (1913), 132-38; and Mrs. (later Lady) Trenchard Cox (M. D. Anderson), "The Twelfth Century Design Sources of the Worcester Cathedral Misericords," *Archaeologia,* 97 (1959), 165-78.

8. Described in M. Chamot, *English Medieval Enamels* (London, 1930), pp 26-31 and plates 5-8. They are in the collections of, respectively, Lord Balfour of Burleigh (on loan to the Victoria and Albert Museum), the Pierpont Morgan Library, and the Victoria and Albert Museum (M.159-1919).

* Association *should read* Associated

9. M. R. James, *"Pictor in Carmine," Archaeologia,* 94 (1951), 141-66, an essay sent in 1932 (perhaps written as early as 1920) to a *Festschrift* for Arthur Haseloff, which in the event did not appear. This is still the fullest account available, but is mostly a summary listing of the headings with a small specimen of verses. See also T. J. Brown in *British Museum Quarterly,* 19 (1954), 73-75; and Floridus Röhrig, *Rota in medio rotae: Forschungen zum biblischen Typologie des Mittelalters,* I (Dissertation, Wien, typed, 1959).

10. For a Latin text of English monastic provenance dating from the first half of the twelfth century, see J. M. Canal, ed., *El Libro "De laudibus et miraculis sanctae mariae" de Guillermo de Malmesbury* (Rome, 1968), p. 69.

11. Based ultimately on the life of Basil attributed, perhaps spuriously, to Amphilocius of Iconium: *Acta Sanctorum, Junii II* (die 14), 944-45; *Patrologia Graeca* 29:ccciv.

12. Benjamin Thorpe, ed., *The Homilies of the Anglo-Saxon Church: Homilies of Aelfric,* I (London 1844), 450-51 (text and translation on facing pages). Through the good offices of Dr. Mary Catherine Bodden, Thorpe's readings have been checked in the Toronto microfilms of MSS Cambridge Univ. Lib. Gg. 3.28 (on which his edition was primarily based), Cbg. Corpus Christi 188, and Brit. Lib. Cott. Vesp. D.xiv. I am also grateful to my colleague Joseph Wittig for assistance with Old English technicalities.

13. N. R. Ker, *Catalogue of Manuscripts containing Anglo-Saxon* (Oxford, 1957), no. 209.

14. Caviness (1981), p. 124 citing Gregory's *Registrum Epistolarum,* bk. III, 64, in MGH Epistolarum I (1887), 225.

15. N. R. Ker, *Medieval Libraries of Great Britian,* 2nd ed. (London, 1964), p. 31.

16. Caviness (1981), pp. 114-15; cf. the diagram in Caviness (1977), p. 170.

17. Caps. 59, 63-86, and 105 respectively: M. R. James, *The Apocryphal New Testament* (Oxford, 1924), pp. 242, 243-50, and 257. The fullest translated collection of versions and fragments is in E. Hennecke-W. Schneemelcher, *New Testament Apocrypha,* transl. R. McL. Wilson, II (Philadelphia, 1965), 188-259.

18. L. Réau, *Iconographie de l'art chrétien,* III.1 (Paris, 1958), 406; *Lexikon der christlichen Ikonographie,* ed. H. Aurenhammer, VI (Vienna, 1974), 99, and VII (1974), 120: all the references are to the raising of Drusiana, and all the examples cited are from the Renaissance. Nor is there anything in the Princeton Index of Christian Art remotely like the Canterbury scene, encapsulated there as "Ministering to poor."

19. Thorpe (1844), pp. 60-61.

20. M. R. James, *Ancient Libraries of Canterbury and Dover* (Cambridge, 1903), p. 51, nos. 305, 309, 316.

21. Sandler (1970), p. 48.

22. T. Symons, ed., *Regularis Concordia Anglicae Nationis Monachorum Sanctimonialiumque,* Nelson's Medieval Texts (London, 1953), pp. 61-62. This juxtaposition of the poor and travellers is made also in the heading to the chapter (X), "Qualiter mandatum cotidianis diebus a fratribus exhibeatur pauperibus, et quo ordine abbas erga peregrinos agat."

23. D. Knowles, ed., *The Monastic Constitutions of Lanfranc,* Nelson's Medieval Texts (London, 1951; reprinted with some additions and different pagination as *Decreta Lanfranci,* Corpus Consuetudinum Monasticarum 7 [Siegburg, 1967]), 31-35. The clause "sicut solet fieri die sabbati ab eis qui mandatum fecerunt" seems to suggest the widely-established weekly observance, but this is not treated elsewhere in the work; and in any case this would have been for the monks only.

24. T. Schäfer, *Die Fusswaschung im monastischen Brauchtum und in der lateinischer Liturgie,* Texte und Arbeiten 47 (Beuron, 1957), p. 39, states that there was a revival of the daily footwashing after the Conquest, under the influence of Ingulf, abbot of Crowland (1086-1109), who though himself English had been prior at St. Wandrille and bolstered the flagging English usage with the vigor of Lotharingian custom; but the evidence adduced does not seem particularly strong and in any case would very likely not be relevant for Canterbury.

25. Ker (1957), no. 186, pp. 240-48, esp. 247.

Professor Caviness wishes it pointed out that the grouping of the clerestory windows of the Trinity Chapel is incorrect in the plan in her 1977 volume (here reproduced), which shows the groupings on the south side to be S:IX-XIII, S:VII-VI, and S:V-IV, whereas they are in fact S:IX, S:VIII-VII, S:VI-V, and S:IV-III. This is shown correctly in the corresponding plan in her 1981 volume, but that from the earlier work has been used here because it is somewhat more legible for my purposes (which in any case have nothing to do with the clerestory windows).

VIII

Martyrological Notices for Thomas Becket

The daily reading of the martyrology, a collection of notices of saints organized (mostly) according to the days of their deaths, was by the twelfth century firmly established as part of the liturgical practice of religious establishments ranging from great cathedrals and abbeys down to - in theory and, as will be seen, sometimes in practice - humble parish churches. As such, it provided, much more clearly than the liturgical calendar for any given year could, a retrospective if unbalanced view of the Christian past.

This past was for the most part remote. What may be called the mainstream tradition of martyrologies in the West, that running from the so-called Martyrologium Hieronymianum of the sixth century to Bede's Martyrology in the early eighth to Usuard's adaptation of it in the mid-ninth, dealt predominantly with the saints of Christian antiquity, and most of all with figures, many of them shadowy, from the age of persecutions. But there was inevitably amplification as well: some supplying of individual omissions, some inclusion of entire groups of saints (say, those of a particular area) not earlier included, and inevitably a certain amount of bringing up to date.

The shape of all such additions was strongly influenced by the traditional form of a martyrological entry. Basic elements of this form are (after something like *eodem die* unless the entry is the first one for the day in question) 1) an indication of the place at which the martyrdom occurred or the saint received renown; 2) the saint's name, with some sort of styling (something like, at the simplest, *virginis et martyris*), always in the genitive case; 3) a brief summary of the circumstances which make the saint noteworthy.

In the case of entries for recent figures the object may be simply to make the record current, or it may be to express a certain view (or views) about the new saint's story. The latter is very markedly the case with Thomas Becket, whose murder in his cathedral at Canterbury on 29 December 1170 was perhaps the most shocking event in the West during the entire twelfth century. The proliferation of miracles and of lives,[1] the swiftness and firm papal management of the canonization proceedings (formal sainthood was declared on 21 February 1173), the magnitude of the rebuilding of the east end of Canterbury cathedral as a shrine to Becket after the disastrous fire of 1174: all these elements kept the memory of Becket's case alive. But his principal feast day, 29 December, fell at an inconvenient time, in the octave of Christmas with all of the complexities that involved, so the degree of actual liturgical commemoration might not have been as great as the fame of his story would lead one to expect. In these circumstances especially, the wording of the entry for him in a martyrology was a prime means by which his memory was preserved year by year - at least until 1538, when by royal order his shrine was destroyed and his cult abolished.

It is the wording of those entries that forms the subject of this paper. I have tried to collect all such notices as I could from the relatively scanty number of surviving English martyrologies. Eight basic forms seem to be discernible. Each is given here in its longest version. After the manner of the *Bibliotheca hagiographica Latina*, they are lettered and referred to by the incipits of the 'narrative' parts (that is, that which begins after the actual styling of the person commemorated):

a. Hic post longos exilii .... uspiam facta leguntur.
b. Qui reversus ab exilio .... et miris decoretur.
c. Qui post relegationem .... septuagesimo primo.
d. Qui ob fidem catholicam .... martirium sumpsit.
e. Qui temporis Henrici iunioris .... celebrata testantur.

---

[1] The basic collection of (Latin) lives is J.C. Robertson, ed., *Materials for the History of Thomas Becket*. 7 vols (vol. VII ed. with J.B. Sheppard; Rolls Series 1875-85); the most important studies those of Raymonde Foreville, now for the most part collected in a Variorium Reprints volume, *Thomas Becket dans la tradition historique et hagiographique* (London 1981). For an ingenious approach to one of the principal lost lives see Margaret Orme, 'A Reconstruction of Robert of Cricklade's Vita et Miracula S. Thomae Cantuariensis,' *Analecta Bollandiana* 84 (1966), 379-98.

f. Qui post multas persecutiones .... miraculis claruit.
g. Qui pro libertate ecclesie .... septuagesimo primo.
h. Qui ob articulos fidei .... in conspectu principum.

a [In Brittania maiori] Cantuarie passio venerandi patris Thome eiusdem civitatis archiepiscopi et martyris gloriosi.
Hic post longos exilii labores quos pro iusticia pacienter pertulit; tandem deo miserante reversus et in ecclesia sua cum honore susceptus; in eadem pro defensione libertatis ipsius gladiis impiorum percussus occubuit. Tali modo fortis athleta agone suo constanter expleto proprio sanguine laureatus ac triumphali morte insignis; ad Christum pro quo fideliter decertavit feliciter pervenit. Cuius glorie miraculorum frequencia testimonium perhibet; que post passionem ipsius e vestigio tanta secuta sunt et adhuc fere cotidie multiplicantur; quanta retroactis temporibus pro aliquo sanctorum vix uspiam facta leguntur.

b [In Anglia] civitate Cantuarie passio beati Thome archipresulis totius angliae primatis et sedis apostolice legati.
Qui reversus ab exilio monachis sinaxim vespertinam celebrantibus in metropoli propria tamquam filius in utero matris a militibus regalibus velut pater a filiis capite cesus et pavimento prostratus exile cerebro mucrone martirum palmam adeptus est. Cuius passio gloriosa deo placere perhibetur; cum miraculis crebris et miris decoretur.

c Cantuarie passio venerabilis Thome archiepiscopi et martiris.
Qui post relegationem septem annorum Cantuariam rediens prius multa passus affligendo carnem Spontaniciam [Pontigny] paupertatem sustinendo; in ecclesia Christi pro nomine Christi et libertate ecclesiae tuenda fortis dei athleta letus ad martyrium accurrens: gladius peremtus occubuit; et ad Christum migravit anno ab incarnatione domini nostri Ihesu christi millesimo centesimo septuagesimo primo.

d [In Anglia] civitate Cantuariensi passio beati Thome eiusdem urbis archiepiscopi.
Qui ob fidem catholicam sancteque ecclesie protectionem, fere per septennium exilio relegatus est; postea vero ad ecclesiam propriam remeans cum tirannicis

adquiescere iussionibus nollet, cerebro percussus, gloriosum ibidem in ecclesia martirium sumpsit.

e [In Anglia] apud Cantuariam sancte Thome archiepiscopi et apostolice sedis legati et tocius Anglie primatis et martiris.
Qui tempore Henrici iunioris pro libertate ecclesie quatuor militum gladiis instanter vespertinali hora in gremio proprie ecclesie eiecto crudeliter cerebro et pro pavimento disperso occubuit. Qui quanti meriti apud(?) deum fuit innumerabilia miracula pro eius merita facta et pro multa terrarum confinia longe lateque celebrata testantur.
Tu igitur martir venerande et pro universalem eccclesiam celebrande pro nostris errantibus apud summum regem dominum nostrum intercede.

f Natalis beati Thome Cantuariensis archiepiscopi.
Qui post multas persecutiones et longum exilium revertens in propria ecclesia tempore regis Henrici secundi quatuor militum gladiis in capite percussus martirum coronam gloriose adeptus est. Qui licet ut aqua sit effusus tunc sceleriter mira(culis) claruit.

g Apud Cantuariam passio beati Thome archiepiscopi.
Qui pro libertate ecclesie dei fideliter decertaret duritium(?) exilium in cilicio lacrimis vigiliis et ieiuniis devota mente sustinuit. Postmodum desiderio patiendi et amore omne(?) ad sedem propriam rediens non multum post quatuor militum armatorum temeraria invasione cum fratres vespertinos ympnos psallerent cervicis et corone diminucione cerebro cum ense extracto; hostiam deo in ecclesia placentem optulit signis et virtutibus clarus anno ab incarnacione domini nostri Ihesu Christi millesimo centensimo septuagesimo primo.

h [In Britannia] ecclesia Cantuarie passio sancti Thome archiepiscopi.
Qui ob articulos fidei catholice et libertatem ecclesie anglicane quievit in conspectu principum.

If we attempt to arrange these in something like chronological order we can perhaps begin to piece together a story. What is probably the earliest witness ('a') seems to be what we would both expect and want: a document from the cathedral priory (Christ Church) where the saint was martyred. At first glance this seems ideal. BL Royal MS 7.E.VI is a Christ Church manuscript of the

Please keep this receipt as proof of Issue

Customer name: Charles, Sara

Title: The twelfth and thirteenth centuries : 1066-c.1280 / edited by Barbara Harvey.
ID: 1915266264
Due: 30-01-18

itle: The liturgy in medieval England : a istory / Richard W. Pfaff.
D: 1917435189
ue: 13-02-18

itle: Liturgical calendars, saints and services in edieval England / Richard W. Pfaff.
: 1916865182
ue: 13-02-18

tal items: 3
tal fines: £6.50
/01/2018 12:25
ecked out: 11
erdue: 0
ld requests: 0
ady for pickup: 0

twelfth century containing a martyrology, the Rule of Benedict, and a set of themes for homilies on the Gospel lessons of the liturgical year (the latter has nothing for Becket). Unfortunately for our purposes, however, the last leaf of the martyrology has been removed and a new one (fol. 73) - the leaf which contains the notice for Becket - substituted. Our text 'a' is written on this new leaf; it is also repeated verbatim in an early fifteenth-century obituary, martyrology, and Rule (BL Arundel 68, fol. 134v), a manuscript apparently copied from the twelfth-century book, and also in an early sixteenth-century Christ Church martyrology (London, Lambeth Palace 20, fol. 80v). So we seem justified in assuming that this is Christ Church's 'official' language, and very probably its authentic martyrological notice.

Additional evidence that fixes this language into the late twelfth century is its appearance in a martyrology of that date which seems to have been used at a religious house of a quite different type and scope from Christ Church. Bodl. Laud misc. 240 is a calendar, martyrology, and chapter homiliary very likely from the Augustinian abbey of St Osyth (Chich) in Essex. The entry for Becket is not in the original hand, which helps to date the writing of the main martyrology to before 1173; rather, it is a marginal addition, for the most part in the same hand which added the Conception of the Virgin on 8 December. But the first words of the martyrological entry were in turn overwritten with a seven-word heading which substitutes *prothomartyris* for the Christ Church entry's *martyris gloriosi*. The St Osyth marginal entry is also a good deal shorter, lacking both the final sentence of the text in the Canterbury manuscripts and seven words in the previous sentence. The calendar, which is somewhat later than the martyrology, has Becket's feast (29 December) as an original entry. What seems to have happened is that a martyrology of the third quarter of the twelfth century was both adapted for use at St Osyth (by, for example, the addition of the Octave of St Augustine's main feast, fol. 43, and of his Translation, fol. 49) and updated from time to time with numerous additions throughout the thirteenth century.

So it is possible that the Becket entry in this martyrology used (almost certainly) at St Osyth came from Canterbury; in any case, it is a prime witness to the textual tradition of 'a'. Further corroboration may be seen in two late medieval manuscripts. The first is a mid fourteenth-century martyrology from Hereford Cathedral (Bodl. Rawl. B.328)). At 29 December there is what looks to have been a long entry, of some twelve lines, but it was later thoroughly erased. Such words as can be read under an ultraviolet lamp correspond exactly to the Christ Church documents. The second, of the fifteenth century (Cambridge, Sidney Sussex College 79), was used at the parish church of West Wretham in Norfolk. Here the entry, in the original hand, is legible and follows the wording we are after, with only small alterations (the most important of which is that it begins 'Apud gentem Anglorum metropoli Cantuarie').

Whatever the origin and, so to speak, status of text 'a' ('Hic post longos exilii'), a second text (our 'b') was also in existence by the last quarter of the twelfth century. The martyrology of the collegiate church of St Chad in Shrewsbury (Bodl. Rawl. D.1225) features an entry of considerable length and interest despite - or perhaps because of - the fact that it seems to have no connection with direct Canterbury tradition. Its primary points of note are three. 1) Becket is styled 'archipresulis totius Angliae primatis et sedis apostolice legati.' 2) Stress is laid on the liturgical occasion at which the martyrdom took place: 'monachis sinaxim vespertinam celebrantibus in metropoli propria.' 3) The gory details of the murder itself include mention of the *pavimentum* where he fell and which came to be a particular focus of devotion.[2]

One further twelfth-century tradition needs to be noticed before we pass onto those entries for which there is only later evidence. The martyrology compiled at Cîteaux in 1173-74 has a notice for Becket which is probably the earliest clearly datable such entry that we possess:

---

[2] There is an additional item of interest at the foot of the facing page (fol. 15): eight lines, six of verse (part of a hymn?) addressed to the martyr, followed by a versicle and response. The last three are in whole or part illegible.

Morbos curat et languores Tome intercessio
Lepram mundat febrem sedat salvat a demonio
Res ac _____ inaudita membrorum subtractio
Reparatur reddit versus martiris suffragio
Atque prestat hanc virtutem sanguinis infusio
____________ fide degustatur cedit omnis ___sio.
V. Assit nobis ________________.
(R) __________ pie pr ___________________.

Hans Walther, *Carmina medii aevi posterioris latina*, I.i: *Initia carminum*, 2nd edn (Göttingen 1969), no. 11209, cites the first two lines, from this MS only.

> In Britanniis civitate Cantuarie, sancti Thomae episcopi et martyris,qui, ob defensionem iusticiae, in basilica sedis suae gladio percussus,migravit ad Christum.[3]

Notable here is the styling of the cathedral as *basilica* - a term used half a dozen other times in this martyrology (though never in quite the same way), but not at all in the English notices we are studying. It is not surprising that Becket should be one of only three 'modern' saints to be included here (the others are Maiolus of Cluny and Bernard of Clairvaux), because it was in the Cistercian abbey of Pontigny that he spent the first part of his long exile in France.

In fact, the next English notice we need to take up, following our roughly chronological pattern, specifically mentions Pontigny (*Spontaniciam*) as well as spelling out the year of the martyrdom. This (text 'c') is found in a thirteenth-century martyrology probably used at the parish church at Bathwick in western Wiltshire or eastern Somerset (Cambridge, Jesus Coll. Q.B.14 [31], fol. 1v). The entry is in the original hand, whereas Gilbert of Sempringham (d. 1189, can. 1202) is an addition, but this is scarcely conclusive. However, another addition at 5 January notes as well as the deposition of Edward the Confessor an octave day for St Thomas, which is rather a rarity. I can think of no reason why, at this obscurely-located parish church, there should have been any special interest in, or devotion to, Becket.

The other entries can be noticed more summarily, though each contains some point or points of interest; none comes from a martyrology earlier than the fourteenth century. Text 'd' ('Qui ob fidem catholicam') specifies that the cause of his death was Becket's unwillingness to acquiesce in *tirannicis iussionibus*. This entry is found in a fourteenth-century martyrology which reflects Exeter use (Cambridge, Corpus Christi College 93)[4] and in one of the following century which was bought in 1489 by the book collector Robert Elyot (Bodl. MS 731).[5]

---

[3] H. Rochais, ed. *Le Martyrologe Cistercien de 1173-1174 d'après le ms Dijon 114 (82).* (La Documentation Cistercienne 19; Rochefort 1972), 4.

[4] Edited from this MS by J.N. Dalton, *Ordinale Exon.* II (Henry Bradshaw Society 38, 1909); cf. the supplementary comments in *Ordinale Exon.* IV (HBS 79, 1941). I am grateful to Prof. John McCulloh for straightening out a confusion here as well as for careful and generous comments on an earlier draft of this paper.

[5] N.R. Ker, 'Robert Elyot's Books and Annotations,' *The Library* 5th ser. 30 (1975), 233-37.

Text ‘e’ comes from another fifteenth-century source, a book used at the Cluniac priory of St Saviour at Bermondsey (Surrey; now Bodl. Rawl. A.371). So one wonders particularly at the opening of this notice, ‘Qui tempore Henrici iunioris.’ What survival of tradition accounts for this specifying of the Young Henry, whose anticipatory crowning by the Archbishop of York in the summer of 1170 was one of the precipitating factors in Becket’s fateful return from exile and who in 1173 was to join his brothers Richard and Geoffrey in an unsuccessful rebellion against their father? Like the Shrewsbury martyrology (text ‘b’), this entry ends with a devotional petition, asking for the saint's intercession ‘pro nostris errantibus.’

By contrast, text ‘f’ is the only one to mention Henry II by name, in a brief entry otherwise not specially noteworthy. It is found in a fourteenth-century martyrology used at the collegiate church at Fotheringhay (Cambridge, St John's E.32 [135]). Both martyrology and calendar have had a great many entries added to them, but nothing suggests a reason for this particular wording.

Elements of several of the preceding entries are apparent in text ‘g’, which is found in a late fourteenth-century book eventually (but perhaps not in the middle ages) at Windsor (now Bodl. MS 821) and in a somewhat later one perhaps used at Norwich (Bodl. Lat. liturg. e.43, given by the executors of Francis Wormald in 1973). We note mentions of the exile (as in most of the other notices); of the four knights (but here ‘quatuor militum armatorum’ rather than the ‘militibus regalibus’ of ‘b’ or simple ‘quatuor militum’ of ‘e’ and ‘f’); of the liturgical occasion (‘cum fratres vespertinos ympnos psallerent’, but quite different from ‘b’s’ ‘monachis sinaxim vespertinam celebrantibus’); of ‘cerebrum’ (the tradition that Becket’s brain gushed out, as in ‘b,’ ‘d,’ and ‘e’); and of the spelling out of the year of death (as in ‘c’). One detail is new, however, the inclusion of the hairshirt (*cilicium*), widely noted posthumously as among the evidences of the archbishop's sanctity.

We conclude this survey of the texts slightly out of chronological sequence, with the briefest of these notices (‘h’). In Cambridge, Trinity College O.9.25(1437), a martyrology from the cell of St Albans at Belvoir in Leicestershire dating originally from the thirteenth century (with considerable material from the following century), the twelve words of the entry include three that we have not seen elsewhere: ‘articulos [fidei]’ rather than the simpler ‘fidem catholicam’ of ‘d,’ ‘quievit’as the verb for Becket’s dying, and ‘in conspectu principum’ rather than any mention of the four knights.

Here we see the kernel of an entirely different tradition from the others of the twelfth or thirteenth centuries ('a,' 'b,' and 'c') - which naturally causes us to wonder how many more such traditions there might have been. It causes us also to ponder the two principal possibilities raised by these eight martyrological notices for Thomas Becket: are these notices better regarded as independent compositions which occasionally pass from one witness to another or as the surviving representatives of a finite number (even if we have not exhausted it) of ways of expressing the Becket story in martyrological format?

If the former is likelier, we can do no more than to collect every possible notice into a corpus which, as such, has no immediately obvious further value. If, however, the latter is at least equally likely, we can contemplate the fascinating dual challenge of trying both to trace relationships among the martyrologies in a roughly stemmatic way and of trying to glimpse what echoes these notices might preserve of the very extensive body of medieval material about Becket.

Such echoes might themselves be of two kinds. The first kind is linguistic. Because of the nature of a martyrological entry - conditioned, as has been pointed out, by the form such entries had come to have through centuries of evolution - it is somewhat unlikely that extensive verbal echoes from any of the extant lives will be traceable. Instead, we shall have to hope that a few key words or phrases will yield some clues as to the context(s) out of which some of these notices arose, though probably not their actual authorship. For example, the word *basilica* in the (French) Cistercian notice of the 1170s (see above), although not found in any of the English martyrological notices, is used also by the contemporary chronicler Ralph Niger, who speaks of Becket being crowned with martyrdom 'in basilica sedis suae.'[6] This seems to have no parallel in any of the English notices we have been looking at, but it is hard to believe that there was no echo in England either of Niger's wording or of the Cistercian martyrological tradition as it passed from France.

The second kind of echo is liturgical. Those aspects of the liturgical commemoration of a saint where original composition is possible are primarily the lessons at matins (the saint's *passio* or *legendum*) and possibly some verse

---

6 The whole sentence is strikingly like the Cistercian notice: 'qui pro defensione ecclesiasticae libertatis exilium VII annis perpessus, tandem in basilica sedis suae martyrio coronatus est... ': *Chronicles*, ed. Robert Anstruther (Caxton Soc. 13; London 1851), 166. This instance is itself a useful caution against supposing that the notices collected here represent the entire body of those composed.

elements like rhymed antiphons or sequences (but any poetic elements will scarcely be discernible in the prose of a martyrological notice). It has been observed that in the absence of a text which would give us the (twelve) lessons used at matins by the monks of Christ Church, the (nine) lessons for the December 29th feast printed in the great Sarum Breviary of 1531 - the text from which the standard modern edition was made[7] - 'probably represent the most ancient tradition emanating from Canterbury, traceable in its origin to the first celebration of Becket's feast day 1173.'[8] But the fact there seems to be no echo of these lessons in any of the martyrological entries we have been looking at must cast doubt on this notion, especially in the light of the existence of the late twelfth century notice preserved in the Canterbury and St Osyth documents.

These martyrological entries have, then, a variety of uses - such as the one just sketched, to act as a kind of control on our understanding of later medieval liturgical texts which survive in greater profusion than those of the high middle ages. But the uses of the entries we have been considering are strictly limited by their paucity. Although it is always possible that many more might be discovered, with this subject, as with so much having to do with the study of the middle ages, making do with less than would be ideal is both a large part of the challenge and a large part of the enjoyment.

---

7 F. Procter and C. Wordsworth, eds. *Breviarium ad usum insignis ecclesiae Sarum.* 3 vols (Cambridge, 1879-86), I. col. ccxlvii-cclviii.

8 A. Duggan, 'The Cult of St.Thomas Becket in the thirteenth century,' in *St. Thomas of Cantilupe, Bishop of Hereford*, ed. Meryl Jancey (Hereford, 1982) 21-44 at 33.

IX

ST HUGH AS A LITURGICAL PERSON

In moving from a Carthusian monastery to the bishopric of Lincoln, St Hugh changed his liturgical context drastically. I want to try to explore some of the dimensions of that change of context. This will be done, not surprisingly, on the basis of relevant evidence from the sources for Hugh's life, for the liturgy of the Carthusians in his day, and (a scanty amount this) for that of the cathedral church at Lincoln. We may find, however, that the information yielded by these sources is insufficient both in quantity and, so to speak, in quality: that is, that we can ask more questions than can be answered. Yet the mere asking of these questions may be seen as part of what we are seeking; and so it may not be out of place to close with some misgivings about where we seem to be left by what we have learned.

Not that the nature of the subject itself furnishes any warrant for flabbiness or imprecision. We have a clearly focused question: what were the dimensions of Hugh's life as a liturgical person? Our sources will, of course, go some ways towards answering that question. But if the dimensions of the question outstrip what the sources tell us, that does not invalidate the question. To take a perhaps apt parallel, the interest of a number of modern historians in *alimentation* has opened a path for historical investigation of one of the most fundamental aspects of human life. Deeply obvious as the limitations of the evidence are, the importance of asking questions about something as basic as the nourishment by which human beings live is clear – even when it is also clear that many of the questions most likely cannot be answered.

So with St Hugh. To be sure, the historian of *alimentation* might well, thanks to the numerous references to diet in the *Magna Vita*, find him a fascinating case study; but it is by no strained analogy that we approach thinking about Hugh's liturgical life in this way. The contexts in which he lived make it axiomatic that liturgical worship must have been a prime element in his existence; and we can infer from our knowledge of the finished product – St Hugh as revealed to us by his biographers – that this

* I should like to express gratitude for assistance at various points to David Farmer, Rodney Thomson, and Joan Williams. All citations from Adam of Eynsham's *Magna Vita Sancti Hugonis* are to the edition of D. L. Douie and (D.) H. Farmer (2nd edn, 1985), whose translation has also been used. This edition is referred to by volume and page numbers in parentheses.

was at least to a certain extent the case. But what can be said beyond this axiom and this inference?

Hugh's liturgical formation was in a small community of regular canons, where he was sent at the age of eight. There were at least seven of these canons, so the *Magna Vita* tells us; almost certainly they used the liturgy of the diocese of Grenoble in which they were located. After some eleven years there Hugh, having been ordained deacon, was put in charge of a parish church run by the same canons. This meant that he went from a fairly small to a tiny liturgical context. He soon imported another canon, who was a priest;[1] what liturgical life there was, was solely up to the two of them.

The case here seems almost like the classical one of the promising young cleric just out of seminary, shocked at the loneliness and isolation of church life in a small parish. Indeed, this may help to explain why Hugh was so overwhelmed by his visit to La Grande Chartreuse.[2] The apparent sanctity of the monks and the fascinating combination of eremetic and coenobitic elements in which they lived aside, we may suppose that Hugh's spiritual imagination was kindled at the prospect of a regular and splendid, if predictably austere, liturgical life. It was as a Carthusian that he was ordained priest. At that point he could have expected to spend the rest of his life functioning as a monk-priest in a medium-sized context, probably somewhat larger than that of the canons' community at Grenoble but not exceeding two or three dozen choir monks at most.

When Hugh entered the Charterhouse in about 1160, its liturgy seems to have been quite clearly fixed. The Constitutions of Guigo I were some thirty years old, and had been reinforced by the directive of the 1142 Chapter General that all Carthusian houses should worship in the same way.[3] Subsequent amplifications of custom had imported hymns into the divine office, made possible the more frequent celebration of mass, and in general brought the Carthusian rite within the normal range of western liturgical practice of the twelfth century – at the simple end of the range, to be sure, but by no means on a lunatic fringe of austerity: plain chasubles were worn by the celebrant at mass, but chasubles nonetheless.

These were the liturgical norms Hugh would have carried with him to Witham. Despite its royal foundation it was not an immediate success; nonetheless, after he arrived as its third prior, in 1179, it is likely that its worshipping life soon approximated that of the Great Charterhouse. And, in the absence of any sources for Witham itself, it seems safe to take the liturgical usages of that mother house as representing what Hugh was accustomed to at the time of his election as unwilling bishop of Lincoln in 1186.

[1] Whether this is the same man as the 'simple priest' referred to in *MV* I.vi (1.20) (*simplici quodam sacerdote*) is not clear.

[2] It may also be that Hugh's reaction to Cluny when he visited it late in his life (*MV* V.xv (2.175): 'Truly, if I had seen this place before I fell in love with Chartreuse, I should have become a Cluniac monk') reflects sympathetic admiration for its complex liturgical life.

[3] *Patr. Lat.* 153.1126.

At Lincoln the situation was of course very different. Whereas Witham had been a new, uncertain, and relatively small foundation, the establishment at Lincoln Minster was of reasonable age, very sure (and proud) of itself, and undeniably large. Monastic bishops were no particular rarity in the twelfth century – certainly not in England – and several recent bishops of Grenoble had been drawn from the ranks of the Carthusians. Nonetheless for the prior of the Witham Charterhouse to become bishop of Lincoln was, so to speak, an enormous jump liturgically. This jump was not only from a monastic to a secular liturgy. Equally drastic, I suggest, were the aspects of size and of *persona*: henceforth Hugh as a liturgical person would be functioning when at Lincoln in a very large context, when travelling in a national (and even international) context; and, save for intervals of respite back at Witham and La Grande Chartreuse, always as a bishop.

There is a key question here to which, though purely factual, no definite answer seems at this point possible: how often did Hugh participate in the liturgy of his cathedral church?[4] There are some bits of evidence, but only partial ones. On the one hand, he is in Lincoln on a Good Friday when the miracle of the hod takes place;[5] and he celebrates there on a St Stephen's day, when another wondrous event occurs.[6] On the other, he is away from the Minster on an Easter Eve[7] as well as at other great feasts. Of course, as a bishop (and a tenant-in-chief) he frequently had to subordinate any purely personal priorities he might have felt to the demands of other duties; so it behoves us to be somewhat cautious about assuming that what he did is in every case what he would like to have done.

Let us begin to consider the transition he made – summed up as it is by the overall title of our Conference as *de cella in seculum* – by looking at three specific examples. The first has to do with the rhythm of the divine, or daily, office. The normal Carthusian practice was that vespers, matins, and lauds (to use the normative later medieval terminology) were said in choir, the other offices privately in each monk's cell.[8] At Lincoln of course this was not the case. In theory – and we would do well to remember that at Lincoln theory was probably a good deal further removed from practice than at a Charterhouse – all clerics in residence met for all of the hours in the Cathedral choir. In practice, of course, this must have meant, besides much absenteeism, a good deal of running of separate hours together, but the theory was a more completely corporate one than the Carthusian.

Another obvious difference that would have been apparent to Hugh in the rhythm of the divine office is that in the shape of its largest component,

[4] Indeed, in the absence of a full itinerary for Hugh as bishop, the question will most likely always remain unanswered; certainly no consecutive account of his movements can be derived from the existing biographical materials.

[5] H. Farmer, ed., 'The Canonization of St Hugh of Lincoln: the text of Cotton Roll xiii.27', *Lincolnshire Archit. and Archaeol. Soc. Jnl* 6.ii (1956), 86-117, at p. 97.

[6] *MV* V.ii (2.80).

[7] This seems to be the correct inference from the story in *MV* IV.v (2.21).

[8] Guigo I, *Consuetudines Cartusiae* xxix.6, ed. un Chartreux, *Coutumes de Chartreuse*. Sources chrétiennes 313 (Paris, 1984), 230.

matins. Whereas the Carthusian office was an adaptation of the monastic (Benedictine), Lincoln of course followed secular practice. While both forms divided the service into three nocturns, monastic use allocated the psalms quite differently from the secular distribution, and arranged the lessons in units usually of four (or, in ordinary summertime, one) compared with three for the secular. And – probably the most noticeable contrast to one experiencing both forms – great feasts have twelve lessons in monastic use as opposed to nine in secular. Though any difference in aggregate duration must depend on how long the individual lessons are, in general it is likely that to one accustomed to the fullness of a monastic matins of twelve lessons, its secular counterpart containing a third fewer seemed somewhat sparse. Certainly the balance is different.[9]

All indications are that Hugh was scrupulous in observing the hours of the daily office; yet a personal devotional practice referred to in detail by Adam of Eynsham suggests that either he found the spiritual nourishment imparted by matins inadequate or that the demands of his own life made the regular observance of that hour impossible (we shall return to this point later).

Occasionally there are signs of what seems to be almost a casual attitude towards the daily office. This is shown in the story Adam tells of Hugh's prevision of the death of his almoner, the Templar Morinus, which led him to order horses to be prepared so that he could meet Morinus's corpse. His vision had caused him to rise earlier than usual, and perhaps it took a while to prepare the horses; in any case, as Adam puts it, 'Whilst the horses were being got ready, the bishop and his clerks were chanting the Prime hymn.'[10] The impression one gets is that the waiting time was put to good use; someone – was it Hugh? – must have said something like, 'At least we can get Prime out of the way.'

Similarly with Compline, which Hugh's entourage were chanting as he died: here Adam explains that, though unwilling to leave the dying man at such a time, they nonetheless withdrew (where, he does not say) to recite the hour.[11] In neither case is any connection suggested between the office and either the church or the cell. In short, the attitude is much more like that of the cleric reading his breviary on the subway than like that which ostensibly, anyhow, characterised the canons of Lincoln, not to mention the monks of Witham.

This question of how liturgical observances are conceived, as well as how they are performed, leads us to the next area of investigation: roughly, how the psalms are understood. By this I do not mean how they are interpreted but how the psalms as (in a rough phrase) liturgical

[9] One obvious factor is that not only are there more lessons by one third, but responsories after each lesson to match; since responsories often took longer to sing than lessons to read, the cumulative musical effect of a twelve-lessons matins would have been much fuller than that of nine.

[10] *MV* V.xviii (2.213). Prime, like compline, could easily be said from memory by those familiar with it; the story does not necessarily imply the possession of breviaries.

[11] *MV* V.xvi (2.198).

artifacts lend themselves to being used. Partly this is a matter of some factors we have just noticed. There is a different allocation of psalms for the divine office in the monatic use than in secular, so that in most cases * individual psalms appear at different points in the week's *cursus*.[12] But of course the psalms are used extensively also in the liturgy of the mass (not, however, as whole and identified psalms) and of the occasional or pastoral offices; and they were the staple of the accretions that grew around the basic core of liturgy from Carolingian times onwards.

So it is not surprising that there are apparent in Hugh's liturgical contexts some peculiarities – we might be tempted to call them eccentricities – in the use of the psalms. This is evident in a passage from the *Magna Vita* which is either unclear or, or taken at face value, astonishing. During Hugh's last days, Adam says,

> As long as he was strong enough, he kept to the custom of alternately sitting and standing for the psalms and made his clerks to do the same. Thus, whilst one sat down to rest his weary limbs, another stood up to show his respect for the presence of God and the angels.[13]

What can Adam mean here by *vicissitudinem standi et sedendi inter psallendum*? Hugh would have been familiar with the practice prescribed in the *Consuetudines Sancti Antelmi* (pre-1170) by which there was quite a lot of shifting of positions during responsories, especially on greater feasts;[14] and there was the usual quota of bowing at various points in the recitation of the invitatory at matins and in other parts of the office.[15] But nothing like the jack-in-the-box effect Adam seems to describe appears as a Carthusian custom.

When, however, Hugh was at Lincoln – and properly even when he was not – he might have taken part in an equally odd practice involving the psalms. This is the custom of dividing the psalter among the cathedral clergy for daily extra-liturgical recitation. This parcelling out of the psalms goes back at least to the 1130s. In Lincoln Cathedral MS 1, the Great Bible, there is a list headed, *Hi sunt ad psalterium canendum*, which lists the psalms allotted to forty-three cathedral clergy.[16] This list itself seems to be a late twelfth-century copy; but since forty-three is the number of clergy – bishop, dignitaries, and prebendaries – known to have existed at the Minster in 1132, it seems likely that the practice referred to in the list dates from that earlier period.

[12] An obvious example is Sunday matins, which in all secular uses includes many of the first twenty psalms but in the monastic distribution employs pss. xx-xxxi.
[13] *MV* V.xvi (2.188). We may wonder whether it is possible that Adam was speaking of the use of misericords. That would be the case only if Hugh invariably observed his offices in a choir – which is what we have just seen he did not do.
[14] *Consuetudines Antelmi* cap. vi, ed. James Hogg, *Die ältesten Consuetudines der Kartäuser*. Analecta Cartusiana 1 (Berlin, 1970; Salzburg 1973), 110.
[15] Cap. vii; *op. cit.* p.111.
[16] Fol. 207ra; printed in D. E. Greenway, ed., *Fasti Ecclesiae Anglicanae 1066-1300 III: Lincoln* (London, 1977), 151-3, and less accurately in *Lincoln Cathedral Statutes* (see note 20) III.788-92.

* **monatic *should read* monastic**

The principle on which the list works is purely numerical – the bishop says the first four psalms, the dean the next four, and so on, with the final eight assigned to an unidentified prebendary William – and the rationale for the practice must be simply that it is in some way a good thing to get through the psalter in a day. That is of course an ancient ascetical practice at what we may call the championship level; St Benedict alluded to it in explaining his own allocation of the psalms into a weekly *cursus* suitable to the 'tepid' monks for whom his Rule was intended.[17] The notion of a daily psalter split forty-three ways can scarcely be considered a championship-level practice. Even less is this true from c.1187 (the year after Hugh became bishop), by which time we know from a second list in the same Bible that the number of members of the chapter has grown to fifty-six, a figure which becomes standard for Lincoln throughout the rest of the middle ages; and this figure does *not* include the bishop.[18] Though there are some difficulties about this list, it is almost certain that the expanded list also related to the allocation of the psalms – as witness the fifty-six stall-back plates with the psalm-incipits on them in the Minster choir.[19] If this is the case, that the second list lacks the bishop's name may be of special importance. The natural inference from that fact is that he was no longer included in the allocation of psalms; and the obvious question is, why not? Could this exclusion, somewhere between Alexander the Magnificent (bishop 1123-48) and Hugh, from participation in the shared-out daily psalter have been the result of a disinclination on Hugh's part to cooperate in a practice he found strange or even incomprehensible?

That suggestion is pure speculation. A likelier answer is that during the seventeen years when the see was effectively vacant – from the death of Robert de Chesney in 1166 through the inconclusive episode of Geoffrey Plantagenet to the accession of Walter of Coutances in 1183 – the combination of the lack of a bishop to take a part plus what is clearly a considerable growth in the number of prebends resulted in the bishop's quota being taken away in the general reassignment of psalms. Whatever the reason, it is curious that in the copy of this list in no less a source than the *Liber Niger* – the great hodge-podge of Minster documents originally collected about 1300 and, with the rest of the cathedral statutes, edited exhaustively but almost incomprehensibly by Henry Bradshaw and Christopher Wordsworth in 1892[20] – calls the document 'Antiqua constitucio pro psalterio et pro missa singulis diebus dicendis'. The headnote further specifies,

> Provisum est ab R. decano[21] adiunctis ei discretis iuris de capitulo et institutum in capitulo presente Domino Hugone Lincolniensi

[17] *Reg. Ben.* xviii; ed. and tr. J. McCann (London, 1960), 66.

[18] Fol. 207rb; ptd Greenway, pp. 162-5.

[19] J. F. Wickenden, 'The Choir Stalls of Lincoln Cathedral', *Archaeological Journal* 38 (1881), 42-61, esp. 49-53.

[20] H. Bradshaw and C. Wordsworth, ed., *Statutes of Lincoln Cathedral*, 3 vols (Cambridge, 1892-7), I.300.

[21] Either Richard fitz Neal, dean probably from Dec. 1183 until 1189, or just

Episcopo et confirmante ut psalmi hoc ordine dicantur ab Episcopo et Decano atque canonicis.

In the arrangement there recorded the bishop had been restored to the rota, pss. i-iii being assigned to him. This list is arranged not by the canons' names but by the titles of their prebends, again fifty-six. By the end of the thirteenth century,[22] then, it was believed that St Hugh was the founder of a practice we have seen reason to think he took no part in. But he cannot have helped knowing about it, and perhaps knowing that some of his predecessors had shared in it. Again, we wonder how it must have struck him.

This basic question of ours recurs also in the third general area we want to look at, that of contrasts between the sanctorale of the Carthusians and of Lincoln. To say 'contrasts in the liturgical year' between the two would be putting it too strongly, because of course the main outlines of that year were standard throughout western Christendom long before the twelfth century. But the contrasts we seek now are not wholly confined to the observance of saints' days. Most notably, when Gerald of Wales tells us that Hugh was conspicuous among his brother prelates for his strict keeping of solemn feasts, and instances specifically Ascension, Pentecost, and Trinity Sunday, we take note;[23] because (if this witness of Gerald's is accurate – a point to be returned to later) Hugh probably never observed Trinity Sunday until he became bishop. It was not included in the Carthusian calendar until much later; as is well known, its popularity spread from England as a by-product of the cult of Thomas Becket, who had been consecrated bishop on that day.

For the sanctorale in the strict sense – in full phrase, the *proprium sanctorum* – the differences between Carthusian and Lincoln use were not all that great. On balance the Carthusian calendar – we take that of c.1134 as normative[24] – was, as would be expected, sparer than that which we can postulate for Lincoln (no more than postulate: no Lincoln calendars of anything like that period survive).[25] But the Carthusian calendar of Hugh's time included no English saints, not even Oswald, widely culted on the Continent. Did it therefore seem to Hugh strange to be the head of a liturgical unit which observed many distinctively English feasts – among which would almost certainly have been Alban, Augustine of Canterbury, Cuthbert, Etheldreda, Swithun, Botulf, Guthlac, Edmund King of the

conceivably Roger de Rolleston c.1195-1223 (Greenway, p. 9).

[22] This list was completed after 1290 when the fifty-sixth prebend, Milton Ecclesia, was re-established; there had during most of the century been only fifty-five.

[23] Giraldus Cambrensis, *Opera* VII, ed. J. F. Dimock (Rolls Series, 1877), 100; cf. R. Loomis, ed., *Giraldus Cambrensis. The Life of St Hugh of Avalon*, Garland Library of Medieval Literature, ser. A, vol. 31 (New York and London, 1985), pp. 22-3.

[24] Printed in Hansjakob Becker, *Die Responsorien des Kartäuserbreviers. Untersuchungen zu Urform und Herkunft des Antiphonars der Kartause*, Münchener Theologische Studien, ser. II.39 (Munich, 1971), 42-5.

[25] Indeed, what scanty evidence there is for a Lincoln 'use' as a whole also comes from much later.

East Angles, perhaps also Ethelbert King of the East Angles, Edward the Martyr, Dunstan, Alphege, and Edward the Confessor, with maybe one or two others like Aidan or Aethelwold?

Of discrepancies the other way round – feasts observed by the Carthusians but not at Lincoln – there would probably have been fewer, though it is possible that a couple of primarily monastic occasions would not have been present in a secular calendar – Paul the first hermit on 10 January and Hilarion on 21 October (and possibly Antony on 17 January). But since on the whole the early Carthusian calendar is no more than that of the fully developed sacramentaries of the same sort as would have underlain the Lincoln calendar also, it is less likely that Hugh would have been struck by any very glaring omissions than by what must have seemed to a Carthusian the filling up of the calendar with a dozen or so of local saints.

A few more pieces of information need to be laid out before we try to sum up this attempt to get inside St Hugh's 'liturgical sensibility'. One further bit concerns his attitude towards celebrating the mass. By his time it had become normal for Carthusian monk-priests to celebrate frequently, and it seems safe to assume that the daily celebration recorded as his practice during his retreats at Witham represents his personal preference.[26] But what were the parameters of that liturgical action for him? This question arises in connection with the episode of Easter Monday of 1199.[27] Leaving Richard's court in Normandy he goes to La Flèche and is there about to say mass when he is told that his wagons and horses have been impounded by the garrison and the pack animals seized by robbers; whereupon his clerks (and, Adam adds, even the bishop of Rochester, who was also on the trip) urge Hugh to give up the idea of a celebration and instead merely to read the Gospel! Hugh refuses, insisting instead on donning full pontifical vestments and adding a pontifical blessing. In the circumstances it might have seemed sensible to postpone the celebration altogether and flee forthwith; what is astonishing is the alternative suggestion, the very making of what presupposes that it was at least within the realm of possibility. Would we have thought that a twelfth-century Carthusian bishop would even remotely consider a reading of the liturgical Gospel to be in any way an adequate alternative, or even substitute, for the celebration of the eucharist, especially on so solemn a day as Easter Monday?

The continuation of that story provides us with another piece of valuable information about one of Hugh's liturgical attitudes. As he proceeds on to Le Mans the danger has not disappeared; nonetheless he declines to permit the lessons at matins to be shortened, insisting, Adams says, 'on having long lessons recited as was his custom'.[28] This suggests that he put a premium on that element of the night office which may be termed basic nourishment, the lessons from scripture, patristic homilies, and the lives of the saints. Yet we are told twice in the *Magna Vita* of his practice of

[26] *MV* IV.x (2.49, 50).

[27] *MV* V.xii (2.146).

[28] *Ibid.* (p.147: *longas more solito recitari facit lectiones*).

having read to him at mealtimes very much the same sort of literature as he would have heard during the nocturns. In the first mention Adam implies that Hugh somehow found the night office readings inadequate, and devised a systematic plan for supplementing them:

> At mealtimes he had the scriptures read to him with such assiduity that at matins and dinner he managed to cover practically all the Old and New Testaments (with the exception of the four gospels) ... and in addition to this the passions of some of the martyrs, certain lives of the saints, and the best known sermons of the fathers for the great festivals.[29]

The second mention explains his *schema* for the gospels:

> Whilst every year he had the other canonical books read to him at the appointed times both at Matins and at meal times, he caused the four books of the gospels to be read in the four seasons of the year at Prime after the Martyrology. He never neglected these readings even when journeying on horseback.[30]

Note that this is not the bishop exercising his *ius liturgicum*; it is Hugh's own private devotional practice we are dealing with, one which we must put into the general category of para-liturgical.

The same word, para-liturgical, could almost be applied also to Hugh's attitude to one of the pastoral offices. This concerns his curious propensity for taking part in funerals, apparently almost at random.[31] Even when he was not officially involved in the funeral, he would, if a book were available, take the priest's part – that is, interject himself into the rite otherwise performed by (so we assume) the parish priest. So great was this propensity that we are told of a book Hugh almost always had with him, *orationes cum psalmis*,[32] which must have been either a separately bound office of the dead or more likely a manual, alias ritual. Since one of these episodes takes place in Normandy we cannot suppose that Hugh's rationale was that as chief liturgical officer of his diocese it was fitting that he should function at any ecclesiastical rite he encountered; rather, his habit of intruding himself into funerals must be seen as an expression of a private, perhaps somewhat morbid, spirituality – and as a practice which he could follow only because he had during his lifetime acquired a great reputation for sanctity and authority.

His liturgical preparations for his own death both show the intensity of his concern for the rites associated with dying and give the one specific bit of light that we have concerning his own awareness of the liturgical dimension of his transition *de cella in seculum*. As he returns from the Continent to England in the late summer of 1200, sensing himself to be fatally ill and realising that his fellow-prelates were all at the session of the Great Council, meeting (as it happened) at Lincoln, Hugh, by this time at

29 *MV* III.xiii (1.126).
30 *MV* IV.xvi (2.194).
31 E.g., *MV* V.i (2.77).
32 *MV* V.ii (2.79).

his London residence, asked for seven or eight monks from Westminster and choir clerks from St Paul's to attend him:[33] that is, he requested a mixed force representing both the monastic tradition from which he had come and the secular element into which he had been thrust. Surely this was not accidental; indeed, having lingered longer than was expected, and still at London, the day before he died he sent to the abbot of Westminster and the dean of St Paul's for the same mixture of monks and clerks. It seems clear that this gesture of his is meant to reflect the mixed liturgical context in which the final fourteen years of his life had been led.

As we reflect on these bits of evidence about St Hugh as a liturgical person, one impression comes through with surprising clarity: that to a large extent the liturgical attitudes we have ascribed to him are those we customarily associate not with the high but with the later middle ages. Among these are the idea of liturgical equivalency (let some action stand for some other, like the reading of the Gospel for the mass); a sense of corporate worship as less vivid than private forms of religiosity (his creation of what is virtually his own lectionary system, supplementing to the point of supplanting that of matins); and the kind of individualism that we see reflected in his idiosyncratic intrusions into funerals, the urgency of rites for the dying somehow cancelling all ordinary notions of liturgical propriety and good sense.

Beyond that conclusion, this brief and *faute de mieux* superficial attempt to get inside Hugh's liturgical sensibility has some ramifications of wider significance than the admittedly rather small number of instances deployed here would seem to suggest. In ascending order, perhaps, of relevance to the business of this conference, they may be termed ascetical, psychological, and historiographical. The ascetical belongs to the theologian's province – which may indeed be that of other papers here. My brief will stretch only so far as to pose a single question, one which those with some experience of a structured liturgical life may want to ponder: is the modern presumption that a liturgically-based spirituality is in general the most normative and healthiest just that, a modern presumption? When every caution has been expressed about the limits of our evidence and so on, it remains true that the spirituality of this great Carthusian saint, as conveyed primarily through the eye of a Benedictine biographer, comes through to us as much less informed by the liturgy than we might have imagined.

And this leads to the second ramification of our story, the psychological or (at the risk of jargon) psycho-historical. Whether or not we are surprised that on the ascetical level the liturgy does not bulk larger than it seems to do in what we know of Hugh's life, on the level of trying to understand the inner workings of a late twelfth century man we are faced with a different kind of enigma. In saying this I am thinking of the interest of many contemporary historians not this time in *alimentation* but in what has come to be called *mentalités*. A sentence from George Duby's recent life of William the Marshal sums up this approach eloquently: 'I

[33] *MV* V.xvi (2.191).

want to try to see the world the way these men saw it.'[34] Thus expressed, our problem is that from the prevailing impression we have of his age, the way Hugh saw the world *should* have been considerably, perhaps even primarily, based on the liturgy. That we cannot with confidence affirm this to be the case makes for a certain uneasiness. If what we had supposed to be one of our lynch-pins in building up a picture of the past proves weak, what else may totter?

Of course, a shaking of received assumptions is no bad thing. It is, however, distressing historiographically – our final ramification – when sources we thought would provide us with a certain kind of information fail to do so. This point is fundamental to my concern (speaking as an historian) because I am aware that it may be not so much that there is something amiss in what we would have thought made Hugh tick (the psycho-historical) nor in what the judgment of prescriptive theologians might suggest ought to have made him tick (the ascetical), as that our sources just do not add up to a believable picture. We have to deal with the factors of both incompleteness and exaggeration. Gerald the Welshman's account of Hugh's faithfulness in keeping Trinity Sunday may be an example of the latter. I think it quite possible that Hugh never kept Trinity Sunday at all and that Gerald either did not know that fact or had no qualms about improving on the existing state of affairs. Similarly, it may be merely the incompleteness of our evidence which accounts for the impression we have of Hugh as a bit liturgically quirky, and that if we had more – some sort of Parson Woodforde-like diary, say, recording with tedious fidelity each liturgical obligation met – we would realise that some of the more or less juicy bits we have been considering were of interest to Hugh's biographers just because they were atypical.

Still, we can only make the best use of what evidence we do possess. If, as promised at the beginning, this paper has raised more questions than it has answered, it does perhaps fill what would otherwise be a sizeable gap in a conference devoted to the life and legacy of Hugh of Avalon, the Charterhouse, Witham, and Lincoln: for no even remotely complete assessment of him will ever be possible without the liturgical dimension's being taken fully – if never quite satisfactorily – into account.

[34] G. Duby, *William Marshal. The Flower of Chivalry*, tr. Richard Howard (New York, 1985), 38.

X

Bede Among the Fathers?
The Evidence from Liturgical Commemoration

In the fascinating and protracted argument as to when the patristic period in the Latin West can meaningfully be said to have ended, a *terminus* sometimes offered is the death of the Venerable Bede (735). This end point is best known, of course, through the Corpus Christianorum Series Latina which, with its *Clavis Patrum Latinorum*, goes a long way towards canonizing the notion that Bede is the last of the Latin Fathers — everything after him being categorized as 'Continuatio Medievalis'. Other well known tools, however, have earlier cut-off dates; for example, what may seem most normative in the context of the present Conference, the *Oxford Dictionary of the Christian Church*, says firmly that from the eighteenth century on 'the patristic period is generally held to be closed with St. Isidore of Seville in the West' (d. 636), though it does allow a date as late as the death of St. John of Damascus [749] in the East[1].

Such things were not at all clear-cut in the middle ages, when, as far as I'm aware, there was no notion of patristics as a subject, though of course some sense existed as to the Fathers of the Church. Of various ways one might attempt to ascertain who medieval people thought the Fathers were — for example, which writers were drawn on as sources for homilies in the Night Office, or which were cited as a matter of course by students of the Bible from the twelfth century on — it seems worth asking what such evidence as can be marshalled for the liturgical commemoration of Bede suggests as to the degree (if any) that he was regarded as one of the Fathers, albeit a late-born and English-bred one. This is a rather narrowly defined query, and the scope of the present investigation is limited commensurately; almost all the material known to me is English and is drawn from liturgical manuscripts rather than from, say, reports of miracles connected with Bede's bones or reverence paid to them.

As might be expected, the great preponderance of the material I have found comes from liturgical calendars. It needs therefore to be stressed that inclusion in a liturgical calendar in the middle ages does not by any means prove liturgical observance; a glance at any handful of medieval service

[1] F.L. Cross and E.A. Livingtone (eds.), *The Oxford Dictionary of the Christian Church* (Oxford, 1974[2]), 504.

books which contain both calendars and sanctorales (that is, forms for individual saints) will quickly establish that. But inclusion in a calendar does make liturgical commemoration feasible, and a person so included can fairly be regarded as within at least the lowest range of such commemoration, that of a *memoria* in the office or an additional set of orations in the mass — depending on what else happens on the day in question.

In Bede's case something quite important occupied the day on which he was reckoned to have died: the commemoration of Augustine of Canterbury, fixed since at least the later seventh century at May 26th (as Bede himself tells us, *Hist. Eccl.* II.iii). Awkward though this is, the tradition of the 26th as also Bede's death day seems firmly fixed as early as there is any evidence of his commemoration; in the middle ages he was only very occasionally commemorated on either the 25th (which was devoted to Pope Urban, with Aldhelm sometimes added) or the 27th (despite its being generally vacant).

Such mention of Bede as is found in calendars may serve our purposes in two ways: through how he is styled and through any indications as to the grading (i.e., importance) of a given commemoration. As to styling, since Bede is one of a tiny number of Fathers or possible Fathers not to have been a bishop, the most useful comparison may be with Jerome, who like Bede was ecclesiastically a 'presbyter', hagiographically a 'confessor', and patristically (if I may coin a word) a 'doctor' — at least that latter term, 'doctor', is one we shall be looking for. So when, towards the end of the middle ages, calendars in missals of York Use, both manuscript and printed[2], list Jerome as 'presbyter, confessor, et doctor' and Bede as 'presbyter et confessor', we can perhaps infer that Bede is not here being regarded in the same way as that most notable of non-episcopal Fathers generally was. But this is slightly misleading, or at least not very informative, since, though Bede is styled 'doctor' in only two calendars, both related to St. Albans[3], 'doctor' does (as we shall see) become a common epithet for him in another kind of source. Otherwise, he is styled either 'presbyter' or, less often, 'confessor' (or both) in nearly every one of the roughly three dozen calendars entries that I have noted; on balance, modes of styling in calendars do not materially advance our enquiry.

The grading of any possible commemoration, inconsistent and almost haphazard though grading 'systems' often are, may be somewhat more useful. In the majority of calendars where comparative indications of liturgical importance are given, Augustine of Canterbury is generally magnified (as having nine lessons, or being observed 'in albis' or 'in cappis', or written in red) while Bede has almost always simply 'commemoratio' or 'memoria' next

[2] As in the composite calendar printed in *Missale ad usum insignis ecclesiae Eboracensis*, W.G. Henderson (ed.), I (Surtees Society 59; 1874), xxxiv, xxxviii.

[3] See notes 5 and 6 below.

to his name. Only in a few cases have I encountered the opposite. One, a late fourteenth century Carmelite breviary[4], preserves the text of nine proper lessons for Bede; we shall return to it momentarily. Another, a calendar of c. 1400 which is perhaps the latest of the ten or so calendars from St. Albans abbey that have survived, has the entry 'Sancti Bede doctoris xii lectiones' — the highest number in the Benedictine office — but no text is extant (the book is a tiny psalter)[5]; and the same grading is found in the mid-fifteenth century calendar of a cell of St. Albans, Tynemouth (the codex was perhaps used also at Wymondham)[6]. Again, a calendar from a North Country Augustinian house specifies, at May 27th, nine lessons; but there Bede is only 'presbyter', not 'presbyter et doctor'[7]. On the whole, though, there is little evidence that Augustine of Canterbury is ever 'trumped' in importance by an awareness of Bede as being of patristic standing.

More instructive may be the inclusion of Bede's name in martyrologies — in those, that is, which bring their contents 'up to date' by including figures later than their base in (most commonly) the ninth century martyrology of Usuard, which is itself modelled closely on Bede's and which does not include him[8]. Most of the sixteen instances I have found date, not surprisingly, from the later middle ages, a period much better represented by such books than earlier centuries are, anyhow. Also not surprising is that among the earliest martyrological mentions is one from Durham Cathedral Priory of c. 1100: the simple entry 'Deposicio uenerabilis Bede presbiteri'[9]. Almost as early is a martyrology from Exeter Cathedral[10], 'in Britannia apud Durelmam [a garbled form of Durham] uenerabilis Bede presbiteri et confessoris' — an entry which puts Bede into the customary *Martyrologium Hieronymianum* form of general place (here, Britannia), specific place if possible (Durham), and saint with styling.

At the same time, the beginning of the twelfth century, a fuller tradition is also in being, one in which Bede is spoken of as 'doctor Anglorum sagacissimus'; but the wording disappoints as it continues with a quite general 'cuius quanta extitunt merita et doctrine fluenta mellita et bonorum operum exempla testantur'. This wording appears in a martyrology from St. Augustine's, Canterbury, of probably just after 1100[11]. It is found also, in precisely the same words, in one from the Augustinian house of St. Osyth in Essex of about 1170[12]; there it is an early marginal addition, and could well have been copied from something like the Canterbury book.

[4] See note 22 below.
[5] Oxford, Bodleian Library (hereafter Bodl.), MS Gough liturg. 18.
[6] Bodl. Lat. liturg. g. 8.
[7] Bodl. Rawl. D. 938.
[8] J. Dubois (ed.), *Le Martyrologe d'Usuard* (Subsidia Hagiographica 40; 1965).
[9] Durham, Cathedral Lib. B.iv.24, f. 23v.
[10] Exeter, Cathedal Lib. 3518, f. 23v.
[11] London, British Library (hereafter BL), MS Cott. Vit. C.xii, f. 130v.
[12] Bodl. Laud misc. 240, f. 27v.

From the next century on a couple of alternative traditions seems to be in effect about Bede's entry in martyrologies. One is to call him 'egregius' rather than 'uenerabilis', as seen in a thirteenth century martyrology for the Cisterican nuns at Wintney in Hampshire[13]. A second, biographically accurate, is to specify the place to which he is ascribed as 'Apud Gyervum', Jarrow, as in a book from Belvoir Priory, another cell of St. Albans, of the thirteenth/fourteenth century[14].

But the most normative wording comes to be that found in, for example, an Abingdon Abbey martyrology of the late thirteenth century[15]: 'deposicio uenerabilis Bede presbiteri confessoris et doctoris'. This tradition, that he should be styled as 'doctor', is widely evident thereafter: in books of the later middle ages from as far apart as Devonshire[16], Suffolk[17], Surrey (the Cluniacs at Faversham)[18], and Northamptonshire (a book used at Fotheringhay)[19]. One, unlocatable[20], goes further in speaking of him as 'doctoris Anglorum gentis', which sounds promising because of the echo of the title of his *Historia ecclesiastica gentis Anglorum*; but it proceeds with only a rather prolix discussion of when he died, which claims that he was 'nonagenarius', ninety years old — a venerable Bede for sure! Odd though this seems, it may hark back faintly to the wording of the standard entry for Jerome in the Usuard family of martyrologies, 'apud Bethleem Iude deposicio beati Ieronimi presbiteri qui obiit anno etatis sue nonagesimo octavo mense sexto'[21]; and if so may imply some indication of Bede's being regarded as a Father like Jerome.

These calendarial and martyrological notices are just that: notices, tantalizing in brevity and difficult to interpret with precision. Fortunately, at least one piece of evidence survives of a fuller sort: a late fourteenth century Carmelite breviary from somewhere in the east of England, perhaps Cambridge, which offers the text of a full nine lessons 'in die uenerabilis Bede presbiteri'[22]. This is described as the 'grata festivitas nostri beati Bede presbiteri confessoris egregii et doctoris catholici': a combination of virtually all of the elements noted above. Among the information offered is a lengthy enumeration of his works, borrowed obviously from Bede's own list at the end of the *Historia*

[13] BL Cott. Claud. D.iii, f. 24.

[14] Cambridge, Trinity College O.9.25, f. 22.

[15] Cambridge, University Library Kk.i.22, f. 56v.

[16] Bodl. MS Bodl. 821, f. 15v.

[17] Bodl. Rawl. liturg. e.42, f. 37.

[18] Bodl. Jones 9, f. 32v.

[19] Cambridge, St John's College E.32, f. 24v.

[20] Bodl. Lat. liturg. e.43, f. 49v.

[21] As in e.g. BL Roy, 2.A.xiii, f. 39, a thirteenth century book possibly connected with Gloucester; cf. Dubois (as in note 8), 312.

[22] Oxford, University College 9. Evidence for Eastern English origin is extensive, for specifically Cambridge provenance somewhat shaky: see my *New Liturgical Feasts in Later Medieval England* (Oxford, 1970), 27-28.

ecclesiastica; ingenious quotation from the letter of Pope Sergius I (d. 701) to Abbot Ceolfrith of Jarrow supposedly asking for Bede's help[23]; and allusion to the monk Cuthbert's letter giving an eyewitness account of Bede's death[24]. The last two lessons present the story of a nearly-blind Bede preaching to the rocks, with angels responding 'bene dixisti, uenerabilis pater'[25]. This is by way of explaining the statement at the beginning of Lesson VIII, that though Bede is most worthily to be enrolled in the catalogue of saints ('sanctus cathalogo sanctorum dignissime sit ascriptus') he is, however, to be called not just 'Saint Bede' but 'Venerable Bede'.

Which of course says nothing as to whether he is or is not to be regarded as among the Fathers. On one level — that of this Conference — it is somewhat disappointing that there is relatively little hard liturgical evidence that Bede was regarded in the same light as the undoubted Fathers; in particular, one might have hoped for some such language in the martyrological entries. On the other hand, it may be gratifying to the multitude of Bede's admirers to learn that such liturgical evidence as exists does seem to put him in, so to speak, a class by himself. Though pride of place goes to the distinctive epithet 'uenerabilis', he was also 'egregius' and quite clearly 'doctor'. The latter aspect is summed up well by the compiler of the Carmelite office in words which can also be our concluding summary:

veluti scriba doctus doctor uenerabilis hic[?][26] scripsit super totum ferme [sc. veterum] testamentum et super novum plurima volumina et preclara.

If such activity does not qualify him as a Father — to a medieval mind or to ours — it is hard to imagine what would.

[23] On the difficulties surrounding this letter, see William Stubbs in *Dictionary of Christian Biography* I (London, 1877), 300-301, and in his Rolls Series edition of William of Malmesbury, *Gesta Regum* I (1897), 62-63; and Rodney M. Thomson, *William of Malmesbury* (Woodbridge, 1987), 172-173.

[24] *Bede's Ecclesiastical History*, ed. and trans. B. Colgrave and R.A.B. Mynors (Oxford, 1969), 580-587.

[25] The story is included in the omnibus chapter on Pope Pelagius towards the end of the late thirteenth century *Legenda Aurea* of Jacobo da Voragine: T. Graesse (ed.) (Dresden, 1890^3), 833-834. I have been unable to find an earlier source.

[26] The abbreviated word thus rendered has defied the combined eyes of Drs Lesley Smith, Rodney Thomson, and Andrew Watson, to all of whom I am grateful; the sense demands 'hic'.

XI

Bishop Baldock's Book, St Paul's Cathedral, and the Use of Sarum

A rather firm division is commonly assumed between English liturgical sources of the high and those of the later middle ages. The codification of the Salisbury Consuetudinary in the middle of the thirteenth century, the nearly simultaneous appearance of service books of the kind generally called 'Sarum,' and of course the vastly greater number of liturgical manuscripts that survive from the fourteenth and fifteenth centuries as compared with the twelfth and thirteenth (not to mention earlier periods), all tend to fix this impression in the minds of students.[1] Understandable though such a division may be in terms of the availability of materials and the emergence of certain aspects or themes,[2] the consequence is that it is hard to get a sense of engagement with liturgical sources that span this division.

The present investigation attempts to do just that: to engage with a single, quite fascinating document which was still being taken seriously liturgically - although, as we shall see, it could never have been used comprehensibly as a service book - a century or more after it was written. This is a manuscript of the late twelfth century (but manifesting in its original state both confusion in dealing with an earlier model and some astonishing and indeed inexplicable

---

1 Note for example the second sentence of Andrew Hughes's invaluable *Medieval Manuscripts for Mass and Office: a Guide to their Organization and Terminology* (Toronto 1982), xi, that, despite the general nature of the title, '[This book] is to introduce students of the later middle ages to the manuscripts of the liturgy.'

2 For example, another work by Hughes, *Late Medieval Liturgical Offices: Resources for Electronic Research: Texts* (Toronto 1994), and Miri Rubin, *Corpus Christi: the Eucharist in Late Medieval Culture* (Cambridge 1991).

experimentation); in the mid-thirteenth century it was adapted, at least in its calendar, to make it suitable for another place than its area of origin; and in the early fourteenth century it was used by an important bishop not only in personal ways - he had obits entered for five people who mattered to him - but also as a vehicle for what it would be fair to call liturgical study, albeit to no more concrete result that we know about than a set of, in effect, doodles on the manuscript.

Manuscript number 1 in the small collection of medieval manuscripts at St Paul's Cathedral in London presents at first inspection a very considerable enigma. That this enigma seems not to have been recognized hitherto probably stems from a rare mis-description by the late Neil Ker. In the first volume of his *Medieval Manuscripts in British Libraries* he calls it 'Psalterium, etc.,' and describes it as though it were an ordinary manuscript psalter, equipped (as indeed it is) with the standard features of calendar, canticles, and litany. The bulk of the book, folios 8-179 (out of a total of 197), he characterized only as 'Liturgical psalter. Hymns, antiphons, etc. noted on 4-line staves in red. Two leaves missing.'[3]

What is misleadingly inadequate about this description will appear presently. For the moment we can use, as students almost always can, the rest of Ker's description to frame our basic understanding of the book. Certainly we shall not quarrel with his general dating, 's. xii/xiii,' the termini inferrable from the calendar being apparently 1173 and 1220 (canonization of Thomas Becket and his Translation, respectively: the 29 December feast of his martyrdom is included but not the 7 July translation feast, which is added in a later hand). Physically the book is rather imposing. The written space is 233 mm high by 125 mm (roughly 9 x 5 inches), with individual letters a generous 7-9 mm high. At least two large hands are noted by Ker, 'one of them (ff. 164-87v) admirable.'

The book was ambitiously illustrated. There are gold and colored initials (two of them historiated) at Psalms 1, 26, 38, 51, 68, 80, 97, 101, and 109. The initial to Ps. 52 has been cut out, and the leaves with those for Pss. 51 and 109 are missing. This is the familiar tenfold division which combines the three 'fifties' (Ps. 1, 51, 101) with the defining psalms at matins in the secular use on the six weekdays and at Sunday vespers. There is nothing specially noteworthy in this, nor in the presence of ornamented initials to the other psalms in a

---

[3] N.R. Ker, *Medieval Manuscripts in British Libraries*, I (Oxford 1969), 240-1.

pattern which alternates red and blue. But it is clear that care has been taken over the book, and expense undergone (the binding is not medieval). It is not, however, inventoried in Nigel Morgan's volume of the 'Survey of Manuscripts Illuminated in the British Isles,'[4] and in fact seems to have been noted in no other work of scholarly reference save Ker's own *Medieval Libraries of Great Britain* (2nd edn, 1964), which places it as having been at St Paul's at some time in the middle ages, while Andrew Watson's *Supplement* to that edition (1987) adds some qualifying information about relevant booklists. Those lists help us to understand the medieval ownership, a subject to which we must turn before we can try to approach questions of ultimate origin, nature, and purpose.

Several lists survive of the books which were at, or came to, St Paul's from the mid-thirteenth century on; but, as with many medieval booklists, the degree to which service books are included is not always either clear or consistent. So it does not necessarily prove anything that in two related lists datable to 1245 and 1255 our book does not seem to be mentioned.[5] The first includes no psalters at all, but in the second (characterized by Ker as 'the 1245 inventory, word for word, with the addition of the treasures acquired in the ten years after 1245') eight are mentioned. How haphazard this is is shown by the fact that a list from the end of the thirteenth century (1295, of which three fair copies survive) notes only one, which is quite clearly the present St Paul's MS 2, a Hebraicum-text psalter with the commentary of Herbert of Bosham, given by Henry of Cornhill, dean from 1243 to 1254; the logical inference here would be that MS 2 was given after Henry's death and did not quite make it into the 1255 list. On analogous reasoning the absence of our book (MS 1) from the 1295 list

[4] Nigel Morgan, *Early Gothic Manuscripts* [I], *1190-1250* (London 1982). He does however mention it in his article in 'Psalter Illustration for the Diocese of Worcester in the Thirteenth Century,' *Medieval Art and Architecture at Worcester Cathedral*, Brit. Archaeol. Assn. Conference Trans. for 1975 (London 1978), 91-104, and notes that it is cited in F.C. Eeles, 'Part of a Kalendar of a thirteenth-century service book once in the church of Writtle,' *Trans. Essex Archaeol. Soc.* 25 (1959/60), 73 [I owe this reference to Nicholas Rogers].

[5] The 1245 list is printed by W. Sparrow Simpson, 'Two Inventories of the Cathedral Church of St. Paul, London,' *Archaeologia* 50.ii (1887), 441-524 at 496-500; those of 1255 and 1295 by N.R. Ker, 'Books at St Paul's Cathedral before 1313,' in *Studies in London History presented to P.E. Jones*, ed. A.E.J. Hollaender and W. Kellaway (London 1969), 41-72, repr. in Ker's *Books, Collectors and Libraries*, ed. Andrew G. Watson (London 1985), 209-42.

in its original form suggests that it may not have been among the cathedral's books by then, but that is far from certain.

This is consonant with what appears to be the earliest reference to our book, in a supplementary note to one of the copies[6] of the 1295 list: 'Item duo alia Phalteria [sic], unum de dono Radulfi Episcopi et aliud de dono Ricardi Episcopi.' The second of those mentioned is further described in an addition to another of the copies of that list,[7] which makes it plain that the donor was Richard [of] Gravesend, bishop from 1280 to 1303. Almost certainly the donor of the first must be Ralph Baldock, bishop from 1304 to 1313. But the hand which added the supplementary note is said by Ker to be the main hand (that is, of the 1295 list) writing between 1300 and 1311, and the words 'ex dono Radulfi Episcopi' do not necessarily imply that the gift was made after Baldock's death.

Ker was surely being too cautious when he noted, à propos this addition, that since our book 'contains obits of the family of Everard de Baldock, s. xiii^{2}, and was in London in s. xiv^{in}, it is tempting to equate it with the psalter given by Ralph de Baldock.'[8] It can scarcely be anything else. The calendar contains obits (in one hand) for 'Matilda Everard de Baudak' (Baldock) on 23 November 1271 and for a 'William Everard de Baudak senior' 22 December 1270 and 'junior' 28 November 1272. That these were people of some substance, or at least had a relative of some importance, is shown by the indulgences for prayers on behalf of William (senior) and his wife Maud granted by Oliver Sutton, bishop of Lincoln (in which diocese the Hertfordshire town of Baldock was located) on two occasions, 25 November 1290 and 20 March 1292 (the latter specifying also their son, William [junior]).[9]

Where mild speculation comes in is to suppose that William (senior) and Maud Everard were the parents of Ralph de Baldock, with William (junior) a brother. (It is almost certain that another brother was the Robert de Baldock, preferred in the diocese of London as prebendary of Holywell and in 1315 as archdeacon of Middlesex, and a key actor in the last years of Edward II's reign.)

---

[6] Oxford, Bodleian Library, Ashmole 845, fol. 185v; Ker, 'Books at St. Paul's,' p. 214, calls it 'not earlier than 1299, added to by the main hand between 1300 and 1311 (f. 185v) and by other hands up to 1333 (f. 187v) in blank spaces.'

[7] London, St Paul's Cathedral, Dean and Chapter, W.D. 3.

[8] 'Books at St Paul's,' p. 235 of 1985 reprint.

[9] *The Rolls and Register of Bishop Oliver Sutton 1280-99*, III, ed. R.M.T. Hill (Lincoln Record Society 48, 1954), 58-9 and 191.

Ralph had the rectory of a church in the diocese of Lincoln (Little Woolston, Bucks.) from 1275 and continuous provision in London, as archdeacon of Middlesex from 1276 and dean of St Paul's from 1294, so he would have been well placed to solicit the granting of indulgences for the Everard de Baldock family on these two occasions, the first issued from Baldock itself and the second from the Old Temple, London.

These details point in the direction of Ralph's being in possession of our book and of his having had added to its calendar, written in a single hand, the obits of the three family members on whose behalf he also secured indulgences. Two further obits were added in a different hand early in the fourteenth century: one for Alice de Vere, countess of Oxford, 7 September 1312, and one which Ker read as 'Alicia de Trok[...], priorissa de Haliwe[ll]' at 27 November (if a year was given it is now indecipherable in the gutter margin).[10] These additions greatly strengthen the likelihood that the book was Ralph's. Alice de Vere, the widow of Robert, fifth earl (d. 1296), left a precious chalice to her second son Hugh, and the inventory of Ralph Baldock's goods taken at Stepney on 12 June 1313 includes 'unus calix magnus deauratus ponderis xliiii s. ii d. legatus domini Hugonis de Veer.'[11] It looks as though Hugh de Vere passed the chalice on to Ralph Baldock immediately on inheriting it from his mother - his gift being possibly connected with the entry of her obit in our book. As for prioress Alicia, the nuns at Halliwell (alias Holywell, the name of the prebend held by Robert de Baldock) had dealings with both Ralph and Robert: most notably an agreement in 1283 between that priory and Ralph that revenues of two marks owing to him should be distributed among the nuns on the day of his obit, with services to be held for his benefit.[12] In that year the prioress seems to have been one Christina; but an Alice is attested in that office ten years later, followed by another Christina in 1314.[13] It seems right to connect both of these non-family obits with Ralph during either his deanery or his episcopate.

---

[10] There is also a note, in what Ker calls the same hand, on fol. 1 to the effect that 'Nox habet horas in Ciuitate Lond' et in confinio eius xv et xlv minuta;' lines to the same effect in two somewhat earlier hands are on fol. 1v and 2.

[11] *Historical Manuscripts Commission Ninth Report and Appendix*, part i (1883), 29b.

[12] Ibid., 19a.

[13] Alice: ibid., 19b;, the second Christina: *Calendar of Patent Rolls, 1313-17* (HMSO 1898), 146. The years of Ralph's episcopate were, as noted above, 1303 to 1313.

* * * * * * * *

We move now a century or more back in time, from indications about probable ownership to the contents of the book, and first to the hagiographical evidence. The peculiarities of the calendar are intriguing but not conclusive. Specially noteworthy saints are signified by being in blue or red, used indiscriminately but as distinct from black; there is no formal grading. Ker suggested that the book was written 'probably for use in a church dedicated to St Andrew,' doubtless on the basis of the vigil and octave for Andrew's main (30 November) feast, where Andrew is in blue capitals, and of a second feast of his Translation (along with that of Nicholas) entered in black at 9 May.[14] Ker noted also two of the additions, the Translation of Becket at 7 July (omission of which helps to date the calendar as before 1220) and Erkenwald on 30 April. That the latter, London's patron saint, had to be added is a strong indication that the book was not originally written for use in the diocese of London. Three other additions, not specified by Ker but all in the same spidery hand as the two noticed above, are Francis ('confessoris et ordinis fratrum minorum fundatoris') at 4 October, Edmund Rich (d. 1240, canonized 1247: the *terminus a quo* for the additions) at 16 November; and Elizabeth of Hungary (d. 1231, canonized 1235) at 19 November.[15]

Among these entries of obvious interest, certainly the treatment of Andrew seems the most noteworthy: to be precise, that his name is written in capitals and that he has a translation feast (his main feast almost always has a vigil and very often an octave as well). The real rarity, though not quite unique, is the joint translation feast with Nicholas. Andrew's translation (to Constantinople) was placed at 9 May at least as early as the mid-ninth century martyrology of Usuard.[16] As such it appears in half a dozen pre-1100 English calendars.[17] When, in one of the most celebrated movements of relics in the entire middle

---

14 *Med. MSS in Brit. Libs.* I (see note 3), 240; by an inexplicable slip, the date for the dual Translation feast is given there as 7 Sept.

15 The only other saints added are Chad, at 3 (not 2) March, faintly, in what looks to be a fifteenth-century hand, and perhaps Wenefred, in a hand so faint as to be scarcely discernible, on 2 or 3 November.

16 J. Dubois, ed. *Le Martyrologe d'Usuard* (Subsidia Hagiographica 40; Brussels 1965), 226-7.

17 F. Wormald, ed. *English Kalendars before A.D. 1100* (Henry Bradshaw Society 72, 1934), nos 3, 6, 8, 15, 16, and 19; it was added in the thirteenth century to nos 12 (see next note) and 13.

ages, those of Nicholas landed at Bari in 1087, which they apparently did also on 9 May, a potential coincidence, or even conflict, was set up.[18] In any case, they appear here together, in a rare combination of both translations.

The prominence given to Andrew aside, we are left with only one other indication from the calendar which points strongly in any direction: the presence of two feasts for Oswald, (arch)bishop, his deposition on 28 February and translation on 8 October, both colored. This of course suggests Worcester influence. Of the two translation feasts known for Oswald (d. 992), the original one, 15 April, marks the translation by (arch)bishop Eadwulf in 1004. A second translation, made necessary by the destruction of Oswald's church at Worcester and its replacement, occurred on 8 October around 1086, under Wulfstan (bishop 1062-95).[19] The October date, liturgically more convenient than the one in April, is the one in the calendar of our manuscript. This means that the Worcester influence discernible in this calendar is probably no older than the late eleventh century.

At the other chronological extreme, a *terminus ante quem* for Worcester influence is suggested by the omission of Wulfstan's feast on 19 January; this would seem to date any such influence, or even model, to before 1203, the year of his canonization. This, in conjunction with the presence of Becket's 29 December feast, narrows the range of probable years for the writing of the calendar to c. 1173-1203. (The other potentially localizing name, that of Erkenwald, is, as noted earlier, an addition of the mid-thirteenth century.) It

---

18 Among the post-Benedictine calendars collected by Wormald (*English Benedictine Kalendars after A.D. 1100*, HBS 77 and 81, 1939-46) the combined translation feast appears only in calendars from Muchelney (in one manuscript , c. 1300; vol. 81, p. 96) and Ely (p. 12); if Wormald's collation is correct, the Ely witnessses to the combined feast include one as early as the mid-twelfth century (pre-1170; Milan, Bibl. Naz. Braidense, AF XI.9) and one datable 1170-89 (the Liber Eliensis MS in Cambridge, Trinity College O.2.1 [1105]). The combined feast may have been added in the thirteenth century to a mid-eleventh century Psalter with Winchester connections (London, Brit. Lib. Cotton Vitellius E.xviii), with the grading 'in albis;' the word which may be 'Andreae' seems to be erased. Nicholas's translation does not appear in any of the six pre-1100 calendars which contain the translation of Andrew by himself. The two translations appear as separate entries in the calendar of the Les(s)nes(s) missal of the early thirteenth century, with chants incipits given in its second sanctorale (*Missale de Lesnes*, ed. Philip Jebb, HBS 95, 1964); my thanks to Nicholas Rogers for reminding me of this.

19 *William of Malmesbury's Vita Wulfstani*, ed. R.R. Darlington (Camden Soc. 3rd ser. 40, 1928), 52, gives the day but not the year.

looks, then, as though the calendar was written in the diocese of, or under the strong influence of, Worcester in the last quarter of the twelfth century.

Evidence from the litany points in the same direction but is no more conclusive. Here too Erkenwald's name has been added, over an erasure and in a fourteenth century hand, as fifteenth among the twenty-four confessors. Ker suggested that the erased name might have been that of Mellitus, whose name is also written in the gutter margin, but surely Oswald is likelier in a sequence that now runs Birinus, Swithun, Æthelwold, Erkenwald, Dunstan. There are two other alterations to the list of confessors. Where the first name should have been is now a blank line, which Ker suggests was originally Benedict, whose name was then 'erased and entered lower down, s. xiv in.' (I cannot myself see either of these readings.) Also erased is the name of the ninth (originally tenth) confessor; the sequence now runs Ambrose, Jerome, erased, Gregory, Augustine (with later addition 'cum sociis tuis'), so the erased name should be that of Augustine of Hippo. The sole name capitalized in the litany now is Andrew; a key indication would have been whether Oswald - if it was he who was erased and replaced by Erkenwald, between Æthelwold and Dunstan - was also in capitals. The omission of Becket is highly puzzling, especially as Blasius (specially prominent at Canterbury) is inserted into the martyrs, at the foot of a column, perhaps in the early thirteenth century. Later medieval hands have added Linus, Cletus, and Fabian to the martyrs, and to the virgins Spes and Caritas (after Fides in the original) in one hand and Wilgefortis and two indecipherable names in another. A third hand has added, much more boldly, Clara.

These details are vital, because trying to establish where the calendar and litany, and therefore presumably the book, were written is basic to understanding why its contents are so striking. The clearest fact is a negative one: that it cannot have been written for direct monastic use, because the pattern of the Daily Office contained in it - the cardinal point to which we shall turn presently - is plainly the secular pattern (the simplest identifying criterion being that there are nine lessons on Sundays and great feasts as opposed to the monastic twelve). So, no matter how strong the Worcester influence is in the calendar - influence probably no more remote than the 1086 (second) translation of Oswald - the book seems unlikely to have been written for use at the monastic cathedral establishment there. St Paul's was by contrast a secular foundation; but the book does not seem to have come into the diocese of London until at least the middle of the thirteenth century (as indicated by the addition of Erkenwald), fifty years or more after it was written. There is no indication as to what its place of residence was during that period, nor of how it got to London.

* * * * * * * *

Nonetheless, we can come at last to the main contents of this codex. We have seen that Ker's catalogue calls the book a psalter, and we return to that term. Without adjectival qualification, 'psalter' usually means just a copy of the psalms, 1-150 in order, plus often some or all of the features mentioned earlier, calendar, canticles, litany, perhaps prayers. A 'ferial' psalter, whether noted or not, distributes the psalms as they are recited in the hours of the divine office throughout the week (the understanding always being that the 150 psalms are to be recited each week): divided, that is, by *feriae*, days of the week. A 'liturgical' psalter (the term Ker used) is, I think, a less precise term, connoting simply a psalter adapted in some way(s) for liturgical worship.

A 'liturgical psalter' is clearly what our book (henceforth P) purports to be - though, as we shall see, it is also something more. In outline its contents are primarily the 150 psalms, in numerical order, but interspersed with many other features which pertain to the hours of the divine office. These may be summed up as follows:

for all or most of the hours: antiphons, noted - only incipits at the beginning of a psalm or group of psalms, written in full at its/their end;
for matins: invitatories (that is, to the Venite, psalm 94), generally not noted; lessons for one week, nine for Sunday, three for each of six weekdays; and responsories after each lesson, all noted;
for lauds and vespers: hymn, capitulum, antiphon to Benedictus or Magnificat, all varying daily, and collect, also variable;
for prime and the little hours (terce, sext, none): hymn, capitulum, and collect of the hour.

This summary list suggests that the book is well on its way to being a compendium from which all the daily offices can be said. Such a book is, of course, called a breviary. But a breviary is a compendium in two senses: it contains all the texts of all the daily offices, and contains them all *per totum annum*, however laid out or organized (as we speak now of 'a breviary in two or four seasonal volumes').

P has all the offices (save for compline, the omission of which seems inexplicable); but that compendiousness is meaningless without some provision for, or at least recognition of, the *per totum annum* factor - precisely what P lacks, for it contains only one week's worth of offices. This means that what P represents might be understandable as a sort of template for the divine office. In part this is what happens in the evolution of the breviary, which has a kind of template in the element called (yet another use of the term) *Psalterium* - in effect, the common of time. But if a *Psalterium* in this sense, whether as part of a breviary or on its own, contains more or less the outline of a week's offices, it cannot be used for a single week - any week - unless it is supplied with the proper parts for some week: preferably as neutral a week as possible.

Two weeks are likely candidates for this distinction (not the first week of the liturgical year, Advent I, because it is such a special season, though often extensive introductory rubrics are found there): the week of the Sunday after (Octave of) Epiphany and that of the Sunday after Pentecost, generally known from at least the thirteenth century as Trinity Sunday. This is the case with P. In several places it supplies forms - specifically, some antiphons and hymns - for each of those two weeks, preference being given to the week after the Epiphany octave. Where there is an additional level of specificity, like the collect for second vespers at Sunday, the form for Trinity Sunday is most often used.

* * * * * * * * *

So far, almost, so good. But the greatest degree of specificity should be found in the lessons at matins, with their corresponding responsories. The basic pool from which the lessons at matins come is of course Scripture, with patristic homilies and saints' legends drawn on as needed. In all of the many *comparanda*, both secular and monastic, that I have consulted, the temporal lessons for the season after Epiphany are invariably taken from Paul's epistles, almost always starting with Romans.[20]

[20] Sarum: *Breviarium ad usum insignis ecclesiae Sarum*, ed. F. Procter and C. Wordsworth, 3 vols (Cambridge, 1879-86); York: *Breviarium ad usum insignis ecclesiae Eboracensis*, ed. S.W. Lawley, 2 vols (Surtees Soc. 71, 75, 1880-83); Hereford: *The Hereford Breviary*, ed. W.H. Frere and L.E.G. Brown, 3 vols (HBS 26, 40, 46, 1904-11-15); Exeter: *Ordinale*

Here any understanding we may have hoped for tumbles down like a house of cards. For P's nine Sunday lessons are drawn not from Romans, nor from Paul, nor from the Bible as such, nor from the Fathers. Rather, they appear to have been taken from a commentary on the psalms, most likely as laid out in a glossed psalter. For example lesson iii (fol. 19v) is clearly commenting on Ps. 2, 'Quare fremuerunt gentes':

> Quare fremuerunt gentes. Hic vox prophetie dicit quare. Ac si dicat sine causa. Quia non potuerunt Christum extinguere, sicut uoluerunt. Inter fremere et meditari hoc interest; quia fremere canum est ut illud. Nolite sanctum dare canibus.

This does not read like a consecutive psalter commentary, and no commentary that I know of is the direct source used here.[21] All nine of the Sunday lessons work this way. They comment on pss. 1.1; 2.1; 6.2, 3, 5, 6, 7, 8, 9, and 11; and the whole of 12; and the psalm verses they comment on are, while consecutive, not allocated neatly among the lessons.

There is some precedent for the appearance of a template of this kind at least in two eleventh-century English office books, either of which could conceivably have been known to the compiler of P or to his source. The first is Cambridge, Corpus Christi College MS 391, usually called the Portiforium of St Wulfstan, a book clearly designed for monastic use, indeed for a persons or persons based at Worcester (though apparently from a Winchester exemplar). This has, in a curious section after its second Common of Saints, forms for a specimen Sunday, headed *Dominicis diebus*. Here each of the first eight of the twelve

---

Exon., ed. J.N. Dalton with G.H. Doble, 4 vols (HBS 37-8, 63, 79, 1909-26-40); Worcester: *Antiphonaire monastique, XIIIe siècle* (Paléographie Musicale, ser. i, 12; Tournai 1922); Hyde: *The Monastic Breviary of Hyde Abbey*, ed. J.B.L. Tolhurst, 6 vols (HBS 69-71, 76, 78, 80; 1932-42); Durham: Cathedral MS B.iii.11, one of the six manuscripts 'Cursus Romanus' in *Corpus Antiphonalium Officii*, I, ed. R.-J. Hesbert (Rerum Ecclesiasticarum Documenta, Fontes 7; Rome, 1963); compare also the six 'Cursus Monasticus' manuscripts in his vol. II, RED 8, 1965 (including Saint Denis as in Paris, BN lat. 12584; but for S. Denis also Paris, Bibl. Mazarine 526, ed. E.B. Foley as *The First Ordinary of the Royal Abbey of St.-Denis in France* (Spicilegium Friburgense 32, 1990).

[21] Recourse to friends expert in this area - I am grateful to the late Margaret Gibson, Philip Pulsiano, and Joseph Wittig for considering the matter - and to CETEDOC seems to confirm my suspicion that the ultimate source may be an unidentified psalter commentary.

lessons for matins on Sundays is taken from a different New Testament epistle, while the last four come from Bede's homily on John 15.26.[22]

Somewhat closer to P, in presenting an entire week as well as in following the nine-lesson secular pattern for Sundays, is London, British Library, Harley MS 863, a psalter almost certainly made for Bishop Leofric for the use of his community at Exeter, 1050-72.[23] Here the Sunday lessons I-VI are taken from the first chapter of Romans, with those for the third nocturn (VII-IX) being the beginning of Bede on John 2.1-11,[24] which in Sarum and most other uses is the Gospel for the second Sunday after the (Octave of the) Epiphany. But in the weekday lessons an eccentricity sets in not wholly unlike that in P. Those for Monday and Tuesday are drawn from Romans 2, but (following a loss of two leaves which contained those for Wednesday and Thursday) the Friday and Saturday lessons are extra-biblical, being drawn from a treatise which deals with the immutability of God.[25]

These partial parallels show that in providing merely a specimen week P is not unique, and it would be desirable to have the peculiarity that both of those MSS manifest explained, or at least studied further. But we must return to P, about which there are three further considerations that make it even more puzzling:

i The responsories are for the most part exactly what one would find in an office book which contained the (ordinary-season) lessons from St Paul; in other words, they are unrelated to the psalter-commentary lessons they are meant to be responding to. Very minor peculiarities aside, they correspond with those found in (mostly later) Sarum, York, and Hereford books - in fact, with many secular uses throughout Western Europe. They also agree for the most part with monastic books from Worcester, Durham, and Hyde (Winchester),[26] but with one crucial exception. This is that the ninth responsory, in our book as in secular use generally, 'Abscondi tamquam ... V.

---

22 *The Portiforium of Saint Wulfstan*, II, ed. Anselm Hughes (HBS 90, 1960), 39; *Homil. in evang. Ioannis* II.16, ed. D. Hurst (CCSL 122, 1955), 292-5.

23 See A. Corrêa, 'Daily Office Books,' in *The Liturgical Books of Anglo-Saxon England*, ed. R.W. Pfaff (Old English Newsletter Subsidia 23; Kalamazoo 1995), 45-60 at 55; cf. P. Conner, *Anglo-Saxon Exeter. A Tenth-Century Cultural History* (Woodbridge 1993), 201.

24 *Homil. in evang. Ioannis* II.14 (see note 22), pp. 94-5.

25 Apparently from Gregory the Great, *Moralia in Job* xii.33, ed. M. Adriaen (CCSL 143A, 1979), 650-51; but with some alterations that suggest an intermediary source.

26 See note 20 for references.

Quoniam iniquitatem,' is the eighth at Worcester, which has 'Peccata mea ... V. Sana mea' after the ninth lesson. This reinforces our impression that the matrix or model for the lessons in our office was almost certainly not a monastic use, where the responsories, like the lessons, travel on Sundays in sets of four, not three. We must still, however, leave open the possibility that whoever first came up with the idea of using a psalter-commentary as Sunday matins lessons may have done so in a monastic context: for our ninth lesson is so much longer than all the others (41 lines of typed transcription long, as against an average of about ten lines for the other eight lessons) that it might have been seen as comprising not one lesson but four (ix-xii, which would then conform to the monastic pattern for Sundays). In any case, the important point is that there is a complete disjunction between P's lessons for Sunday matins and their responsories, which are those meant to follow lessons from Romans in the week after the Epiphany octave.

ii The use of the psalter-commentary is confined to the Sunday lessons. The weekday lessons pick up with readings from Romans (starting in mid-chapter 2), just as they would have had the Sunday lessons come from the beginning (chapters 1 and 2.1-9) of that epistle. This pattern extends through Friday, with lesson iii on that day ending at Romans 4.16.

iii But the Saturday lessons are taken not from Romans (4.18-19, 4.20-24, 5.1-5 would be expected) but from Sap. 1.6-7, Ecclus. 5.1-2, and Ecclus. 7.31-33. Again, the responsories are exactly the usual ones which accompany Pauline lessons.

So there is a double dislocation in the lessons - those for Sunday seem wildly eccentric and for Saturday are surprisingly non-Pauline - but no discernible dislocation in the responsories. This means that the book we are dealing with, written in the quarter century or so before 1200, must itself be a conflation of two sources, an office pattern, already of some antiquity, for the responsories, and a psalter commentary or glossed psalter for the Sunday lessons.

* * * * * * * *

All this is put together by an unknown person for an unknown purpose. Moreover - a further complication - it is pretty clear that whoever this was (or at least the scribe of the present book) did not understand the model or models from which he was working. This is evident at fol. 145v, where, at the end of psalm 116 with its antiphon 'Laudate dominum omnes gentes,' there suddenly breaks in, with no indication or rubric beyond the bare word *hymnus*, the hymn for prime, 'Iam lucis orto sidere.' This is presumably because the numerical order of the psalms, which is the basic principle of arrangement in our book, does not fit neatly into a division between liturgical offices. So psalms 114, 115, and 116 are the first three (of five) psalms for vespers on Monday, whereas psalms 117 and 118 are psalms used at prime and the little hours. Apparently the scribe (at least) has not noticed that there is anything unusual in interrupting the liturgical sequence of the psalms for Monday vespers with the forms for a liturgical office (prime, followed by the little hours) which requires the next two psalms from the numerical sequence. After the forms for the office of nones, which uses the last six sections of psalm 118, Monday vespers picks up again, there being once more no notice that anything unusual has happened, with psalms 119 and 120. Again we are reminded that no one could have used this book liturgically - even though it is considerably noted, as though it were going to be sung from; indeed, no one could even remotely understand it without subjecting it to the kind of analysis we are trying to apply.

There is a hint that, a century or so later, this confusion was noticed; for the vespers of all the subsequent weekdays are firmly marked, in what looks like an early fourteenth-century hand, 'fferia 3 [or whatever] ad vesperas.' This hand can be seen, for example, on fol. 179, where it also supplies for the canticles biblical references (with Arabic numerals) and titles. This is part of a fitful marking up and correcting of the book done, I want now to suggest, after it came into the hands of Ralph de Baldock.

This brings us back to the question of the book's putative attraction for him. As we have examined it, it seems unlikely to have appealed to anyone save the most determined liturgical archaeologist, whether of the twentieth century or of the thirteenth. But the carefully added obits (and also the additions to the calendar and alterations to the litany) show that in the years around 1300 it was being used for some purpose, if not for a properly liturgical one. One simple but unsatisfactory explanation is that Baldock thought it was a nice book and 'personalized' the calendar, perhaps even using it as a kind of devotional memorandum-list, while taking no notice of its peculiar contents. Should this be the case, there is little more to be said.

Alternatively, it seems possible that he was attracted by the character of the book as a kind of model text or template - towards, we would then have to go on to assume, some renewal or improvement of liturgy of the cathedral church of which he was a dignitary and then bishop (archdeacon of Middlesex from 1276/8, dean from 1294, and bishop from 1304/6).[27] Baldock was a considerable bookman, who left to his cathedral some 126 *libri scolastici*, the list of which does not appear to include our manuscript.[28] Nor would it be expected to: none of the other books seems to be a service book as such, although there were a *Legenda sanctorum* and a *Liber de officiis ecclesie*, and among the twenty-eight books inventoried from his study after his death was a *Legenda sanctorum duplex*.[29]

Baldock was, as well, a vigorous churchman; the statutes of St Paul's compiled by him in the context of his decanal visitation of 1295 have been called 'the fullest and best arranged collection of cathedral statutes and customs in any English secular cathedral.'[30] One provision, apparently added when he was bishop, may be pertinent here: 'in ferialibus officiis plane cantentur omnia, prout in libris correccioribus sunt notata.'[31] Is P conceivably one of those books that are 'more correct' with respect to the weekday office?

Beyond the immediate confines of the cathedral, there survives evidence of considerable interest in the 'correctness' of liturgical books in the diocese of London in the mid-thirteenth century and again at its end: as it happens, at precisely the stages when our book seems to have come into the diocese and when corrections are made to it. Visitations of parish churches belonging to the

---

[27] D.E. Greenway, comp., *John le Neve. Fasti Ecclesiae Anglicanae 1066-1300*, I: *St Paul's London* (London 1968), 17 and 18.

[28] Printed in A.B. Emden, *Biographical Register of the University of Oxford*, III (Oxford 1959), 2147-9; cf. N.R. Ker, *Medieval Libraries of Great Britain*, 2nd edn (London 1964), 120.

[29] There was also meant to be a glossed hymnal (*ympnar'glos'*), but as this could not be found a tantalizingly-titled *libellus de coronacione Regis et Regine* was allowed to be substituted (Emden, 2148).

[30] Emden, 2147; cf. Kathleen Edwards, *The English Secular Cathedrals in the Middle Ages*, 2nd edn (Manchester 1967), 25.

[31] W. Sparrow Simpson, ed. *Registrum Statutorum et Consuetudinum Ecclesie Cathedralis Sancti Pauli Londiniensis* (London 1873), 175: Pars VII, cap. 22 in the 'Statuta Minora,' Simpson's MS B.

cathedral chapter were held in 1249-52 and 1297 - the latter under Ralph Baldock as dean.[32] Even in the earlier visitations awareness of a 'usus Sancti Pauli' is manifest, though what its distinctive points were thought to be we do not know.

Nor do we know precisely that the kind of book P approximates would always have been called 'psalterium.' I think it possible that a book as heavily noted as P might have been referred to alternatively as 'antiphonarium.' Particularly striking is the description of a book seen at Willesden: 'Antiphonarium cum kalendario continens legenda de bona litera et bene notata, habens literam auream in principio libri, et poc'[?] secundum ordinem ecclesie London.' At Heybridge there were 'Duo psalteria, unum vetus et unum bonum novum ex dono domini Gosselini in presencia domini Decani;' and at Aldbury a 'liber breviarius cum antiphonario notato de bona litera, veteri male ligatus et male custoditus, habens in capite kalendarium vetus.'[33] Any of those descriptions might fit a book like P.

By the time of Baldock's 1297 visitations nine of the twenty churches visited possessed an 'Ordinale de usu S. Pauli' and three had an 'Ordinale de usu Sarum.'[34] At Barling, where it was specified that a St. Paul's Use ordinal was lacking, there was an 'antiphonarium notatum cum ympnario, psalterio, et kalendario.' The same was true at Cardington, and both cases may be distinguished from the situation at Wickham, which possessed 'unum portiforium de usu S. Pauli bene notatum.'[35]

Whatever was understood by those somewhat unclear terms 'Use of St Paul's' and even 'antiphonarium,' the corrector of P (or correctors, for possibly two hands were involved: in any case, henceforth C) must have thought that he was performing some useful service in supplying and emending the book. Guesses as to what kind of service must depend in part on the nature of the emendations. These can be summarized as follows:

---

[32] Both ed. W. Sparrow Simpson in 1895: *Visitations of Churches belonging to St Paul's Cathedral 1249-1252*. (Camden Soc. n.s. 53 [Camden Miscellany IX]), and *Visitations of Churches belonging to St Paul's Cathedral in 1297 and in 1458* (Camd. Soc. n.s. 55).

[33] *Visitations 1249-1252*, 1, 11, 16. I cannot find the Gosselin or Joscelin who is referred to here.

[34] *Visitations 1297*, lii (Sparrow Simpson's reckoning).

[35] *Visitations 1297*, 9, 51, 34.

a The response following the versicle after the psalm of each nocturn at matins, which is in all save one case missing from original P, is regularly supplied (with what seem to be standard texts) by C.

b Likewise, the versicles and responses commonly found at the beginning of lauds for each day (and variable to the day) are lacking in original P and supplied.

c Corrections are made to the invitatoria (i.e. to the Venite) in which P's for Saturday becomes C's for Thursday, P's for Thursday C's for Friday, P's for Friday C's for Saturday.

Unremarked and unaltered are a number of differences between P and the Sarum office in at least its late medieval form. To begin with, P lacks five elements which a fully developed breviary would have contained:

i The texts of the canticles are not included in the offices of which they are part but rather comprise a discrete section after the psalms proper - that is, in the manner of earlier psalters.

ii Similarly, the texts of the Venite (Ps. 94) and of the Laudate psalms (148-50) used daily at lauds are not given in their respective offices, and appear only in course.

iii There are no rubrics of a sort which indicate when psalms appearing in course are not used in the liturgical context one might expect ('non dicitur ad nocturnas' is a frequently encountered wording for such a rubric).

iv There is no indication of the first psalms of prime (21-25) at fol. 32.

v Finally, and as mentioned earlier, compline is missing entirely.

None of these omissions is surprising in a book which seems to mark a transition from a psalter of the older kind to a ferial psalter of the type that lies at the heart of the breviary; but to the extent that they are not supplied the book becomes more difficult to use liturgically. On the other hand, in one respect P is witness to a practice somewhat more convenient liturgically than the definitive arrangement of Sarum breviaries: it includes proper collects at lauds and vespers for each day of the week, and also specific collects for each of the little hours.

Tiny differences in text, though very small in number, might be thought the most promising avenues towards tracing P's particular lineage; unfortunately, this approach does not seem to yield any light. In two instances in the second nocturn of Sunday matins there is variation in antiphons, and in the capitula at lauds in three (Tuesday, Wednesday, and Thursday), while P's capitulum at sext is Sarum's at nones. A couple of the points of variation are even more miniscule: P's Monday antiphon to Magnificat begins 'Magnificemus Christum regem,' Sarum's 'Magnificet et semper anima mea;' while for Friday P's is in effect only the second half of Sarum's.[36]

It would clearly be rash to try to argue anything conclusive from such tiny details, above all in the light of the fact that there survive almost no complete Sarum office texts as early as c. 1300. I find it equally conceivable that the corrector thought he was adapting original P either to something like the Use of St Paul's or to whatever level of specificity is meant by the phrase 'Use of Sarum' in the visitation records quoted earlier.

* * * * * * * *

In trying to sum up the particular interest, and particular intransigence, of this manuscript, we must note that both interest and unsolved puzzles exist at three levels. The first has to do with the nature and purpose of the book as it was written around 1200; at this stage its most distinctive feature is that the Sunday lessons are drawn from a psalter commentary (perhaps in the form of a glossed psalter). Its calendar makes sense only in terms of Worcester influence, but the book as we have it seems to reflect a secular rather than monastic office-pattern. Further, it is likely that our book is a copy of another (not necessarily much earlier) codex, for the apparently unnoticed interruption of Monday vespers by forms for the little hours makes a nonsense of the text; this must reflect some misunderstanding by the scribe of his instructions. Moreover, the fact that there is additional dislocation in the lessons for Saturday, which appear

[36] P: 'Abraham et semen eius usque in seculum magnificet dominum;' Sarum: 'Suscepit deus Israel puerum suum sicut locutus est Abraham et semini eius; et exaltavit humiles usque in seculum.'

to be absolutely without parallel, shows that the book's experimental nature is not confined to the fact that it appears uniquely to draw on what seems to be a commentary on the psalms as the nine Sunday lessons. The book would be an astonishing *unicum* even if it showed no signs of subsequent use.

The second level of interest-cum-puzzle is how it got to the diocese of London and there had additions made to its calendar (which in the original form was almost certainly written before 1203) sometime after 1247. This is most likely the stage at which Erkenwald is added, but so are Francis, with the expansive styling 'confessor et ordinis fratrum minorum fundator' and Elizabeth; we naturally wonder what the appeal of the latter was, and can observe that the absence of Clare, canonized in 1255, may help to date these additions quite narrowly (it was noted earlier that she had been added to the litany). This is also the point at which visitations are made to churches belonging to St Paul's, special attention being paid to the nature and condition of their service books and awareness being shown of a distinction between St Paul's and Sarum Uses - though to be sure no specific connection with our book can be demonstrated.

From being in the diocese of London, then, and in ownership which shows special awareness of Francis, the book passes to its third stage of interest and enigma. Ralph Baldock, whom it seems fair to characterize as able, ambitious, and bookish, came to possess the codex, which appears to have had special importance for him. Two sets of obits distinctly personal to him were entered in the calendar, one for three family members and one for two benefactors. He left the book (along with, as far as we know, all his other books) to his cathedral. At some point, either during his lifetime or not too long thereafter, some corrections and additions were entered: a few to straighten out possible confusion about what has happened in the psalms for vespers, others to supply or substitute for forms which seemed to be defective. Since we lack reliable bases for comparison of such tiny details as these as early as c. 1300, whether for St Paul's or (surprisingly) for the Sarum Use as a whole, it is not possible to say that these alterations reflect a conscious attempt either to construct a distinctive St Paul's Use (such as is widely postulated for the later middle ages) or to bring the cathedral's texts for the divine office into conformity with what Sarum Use was thought at that point to have been.

'Liturgical doodling' might be a not inappropriate summary for what happens to this book in its third - and as far as we can tell, final - stage; but what intriguing doodles they are, even though we cannot pin down their exact purpose. In roughly another hundred years or so (probably 1415) the Use of St Paul's was to be abrogated in favor of that of Sarum,[37] and our book can have had no more value than that of a curiosity. In Baldock's time this does not seem to have been the case; to him, or to the contemporary of his who wrote the doodles if it was not Baldock, the late twelfth-century book was worth working through as the basis for thinking about the liturgy of the daily office in the early fourteenth. I wish I could grasp just what his purpose was.[38]

---

[37] William Dugdale, *History of St Paul's Cathedral* (London 1716), 24.

[38] I am grateful to Christopher Brooke and Andrew Hughes for general advice and assistance, and to J. Joseph Wisdom, Librarian of St Paul's Cathedral, for smoothing access to the manuscript.

XII

Prescription and Reality in the Rubrics of Sarum Rite Service Books

The subject of this essay is the relationship between service books as they have come down to us and as they seem actually to have been used in English medieval parish churches. Its concrete starting point is the information about books which can be assigned to specific parish churches in N.R. Ker's *Medieval Libraries of Great Britain* and its *Supplement*:[1] For the something like 8,000 to 10,000 parishes and chapels probably operating in England by the end of the middle ages, just over one hundred books of a liturgical sort (including a few books of hours and kalendars) have been identified as having belonged to a specific one. As might be expected, missals are far better represented than any other types of books: forty-two have been so identified, all save two apparently of the Sarum Use, the overwhelming majority from the fifteenth century. All other major types of books together number about the same: eleven breviaries, fourteen psalters, four antiphoners, three graduals, eight manuals, four martyrologies (forty-four in all). About two-thirds are of the fifteenth or early sixteenth centuries; twenty-seven are dated fourteenth or fourteenth/fifteenth; a mere two are of the thirteenth century. There seems to be nothing at all earlier than that.

The survival of such books, and therefore their appearance on this list, is of course a purely fortuitous matter; so that if we look for well-known parish churches from which we might most wish to study service books – for example, Tideswell in Derbyshire, St. Mary Redcliffe in Bristol, Howden in the East Riding, St. Peter Mancroft in Norwich, Escomb in County Durham, all of which would fall into expected categories of noble, beautiful, picturesque or at least very ancient – we will be sadly disappointed. In any case, rather than choosing our books by the churches which possessed them, we shall need to consider the evidence from some of these surviving books – none, as it

[1] N.R. Ker. ed., *Medieval Libraries of Great Britain: A List of Surviving Books*, (2nd edn., London, 1964) [hereafter *MLGB*]: Andrew G. Watson, ed., *Supplement to the Second Edition* (London, 1987).

happens, belonging to churches of any particular fame – in the light of certain aspects of their contents. In doing so, we shall have to assume something not absolutely provable, that on the whole these books were not only owned by but also used in the churches to which they belonged and that it should therefore be possible to consider them as evidence for the practice of the liturgy in those places.

Let us look, to begin with, at a breviary used in the fifteenth century at Launton in north Oxfordshire.[2] The book is very large: 415 by 290 mm. are its present dimensions (but it has been cropped somewhat) it weighs about twenty-eight pounds. It was made somewhere in southern England (i.e., province of Canterbury) in the first half of the fifteenth century. By about 1530 it belonged to John Cottisford, then Rector of Lincoln College, Oxford. At some time in the previous hundred years or so it came to the church at Launton, whose feast of dedication was added to the calendar at 3 October to be kept on the first Sunday of that month, and whose *yconimi* are twice noted as being bound to offer twelve pence to the church at Bicester on the feast day of St. Edburga. Though not elaborately illuminated, it is well enough decorated to have found its way into Pächt and Alexander as 'Good borders and initials. Some borders added xv^{med} – most likely when the book went to Launton, which indicates that a degree of special attention was paid to it at that time.[3]

It would seem a suitable vehicle out of which to conduct the divine office there – physically congruous with, for example, the rubric for the ceremony surrounding the reading of the genealogy of Christ from Matthew at matins of Christmas Day (fo. 30): a rubric which specifies that after the final responsory and its versicle the deacon goes with subdeacon, thurifer, candlebearer and crucifer, all solemnly apparelled, to cense the altar and be blessed by the officiant before mounting the pulpit to sing the lesson. This sort of prescription, implying as it does a liturgical force of three sacred ministers and at least three attendants, naturally leads to an impression of considerably elaborated worship; a feeling that the services at Launton must have been splendid.

Some questions begin to arise, however, when we look at the standard modern printed edition of the Sarum breviary, that of Procter and Wordsworth, which is for the most part a printing of the 'Great' Breviary of 1531, and see there largely the same rubric:[4] but we note that the rubric continues, as it does not in the Launton breviary, by specifying a second censing of the high altar (apparently with the aid of a second thurifer), the other altars not being censed. Are we entitled to infer from this detail that at Launton a second

[2] Oxford, Bodleian Library, MS Laud Misc., 299.

[3] O. Pächt and J.J.G. Alexander, *Illuminated Manuscripts in the Bodleian Library*, iii: *English etc. School* (Oxford, 1973), no. 827.

[4] F. Procter and C. Wordsworth, eds., *Breviarium ad usum insignis ecclesiae Sarum* (3 vols., Cambridge, 1879-86), i, clxxxvi.

thurifer was not used, or that there were no other altars besides the principal one in that church, or both?

Certainly the latter inference looks dubious in the light of a rubric for first vespers of St. Nicholas, which falls within the Octave of St. Andrew. The Launton breviary's rubric spells out that there should be a procession to the altar of St. Nicholas, during which both the altar and the image of that saint are censed (fo. 309 v). But the rubric in the 1531 Great Breviary specifies that this should happen only (and reasonably) 'si habeatur', if there is such an altar; it makes no mention of an image.[5] In this case does logical inference convince us that at Launton there were such an altar and such an image? That is certainly conceivable, though the church was not dedicated to St. Nicholas but to St. Mary (her Assumption), and it probably had only two altars in addition to the principal one.[6]

If one of the altars was dedicated to Nicholas, was the other to Thomas Becket? Another rather elaborate rubric, at the end of second vespers of Holy Innocents, indicates that after the Boy Bishop ceremonies sometimes associated with that day are concluded there is a procession to the altar of St. Thomas the Martyr (whose first vespers it is also). In neither the Launton (fo. 44 v) nor the 1531 breviary (i. ccxlv) is the stipulation 'if there is one' added; how likely does this make the existence of such an altar in a small Oxfordshire parish church?

Similar questions are raised when we turn to a slightly earlier book of the same sort, a breviary used at Denchworth in Berkshire.[7] This is another very large codex, 425 by 375 mm. in present outside dimensions, made in the last decade or so of the fourteenth century, and probably given to the parish church in the Berkshire village of Denchworth by a member of the Hyde family: obits of other members of this family dating back to 1135 were apparently entered in this book out of an older one.[8] Indeed, some such history is suggested by the rubric on fo. 262 v, following the entry about the Translation of Thomas Becket (7 July), in which we read that on the next Sunday after the Translation, 'celebratur festum reliquiarum Sarum ecclesie quod nuper celebratum consuevit in octava die nativitatis beate Marie'. As the change of date for the Sarum Feast of Relics was made in 1319, well over a century before this book was written, the long-obsolete information contained in the present rubric is best explained by its having been copied from an earlier one.

This context intensifies the interest with which we may note the extensive rubric on fo. 283 v dealing with the question of when St. Matthias's feast (usually on 24 February) falls in leap years – a quadrennial problem given that

5 Procter and Wordsworth, iii.25.

6 Jennifer Sherwood and Nikolaus Pevsner, *Oxfordshire*. The Buildings of England (Harmondsworth, 1973), p. 681.

7 Oxford, Bodleian Library, MS lat. liturg., b. 14.

8 Printed by H.B. Hyde in *Notes and Queries*, 7th ser, v (7 Jan. 1888), pp. 2-3.

the Roman dating-system for the later half of a month works towards the beginning of the next month – and also if it should coincide with Ash Wednesday. There is a fairly standard form for such a rubric, one which appears with only a few variations in wording in, for example, the Launton Breviary (fo. 337 v) and a third parish church breviary, that used at Coltishall church in Norfolk.[9] Yet into the Denchworth rubric is tucked the entire entry from the martyrology for 23-25 February. Of all the breviaries consulted for this enquiry, the Coltishall book is the only other one that has any mention of possible complications in the reading of the martyrology, though somewhat shorter than that of the Denchworth book. Is it likelier to be the case that the incumbents of just these two parish churches, one in the Berkshire Downs and one in the Norfolk Broads, had a particular desire to keep their martyrology reading tidy, or that both breviaries have some distant family likeness witnessed to by this peculiar trait?

Next we consider the question of the rubric 'Ubi vero dedicata est ecclesia in honore'. In most of the late Sarum breviaries there is a direction about the observance of first Vespers on a feast day when it is also what we would call the patronal feast. Since the matter of first vespers is one of the trickiest questions in the higher reaches of liturgical minutiae, this would make good sense were it not for the fact that only two or three feasts are so treated, and these are the same feasts in all the breviaries checked for this detail. Every one of nine large manuscript volumes – the Launton, Denchworth and Coltishall breviaries plus service-books used at Arlingham (Gloucs.), Great Bedwyn (Wilts.) and Ranworth (Norfolk),[10] and three which have no identifiable connection with a specific parish,[11] has such a rubric only for two or three feasts: the Decollation of John the Baptist (29 August); Michaelmas (29 September); and sometimes also Anne (26 July). The 1531 Great Breviary has such a rubric at four places, the three just mentioned plus Andrew (for a slightly different case, when it coincides with the First Sunday in Advent, which would trump even the vespers of the patronal feast). It may be objected that such instruction is necessary for the feast of St. Anne, which came to enjoy universal popularity only from the end of the fourteenth century and which follows immediately another important feast, that of James. But there is no major observance before either Michaelmas or the Decollation of John the Baptist (to which we shall return in another context); and it is thus striking that there is no rubric of this kind for David, Gregory, Augustine of Canterbury, Alban, Etheldreda, Nativity of John Baptist, Peter, Paul, James, Laurence, Bartholomew, Denis, Luke, Martin, Nicholas, Thomas the Apostle, or Thomas Becket – that is, for

[9] Durham, University Library, MS Cosin V.i.3, fo. 393 v.

[10] Salisbury, Cathedral Library, MSS 152 and 224, and a manuscript at Ranworth parish church (an antiphonal), respectively.

[11] Oxford, Bodleian Library, MSS Bodl. 976, Hatton 63 and Lat. Liturg., f. 29.

those saints to whom, besides Mary, the vast majority of English churches were in fact dedicated.

This example, while it does not cast any particular doubt on the veracity of the books in which it appears, highlights a somewhat misleading aspect of many manuscript service-books: that, while we tend to think of such manuscripts as to a large extent 'purpose-written' books, any given one will in reality contain a large amount of material irrelevant to the church where it came to be used. In this case we are told what to do on patronal feasts only when the church is dedicated to the Beheading of John Baptist, Michael and sometimes Anne.[12] Since none of these is the dedication in any of the instances in which we know the church where one of these books was used, we must suppose that this rubric was simply passed over, year after year, as an irrelevance. Where it comes to make some sense is, of course, in a printed book like the 1531 edition, presumably made to be circulated to churches of many different dedications. This obvious fact does not explain the appearance of the rubric in manuscript books of a hundred years earlier.

When we turn from breviaries to missals, the situation is even more productive of curiosity; for missals are more likely to contain ceremonial directions – fitfully but, with the fully developed Sarum missals, often in considerable detail. When and how these rubrics, here called ceremonial (what to do, as distinct from what to say), came into the Sarum missal is not yet clear. Nor is the situation ever wholly uniform. By the time of several notable missals which can be connected with specific parishes – as with breviaries, mostly not until the later fourteenth century – several such rubrics are often found, though never uniformly. While their appearance or non-appearance is not coherent enough to be said to tell an entire story in itself, the diversity involved is marked enough to further our argument.

The first 'ceremonial' rubric to attract our attention is found in every manuscript Sarum missal examined. It concerns not action inside the Mass but the location of a Mass. The feast of the Decollation of John the Baptist, 29 August, was also the day on which a virgin martyr of great antiquity, Sabina, was commemorated. Sabina's seems in fact to have been the earlier observance, but the secondary feast of the Precursor (which, along with the tertiary one of his Conception, may have been more popular in England than on the Continent) received the greater liturgical attention. Hence the widely-encountered rubric, which generally reads something like this: 'dicitur missa in cap° [capitulo] de Sancta Sabina virgine post primam ante terciam more solito et missa de Sancto Johanne post sextam dicitur'. The meaning of 'in capitulo' is

[12] In fact, there appear to have been virtually no churches dedicated to the Beheading. One possible exception is Coln St. Aldwyn's (Gloucs.); another, but highly dubious, is Tadcaster (Yorks): F. Arnold-Forster, *Studies in Church Dedications*, i (London, 1899), p. 61. But it is notoriously difficult to get accurate information about medieval English parish church dedications. Without question many churches were dedicated to Michael, a few to Anne.

not clear; the likeliest explanation, that there was an altar in the chapter house which could be used for subsidiary masses, is only an explanation *faute de mieux*. It has been observed that chapter houses – that the one at Salisbury is the ultimate point of reference for this rubric is made plain by the addition of the words 'sicut mos est in ecclesia Sarum' in, for example, missals from Closworth (Somerset) and Colwich (Staffs.)[13] – are singularly unsuited to altars, and furthermore that there is no evidence that altars were ever placed there.[14] For our purposes this does not matter greatly, for the one clear point is that the rubric makes sense only where there is a chapter house, however it is (or is not) involved. Every one of the missals we are considering has here a direction which, almost by definition, cannot have been followed in the parish churches in which these books were used.

Then there is the question of the persons, places and vesture involved in certain chants. This can be seen clearly in rubrics often found for the Saturday Ember Mass in Advent – itself an unusually elaborate service involving twelve lessons with appropriate responses. After the epistle, the tract (in place of a gradual during the penitential season of Advent) is to be sung in the following way: 'Duo clerici de secunda forma in superpelliciis ad gradum chori dicant [*or* cantent] hunc tractum . . . Chorus idem repetat; clerici versum chori dicant'. Then, towards the end of this very extensive piece of singing, there is a further instruction that: 'Duo clerici de secunda forma in cap(p)is nigris ad gradum chori simul dicant totum et integrum istum tractum'. Remembering again that our concern is not with the elaborateness of this exercise, as it might have been performed in Salisbury cathedral, but with the relation between the written page in a missal and the parish church in which that missal was used, we observe that this rubric presupposes (a) two pairs of singing clerics (for the 'solo' parts): (b) a larger body of clerics out of which both pairs are of the second form or rank – again, a point the meaning of which is itself not entirely clear: (c) a body of singers (*chorus*) to respond: (d) at least one step (*gradus*) into the architectural feature called the choir; and (e) surplices for the first pair of clerics and *cappae nigrae* ('in habitu quotidiano', as some of the missals gloss this) for the second pair. Of these features a typical parish church would probably have had the last two: a step at the entrance into the choir and a couple of surplices, along with perhaps the *cappae nigrae*. The rest of the rubric is likely to have been honoured only in the breach. This is again a widespread rubric, appearing in missals used all over the country, for example,

[13] Oxford, Bodleian Library, MS Don.b.6, fo. 199 and London, B.L., MS Harl., 4919. fo. 274.

[14] F.H. Dickinson, ed., *Missale ad usum . . . Sarum* (Burntisland, 1861-83), p. vii, note n, with respect to Requiem Masses to be celebrated 'in capitulo'.

in Adderbury (Oxfordshire), Gawsworth (Cheshire), St. Margaret Lothbury (London), and probably Maldon (Essex).[15]

The third Mass rubric to consider is, unlike the previous instance, found only in certain manuscript missals. This is a bit of delicate liturgical symbolism for the feast of the Seven Brothers on 9 July. Here the instruction is that at the Alleluia the two verses should be sung 'a duobus pueris in superpelliciis' – sometimes the words 'sicut in ebdomade pasche domini' being added. Missals in which this rubric appears include ones used at St. Botolph's and St. Laurence Jewry (both in London),[16] as well as the St. Margaret Lothbury, Colwich and Maldon books cited above, and several not at present to be ascribed to specific parish churches but almost certainly used in such a context.[17]

This way of marking the 9 July feast is not found in the three earliest known Sarum missals: the Crawford (mid thirteenth century), Arsenal (early fourteenth), and Bologna (only a little later than Arsenal).[18] The Bologna missal, which is thought to have some possible connection with Oxford, may however reflect knowledge of the practice, because after the words 'Laudate pueri' it continues 'require in sabbato'. The Saturday in question must be Easter Saturday, though on that day there is no special rubric at the Alleluia in the Bologna missal. Yet the printed missals all contain a rubric about the Easter Saturday Alleluia which begins, 'Duo pueri in superpelliciis in pulpito dicant'; after these two boys have sung a 'Haec dies' verse two other boys, also in surplices, stand at the entrance to the choir and sing (with obvious appropriateness), 'Laudate pueri'.[19] By this time, as again in the printed missals show, * the practice had spread to the feast of the Seven Brothers, for the rubric for that occasion reads, 'Et dicitur cum utroque versu hac die sicut in Sabbato in hebdomade Paschae',[20] Then the same boys pick up again, alternately with the choir, on the verse, 'Sit nomen domini . . . '

Because the Easter Saturday practice is hinted at, though not specified, in the Bologna missal – why else would the words, 'Require in sabbato', have been added at the Alleluia in the Seven Brothers Mass? – but not in the markedly earlier Crawford or slightly earlier Arsenal missals, we may suspect

[15] Respectively, Oxford, Bodleian Library, MSS Don.b.5, fo. 18 v and Barlow 1, fo. 13; Cambridge, University Library, MS Dd.1.15, fo. 17; and London, B.L., MS Harl. 2787, fo. 22. It is noteworthy that in the printed missals mention of the second pair of clerics is omitted (Dickinson edn., col. 38).

[16] Oxford, Christ Church, MS 87, fo. 207 and London, B.L., MS Arundel 109, fo. 187 v, respectively.

[17] Oxford, Bodleian Library, MSS Barlow 5, fo. 202; Rawl. A. 387^{A}, fo. 119; Rawl. liturg. c.2, fo. 199 v; Oriel College 75, fo. 246 v; and Pembroke College, 1, fo. 198.

[18] As in J.W. Legg, ed. *The Sarum Missal* (Oxford, 1916): Manchester, John Rylands University Library, MS Crawford lat. 24; Bologna, University Library, MS 2.565; Paris, Arsenal, MS 135. The first is mid thirteenth century, the other two early fourteenth.

[19] Dickinson ed., col. 379.

[20] Dickinson ed., col. 807.

* again in the *should read* again the

that this bit of elaboration was the invention of a cleric (or just possibly a patron) of the early fourteenth century with a taste for elegant touches in the liturgy. We may suspect also that the inclusion of the Seven Brothers rubric in a limited number of manuscript missals is rather a sign of some affinity between them as books (though not one which can be exaggerated into a close family likeness) than an indication of a sub-use within the Use of Sarum. The printed missals (Caxton's of 1487 is the earliest) seem to have been based on an
* examplar or examplars which contained the rubric; and so what appears to be a standard if trivial part of the late medieval Sarum rite is in fact attested to in only a small minority of manuscript service-books.

Such conclusion as a preliminary enquiry like the present one can have may be stated briefly. It begins with the observation that the mentality we bring to the study of medieval liturgical manuscripts tends to be coloured by the presuppositions of those who worship according to printed liturgical books, especially if such worshippers are of either the Anglican or the Roman tradition – in both of which the use of authority to mandate uniform observance complements the identity-in-multiplicity which the technology of printing makes possible. This mentality is deeply unhelpful when applied to manuscript service books, characterised as they are by a high degree of individuality. Furthermore, the fact that medieval English service-books tend to be classified by Uses, and that only one such Use (that of Sarum) had any very widespread currency, encourages us to think that there is something like a normative Sarum missal or Sarum breviary as prototypical of the *Book of Common Prayer* or the Roman breviary or missal of 1568/70. In very broad outline this may be true, at least negatively: one can say that a book is not Sarum because it lacks such and such features, and to a degree that it is Sarum because it contains this or that. But the variation among those books nominally classed as of the Sarum rite is enormous.

Discrepancies of the kind here discussed, between rubrical prescription and (putative) practice, underline the necessity of careful study of individual manuscripts as discrete pieces of evidence each possessing intrinsic worth, rather than as generalised precursors or models for the printed books which emerged at the end of the fifteenth century. Though those books, cut off as they are by the changes of the English Reformation, can easily seem normative to the liturgical scholar, they may in important respects be misleading to the historian.

Margaret Gibson has commented, addressing another problem, that, 'The relation of the written text of a sermon to the mode and language of its actual delivery is not yet [1984] fully understood'.[21] The same thing can be said of the

[21] Her n. 43 on p. 92 of R.W. Hunt, *The Schools and the Cloister: The Life and Writings of Alexander Nequam (1157-1217)*, ed. and rev. by Margaret Gibson (Oxford, 1984).

* examplar *should read* exemplar

relation between the written text of a manuscript service-book – at least when used in medieval English parish churches – and the performance of that liturgical worship for which it was meant to provide. In both areas there is plenty of work to be done.

XIII

THE ENGLISH DEVOTION OF ST GREGORY'S TRENTAL

THE devotional practice called St Gregory's Trental is not unfamiliar to students of both late medieval liturgy and Middle English literature. Though the verse legend which contains the story received considerable attention around the turn of the century, the liturgical observance itself has never been systematically studied.[1] The aim of the present article is to lay at least the groundwork for such a study, though it will not be possible to solve all the questions which emerge.

A recent article in the *Revue Bénédictine* has raised in somewhat more scientific form than ever before the question of the origins and peculiar character of this practice in France.[2] Dom Hesbert would trace its origins ultimately to the story of the greedy monk Justus in book IV of the *Dialogues* of Gregory the Great. Though one cannot argue from this story that Gregory "instituted" trentals, the story's influence, especially on monastic milieux in the high middle ages, may have been sufficient to put the practice of trentals into widespread use. Dom Hesbert cites examples from eight monastic houses throughout western Europe, and instances could easily be multiplied. But all this is about simple trentals which, though sometimes referred to as Gregorian Trentals, are not the same thing as what in English is called St Gregory's Trental. The difference is that a Gregorian Trental is simply the celebration of mass for the repose of a particular soul for thirty consecutive days (or as close to this as possible), usually by the same priest. St Gregory's Trental, on the other hand, is a trental spread out over an entire year and involving, as of its essence, a "recapitulation" of the liturgical year. It is also frequently connected with a distinctive legend, and augmented by certain stipulated devotions.

Dom Hesbert devotes himself principally to two pieces of evidence. One is a missal from the abbey of St Claude in the Jura, of the mid-14th century.[3] Fols. 70–72 contain the Trental headed by the rubric,

> Sequitur rubrica triginta missarum per sanctum Gregorium papam Sextum approbatarum, de quibus in libro suo dyalogorum ut asseritur fit mensio. In quibus talis ordo

The following abbreviations have been used for libraries: BM = London, British Museum; Bodl. = Oxford, Bodleian Library; CUL = Cambridge University Library.

[1] For editions of the verse legend, see notes 10 and 11. The treatise of K. Eberle, *Der Tricenar des hl. Gregorius* (Regensburg, 1890) is cited by both Adolph Franz (see note 14) and Henry Thurston, *The Memory of our Dead* (London, 1916), p. 151; but as far as I have been able to discover there is no copy in either England or the United States, and the inference from Thurston's reference would be that the work was about Gregorian trentals, not St Gregory's Trental in the form which concerns us.

[2] R. J. Hesbert, "Les Trentains Gregoriens sous formes de cycles liturgiques," *Rev. Bén.* LXXXI (1971), 108–22.

[3] Lons-le-Saunier, Archives Départ. du Jura 10; described in V. Leroquais, *Les Sacramentaires et Missels des bibls. publiques de France* II (1924), 339.

servari debet videlicet quod per triginta dies continuos per eundem sacerdotem existentem in gratia quantum in ipso est celebrantem vel celebraturum omni die.

The litany, and two prayers (the text of which is given) are to preface each mass. The specified masses are (in shorthand form) those of Adv. I, Nativ., Stephen, Jn. Evang., H. Inn., Epiph., Oct. Epiph., Sunday after Oct. Epiph., Purif., Septuag., Lent I, Lent II, Lent IV, Palm S., Maundy Th., Easter, Asc., Pentec., Trin., Pentec. XX, Pentec. XXIV, Jn. Bapt., Peter and Paul, Mary Magd., Lawrence, Assumption, Annunc., Nativ. BVM, Holy Cross, Michael.

Of this dauntingly elaborate devotion Dom Hesbert says, "L'idée qui a guidé l'organisateur de ce trentain est désormais bien claire: il l'a conçu comme une réduction de l'année liturgique; une année liturgique bloquée en un mois" (p. 112). The form of the Trental contained in this missal is indeed a recapitulation: the "highlights" of the liturgical year "per triginta dies continuos."

His second piece of evidence is a 15th century missal from the church of St Nizier in Lyon.[4] Its initial rubric is slightly different from that of the St Claude missal:

Hec presens rubrica est de missis beati Gregorii pape sicut continetur in libro dyalogorum, quod fuit quidam episcopus qui celebravit et dixit xxx. missas eas continuando pro anima cuiusdem hominis existentis in penis purgatorii. . . .

The preliminary devotions are also changed, and the list of prescribed feasts is slightly but importantly altered. Even more important, there is no specification that the masses must be said on thirty consecutive days.

After exploring the possible connections between the two missals — the Lyon book, Dom Hesbert feels, is probably dependent on, or heavily influenced by, St Claude, and he notes that this form of trental is not found in any other Lyon missals — he mentions, as almost an afterthought, that another form of St Gregory's Trental is to be found in late medieval English missals. He cites ten English missals (not all of them Sarum, as he thinks),[5] prints the introductory rubric from one of them, and lists the specified feasts. These feasts are the most immediately distinctive things about the English form of St Gregory's Trental: there are only ten of them (Nativ., Epiph., Purif., Annunc., Easter, Asc., Pentec., Trin., Assumption, and Nativ. BVM — with, as we shall see, some variation for the last two), of which each mass is to be repeated three times, within the octaves of the respective feasts. (There are also other specifications and distinctively English characteristics which Dom Hesbert does not note: these will be discussed presently.)

II

In trying to trace the development of this curious practice in England it is necessary, if confusion is to be avoided, to understand two things from the start. The first is that St Gregory's Trental has nothing integrally to do with Gregory

[4] Poitiers, Bibl. de la Ville 29; descr. in Leroquais, *op. cit.* III (1924), 205.

[5] Oxford, Univ. Coll. 78A is a Hereford missal, not Sarum, and is of the 15th century, not the 14th. The MS cited by Hesbert as CUL 151 should be 451.

the Great:[6] as we shall see, frequently (and probably in the earliest forms) he is not even named, and occasionally some other pope will be the subject of the legend. Secondly, the form in which St Gregory's Trental appears in England is the result of the conflation of a literary story of the exemplum or perhaps fabliau type and a liturgical practice. This conflation is hard to see because it has taken place by the time both of the earliest literary accounts of St Gregory's Trental we have and of the earliest liturgical evidence. But that such a conflation did occur seems incontrovertible.

It may be well to start with a summary of the literary story in its final form. One day at his mass Gregory (or whoever, named or simply "quidam apostolicus," is the subject of the story) prays to know the estate of his mother, who had died renowned for her sanctity. As he prays a monstrous apparition fills the room — its stench is particularly emphasized — and upon being conjured by Gregory reveals itself to be his mother, who is suffering hideous torments because she bore, and to avoid scandal strangled, two illegitimate children. Gregory can relieve her pains by saying thirty masses, three commemorating each of ten principal feasts of the year. He does so, and at the end of the year a vision appears to him, of a woman in such glory that he takes her to be the Blessed Virgin. But she is, of course, his mother, now delivered from her pains and exalting the powers of the Trental.

The literary story can be traced back into the 13th century. Though elements of it go back still further — indeed, to Gregory's *Dialogues* inasmuch as they are beyond comparison the most influential collection of miracles showing how the mass can aid souls in purgatory — the 13th century appears to have been the time when the two aspects which define the story were juxtaposed. These aspects are the secret wickedness of a pope's or priest's mother, unsuspected until she appears as a ghastly spectre to her praying son; and the deliverance of a soul from Purgatory through the efficacy of a trental of masses said for it. Though the ultimate origin of the story is a matter of some obscurity, and some controversy, it would appear that a satisfactory starting point for our purposes (which, it must be remembered, are to follow the story only as it comes to be an element in the liturgical practice) will be found in one MS of the fables of the English writer Odo of Cheriton (d. 1247). This MS (BM Harl. 219) contains some twenty-five interpolated fables, of which one, "De muliere adulterina mortua, filio suo sacerdoti apparenti," provides most of the first half of the St Gregory's Trental story:[7] the woman with one legitimate son, who becomes a priest, and two illegitimate ones; the priest-son, who has prayed to know her eternal fate, con-

[6] This point was made in a brief and oblique contribution which is practically the only modern literature on the subject in English: J. R. Hulbert, "The Sources of *St. Erkenwald* and *The Trental of St. Gregory*," *Modern Philology* XVI (1918–9), 485–93.

[7] Of the various MSS of Odo discussed by L. Hervieux, *Les Fabulistes Latins* . . . IV. *Eudes de Cheriton et ses Dérives* (Paris, 1899), only BM Harl. 219 (fol. 14) contains this story, one of those added to Odo's collection by an unknown supplementor. This MS, also including the *Gesta Romanorum*, was written at the end of the 13th century and beginning of the 14th, and is almost certainly of English provenance: see Hervieux, p. 149.

fronted by a horrid apparition (described in grotesque detail); confession by the mother that these torments are the penalty for her sins. At this point the fable ends, with no mention of the trental. But that element is provided by another story, almost certainly by Odo (though it appears in only two of the many MSS of his collection),[8] about bishop Theodosius and the block of ice, which fishermen bring to ease the bishop's gouty foot, and which turns out to contain a soul whose deliverance can be accomplished only through a trental of masses. This, however, is a simple trental, which must be said in thirty consecutive days, and an important element in the story is that the bishop has to try three times before he can overcome the wiles of tempters working to prevent him from finishing the trental. So, though both aspects of our story are present in this collection of fables, even putting them together would not provide us with what we now recognize as St Gregory's Trental.[9]

By the mid-14th century these two stories have been put together into a Middle English verse tale called "The Pope trental."[10] This is the title in the celebrated Vernon MS (Bodl. Eng. poet. a.1), a vast compilation of pieces, in south English dialect, written about 1382. (There are actually two versions of our tale in the Vernon MS, with only insignificant verbal variations; the title of the second version, insofar as there is one, seems to be "The guldene trental.") The numerous MSS which contain the poem under titles like "Trentalle Sancti Gregorii" are of the 15th century.[11] By the time the tale in the Vernon MS has

[8] Bodl. Douce 98 (fol. 48), an English(?) miscellany of the 14th(?) century; and Berlin, Meerman lat. 147, a late 13th century book from Battle Abbey (N.R. Ker, *Medieval Libraries of Great Britain*, 2nd edn. 1964, pp. 8, 229), where it is the last story (fol. 144) in the "Parabole" of Odo.

[9] These two stories reappear in a late 14th century English MS, BM Harl. 1288 (not 1228 as in Hervieux) containing a variety of religious pieces, including at the end a Latin version of the French translation of some of the Odonian fables made by Nicholas Bozon, c. 1320-50 (ed. under the title *Contes Moralisées* by Lucy Toulmin Smith and Paul Meyer, Soc. Anc. Textes Fr. xxvii, 1889, 1–189). Though Bozon translated neither the adulterous mother story nor the block of ice story, both have reappeared in the Latin retranslation in Harl. 1288 (fols. 51v and 17v respectively). There is a small puzzle here which needs untangling.

[10] Ed. C. Horstmann, *The Minor Poems of the Vernon MS*, part i (Early English Text Soc. 98, 1892), 260–8.

[11] Among which may be mentioned especially BM Cott. Calig. A.ii, fol. 86, ed. Furnivall, EETS 15, 1866 and reprinted at the foot of Horstmann's edn., cited above; Lambeth 306, fol. 110, used as a base MS by A. Kaufmann, *Trentalle Sancti Gregorii . . . in zwei Texten herausgegeben* (Erlanger Beiträge zur englischen Philologie iii; Erlangen, 1889), the second text being that of CUL Kk.i.6, fol. 242; BM Harl. 3810(I), fol. 76v, ed. R. Jordan, *Englische Studien* xl (1909), 351–71; Edinburgh, Advocates 19.3.1, fol. 213, ed. K. Bülbring, *Anglia* xiii (1891), 301–8. Others are Oxf., Balliol 354, fol. 139 (of the early 16th cent.), discussed by E. Flügel, *Anglia* xxvi (1903), 94–285 esp. 150–1; Princeton, Garret (s.n.), fol. 38, discussed by R. K. Root, *Englische Studien* xli (1910), 360–71 esp. 363; Aberystwyth, Nat. Lib. Wales, Peniarth 394, fol. 71; and Oswestry, Lord Harlech's Collection, Porkington 20, fol. 94: see C. Brown, *Register of Middle English and Didactic Verse* (Oxford, 1920) nos. 358, 999, 2056 (there are no additions to these MSS in Brown-Robbins 1943 or Robbins-Cutler 1965). The various MSS have been divided into two versions (J. E. Wells, *A Manual of the Writings in Middle English*, New Haven, 1916 and nine supplements, p. 172): the first (Vernon, Calig., Lambeth, Princeton) being more straightforward, and the second (Edinburgh, CUL, Harl.) including various temptations Gregory is afflicted with before concluding the Trental. Of the unprinted MSS, Aberystwyth and Balliol are of the first version, Porkington of the second (*First Supplement*, p. 956). For our purposes, the variations between the two versions are relatively unimportant.

been composed, the liturgical practice of St Gregory's Trental is complete in the form in which we have it. Not only does the Vernon MS poem specify the ten feasts of the peculiarly English sequence (though the last two are Nativ. BVM and Conception rather than the more usual Assumption and Nativity: this point will be returned to later); it also includes a verse translation of the prescribed collect which is to be added after the collect of the feast at each mass within the Trental. We know, then, that the liturgical practice is in existence by about the mid-14th century, from the evidence of the literary story. It would seem time now to turn to the liturgical practice itself.

III

As was mentioned earlier, Dom Hesbert cites ten MS English missals. To this evidence may be added information from a further half-dozen or so English MSS as well as the witness of the two modern editions of the Sarum missal. That of J. W. Legg (Oxford, 1916) was made from the three earliest MS missals known to him: the Crawford Missal (now Manchester, John Rylands Lib., Crawford lat. 24), of the mid- or later 13th century, as his base MS, with collations from Paris, Arsenal 135 (probably second half of 13th century, and later carried from England into France), and Bologna, Univ. Lib. 2565 (probably first quarter of the 14th century, with a number of leaves missing). Of these three, only the Crawford Missal contains St Gregory's Trental, but there it is not in the original hand, having been added in a smaller hand at the end of the original contents (fol. 233v: Legg, p. 460). It has neither title nor rubric, and begins simply "Hec sunt festa in quibus iste oraciones subsequentes dicantur, videlicet Infra octab(as) Natalis domini iii," etc.; it then lists the other nine feasts and gives the texts of the three mass-prayers which we shall notice presently. The fact that there is no mention of Gregory or of the story of the pope's mother leads us to suspect that the addition was made fairly early, but there is no way to tell whether it was before or after the earliest securely dated references we have.

Next it is useful to notice the other extreme chronologically; evidence from the printed editions of the late 15th and early 16th centuries, as contained in F. H. Dickinson's edition (Burntisland, 1861–83) of the Sarum missal. Here we find a long rubric (p. 883*) mentioning St Gregory's Trental by name, specifying the ten feasts, containing detailed instruction for the celebration of the masses in the Trental (including the daily recital, throughout the year, of Placebo and Dirige with nine each of psalms, lessons, and antiphons, except during Eastertide when three suffice, as well as daily Commendation of Souls), and concluding with the three collects.[12] There is, however, no reference to the story. In the printed editions we have what we can regard as the most highly developed form of the practice.

Between these "earliest" (?addition to the Crawford Missal) and "latest" (printed missals c.1487–1557) mentions comes the evidence of the group of late 14th and early 15th century missals we must now notice. Of these the two

[12] These are followed by the "Dies irae," headed "Prosa pro defunctis qui voluerit"; it is not clear whether this is meant to be connected with the Trental or not.

earliest are probably Oxford, Keble 54 (c. 1383) and CUL Ff.ii.31 (dated 1397). The Trental in the Keble missal begins with a very long rubric, mentioning Gregory by name (p. [sic] 499). The Cambridge MS likewise has a long legend (fol. 245v, in the same hand as the sanctorale), and also a long rubric following the prayers. So we know that Gregory's name was connected with this form of the trental in at least some English liturgical books of the end of the 14th century. Evidence from missals of the following century is more common: for instance, a short rubric, but naming Gregory, in a Sarum missal (CUL Ee.ii.2, fol. 160v); and in the Hereford missal from Whitchurch, Mons. (Oxford, Univ. Coll. 78A; ed. W. G. Henderson, Leeds, 1874, p. 436). But in the York missals — of those in manuscript as opposed to printed editions, Oxf., Univ. 78B (ed. Henderson, Surtees Soc. 60, 1872, p. 189), and Cambridge, Sidney Sussex 33 are the only ones with long legends — both the MSS and the printed books fail to include Gregory's name. The heading is simply "Modus celebrandi trentale pro anima alicujus," and where the legend is included it speaks merely of "Papa familiarus filius ejus."

In fact, inclusions in English MS missals of what we call St Gregory's Trental without any mention of Gregory are no less common than those which specify his name. Instead of a name, the short legend prefacing the prayers often speaks of "quidam apostolicus" (Sarum missals CUL Add. 451, late 14th century; and of the 15th century, CUL Gg.v.24, BM Arundel 109, Bodl. Barlow 1 — the preceding four all noticed by Hesbert —, and Bodl. Rawl. liturg. e.41, added in a different hand at fol. 149v). Even more noteworthy is BM Add. 25588, an early 15th century Sarum missal from the diocese of Norwich in which the observance appears as St Leo's Trental! A French rubric on fol. 246 begins, "Ceo est la trental que seynt leo apostoile de rome chaunta pur lalme sa miere, ceo est a sauer, iii messe de la nativite nostre seygnor . . . ." Certainly the connection between 'quidam apostolicus' and Gregory was not indissoluble.

Additional light is cast by two MS service books originating in continental Europe. Bodl. Canon. liturg. 3, a Cistercian breviary and votive missal from Pannonia, dated 1373, contains an order of thirteen masses of a pope Clemens to obtain any grace asked for (fol. 210), the masses being specified by their introits: Adv. I, Nativ., Epiph., Septuag., Palm S., Easter., Asc., Pentec., Trin., and votive masses of the BVM, the Angels, the Apostles, and All Saints.[13] Here we see the idea of the efficacy of masses spanning, or (perhaps better) subsuming, the liturgical year, and connected with the name of a third pope, Clemens (without number). A second variation is contained in a Maguellone (Montpellier) missal, of around the mid-15th century (Bodl. Lat. liturg. d.8, fol. 332): "Hec sequens tabula est de misse (sic) beata (sic) gregorii pape sicut continetur in libro grisologorum ubi legitur que fuit quidam episcopus qui celebravit ea . . . ," continuing with a story of the liberation of a soul from purgatory

[13] I am grateful to Dr A. C. de la Mare for supplementing my imperfect notes by an ultraviolet scrutiny of this MS.

through the trental. There follows a list of thirty specified masses. Twenty-five of these are the same as those stipulated in the mid-14th century St Claude missal discussed by Hesbert; peculiar to the Maguellone missal are Lent III, Pentec. I, Pentec. II, All Saints, and (with a certain logic) Gregory, in place of the St Claude missal's Octave Epiph., Sun. after Oct., Pentec. XX, Pentec. XXIV, and Nativ. BVM. The Maguellone rubric, while specifying Gregory's name, offers a literary reference where one can read a story about, not necessarily Gregory, but "quidam episcopus." It may be conjectured that "grisologorum" is a corruption, or scribe's misreading, of "dialogorum," and that the reference marks a stage of confusion between the story of St Gregory's Trental and that of the trental ordered by Gregory in the *Dialogues*. Here it may be pertinent that the Maguellone missal is about a century later than that of St Claude.

We cannot become diverted here into the immense subject of "Messreihen" of which Adolph Franz collected a large number;[14] but it is worth noting that he includes a few forms which are very close to the one we are concerned with. One is the "Trental of St Sebastian," which seems to be in reality a variant form of St Gregory's Trental, disguised by a confusion with the idea of a privileged mass or privileged altar arising from the story of Gregory's celebrating at the church of St Sebastian in Rome when an angel announced to him special benefits attached to masses there.[15] St Sebastian's Trental is connected with Gregory not only by this story but by the fact that it consists of thirty masses spanning the liturgical year. Furthermore, these masses are the same as those of St Gregory's Trental in the St Claude missal; except that St Sebastian's has Pentec. I and II instead of XX and XXIV, and Gregory "vel de omnibus sanctis" and "de mortuis" instead of Sunday after Oct. Epiph. and Nativ. BVM. This trental is included in the Roman missals printed at Paris in 1515, 1530, and 1540, and is indulgenced — modestly: "plures annos et quadragenas indulgentiarum" — by a pope Innocent.[16] This is probably meant to be Innocent IV (1243–54), who seems frequently to be mentioned in these connections; but the number is unlikely to convey any particular accuracy, and indeed Innocent VI (1352–62) would be an altogether more probable choice.

The next among the mass-series Franz describes which is important to us is one which he cites from a St Alban MS now at Trier.[17] This is a set of "Misse pro defunctis, ut meritis subscriptorum festorum liberentur": three masses each of Annunc., Nativ., Jn. Evang., Epiph., S. Cruce, Resurr., Asc., S. Spir., Trin., Nativ. BVM, these being presented as the masses St Egidius celebrated for Charlemagne! This series is, in its provision of the ten masses to be repeated thrice each, very close to the English form of St Gregory's Trental; but the Trier MS is of the 15th century, and as we have seen, the English form is fully extant by the second half of the 14th, so we are not carried much further in our search

[14] A. Franz, *Die Messe im deutschen Mittelalter* (Freiburg-i-B, 1902), 218–67.

[15] Ibid., pp. 248–9.

[16] *Missale Romanum 1474*, ed. R. Lippe, II (Henry Bradshaw Soc. 33, 1907), 366–7.

[17] *Op. cit.*, p. 252.

for the origins of the English form. The form contained in the Trier MS is very unusual in starting the sequence with the Annunciation.

One more continental analogue must be mentioned, this time not a trental but a "septenar," a series of seven masses. Franz describes, from a south German book of masses of the 15th century, a septenar in honor of the suffering of Christ and the Blessed Virgin.[18] Of particular note to us are not the specified masses, concentrating as they do on just the Passion, Resurrection, and Assumption, but rather the introduction, which explains,

> Sequuntur hic septem misse que videntur efficacie magne pro animabus in purgatorio existentibus pro celeriori liberacione prout manifestate sunt Gregorio pape ut ipse legeret pro expiacione reatus matris sue.

Here it is very likely that there is some influence *from* the English poetic legend — which Franz mentions without adducing any continental parallels; the MS is late enough for this to have been possible.

IV

The process which it is at this point possible to suspect would be one by which a liturgical practice begins (or is developed from a hint in a patristic source, i.e. the *Dialogues*); is then attached to a literary story which has its roots in, most likely, a sermon exemplum designed to show the efficacy of masses for the dead and to encourage support by the faithful for such masses; and enjoys widespread circulation in usual but not invariable connection with the story. Such a process would seem to correspond to what facts we have about St Gregory's Trental. The alternative would have to be that the story and the liturgical practice were connected from the beginning, which would in turn require either that the fabricator of the story was the inventor of the practice, or that the story was concocted to justify and authenticate someone's liturgical innovation. Neither of these possibilities seems at all likely.

Analysis of the mass prayers which were apparently attached to the English form of St Gregory's Trental from its inception may help a bit in our search for the origins — or at least the original character — of the practice. These prayers are to be said after the proper mass prayers for each feast: "ita quod Orationes subsequentes cum Oratione de festo sub uno *Oremus* et sub uno *Per Dominum* dicantur," in the words of the rubric to the printed missals. They are therefore presumably connected in an integral way with the efficacy which is supposed to be attached to the Trental. Though the prayers are substantially the same in the missals of the three English uses, there are sufficient variations to be worth having laid out in critical form. (Base text from Legg's edition of the Sarum missal, i.e. the Crawford missal; D = Dickinson's text, from the printed Sarum missals; Y = the printed York Missal; H = the printed Hereford missal.)

> *Oracio.* Deus qui es noster redempcio, et[a] in terra promissionis ante omnes terras nasci elegisti, mortemque ibidem sustinuisti, libera propicius animam famuli tui .N. de manibus demonum[b] et eandem terram[c] de manibus[d] paganorum ut[e] populus qui in te

[18] Ibid., p. 255.

non credit, per virtutem tuam emendacionem habeat[f], et illis omnibus qui in te confidunt, pro tua magna succurre pietate[g], per dominum nostrum[h].[19]

a. Deus summa spes nostrae redemptionis, qui D,H
b. et de poenis purgatorii *add.* H
c. celeriter *add.* H
d. potestate D,Y
e. et H
f. habeat emendacionem Y
g. pietate succurre D,Y; per tuam magnam succurre pietatem D *var.* (1501L, 1515, 1557)
h. Qui vivis Y,H; Qui cum deo Patre et Spiritu D.

Secretum. Omnipotens sempiterne[a] deus, redemptor animarum salvandarum et precium redempcionis tocius[b] humani generis[c], miserere[d] anime famuli tui .N. et quicquid[e] viciorum fallente diabolo et[f] propria iniquitate[g] contraxerit[h], tu pius et misericors abluas indulgendo, et terram quam ihesus christus filius tuus dominus noster[j] sanguine proprio[k] dedicavit[l] de manibus inimicorum[m] tuorum[n] eripias, vota filiorum israel ad eius liberacionem[o] instancium in viam salutis eterne misericorditer dirigendo. per.[p]

a. et misericors *add.* D(1494), H
b. tocius *om.* D
c. generis humani D,Y,H
d. clementer *add.* D,Y,H
e. in eo *add.* D
f. et *om.* H
g. seu fragilitate *add.* D(1494)
h. contraxit Y
j. ihesus . . . noster *om.* D,Y
k. proprio sanguine H; sanguine proprio tuo D
l. dedicasti D,Y,H
m. crucis *add.* D,H; per virtutem sanctae crucis Y
n. tuorum *om.* Y
o. liberacionem eius H
p. Qui vivis et regnas D,Y

Postcommunio. Deus cuius misericordie non est numerus, cui soli competit medicinam prestare post mortem, qui es vita viventium, spes moriencium[a], salus omnium in te credencium[b], qui terram hereditatis tue per peccata filiorum esau pollutam precioso sanguine tuo consecrare dignatus es[c]; tu animam famuli tui .N. per huius virtutem sacramenti, et[d] a peccatis omnibus exuas, et a penis quas pro his meretur[e] eripias, et populorum incredulum ac rebellem per graciam tuam facias peculiarem, illis et[f] omnibus[g] que in tuam misericordiam[h] confidunt, manum auxilii tui piissimi[j] largiendo[k]. per dominum.[l]

a. et *add.* D,Y
b. sperancium D,Y,H
c. dignatus es consecrare D
d. et *om.* D
e. benignus *add.* H
f. illis que D,Y
g. omnibus *om.* H
h. tua pietate et misericordia Y; tua misericordia D,H
j. piissime D,H
k. largiaris Y
l. Qui vivis et regnas cum Deo D

[19] Compare the Middle English gloss inserted in some versions of the vernacular story, e.g. in that of the Vernon MS (EETS 98, p. 265):

God, ur verrey Redempciun,
Ur sothfast soules savaciun,
That chose al othur londes bi-forn
The lond of bi-heste In to beo born,
And thi deth suffredest in that same,
Dilivere this soule from gult and blame,
Tak hit out of the fendes bond,
And that lond from the hethene hond,
And peple that leveth not in the
Thorwh thi vertu amendet mote be;
And alle that trusteth In thi Merci,
Lord, save hem sone and sothfastli!

(The thorn has been printed as 'th,' and u's and v's regularized.)

Only one of these variations is of any real importance, the beginning of the collect which in the earliest Sarum version and in the York missal begins, "Deus qui es noster redempcio," becomes in the later Sarum missals and in the Hereford, "Deus summa spes nostrae redemptionis."

The immediately striking thing about these prayers is that they combine two not obviously related elements: concern for the redemption of the soul for whom the Trental is being offered, and hopes that the Holy Land can be recovered from the Infidel. These two elements are in fact so unrelated in the language of the prayers as well as in theme that it would almost be possible simply to remove the clauses mentioning the Holy Land and have prayers much more directly suitable to the Trental. Yet the "crusading" element, if we may so call it, is present from the earliest versions of the prayers we possess. By contrast, the literary stories make no mention of the "crusading" element whatever. If this element is, as at first glance it seems to be, the secondary one, it is very difficult to conceive why it should have been added to prayers concerning themselves with the ostensible purpose of the Trental, the delivery of souls from Purgatory. But what if the situation was originally the reverse?

V

The verse tale of St Gregory's Trental, considerably expanded (version B), in the late 15th century MS BM Harl. 3810.I includes detailed specifications which perhaps provide a clue to this central puzzle of the text of the mass prayers.[20] The story is prefaced by a long set of Latin directions for the performance of the Trental. These directions, which read exactly as though they could have been taken from a service book, begin (fol. 75v), "Sciendum vero est quod sequenti modo debet trentale quod dicitur sancti Gregorii celebrari." The supplementary devotions for the fullest form of the Trental are then specified: "Placebo" and "Dirige," i.e. daily vespers and matins of the dead, with commendation of souls, the latter spelled out in exact detail as though taken from an ordo. Then there follows immediately, without any explanation, the text of the three mass prayers — the implication being presumably that they are to be said as part of the commendation of souls. The first (the mass collect) begins "Deus summa spes nostre redempcionis" as in the later (printed) Sarum and the Hereford missals, but over the words "summa spes" a second hand has written "qui es summa spes (and then struck through "spes") nostra redempcio": that is, a correction has been made to bring the text into line with that of the *older* Sarum (e.g. addition to the Crawford missal) and York missals. But there is a further complication. At the conclusion of the Middle English story, a new folio (85v; 85 is blank) begins "Hec est regula generalis huius trigintalis dicendi. Inprimis celebrans cotidie primum mane surgens dicat psalmus 'De profundis' cum oracione dominica et salutacione angelica et oracione 'Inclina domine' et cum hac oracione 'Omnipotens sempiterne Deus nostra existens redempcio, qui in

[20] My account is taken from the careful description and transcript of this part of the MS by Richard Jordan, art. cit.: see n. 11.

terra promissionis . . . '": the mass collect with a different beginning formula and so many variations from the basic text we have seen in all the English missals as to make inevitable the suspicion that that text and the one contained on fol. 85v of the Harley MS are two versions of a common original. There is no clearer way to indicate the relation between the two than to print them in an interlinear form, the text from the the Crawford missal on top and that of Harley fol. 85v on the bottom:

Deus qui es noster redempcio et in terra promissionis
O.s.d. nostra existens redempcio qui in terra promissionis

ante omnes terras nasci elegisti mortemque ibidem sustinuisti
super omnia alia loca nasci dignatus es et mortem passus es

libera propicius animam famuli tui .N. de manibus demonum
presta quesumus ut eam propicius de manibus paganorum

et eandem terram de manibus paganorum
liberare digneris et animam famuli tui ab omni pena conserues

ut populus qui in te non credit per virtutem tuam emendacionem habeat
et populum in te non credentem per virtutem tuam corrigere digneris

et illis omnibus qui in te confidunt
et omnibus in te fiduciam[21]

pro tua magna succurre pietate
per tuam potenciam in presenti graciam et in futuro gloriam sempiternam largiri.

The obvious substantive difference between the two versions is that, after the introductory clause in both, the Crawford version prays for the deliverance of the soul first and of the Holy Land second, while the Harley version reverses the order. In other words, it looks as though the latter may point to a stage in which the prayer was *primarily* one for the delivery of the Holy Land, i.e. with our "crusading" element foremost.

In summary, then, the Harley MS provides us with two versions of the prayer which in the missals is the mass collect: one (fol.75v) being basically the text of the English missals, with the later opening phrase corrected to approximate to the earlier; the other with marked variations not only in its opening phrase but also in the order of its petitions, and in consequence more clearly "crusading" in tone. There is no need to try to reconcile these two versions in the same MS, nor even the sets of directions which contain them. In fact, the second (fol. 85v-86) reads like a quite independent set of directions for the execution of the Trental. This is borne out by what follows the variant version of the prayer: directions that the celebrant should fast Wednesdays and Fridays "si sit dispositus"; that he should say Placebo, Dirige, and Commendation of Souls "cum predicta oracione scilicet 'Omnipotens sempiterne deus' cum oracionibus consuetis que sunt iste oraciones: 'Deus cui proprium misereri,' 'Inclina domine aurem tuam,' et 'Tibi domine commendamus'." Next the ten feasts whose masses

[21] Jordan supplies "habentibus" here.

are to be celebrated are specified, to be said within their octaves. Then comes the most illustrative point:

> Et notandum quod collecta appropriata trigintali[22] que sic incipit 'Deus qui es summa redempcio' cum qualibet propria collecta cuiuslibet misse et hoc secretum 'Omnipotens' et 'Videmus' cum proprio secreto cuiuslibet misse et haec postcommunio 'Deus cuius misericordie' cum propria postcommunione cuiuslibet misse cotidie per annum dicende sunt sub una conclusione.

This shows that the same mass prayers as in the English missals are known to whoever composed this rubric; he does not, however, appear to realize that "Deus qui es summa redempcio" is simply an alternate version of the prayer he has just given in extenso, "O.s.d. nostra existens redempcio." (The meaning of "Videmus" as applied to the secret is not clear.)

VI

At this point the investigation seems to run up against a blank wall. At least three possible avenues can be imagined. What would most of all open a new way would be a manuscript — ideally from a context which had some clear connection with the crusades — containing the prayer in the form of fol. 85v of Harl. 3810, i.e. in which the references to the Holy Land come first. No such manuscript of this sort is known to me, but it seems more than likely that such a thing does exist.

Secondly, a clue might be provided if a satisfactory explanation were found for the alternative term used for the Epiphany in the rubric of the York missals: "tres de Apparatione, scilicet de Epiphania." The name "Apparitio" ("Apparatio") to refer to the Epiphany (which is the term used in all other English instances) seems to be extremely rare. It is employed in a book of Hours for the use of Reims in the late 13th century (London, Victoria and Albert Mus. Reid 83),[23] and in a 14th century breviary from Apt in Provence, but apparently not in other surviving Apt breviaries.[24] Such fragmentary evidence does not seem to be of any immediate use to us.

Thirdly, it might be possible to extract some help from the discrepancy between the lists of specified feasts in the Vernon MS (the earliest extant MS of the verse legend) on the one hand and all the other MSS of the legends and the service books on the other: that whereas the list normally concludes with the Assumption and the Nativity of the BVM, the Vernon list ends with Nativ. BVM and Conception. If, in a MS older than c. 1380, another list of feasts were to be found ending as does that in the Vernon MS, it might give a hint as to the source of the variant list, and hence of the devotion as a whole.

These three points by no means exhaust the possibilities for new light on the question of the origins of St Gregory's Trental in, at any rate, its English form.

[22] Note that the form on fol. 75v was "trentale," not "trigintalis."

[23] I owe this reference to the kindness of Dr Alison Stones, transmitted to me by my colleague Professor J. Folda.

[24] V. Leroquais, *Les Bréviaires mss. des bibls. publ. des France* I (1934), 33: Apt, Trésor de la Cath., MS 1.

"Origins" must be left in the plural because as we have seen there are at least two: i) the development of the literary story to the point at which it is supplied with precise liturgical details; and ii) the development of a liturgical practice from some combination of a) devotions connected with recovery of the Holy Land and b) the idea of a trental for the delivery of a soul from purgatory amplified by the notion of some special efficacy inherent in the liturgical year. It seems clear that a) and b) were combined into ii) before ii) was conflated with i). The latter conflation, of already developed liturgical practice with literary story, has taken place in England by the third quarter of the 14th century; when, and in what circumstances, the two elements of the liturgical practice were joined together, is a question whose answer must await the discovery of new evidence, or re-evaluation of old.

VII

Something can, however, be said about the reception, and to a degree the understanding, of this devotion in late medieval England. What evidence there is for this — aside from what we have already considered, inferences that can be drawn from the transmission of the literary story and from service books — comes largely from wills. Undoubtedly an enormous number of references lie in the mass of unpublished English medieval wills; even a selection from those which have been published[25] provides ample information: the problem is how to interpret it. The chief difficulty is that the term "St Gregory's Trental" is not infrequently used in wills in contexts which make it either impossible or unlikely that anything other than a simple ("Gregorian") trental is meant. One way to tell this is by the stipends indicated. Trentals provided for at the "cheap" rate of ten shillings each are likely to be of the simple kind. In 1395 Sir Robert Bardolf, after making provision for an enormous number of masses to be said for himself and souls dear to him, leaves also forty shillings for four "trentals of St Gregory."[26] This amount works out to four pence per mass — a standard minimum rate for which, in the somewhat transactional atmosphere of late medieval piety, one would be unlikely to expect, or get, anything "special." A century later trentals are still being provided for at this minimum, and by those who are wealthy and important enough to do better if they wished. Dame Jane Stonor in 1493 left fifteen pounds for thirty "trentals of St Gregory";[27] six years later the vicar of Bampton (Oxon.) provided that the fellows of Oriel College should celebrate "five trentals of St Gregory . . . so that they begin within three days after my decease and so continue, and they are to receive for each trental ten shillings."[28]

[25] The most fruitful collections have been *Somerset Medieval Wills* (abbrev. SMW), vols. I and II, ed. F. W. Weaver (Somerset Record Soc. 16, 1901; 19, 1903); *Some Oxfordshire Wills* (abbrev. SOW), ed. J. R. H. Weaver and A. Beardwood (Oxfordshire Rec. Soc. 39, 1958); and *Testamenta Eboracensia* (abbrev. TE), vol. I, ed. J. Raine (Surtees Soc. 4, 1836).

[26] SOW, p. 8.

[27] SOW, p. 50.

[28] SOW, p. 65.

A higher rate of mass stipend, and occasionally a different designation, indicate at least sometimes unambiguous references to St Gregory's Trental as we have studied it. The difference in stipend is apparent as early as 1383: Sir Maurice Wyth leaves four pounds ten shillings for thirty trentals to be celebrated within a month after his death (thirty-six pence per trental), and ten pounds for a Trental of St Gregory.[29] It seems that a confusion of nomenclature existed from at least the late 14th century, as Sir Robert Bardolf's will, cited above, shows; soon, it would appear, the term "great trental" was used to indicate our more elaborate devotion. An early instance of this is in 1426;[30] a very clear one is in the will of Thomas Tremayll of 1508. He leaves two shillings and sixpence to each of six houses of London friars for a simple trental (at thirty pence each, or one penny per mass, this is likely to mean nothing more than a mention by name at the Lavabo), four pence or six pence per priest "as the place requires" for a trental to be celebrated on one day in the church of the parish in which he happens to die; and if it can be provided for out of his goods, a special trental called "le grete trental" by any good and honest priest thereto called, at a stipend of twelve marks — a rate of five shillings and four pence per mass![31] Another Somerset man leaves, in 1529, ten pounds "to have a priest to sing the great trental in the said church for one whole year."[32] By contrast the simple trental is sometimes called "the lesser trental": Sir John Tower referred to it in this way when he left half a mark to a specified priest "to the celebration of a lesser trental for my soul to be said by note"[33] (this rate, eighty pence for thirty masses, is again very low).

Even without being aided by the distinctive nomenclature or higher rate of stipend, we find a few references to St Gregory's Trental which are unambiguous because they refer to distinctive features of the devotion. One trental of St Gregory 'according to the feasts accustomed' is specified by John Hertylpoole, himself a priest, in 1431.[34] Sir John Bigod in Yorkshire (1426) provides that in addition to the celebration of St Gregory's Trental for two years there is to be said every day "unam collectam specialem, videlicet 'Deus summe [sc. 'spes'] nostre redempcionis' "[35] — the later form of the collect we have studied. And it is presumably the cumbersome supplementary devotions which Richard Best of Taunton (1502) refers to in ordering "St Gregory's trental with all observance according to the same" every year for three years.[36]

But the ambiguity remains, and in a number of instances it is impossible to be sure which kind of trental the testator had in mind. What did Henry Bowet, archbishop of York, mean when in 1421 he left "pro mille missis celebrandis

[29] SMW II, p. 288.
[30] SMW I, p. 404.
[31] SMW II, p. 116.
[32] SMW II, p. 281.
[33] SMW II, p. 78.
[34] SMW I, p. 135.
[35] TE I, p. 410.
[36] SMW II, p. 30.

more trentalis Sancti Gregorii, pro anima mea, et animabus parentum meorum, et omnium fidelium defunctorum, infra mensem a die obitus mei xx 1."?[37] A thousand masses within a month, at just under five pence per mass, scarcely corresponds to our understanding of the way the devotion works. What did the ten shillings which the London butcher Hugh Mason left in 1385 to each of two Franciscans "sub condicione quod quolibet eorum celebret pro anima mea trigintale Sancti Gregorii" actually procure for him?[38] Did the "magna festinacia" with which Isabella Salwayn in 1429 specified her St Gregory's Trental celebrated make the provision impossible to carry out?[39] How could Elizabeth Byconyll in 1504 expect four Trentals of St Gregory to be accomplished within a month after her death?[40]

A possible solution, which can only be suggested rather than proved, is that St Gregory's Trental may have been as often celebrated in the breach of its elaborate rules as in their observance. The distinctive point of the devotion, that the masses of the ten chief feasts should be said rather than requiem or other masses, could be preserved, along with the collects and other specified devotions, even if the subsidiary provision, that the masses of each feast were to be said within their respective octaves, was ignored and the whole thing condensed into a calendar month. In the words of the vernacular story, "These ben the chefe festes ten / That sokour the sowles that ben fro heven" was the essence of the practice (thus preserving what Dom Hesbert stresses, the idea of the virtue inherent in the liturgical year), while the instruction "Lette say these masses be your hestes / With-inne the utas [octave] of the festes!" was secondary and could be ignored. (It might be pointed out that to find, during an octave like that of Christmas crowded with other feasts of a high grade, three mass-days free for masses of St Gregory's Trental would for many priests be an impossibility.)

This suggestion — that in practice St Gregory's Trental was often watered down from its rubrical elaboration by being compressed into a month — is strengthened by a corresponding dilution of the idea of the benefits produced by the devotion. Whereas the point of the literary story is the deliverance from torment of a particular soul (the pope's mother) and the proper mass-prayers mention only a single soul,[41] testators regularly establish trentals for the souls of relatives and others to whom they are bound as well as for themselves. As the appendix to the poem in the Harley MS reads,

> Sone, on thynge of charite I the rede,
> Do it as well for the quyk as for the dede.
> Synge it as wele for V as for one,
> Ffor it may save the sawles everechone.

[37] TE I, p. 398.

[38] C. L. Kingsford, "Additional Materials for the History of the Grey Friars," *Collectanea Franciscana* II (Brit. Soc. of Franciscan Studies 10, 1922), 80.

[39] TE I, p. 418.

[40] SMW II, p. 72.

[41] Compare the rubric in the Hereford missal (ed. Henderson, p. 436): Et qui vult deliberare animam cito de poenis purgatorii, dicat istas missas sequentes.

It may be suspected, then, that what the devotion most often boiled down to in practice was a slightly more elaborate — and therefore expensive — way of offering masses for the dead, with some notion of added efficacy probably incorporated through the connection with Gregory, and made popular by the colorfully told vernacular story. The very elaborateness of the devotion doubtless helped to enhance its popularity, and at the same time this popularity ensured that St Gregory's Trental would in practice tend to become conflated with ordinary trentals. What stuck in the minds of those who were attracted to this devotion was probably an idea — the recapitulation of the liturgical year — and a story. How the story, and by extension the practice, of St Gregory's Trental, would strike a subsequent generation is shown by a 16th century gloss in the Balliol MS: "This tale of pope gregorius is a lye & y(at) a monstrous on(e), a deceaver of Sathan to deceave him or a devise of his owne."[42]

[42] E. Flügel, "Die Lieder des Balliol MS 354," *Anglia* XIII (1891), 105–6.

INDEX OF MANUSCRIPTS

GENERAL INDEX

Individual saints have been indexed when their presence is noteworthy, but not when they are part of a list or occur incidentally to the main argument. Nicknames of manuscripts (e.g., Bosworth Psalter) are cross-referenced to the index of manuscripts; conventional abbreviations have been used for brevity: BL, Bodl., CUL are obvious; BN = Paris, Bibliothèque nationale; B.m. = Bibliothèque municipale. The main topics in each article are indicated by *passim*. Modern scholars' names are not included, and the Introduction has not been indexed. Nor has part ii of number V, for it is the edition of William of Malmesbury's *Abbreviatio Amalarii* for which part i is explanation and commentary.